Mafalda

A book in the series
LATIN AMERICA IN TRANSLATION / EN TRADUCCIÓN / EM TRADUÇÃO
*Sponsored by the Duke–University of North Carolina Program in
Latin American Studies*

Mafalda

A Social and Political History of Latin America's Global Comic

ISABELLA COSSE

TRANSLATED BY LAURA PÉREZ CARRARA

Duke University Press *Durham and London* 2019

©2014 Fondo de Cultura Economica de Argentina, S.A.
El Salvador 5665, CP, 1414, C.A.B.A. – Argentina

English Edition © 2019 Duke University Press
Printed in the United States of America on acid-free paper ∞
Cover designed by Matt Tauch.
Text designed by Drew Sisk.
Typeset in Garamond Premier Pro, Folio, and ITC Lubalin Graph
by Westchester Publishing Services

The Cataloging-in-Publication Data is available at the Library of Congress.

ISBN 978-1-4780-0513-1 (ebook)
ISBN 978-1-4780-0507-0 (hardcover)
ISBN 978-1-4780-0638-1 (paperback)

Cover art: Mafalda cartoon © Joaquín Salvador Lavado (Quino).

For Emilio and Tomás

CONTENTS

ILLUSTRATIONS

ACKNOWLEDGMENTS

I began my research with the aim of understanding the relationship between family and class in the turbulent Buenos Aires of the 1960s, but I soon realized I was dealing with a phenomenon that exceeded by far that period and space. That realization led to this book, which tells the social and political history of *Mafalda*—Latin America's most popular comic strip both on the continent and in the world—and, in doing so, offers a narrative of the recent past, a past that is still present in the dilemmas faced by the region and by societies today. Undertaking research on a continental and transnational scale in Argentina is not a simple task, and neither is it easy to have the outcome of that research published in English, much less by a publisher as prestigious as Duke University Press. I am fully aware that if I have had the satisfaction of overcoming the many obstacles and challenges posed by this work it is because Mafalda opened many doors for me, because I had the support of countless accomplices (friends, colleagues, publishers, archivers, Mafalda fans) who were willing to help, and because I worked under institutional conditions that allowed me to concentrate on my research. I would like to begin these acknowledgments by giving thanks for all of that.

I conducted this study in my capacity as career researcher of the National Scientific and Technological Research Council (CONICET), headquartered at the Interdisciplinary Institute of Gender Studies (IIEGE) of the School of Philosophy and Literature, Universidad de Buenos Aires. As I write these pages, I fear for research activities in the country, as the government's science policy suffers under budget cuts and the application of business criteria to measure intellectual production. In this sense, I would like to highlight that an offshoot of an investigation—because writing a book on Mafalda was not part of my original research plan—led to a book that won the Premio Iberoamericano Book Award from the Latin American Studies Association (LASA), and which was picked up by Duke University Press to be translated and published in English, and whose appeal goes beyond colleagues and people in academia. It is a book that can interest, and even excite, a wide range of people, from my Bolivian neighborhood grocer (who carefully weighed copies of my book so I could mail them) to the children in the "Mafalda" school in Buenos Aires where I first presented my book, to the many people in Chile, Mexico, New York, and other places who shared with me their ideas about the comic strip and their memories.

I said that the project was an offshoot because I did not originally intend to focus on the comic strip, but this research is very much connected with concerns (family history, the 1960s, memory, and the dictatorship) that have interested me since my undergraduate years at Universidad de la República, in Uruguay, and my PhD dissertation work (on family mandates in the 1960s), conducted under the aegis of the History Program at Universidad de San Andrés, in Argentina. Nonetheless, I knew that I owed myself a more thorough study on these subjects. I discussed an initial idea at a 2010 workshop titled "Laughter in History: Everyday Life, Family, Gender, and Sexualities in Argentina through Humor, 1910–2010," jointly organized by Karina Felitti, Valeria Manzano, and me (as all three of us were very interested in humor in connection with our research) and sponsored by Universidad de San Andrés, the Institute of Higher Social Studies (IDAES) of Universidad Nacional de San Martín, and the IIEGE of Universidad de Buenos Aires. The project gained strength with the feedback I received from the anonymous readers of the *Hispanic American Historical Review* (*HAHR*) when I submitted a manuscript that was a condensed version of what would become the first chapter of this book. The review process for the *HAHR* article, edited by John D. French and Sean Mannion, was also enriching. As I advanced with my research, I discussed my findings in the Program of Studies on the Middle Classes of the Economic and Social Development Institute in Buenos Aires, coordinated by Sergio Visacovsky; the Recent History Hub at Universidad Nacional de San Martín (Argentina), where I was hosted by Marina Franco and Valeria Manzano; and in the Recent History Seminar of Universidad Nacional Autónoma de México (UNAM), which Eugenia Allier invited me to participate in. I would like to mention in particular the members of the Group of Childhood and Family History, which I coordinate in my own institution (IIEGE), and the students in the courses I have taught during these years, in particular the students in the PhD dissertation workshop of Facultad Latinoamericana de Ciencias Sociales (Argentina). Many colleagues in each of those spaces generously contributed their thoughts and forced me to review and strengthen my arguments. In addition to those mentioned above, I would like to thank Lila Caimari, Eduardo Míguez, Ezequiel Adamovsky, Enrique Garguin, Laura Vázquez, Marcela Gené, Florencia Levín, Mauro Pasqualini, Emilio Burucúa, Mara Burkart, Rebekah Pite, and Susana Sosenski, for listening to me and for their thoughtful suggestions.

I was lucky to have the Spanish version of this book published by Fondo de Cultura Económica, in 2014. I thank Alejandro Archain, director of the publishing house, for his unconditional support and for kindly giving the necessary permission for this version in English. I would also like to thank the publishing house's talented editor, Mariana Rey, who worked with a first-rate team. The English translation and edition would not have been possible without the unwavering support of my "gringo" friends Nara Milanich, Heidi Tinsman, Charles Walker, and Pablo Piccato, the interest of Duke University Press, and the sensitivity and insight of Gisela Fosado. While I explored the comic strip's international circulation I learned that humor is one of the most difficult things to translate, as *Mafalda*'s English translator, Andrew Graham-Yooll, explained to me. Laura Pérez Carrara, my translator and friend, took on the challenge of translating this book with intelligence and relentless logic.

Many people made this investigation possible. I turned again and again to Daniel Divinsky, director of *Mafalda*'s publishing house Ediciones de la Flor, who gave me access to his company's archive. Alba Lampón and Sergio Morero helped me enormously with their memories, material, and contacts for interviews with Quino himself and with his wife, Alicia Colombo, who was also his agent and is no longer with us. It was a privilege to be able to talk with both of them at length and to finally meet them personally after years of studying *Mafalda*. As I was only able to examine part of Quino's archive—which was very important for my work—in order to complete my research I resorted to multiple other archives, large and small, specific and wide ranging. My investigation would not have had the scope it achieved were it not for the support of Patricia Reynal at Editorial Perfil's documentation center and of Claudio Martyniuk, who allowed me to consult the archives of the newspaper *Clarín*. I would also like to express my appreciation to the archivists and librarians of the documentation center of Círculo Sindical de la Prensa y la Comunicación de Córdoba, the archive of the Córdoba newspaper *La Voz del Interior*, the archive of the newspaper *Río Negro*, the documentation centers of the newspapers *El País de Madrid* and *La Vanguardia* in Barcelona, and the documentation center of the newspaper *Excélsior* in Mexico. In Argentina I would like to thank the Library of Universidad de San Andrés, the library archive of Universidad Torcuato Di Tella, the research center and libraries of Instituto Ravignani, and the IIEGE. I would also like to mention Vanessa Fuentes, who gave me access to the press material of the publishing house Tusquets in Mexico; Antonio Torres, of Club del Comic, who gave me access to his collection of magazines and invaluable toys; and Doctor Pablo Yadarola, the legal director of Department 23 of the Twelfth Federal Criminal and Correctional Court, who allowed me to consult the criminal files on the Pallottine murders. My work would have been impossible without those sources and documents. No less important was the help and support from colleagues, friends, and relatives who provided me with material and contacts: Esther Acevedo, Paula Alonso, Martín Bergel, Paulina Brunetti, Avina Celotto, Julieta Di Corletto, Leny Durán, Ana B. Flores, Judith Gociol, Rafael Grompone, José María Gutiérrez, Micaela Libson, María Inés Loyola, and Coleta Ravoni.

The interviews I conducted were invaluable for my research. They are included in the list of sources but I would like to express my thanks here in particular to Rodolfo Capalozza, Francisco Chirichella, Norberto Firpo, Miguel García, Andrew Graham-Yooll, Pablo José Hernández, Pablo Irrgang, "Chiche" Linari, Eduardo Longoni, Rolando Sabino, Juan Sasturain, Sergio Suppo, Carlos Torrengo, Jorge Tovar, and Luis Tovar. Equally important were the readers of *Mafalda*, whom I do not identify by name so as to respect their privacy, but who shared their individual stories and allowed me to explore their subjective experience. Also valuable were the countless informal conversations and impromptu talks I held with a range of people, as well as the discussions triggered by the publication of the book in Spanish.

The research moved forward almost effortlessly. It was in itself an enjoyable experience for me, even though it had its share of obstacles and tough moments. Encountering the many readers and fans of the comic strip and the surprises that writing this book brought me has been enormously gratifying. Similarly of great value were the feedback from colleagues who reviewed the Spanish edition and the discussions at the many book presentations I gave, not just in Argentina but also in Chile, Uruguay, Mexico, the United States, and Peru. Bearing those contributions in mind, I made some changes to the original book, but the English edition is essentially the same. Also useful were the very interesting discussions I had with Nara Milanich, Heidi Tinsman, Pablo Piccato, and Elizabeth Hutchinson, colleagues I met during my time on a Fulbright-CONICET postdoctoral fellowship at Columbia University's Institute of Latin American Studies. Moreover, my contact with Paulo Drinot led me to build on some of the ideas developed in chapter 5 and to contribute a chapter to *Comics and the Past in Latin America* (University of Pittsburgh Press, 2017), a book he coedited with Jorge L. Catalá Carrasco and James Scorer.

My research was supported by a CONICET grant to the Multiannual Research Project "A Micro-Historical Study on Couples" and assisted by the Hada and Ruper Foundation. I was able to conduct interviews and consult newspapers and archives in Mexico City thanks to the opportunity afforded by an invitation to participate in the colloquium "Los niños, fuentes y perspectivas," coordinated by Delia Salazar and Eugenia Sánchez Calleja. Unfortunately, I was unable to travel to Italy and Spain, but I made extensive use of digital newspaper libraries and conducted many interviews over the telephone. I also had the determined help of Giulia Venturi in Verona, Guillermo Aquino Falfan in Mexico City, David Candami in Barcelona, and Caitlin Reilly in Washington, DC. In Buenos Aires, Inés Ibarlucia helped me put a sensible limit to my ever-growing sources, and for specific matters I had the support of Claudia Patricia Ríos in La Plata and of Cristina Fuentes in Córdoba.

With *Mafalda*, as never before, I had an object of study that met with passionate interest at social gatherings and casual meetings, prompting stimulating conversations. The full list of those who helped me is too long to include, but I would like to thank some not yet mentioned who understood (and put up with) my Mafalda obsession: Mariana Alcobre, Paula Bruno, Marcela Cerruti, Rosa Czerniuk, Verónica Devalle, Ana Rita Díaz, Christine Ehrick, Mercedes García Ferrari, Mateo García Haymes, Sandra Gayol, Patricia Gonzalez, Karin Grammático, Valeria Llobet, Vania Markarian, Daniel Mingorance, Emiliano Núñez, Camila Núñez Pérez, Sandra Olstein, Valeria Pita, Amanda Salvioni, Cristiana Schettini, Leandro Stagno, Carla Villalta, and José Zanca. I also enjoyed talking to my parents, Gustavo and Silvia, about this project as I was working on it. I valued Marta Crenzel's help, Mariana Cosse's and Isabel Larghero's enthusiasm, and the "commitment to the cause" displayed by Rafael Grompone, who was willing to lug the heavy Italian editions of *Mafalda* all the way down south to Argentina for me.

I never would have been able to turn my research into a book were it not for my husband, Emilio Crenzel. He—my representative of the anti-Mafalda public—convinced me of its importance. He discussed the key arguments of my interpretation with me, revised each and every page, and when he sensed my exhaustion, he surrounded me with loving care. My son, Tomás, was only two when I came upon him staring entranced at the image of Mafalda in the bright orange cover of the *Mafalda inédita* compilation. Today, more than ten years later, I am pleased to discover in him a sense of humor that is all his own. These pages are dedicated to them both, my treasures.

INTRODUCTION

It is impossible not to come across Mafalda in Buenos Aires. Her lively eyes are there at the port, welcoming visitors as they disembark. Tourists and locals will also see her in the heart of the city, sitting on a park bench in San Telmo surrounded by fans, and, again, in the city's busiest subway station, on a huge mural. Her image looks back at you from T-shirts, mugs, refrigerator magnets, and assorted knickknacks sold in shops in cities across Argentina, alongside items featuring national icons such as Che Guevara, Evita, and tango legend Carlos Gardel. Nobody is surprised by the fact that she is merely a cartoon character. Neither are they surprised that Mafalda and friends have become so well known outside Argentina. *Mafalda* is the most famous and popular Latin American comic strip in the world. Readers from different countries and continents have found social, political, and subjective meaning in it. It has now been translated into more than twenty languages and continues to conquer new markets and attract new readers around the globe, including in places as remote as China, South Korea, and Indonesia, with new editions still selling out everywhere. *Mafalda* has millions of followers on Facebook and the cartoon's creator receives mail from all over the world.

Mafalda was born more than fifty years ago without much fanfare. In 1964, Joaquín Salvador Lavado—already a well-known cartoonist working under the pen name Quino—introduced a new cartoon for adults in the pages of a political magazine. He never imagined then that his creation would turn out to be such an unprecedented success. The comic strip's main character, Mafalda, was a little girl from a middle-class family who was wise beyond her years and had a rebellious attitude. She lived in a small apartment in Buenos Aires, the city that served as backdrop for her adventures. Drawn with androgynous features, this brainy tomboy could be a handful for her parents, as she continuously baffled and challenged them. She caused her dad many sleepless nights with her endless queries about politics and the state of the world, and she unsettled her mom with her feminist quips, even driving her to tears. In a nod to readers, she diagnosed both parents (and grown-ups in general) as suffering from "mass hysteria." Two years after it first appeared in print, *Mafalda* was read daily by an estimated two million people and the collections released in book format were sold out in just a few days. The comic strip's popularity quickly spread beyond Argentina. In 1969, an Italian edition with a prologue penned by Umberto Eco opened the doors to the European market. Meanwhile, in Latin America its readership continued to grow and by 1972 the strips were featured in sixty newspapers and magazines across the region. During those years it was also published in book format in Portugal (1970), Germany and Finland (1971), and France (1973). But the cartoon's fame was not limited to the printed page, as dolls of the characters were manufactured and sold in several countries; their images stamped (mostly without the author's permission) on everything from T-shirts, ads, and posters to wedding invitations; and in Paris there was even a boutique named after the main character. *Mafalda* had become a social phenomenon. Its impact had transcended individual experiences and subjectivities and entered the realm of collective identities and political and social realities, both in Argentina and outside the country. It is these meanings that are at the core of this book.

How did *Mafalda* become so popular and retain its popularity for so long? And why is it still so relevant? What social, political, and cultural meanings did it have throughout the more than fifty years since it was first published? These questions are woven together to form the fabric of this book, which tells the story of the iconic character and comic strip and the social relations, political dilemmas, and cultural and economic dimensions that explain how Mafalda and her universe came alive outside the page and why they remain so current today. These questions entail examining a number of issues that are key for understanding the recent history of Latin America, as well as contemporary history in general: namely, middle-class identities and sociocultural modernization, generational and gender ruptures, political violence and authoritarianism, the construction of a global antiestablishment sensitivity, and the dilemmas posed by recent history and collective memory. These issues provide a central thread for each chapter, but the book follows a chronological order, so that it also contains a narrative of the past half century from the unique perspective of pop culture, shedding light on a period that is critical for gaining insight into the present.

The significance that *Mafalda*'s fifty-plus years have for our present cannot be overstated. The comic strip was born at a time when young people in Latin America could still recall the struggles for political and social rights waged by the masses and when the bombings of World War II were still fresh in the minds of Europe's youth. On both sides of the Atlantic, the postwar generations were enjoying unprecedented economic growth and a remarkable expansion of their social rights. This prosperity allowed them, like no generation before, to distance themselves from the experiences of their elders. It was these young people who were behind the political and cultural upheaval of the 1960s, as they strove to realize their utopian dreams of a more just society. In Latin America, these demands—raised in the midst of the Cold War—questioned the hegemony of the United States and made it possible to imagine a new world order. The region joined the rest of the Third World in spearheading a vigorous movement. The Cuban Revolution was shaking the foundations of the Latin American left in societies where the expansion of the middle class made the historical exclusion of the lower classes all the more evident. Social and political protests spread like wildfire across a continent that seemed to be on the brink of a revolution. But that optimism descended quickly into hopelessness. The 1973 oil crisis symbolized the structural decline of capitalism and the beginning of a new era shaped by a neoliberal reorganization of the economy. The dismantling of the welfare states in Latin America was driven by ruthless dictatorships that in the Southern Cone left countless dead in their wake. The 1990s were characterized by growing social exclusion, a cult of individualism, and rampant privatization, which only recently have been questioned within a new political and social scenario.

This book explores these pivotal decades of recent history by following *Mafalda*'s tracks and, in the process, addressing issues that are key for unraveling that period in history. My premise is that the comic strip's social and political significance makes it a unique gateway into understanding the political, social, and cultural upheavals of this half century. Fully aware of the complexity of that starting point, I take an approach that regards humor as a powerful lens that enables us to gain insight into the human condition and social phenomena, in line with Mikhail Bakhtin, for whom certain essential aspects of the world can only be accessed by means of laughter.[1] Moreover, humor—what is considered funny, the comedic strategies employed, the way in which humor questions reality, and laughter itself—presupposes shared codes that require a tacit understanding between those who produce it and their audiences (listeners, readers, viewers). As Peter Berger has said, humor strengthens group cohesion, draws boundaries, and contributes to social self-reflection.[2] That was what Sigmund Freud meant when, in the bourgeois Vienna of the early twentieth century, he explained that laughing with others expressed the existence of broad psychic agreement.[3]

The social nature of humor entails assuming that what people find funny varies in time and across social settings, but also that laughter itself changes over time. Hence the challenge involved in analyzing humor produced in a historical context different from our own. As historians we must discover what is not made explicit in a joke, that is, what is implicitly conveyed to the readers or audiences of the time in which the humor was produced. The unique social and cultural significance of *Mafalda* and the richness of Quino's comedic creation offer enormous possibilities for such an analysis. Ultimately, the historiographical aim of this book is to contribute to a social history of humor.[4] With that in mind, I take on three conceptual and methodological challenges: exploring the mutual feedback between the symbolic and the material, highlighting the intersection of the domestic and the political, and mapping national, regional, and transnational dimensions.

For the first challenge, I draw on a long tradition of studies that focus on culture as an object of analysis of social phenomena. While a discussion of the many works in this sense exceeds the scope of this book, I would like to acknowledge how this tradition informs my approach. On the one hand, my contribution poses questions about the relationship between the material and the cultural in terms of social history. In writing this history of *Mafalda* I have assumed, in line with Raymond Williams, that culture is mediated by social relations that make it possible, and that, at the same time, it constitutes a "signifying system through which . . . a social order is communicated, reproduced, experienced, and explored."[5] This assumption raises two problems that I have addressed here: understanding how an artistic form emerges, and elucidating its social "mediations," meanings, and effects. On the other, I incorporate the challenges of conceiving those who read, use, and experience cultural productions as active subjects.[6] My aim was to understand the meanings and uses that my cultural object—*Mafalda*—has had over the years for various subjects, both collective and individual, and how these meanings and uses changed in each historical context. With this in mind, I set out to historically reconstruct the processes of the production, circulation, and resignification of *Mafalda*. To do that I have considered the cartoon as a representation produced by and embodied in practices and objects, which turned it into a social phenomenon that draws on materials from society but, at the same time, operates on them.

The second challenge involves understanding how family and everyday life are articulated with the political as a decisive dimension of the social. It is at that intersection that individuals establish relationships, confront others, and shape their values and customs. From this perspective, I argue that the ways in which individuals behave and conceive their family relations contain a political and ideological element inasmuch as they involve power relations (within the family and outside it) that create gender, social, and intergenerational inequalities.[7] There are numerous studies that have explored this in Latin America, where family, moral, and sexual values played a crucial role in the establishment of social hierarchies.[8] Working- and lower-class families were in fact not contemplated in the civil codes adopted by the new nation-states in Latin America modeled on the Napoleonic Code, and they were marginalized by social norms (often associated with the middle class) that naturalized a standard family model. That standard family was formed by a legally married couple and their biological offspring, with a division of roles in which the husband was the breadwinner and the wife the homemaker. Anything that differed from that model was viewed as deviant. The antiestablishment youth of the 1960s challenged—in different ways and to various extents—certain foundations of those family mandates, thus sparking powerful conflicts over the values of the middle class and its role in Argentine society and explicitly connecting family matters with political issues.[9]

The third challenge consists in analyzing the centrality of national, regional, and global connections for understanding historical processes. In that sense, my approach is based on recognizing the historically uneven nature of such connections and the role they have played in determining the dominant position of the most powerful capitalist countries, in the context of the emergence of a transnational economy.[10] But at the same time, in line with pioneering studies on Latin America, I argue that Latin American societies had an active role in transnational dynamics, and I am interested in analyzing the complex relations established between global markets, state policies, and cultural movements.[11] These transnational dynamics, which extend far back in time, took on particular significance in the 1960s as the connections between various processes, actors, and movements expanded and the flow of goods, people, and ideas intensified. Studying cultural productions such as *Mafalda,* which emerged in noncentral countries, expressed and fed an antiestablishment sensitivity (whose global scope was evidenced by the protests of 1968), and operated independent of multinational companies, is key for understanding these dynamics.[12]

Prior studies on *Mafalda* can be grouped in one of two approaches. On the one hand, the pioneering studies by Umberto Eco (in Italy) and Oscar Masotta (in Argentina) gave way to many works that have examined Quino's conceptual humor through the lens of fields such as social communication, linguistics, and semiotics.[13] These works have focused on analyzing narrative structures, the relationship between images and text, comedic strategies, and the context in which the comic strip was produced. On the other hand, there are studies that have approached it from quite a different perspective. They have analyzed the strip with the aim of identifying what it says socially and politically. From this angle, the strip has been interpreted as a reflection of certain political moments and of phenomena such as intergenerational relations, changes in the family, and national identity in Argentina.[14] These contributions have informed my research enormously, as have the studies on the field of humor during those years.[15] But as I read them I realized that I had an approach that was somewhat unique in that it straddled the two perspectives. My approach entails examining the link between the two levels—that of the comic strip itself and of a social reading of it—and producing a reconstruction that is purely historical and addresses in equal measure the cartoon's artistic production (including the analysis of its images) and the social nature of its production, circulation, and meaning.

My work on *Mafalda* was the result of more than six years of research that involved a thorough study of numerous primary sources. This included consulting the original versions of the comic strip published in Argentina in *Primera Plana*, *El Mundo*, and *Siete Días*, in Mexico in the newspaper *Excélsior*, in the Spanish newspapers ABC and *La Vanguardia*, the Italian dailies *L'Unità* and *La Stampa*, and the comics magazines *El Globo* (Spain) and *Il Mago* (Italy). I also reviewed all the compilations released in Argentina, Italy, Spain, and Mexico, and I watched the film adaptations of the comic strip. Throughout my research, I explored at length the archives held by the newspapers and magazines that originally featured the comic strip in Argentina, Mexico, Italy, and Spain. I was also given access to part of Quino's personal archive. More recently, as I worked on this English edition, I had a chance to consult new sources under the National Comic Strip and Graphic Humor Research Program of Argentina's National Library. Moreover, I consulted the archives of Instituto Torcuato Di Tella, the documentation center of the publishing house Perfil, the National Libraries of Argentina and Chile, the Library of Congress, and the Library of Universidad Nacional Autónoma de México. For specific time periods, I researched other Argentine and foreign newspapers and magazines. I read numerous essays and tributes, conducted more than sixty formal interviews, and held countless informal conversations. I spoke at length with Quino and Alicia Colombo, his wife and agent, and with editors, publishers, printers, booksellers, readers, and fans who visited the Mafalda statue in Buenos Aires. I contrasted the multiple sources consulted and the facts gathered, paying close attention to the discourse characteristics of each type of source and the contexts in which the various uses and the different appropriations of the strip took place. I was especially careful to take into account the subjective nature of personal memories and how the view of the past that they evoke is shaped by the perspective one has in the present.

I applied an analytical strategy that combined a densely synchronic analysis with a long-term diachronic reconstruction, driven by the conviction that it is possible to write a recent history that extends into the present without affecting its specifically historical perspective. If, when I started out, this was an intuitive strategy, in the course of my research it became an epistemological decision. A recent phenomenon—even as recent as a few years—can be an object of historical study because its historical nature is not determined by the number of years that have passed since its occurrence; rather, it depends on the researcher's ability to distance themselves from it. There is no positivist illusion behind these precautions. The delimitation of this history was defined by me based on a dialogue between my hypotheses and my analysis of the sources. In this sense, I would like to close this introduction by presenting the main ideas of this long-term perspective, which provides an account of the last half century structured by different issues. Each chapter is, in turn, organized around one of those issues.

The first chapter examines the birth of *Mafalda*, with Quino's preliminary sketches for an advertising campaign, and the strip's public debut in a political magazine in 1964. Through this reconstruction, I illustrate how humor offers a privileged means of gaining insight into the middle class and the process of sociocultural modernization in the 1960s. My analysis challenges simplified views that assume that the middle class leaned either to the left or the right in the country's social and political processes. Instead, I posit two ideas. The first is that from the start the comic strip was permeated by the cultural, social, and economic dynamics that characterized the mid-1960s. In particular, I argue that *Mafalda* echoed the generational and gender tensions that were shaking the foundations of Argentine society at the time, and I examine the contradictions (the impossibilities and frustrations) encountered by the middle class in the face of social modernization. The second idea is that *Mafalda* not only spoke to the world in which it emerged but also influenced that reality. I maintain that it put into circulation a certain representation of the middle class and a form of humor (employing irony) that was intertwined with the identity of the middle class. It contributed to the consolidation of that identity at the same time that it discussed and reflected on it through an unprecedented and extremely complex depiction—a heterogeneous view of the cultural values and social aspirations of the middle class that combined the everyday with the political.

The second chapter looks at the social and political divisions that gripped Argentina between 1967 and 1976, a time marked by cultural and political radicalization and increasing violence, which culminated in state terrorism. It examines the growing complexity of the strip (with the introduction of new characters and more detailed drawings) as of 1968, when it began to be featured in the pages of the photojournalism magazine *Siete Días*. It also analyzes how the comic strip commented on and reflected the repression by the Onganía dictatorship (1966–69), which dissolved parliament, placed the public university under its authority, and stepped up censorship and moralist campaigns in a context that saw the emergence of new left-wing organizations, including armed groups, and popular movements. It then reconstructs the controversies triggered by *Mafalda* from 1969, in the heat of labor and student struggles, until 1973, when the strip bode its readers farewell while the country was still under democratic rule but in a climate of rapidly escalating political violence. Against that backdrop, it gives an account of the different interpretations that saw the "intellectualized little girl" either as a dangerous expression of youth rebellion or as a timid petit bourgeois, depending on which end of the political spectrum the critic stood. This provides insight into the unprecedented ruptures that political polarization and the rise of state violence caused in the middle class and in Argentine society as a whole. It also sheds light on the views of those who, while assuming a political commitment, were reluctant to accept armed struggle as the only solution available and, in terms of their personal commitment, to place art at the service of the revolution. Finally, it addresses the new discussions about *Mafalda* that the various actors engaged in and, especially, the new ways in which they used the strip in the context of the rising authoritarianism that would lead to the coup d'état and Quino's exile.

Chapter 3 focuses on the global scale achieved by *Mafalda*. How did this little girl from Buenos Aires become such an internationally famous figure? What does this success tell us about the place of Third World cultural production at a transnational level? I argue that the broad distribution achieved by the comic strip occurred as a result of a combination of favorable contexts, contingencies, and unique appropriations in each social space and historical moment. I address each of these aspects by looking at *Mafalda*'s arrival in Italy, Spain, and Mexico. By taking these moments as the starting point I am able to highlight the role that small cultural ventures, informal social networks, and specific individuals—with different positions and identities—played in the development of a cultural market of political antiestablishment products that operated by linking the local and global scales. This also reveals the existence of a more or less transnational body of readers who could laugh at a conceptual humor in which they saw themselves reflected, because it operated on the ruptures produced by a number of shared phenomena—including sociocultural modernization, the political and cultural radicalization of young people, global inequalities and the emergence of the Third World, and the visibility achieved by feminist demands. This helps explain the emergence of an antiestablishment and progressive sensitivity in the 1960s and '70s and the change of direction of cultural exchanges between the North and South that made it possible for the South to supply cultural products to the North.

The fourth chapter takes us back to Argentina. Here I look at how cultural productions were resignified by state terrorism and the disappearance of activists during the dictatorship that began in 1976. It opens with an analysis of a macabre episode involving a poster—one that had become immensely popular in the country—that depicted Mafalda pointing critically at a police officer's baton and calling it the "ideology-denting stick." In 1976, after brutally murdering a group of Pallottine priests and seminarians, members of the government's repressive forces placed a copy of this poster on the lifeless body of one of their victims. This perverse co-opting recognized the antiauthoritarian political significance of the comic strip, which was also evidenced by the objections made by censors to the *Mafalda* movie that came out in 1981, near the end of the dictatorship. Despite this awareness of the comic strip's antiauthoritarianism, and while its publishers were censored, jailed, and exiled for other publications, *Mafalda* continued to be available to the public throughout the dictatorship. To understand this paradox, my analysis examines the cracks left open by the regime's cultural repression policies. The second section of the chapter centers on the country's return to democratic rule. It looks at how the relationship between political commitment and humor was redefined based on the oppositional role played by humor in the final years of the dictatorship. I argue that the comic strip's identification with the democratic creed, to which broad sectors of society adhered, renewed *Mafalda*'s widespread success. The twenty-fifth anniversary of *Mafalda* was commemorated with a widely attended exhibit and the publication of previously unpublished material, and this celebration fueled a new resignification of the strip among the public, as Quino imagined that Mafalda could have been among the country's disappeared.

Chapter 5 is devoted to reflecting on the comic strip's lasting relevance in Argentina and around the world. The past two and a half decades have been defined by the consolidation of *Mafalda*'s global success in a social and cultural myth-building process. With that idea in mind, I first focus on the context of rising neoliberalism, looking at how the comic strip channeled a resistance to that order through a nostalgic echoing of the 1960s that asserted the continued relevance of that generation's utopian dreams. After examining the establishment of ritual spaces and events such as the successful "Mafalda's World" exhibit in Madrid, I analyze the new forms of intergenerational transmission and the expansion of the comic strip's readership. Last, I reconstruct the celebrations held on the anniversaries of the cartoon and the building of commemorative spaces (squares, murals, statues) and look briefly at the use of Mexican death imagery in connection with *Mafalda* as an example of how the liminal nature that characterized the cartoon from the very start allowed it to take on specific meanings.

In the conclusion I return to the questions posed at the start and venture possible answers, arguing again that Quino's genius created an unprecedentedly powerful cultural product. The comic strip offered a philosophical and atemporal reflection on the human condition, which also operated productively on decisive phenomena of the 1960s—authoritarianism, generational conflicts, feminist struggles, the expansion of the middle classes, and the challenges to the established family order. I stress, however, that *Mafalda*'s lasting appeal is explained by the interweaving of phenomena, decisions, interventions, and concrete junctures that enabled its circulation, expansion, and resignification in different parts of the world throughout half a century. It was in that crisscrossing of random occurrences, singularities, and recurrences that this unique phenomenon emerged—a paper-and-ink creation that took on a life of its own and has become a global myth. As such it gives meaning to human existence.

As soon as I began my research I realized that my subject of study was important not only on a social level but also on a personal and affective level for a readership that at its core may be middle-class and antiestablishment but which has expanded far from that core to include different cultural and social sectors and characteristics across various generations. I also became aware of how that significance affects each and every analysis of and reflection on *Mafalda*. As a colleague warned me after I was bombarded with questions and comments when I presented a very early draft of part of my research: "If you mess with our *Mafalda*, you're going to have to answer to us." As I wrote this book, I remembered her warning. At the time, I did not imagine that I would meet with a similar reaction when speaking about *Mafalda* in New York. When that happened—at Columbia University's Institute of Latin American Studies—I was surprised once again by the cartoon's ability to mobilize a *we* that transcended its Buenos Aires roots. I now deliver these pages in the hope that they will contribute to the understanding of Latin American culture in general and of *Mafalda* in particular—of its capacity to imagine a *we* that overcomes language barriers, borders, and sociocultural differences. I hope

I have succeeded in my effort to show how at the intersection of an artist's creativity and local and global sociocultural processes, as well as multiple interventions and contingencies, a remarkable phenomenon emerged: a unique fictional character that jumped off the page and became very real for many people around the globe, taking on mythical proportions and helping them make sense of the world.

CHAPTER 1

Marks of Origin
Middle Class, Modernization, and Authoritarianism

In 1963, the cartoonist and illustrator Joaquín Salvador Lavado (Quino) created *Mafalda* upon the request of a local ad agency that was preparing to
launch a new line of home appliances for Siam Di Tella, then a major manu-
facturer in Argentina. The agency planned to place the Mansfield brand on the
market through a subliminal campaign consisting of a comic strip based on a
"typical family" of husband and wife with two children. Quino was asked to
deliver a cartoon along the lines of contemporary US comics, such as *Peanuts*
and *Blondie*, and to give each of his characters a name starting with the letter
M to match the brand name. Following these instructions, Quino included a
little girl in his fictional family whom he called Mafalda, a name he took from
a recent movie. In the end, the agency had to abandon the project when the
newspaper realized the comic strip was actually surreptitious advertising, and
the brand was never launched for reasons unrelated to the campaign. Quino,
however, had already drawn eight trial strips, and the following year three of
these were picked up by his friend and fellow cartoonist Miguel Brascó, who
featured them in "Gregorio," the humor supplement he directed for *Leoplán*
magazine (see figure 1.1). Shortly after, Quino took the original idea and turned
it into what would become his most famous cartoon. In September 1964, the
magazine *Primera Plana* began publishing *Mafalda*.[1]

The story of how *Mafalda* was born is well known throughout the world,
in the many countries where the much-loved cartoon character is not only read
and quoted but also considered a cultural icon. But in this chapter I would like
to look more closely at the comic strip's origins with the aim of shedding light on
the social, cultural, and economic interconnections it reveals. This effort will be

guided by two ideas. The first is that from the start the comic strip was permeated by processes that in the mid-1960s made Argentine society unique. The second is that while Quino was undoubtedly a keen observer of reality and incorporated it brilliantly into his strips, *Mafalda* did not just speak to the world in which it emerged; it also influenced it. I draw here on the work of Raymond Williams, who posits that there are social phenomena "in which certain crises which cannot otherwise be directly apprehended are 'crystallized' in certain direct images and forms of art—images which then illuminate a basic (social and psychological) condition."[2] That is, there are cultural forms that can shape social phenomena and conditions and thus provide a unique lens for examining such phenomena and conditions. Building on this idea, this book seeks to provide further insight into Argentina's middle class in the 1960s and early 1970s by historically reconstructing the production, circulation, and social resignification of *Mafalda*.

The new historiography on the middle class in Latin America is filling a long-standing void in the research on social classes, which for decades focused only on the working and upper classes. This work emerged in the context of poststructuralism and as cultural studies was gaining ground, prompting thought-provoking discussions on the origins of Latin America's middle class.[3] These discussions are still ongoing and have raised new questions connected with epistemological concerns (such as the link between the material and the symbolic; or historical temporality), giving way to a particularly stimulating debate.[4] In any event, they have shown the importance of avoiding a simplistic approach to the middle class and of connecting it with a historical process that is not determined beforehand.

With that in mind, in these pages I would like to shift the focus away from the origins of the middle class to examine that class in the 1960s, when there is no doubt about its importance in political, economic, and sociocultural processes. By then it participated openly and directly in such processes and was at the center of countless debates, interventions, and strategies across Latin America. Research conducted in the early twenty-first century took a new approach to the 1960s and '70s, and although these works do not address the middle class specifically as a subject of study, they do underscore the major role it played during that period.[5] They show that while in the first decades of the twentieth century the middle class may have appeared ubiquitous in many Latin American contexts, as of the 1960s it stood out for its centrality. Only recently, however, have studies of the 1960s treated the middle class as substantive in and of itself—in historical and nonsimplistic terms (as is the case in this book).[6]

In Argentina, these discussions entail revising the persistent idea that by the 1960s the country had a long-established middle class formed by waves of upwardly mobile European immigrants dating back to the second half of the nineteenth century. This large, solid middle class had come to be seen as a typical feature of Argentina's national identity.[7] The foundations for this interpretation were laid down in the mid-twentieth century by the scientific sociology of Gino Germani. This Italian sociologist—who immigrated to Argentina and deeply influenced the field there and across the region—used statistical data to lend authority to the claim that the middle class represented a major segment of Argentine society (around 40 percent, according to his estimates). Germani explained its growth as resulting from the modernization and urbanization processes of the late nineteenth and early twentieth centuries.[8] More recently, the Argentine historian Ezequiel Adamovsky has offered an interpretation that challenges this idea. Drawing on public discourse and image analysis, he argues that the identity of the middle class was not consolidated until the emergence of the Peronist movement (1943–55), when it coalesced as an antipopular reaction against the political irruption of the working class.[9] His theory has sparked great controversy as it undermines notions that are firmly rooted in both academia and society, not only plays down the importance of structural economic and social dimensions but also of everyday life, and reopens a recurring discussion—particularly intense in Argentina—of the middle class's political and social significance.[10]

As noted earlier, I steer the discussion of Argentina's middle class away from the question of its origins and consider instead how it can be interpreted and what characteristics it had in the mid-1960s, when not only is there no question that it existed but it can be said to have been at its strongest.[11] Along these lines, studies have highlighted a conservative streak in the middle class in view of the role it played in contributing to legitimize the coups staged during this period, lending its support to moral crusades, and condoning the "war against subversion" waged during the last dictatorship and in the years leading up to it. But examining the role of the middle class has also been instrumental in explaining the radicalization of young people, the enormous popularity of psychoanalysis, and the changes in family values.[12] In sum, there is no doubt about the middle class's importance in the 1960s and '70s, but there are no studies that explain its contradictions historically.

Thus, through an analysis of *Mafalda*—a comic strip that initially appealed primarily to middle-class readers and was read, discussed, and held up as an emblematic representation of that social class—this chapter attempts both to examine the middle class during that period and to understand its conflicting views. My premise is that the huge commercial success of the comic strip, the debates it sparked among the public, and its social significance turned *Mafalda* into a representation—embodied in objects and practices—that is extremely valuable for studying the middle class at that particular moment in history. First I examine the social and cultural practices that made the cartoon possible and gave it meaning. I then look at its original cast and characteristics, pointing out gender, generational, and family dimensions. I go on to consider the limits between the public and the private and how *Mafalda* deals with those boundaries. Finally, I discuss the growing complexity of the comic strip—starting with its move to the newspaper *El Mundo* and up to the 1966 coup staged by General Juan Carlos Onganía, when it became a symbol of antiauthoritarianism—observing the relationship between sociocultural and political conditions and its representations of middle-class identity.

My core argument is that Quino produced *Mafalda* by drawing on elements from society but that, at the same time, the comic strip contributed to shaping reality. It "crystallized" a middle-class identity that reflected—and generated—concrete practices that operated socially, culturally, and politically. Employing a form of humor—a critical self-reflective irony—to engage in dialogue with the sociocultural environment and identity of the middle class, it put into circulation a certain representation of the middle class that depicted it as a heterogeneous whole marked by the ideological and cultural differences that pierced it. I propose that instead of adopting a one-dimensional approach to the middle class that looks at either structural or discursive factors, we examine the (always shifting) connection between the sociocultural conditions of individuals and groups (with their concrete social relations) and the images and representations of their identity produced by them or by others. In line with the work of E. P. Thompson, I posit that to understand the middle class we need to think about its identity in relation to material, social, and political conditions.[13] That is, I conceive the middle class at the intersection of practices and representations involving the struggles, experiences, and ideas of concrete individuals within the fabric of their social relations.[14] This approach also entails transcending dichotomous views that imagine the middle class as leaning either to the left or to the right politically. At the same time, it reveals how discourses and representations concerning the middle class exposed—and even used—its contradictions and ambiguous stances toward democracy, social modernization, authoritarianism, and countercultural trends.

Quino Finds Mafalda and Mafalda Finds an Audience

We invited Quino to contribute to the pages of *Primera Plana* even before we launched the magazine. It has taken him almost two years and he only agreed once he was sure he could deliver something different from his usual work: a comic strip almost mirroring real life, peopled by an intellectually-precocious little girl—Mafalda—and her unique universe of family and friends. Quino—who at thirty-two is undoubtedly the most brilliant cartoonist of his generation—joins our magazine with Mafalda and he does so with his characteristic humility, placing the strip at the foot of the page. In the future, it may change form or take up more space. That's up to him. Our doors are wide open to his talent.

— "Carta al lector" (note to the reader), *Primera Plana* (Buenos Aires), no. 99 (September 29 1964), 1

With these words, *Primera Plana* introduced *Mafalda* to its readers. It is not surprising that it chose to highlight the singularity of the comic strip and its author. As of 1962, with Jacobo Timerman at the helm, the magazine had established itself as part of a new wave of journalism. It targeted a male middle-class audience that according to a market study totaled some 250,000 readers, mostly businessmen, intellectuals, and professionals.[15] Editorially it was somewhat contradictory. In economics it adhered to developmentalism (which assigned an active role to the state and encouraged foreign investment to boost industrialization); in politics it favored military interventionism; and in culture it promoted social modernization and literary vanguardism. Its pages featured celebrated writers such as Tomás Eloy Martínez, Ernesto Schóo, and Jorge Romero Brest, whom the magazine saw as helping to steer the country in a new, modernizing direction. While it aspired to educate the public, it did not make that aim explicit. Rather it assumed active, intelligent, and knowing readers who enjoyed the illusion of belonging to an exclusive, discerning, and uninhibited circle.[16] The praise for Quino was part of the magazine's strategy to shape a sophisticated readership that was capable of appreciating the cartoonist's originality and vanguardism. This ideal audience was often probably far from reality, but the strategy was key at a time in which several new magazines were being launched, pitting publishers against each other in a fierce competition for readers.[17]

While *Primera Plana*'s claim that it had failed in previous attempts to recruit Quino may or may not be true, there is no doubt that by 1964 the artist was one of the most celebrated in his field. In 1962, when he received the commission for the home appliances campaign, Quino had just held his first show in Buenos Aires. The following year, he published *Mundo Quino*, his first collection of caricatures. That book—remembered even today—proposed a conceptual humor in single-panel cartoons with no captions and an original style inspired by the renowned *New Yorker* cartoonist and illustrator Saul Steinberg. Quino's work was part of a cartoon art boom in Argentina that had begun in 1957 with the publication of the widely successful magazine *Tía Vicenta* under the direction of the Argentine caricaturist and humorist Juan Carlos Colombres (Landrú) and with the participation of famous cartoonists such as Oscar Conti (Oski), Raúl Damonte Botana (Copi), and Quino himself. With a combination of genres and a style open to surrealism and the absurd, the magazine quickly reached a monthly print run of 100,000 and invigorated the country's field of graphic humor.[18]

In that renaissance, Quino's career took off. He had known from an early age that he wanted to draw. A shy boy from a family of politicized Spanish immigrants with a tradition of republicanism and anticlericalism, he had spent long hours drawing in his childhood home in the province of Mendoza. His mother, moved by his enthusiasm, had surrendered her kitchen table so he could use it as a drawing board. His first teacher had been his uncle Joaquín, an artist who worked in advertising, and Quino loved poring over the American magazines his uncle received. In 1945, when he was only twelve, his mother died and he decided to enroll in art school, but he dropped out three years later, when his father passed away. By then he was already set on becoming an illustrator and hoped to be hired as an assistant to Guillermo Divito, who was at the time a very prominent cartoonist and caricaturist. In 1950, Quino received his first commission—a comic strip to advertize a Mendoza silk shop—and in 1954 he published his first contribution in *Esto Es*, a political magazine similar in style to *Primera Plana*. After a first failed move to Buenos Aires, he settled down permanently in the capital in 1958. His workload increased and he began publishing in a number of magazines, including *Rico Tipo, Vea y Lea, Panorama,* and *Atlántica,* and in newspapers such as *Democracia.* He made friends among the editorial staffs in all these publications. During this period he met Miguel Brascó, who would play a key role in the history of *Mafalda,* as he recommended Quino for the Mansfield campaign and later featured the trial strips in his magazine. Around this time Quino also met the journalist Julián Delgado, *Primera Plana*'s future editor in chief, who would invite him to join the magazine's staff. In those early years in Buenos Aires, the two young artists lived in the same boarding house. It was a time of intense activity and little money, and Quino remembers having to work through the night in order to meet the deadlines he agreed on just to eke out a living.[19]

The groundwork for *Mafalda* was thus laid down in a fertile and vigorous field, where Quino was able to grow creatively, intellectually, and artistically, and in a climate of journalistic renewal that was part of a general surge in cultural creativity. Cultural productions have a complex but undeniable relationship with social phenomena. We cannot fully understand them without taking into account their social and economic underpinnings. In this sense, from the very first strip, Quino's cartoon struck a dialogue with events and developments in Argentine society, and it reflected and commented on phenomena that were affecting the middle class in particular.

In 1964, when *Mafalda* began its run, nobody questioned the statistical importance of Argentina's middle class.[20] Over the following decades it continued to grow as the number of independent shopkeepers, white-collar workers, technical experts, and professionals increased.[21] Its numerical significance was reflected in the country's social and demographic development. The early 1960s saw the coming of age of a generation that had benefited from the expansion in secondary school enrollment during the first governments of Juan Domingo Perón (1946–55), a process that continued over the following years with the growth in higher education. Between 1950 and 1960 the number of students enrolled in standard education and technical studies at the secondary level nearly doubled nationwide, somewhat less in the capital. University students throughout the country increased more than twofold in that period. In 1961, one out of ten Argentines aged twenty to twenty-four was enrolled in university or other higher studies (including teacher training), and a decade later, in 1971, that proportion had again doubled. The number of white-collar workers—in offices, commerce, public services, and education—had also been on the rise since the 1940s. This form of employment had intensified under developmentalism, which had advanced the fields of services, marketing, advertising, and human resources. In 1960, according to census data, there were 822,450 commerce workers and 706,277 office workers in the country, which combined accounted for 20 percent of the economically active population, and in the capital these two groups totaled 32 percent, with 230,025 and 168,715 workers, respectively. These workers—both male and female—were avidly participating in the changes in consumption patterns that were under way. The improvements in income distribution as a result of Peronist policies, the expansion of public services (gas, electricity, sewers), and the decreasing prices of electrical goods made it possible for many households to acquire television sets, stoves, refrigerators, and other major appliances. Manufactured clothing and food purchases also increased. None of these trends were entirely new, of course, but in the 1960s they became more widespread and were strongly associated with a middle class that had swelled in numbers under an economic developmentalist agenda that promised to modernize the country, but in the context of a more restrictive political democracy in which Perón and his movement were banned.[22]

The ad agency wished to target this middle class when it asked Quino to create a comic strip to sell home appliances. The idea of using a cartoon for subliminal advertising entailed a belief—perhaps naive—in the power of creativity, and it followed the trends that characterized the developmentalist expansion furthered by the government of Arturo Frondizi (1958–62). The focus on strengthening productive sectors and the role that companies were expected to play in national development required both boosting foreign investments and a social, cultural, and economic modernization program to support these goals. The Siam Di Tella business group, which manufactured the Mansfield appliances, adhered completely to this developmentalist creed. The group had been one of the driving forces behind modernization efforts. But it had also shown its commitment to promoting the latest artistic and cultural productions, most notably with the establishment of the Torcuato Di Tella Institute, where Germani's school of scientific sociology interacted with avant-garde artists and designers who were changing the world of art and advertising.[23] The group's ad agency had originated at the institute, from which it had recruited several artists and intellectuals, including Pérez Celis, Paco Urondo, and Norman Briski. These admen and market experts drew on developments in the social sciences, which Germani had helped consolidate as a discipline in Argentina. For example, they hired the services of the Applied Social Psychology Institute (Instituto de Psicología Social Aplicada), founded in 1961, whose surveys—along with those of similar companies—were instrumental in mapping out the middle-class market. At the same time, they popularized a certain hierarchical segmentation of society by including it in studies and news articles. That intellectual and artistic hub fostered by the Di Tella group, in which the modernizing forces of avant-garde artists and Germani's scientific sociology converged, contributed to *Mafalda*'s birth.

It is, however, telling that Quino chose to name his protagonist after a character in the 1962 film *Dar la cara*, as the script was based on a book by David Viñas, a young writer whose views were diametrically opposed to those held by scientific sociologists. He belonged to a generation of left-wing intellectuals who distanced themselves from their modernizing and anti-Peronist elders. "This generation—my generation—is Peronist," Viñas had declared in 1959. The movie expressed the emergence of a group of young intellectuals who produced a "literature of mortification and atonement," as the Argentine sociologist Carlos Altamirano has described it. They reproached the middle class—their own class—for disparaging the *cabecitas negras* (literally "black heads," the derogative term used for Argentina's indigenous population) and blamed it for the downfall of Peronism.[24] While Quino only took the name of a minor character in the movie (that Mafalda was a baby who appeared only briefly on screen), his choice is nonetheless significant. It links the comic strip, a future symbol of the middle class, to an ideological tradition critical of that social sector. Quino was, in fact, part of a group of friends that included left-wing writers and journalists such as Rodolfo Walsh—who lived in the same boarding house as Quino—and Paco Urondo. They met regularly, joined occasionally by Viñas himself, to engage in serious political discussions but also to enjoy themselves.[25]

In short, *Mafalda*'s origins—from the initial idea to its production and circulation—were situated at a convergence where the field of culture (humor, artistic and intellectual productions, the media) met commercial efforts (the ad agency and Siam Di Tella's strategies) and social processes that affected the middle class in particular but not exclusively. The comic strip took up the social, political, and cultural contradictions of this class. In particular, *Mafalda* initially touched on the phenomenon of social modernization, and especially on the changes in family relations, the status of women, generational gaps, and authoritarianism. Quino drew intuitively on all these processes, employing them as key devices—what Williams called "social material"—and returning to them over and over again.

FAMILY, GENDER, AND GENERATIONS

Mafalda staged a representation of a nuclear family, with first one and then two children and the traditional division of roles in which the husband was the breadwinner and the wife the homemaker. This family model was not new to the Argentina of the 1960s, as in the early years of the twentieth century the birth rate had dropped and the marriage rate had gone up. Neither was its association with the middle class. In creating his fictional family, Quino drew on a long line of emblematic representations that reflected the link between family models and social status. These images had contributed to shape the "typical" family, with its homogeneous and exclusionary makeup that left out countless family situations, and which had become a normative yardstick and an ideal associated with improved living conditions and aspirations of respectability and upward social mobility.[26]

The novelty of Quino's portrayal was in the specifics of his family—the concerns and anxieties of the parents and the confrontational attitude of the little girl—which produced a modern rendering. By giving his characters these traits, Quino also addressed the issues that *Primera Plana* presented to its readers in other sections. The magazine published a weekly "Modern Life" section that covered trends and topics that its editors thought would be of interest to the middle class: psychoanalysis, new child-rearing practices, the generation gap, the role of television, and shifting authority within the family. While the editors were undoubtedly trying to call attention to such matters, they were not merely pushing an agenda, as these were indeed concerns of the middle class. People were convinced they were living in an era of inexorable changes in family relations and social norms, although they were not as certain of the direction such changes would take.[27]

According to his own account, Quino modified his original version of the comic strip to adapt it to *Primera Plana*. He first changed certain details of the drawings and discarded elements that were associated with the past to achieve a sleeker style that matched the magazine's editorial line. He modified the father's appearance, making him more modern and pleasant, traits that were essential for the dialogue the comic strip wished to strike with its male readers. Quino also revamped the office and home settings, replacing the old-fashioned furniture with new pop-style pieces, and the harsh lines with more rounded ones.

But the most important change Quino introduced was in the makeup of the family. In line with Siam Di Tella's commission, which called for a cartoon somewhere between *Blondie* and *Peanuts* and centered around a typical family, he had originally drawn a married couple with two children: a boy and a girl (figure 1.1). In the final version, the son was cut out and the daughter was the only character in the strip that retained the same facial features. By eliminating the son, the daughter no longer had a marginal role and instead became the lead character and the driving force behind the storylines. This change, which was probably not intentional, would prove key for the development of the cartoon's themes.

FIGURE 1.1 Quino, untitled strip published in the "Gregorio" supplement of the magazine *Leoplán* (Buenos Aires), ca. June 1964, reproduced in Quino, *Mafalda inédita*. © Joaquín Salvador Lavado (Quino).

On September 29, 1964, *Mafalda* was featured for the first time in *Primera Plana*. By giving the comic strip the name of the child character, Quino established her central role and defined her characteristics and the place she occupied in the family. The strip with which *Mafalda* premiered shows the little girl asking her father if he was a good father (figure 1.2). This entailed an inversion of normal parent-child relations in which the adults asked the children about their behavior. Her father answers that he *thinks* he is a good father but that there might be better fathers out there, and in doing so he displays a reflective and unassuming attitude that undermines his position of authority, as it prevents his daughter from seeing him as the best father in the world. The girl's reaction is paradigmatic of what the character's personality would be throughout the comic strip's run: her father's response seems to confirm her suspicions and we see her turning her back on him disappointed, the sweet, smiling face from the first panels transformed with anger.

The following week, readers would discover (figure 1.3) that this little girl could curse and had a range of furious expressions and attitudes that clashed with the gentleness that was expected of her age and sex. For the humorous device to work, readers had to empathize with the situation. These early strips, then, introduced a core aspect of the cartoon, as Mafalda, the character, encapsulated two tensions—generational conflicts and changing gender roles—that Quino would address through his humor over the following years. In generational terms, Mafalda was a hybrid whose biological immaturity was out of sync with the intellectual development she displayed. She reasoned like an adult, or, rather, like a rebellious teenager or youth who defied her parents. But she was just four years old. The resulting incongruous effect was comical. It exposed the weaknesses of adults, but it did so while at the same time evoking the tender feelings naturally inspired by children, thus tempering the irony. This strategy—which combined tenderness with caustic criticism—was especially effective because it brought into play basic notions regarding children and youth that were held by many at the time. The reference to the new generations was reflected in the drawings. The way the character Mafalda—and later her friends—was drawn was distinct from the way the adults in the comic strip were drawn, with different proportions that were meant to stress the changes in the human body at the various stages of life. Mafalda was given a large, round head—a simple closed shape that alluded psychologically to the mother's womb and the globe.

The storyline upset the prevailing glorification of childhood whereby children symbolized the expectations of progress and future well-being of their families, the nation, and even the whole of humanity. This exaltation rested on

FIGURE 1.2 Quino, "Mafalda," *Primera Plana* (Buenos Aires), September 29, 1964, 22.
© Joaquín Salvador Lavado (Quino).

FIGURE 1.3 Quino, "Mafalda," *Primera Plana* (Buenos Aires), October 6, 1964, 26.
© Joaquín Salvador Lavado (Quino).

a social and cultural view of childhood as a unique and decisive stage in the life of the individual. But the comic strip also addressed changing child-rearing practices, which relied more and more on ideas based on psychology and entailed revaluing the spontaneity and autonomy of children. As *Primera Plana* highlighted, this psychological approach to understanding family relations was having a big impact on Argentine society. Eric Fromm's *The Art of Loving* (1956) was a best-seller in the country; several magazines featured the child care advice of Dr. Benjamin Spock, who had even visited Argentina; the newspaper *La Razón* (which sold half a million copies a day) published a regular column on modern parenting practices penned by the Argentine psychologist Eva Giberti; and it was common for couples to sign up for courses that offered psychological guidance on how to raise their children.[28]

In *Mafalda* these new approaches to childhood were connected with the perception of the generational gaps and the new protagonism of young people.

In the 1960s these issues were part of a global phenomenon, and they were just as important in Argentina—particularly in urban settings—as elsewhere. As could be read in the pages of *Primera Plana*, adults were troubled by the behavior, tastes, and fashions of young people because they challenged hierarchies within and outside the family through attitudes and ways of understanding all aspects of life—from sex to social conventions—that to a greater or lesser extent defied the establishment.[29] This alarmed educational, religious, and political authorities, whose fears grew as the confrontational stance spread to the domain of politics. Following Perón's ousting in 1955—with the coup that banned his movement—many young people joined the Peronist resistance. University and high-school students also turned to politics when they stood up to defend the state monopoly over higher education that came under threat with President Arturo Frondizi's chartering of private universities. Many other youth became politically active with the Cuban Revolution of 1959, which opened up the possibility of radical change that, in Argentina, with its restricted democracy and constant military interventions, seemed more urgent than ever. Young people thus emerged as vital political players, channeling their actions through the countless organizations that sprang up in an increasingly vibrant social, cultural, and political setting. In sum, *Mafalda* called attention to the various questionings voiced by the new generations that were setting off alarms among the authorities and in the media, which, in turn, alternatively glorified and demonized youth.[30]

With respect to gender, Mafalda presented certain androgynous ambiguities or fluctuations. In the trial sketches, Quino had already drawn her as a boyish girl. In one strip she was shown wielding a large hammer and building what appeared to be a bed for her dolls. In the last panel, however, she revealed that it was meant to be a therapist's couch, thus deviating from standard female behavior in both the activity and the end result (as psychoanalysts were still primarily male). In the first strips published in *Primera Plana*, the malicious attitude and mischief of the "intellectually-precocious little girl," and her use of curse words, suggested a character with personality traits that society expected to see in males. Gender ambiguity could also be observed in her facial features: her knitted brows, angry eyes, bellowing mouth, and annoyed expressions stood in stark contrast to the sweet, angelic, tender faces normally associated with little girls. Thus she adopted typically masculine attitudes that had defined—traditionally and still—socially constructed gender roles, thereby representing the ways in which gender was being redefined and the discussions such redefinitions prompted.

In contrast to Charlie Brown—the character the ad agency had asked Quino to draw inspiration from and whose universe was populated exclusively by children—*Mafalda* was centered around generational conflicts and the provocations of young people. As the gender and generational orders were disrupted, the adults appeared helpless, adrift. This was evident in the father's expression in the first strip, when Mafalda turned angrily away from him as he confirmed her suspicion that she did not have the best dad in the world. One of the following strips showed this disruption in a paradigmatic way. In the first panel the little girl asks her mother if she could draw in a booklet she had found. Her mother says no, explaining that it is not just any booklet but contains her marriage certificate. Upon hearing her mom's explanation, Mafalda exclaims, "What do you need a booklet for? I thought people got married upfront." This was a play on a common practice at the time, which involved buying groceries on informal credit from the neighborhood store (running a tab) and the use of booklets to keep a record of what was owed, and a kid's innocent association linking two things that on the surface are vastly dissimilar: money matters and affairs of the heart. In that way, it alluded to the importance of material considerations in marriage decisions rather than love. The result is ironic, as such formulations convey the opposite of what is literally said and serve to capture a contradiction. They express skepticism and make it possible to adopt a critical stance, often building on a paradox, in this case the two unrelated booklets prompting a reflection on marriage. Used in humor, these constructions are even more significant, because they require an actively engaged target audience that has to fill in the gaps with what is left unsaid to discover the cracks in the reality they inhabit.[31]

By subverting the gender and generational orders, the strip portrayed the adult characters as vulnerable and out of place. This was particularly the case with Mafalda's mother, Raquel, a stay-at-home mom and full-time housewife who represented the female ideal—a homemaker wholly devoted to her children—fostered early in the twentieth century by the policies, ideologies, and discourses of the country's intellectual elites, the state, and the Catholic Church.[32] In the 1960s, this ideal—which had been a symbol of prosperity, respectability, and family values—was in flux. The number of women in the workforce—often underreported—increased from 21.7 percent of the economically active population in 1947 to 24.8 percent in 1970 nationwide, and from 31 to 35 percent in the capital during the same period. This increase was more pronounced among women aged 30 to 39, going from 25 to 33 percent in that age range, which was also when women traditionally married and became mothers. The change in the status of women was also reflected in education. More than two-thirds of young women aged 20 to 24 had a high-school education and almost half had reached higher education or university level.[33] At the same time, women began to look outside the home for personal fulfillment, emulating the new female ideal of the "modern," "independent," and "liberated" woman associated with the younger generations and the cultural prestige afforded by professional, intellectual, and artistic careers. In fact, *Primera Plana* and other "modernizing" media claimed to echo these generations and celebrated young women such as Dalila Puzzovio, an artist sponsored by the Di Tella Institute, who provocatively declared that women wanted to "improve our situation, satisfy our desires, do whatever we please," thus challenging their mothers' generation.[34]

Quino incorporated these tensions into his storylines. Mafalda questioned the traditional feminine ideal embodied by her mother, forcing Raquel to become aware of her own frustrations. Her opposition was such that it defined Mafalda's identity. One of the first installments of the cartoon was a series of sequenced strips that dealt with Mafalda's disappointment upon discovering that Raquel had dropped out of college. Mafalda begins by making her case with a string of cause-and-effect arguments (figure 1.4): "If you hadn't married, you would've gone on studying and you would've finished college and . . . you'd have a degree and you'd be SOMEBODY and . . ." At that point she is interrupted by her mother's frustrated sobbing. Mafalda's blunt logic (which at that time was being identified by psychological theory as typical of the child) laid bare the essence of the adult's condition.[35]

FIGURE 1.4 Quino, "Mafalda," *Primera Plana* (Buenos Aires), October 20, 1964, 64. © Joaquín Salvador Lavado (Quino).

As the realization of her mother's past dawned on Mafalda her reaction produced a humorous effect that was amplified by the double inversion created by the situation depicted in the strip. Here it is the mother, not the child, who cries while the daughter appears as the voice of reason and—in later strips— would play the parental role of comforter. The value of motherhood was also inverted, as the daughter's demand entails that being "somebody" requires a "degree," in contrast to the traditional idea that motherhood is the natural female vocation. The irony resonated clearly with both male and female readers alike: the intellectualized little girl and her mother embodied the conflicts sparked by the new styles of womanhood and the clash between generations, which not only were expressed in the media but also were present in the relationships many ordinary mothers had with their young daughters. Mafalda's invective, however, was softened because it was voiced by a child: a little girl did not compete with her mother in the same way a teenager would, because her reasoning inspired tenderness and, thus, opened up for the mother the possibility of reparation, giving her hope that her own frustration would not be mirrored by her daughter.

Generational conflicts and shifting gender roles took on a different meaning when it came to men. Mafalda's father—the leading male adult character in the strip—was a modern provider: a white-collar worker who enjoyed domestic life, tending to his plants, and reading parenting books.[36] In addition to softening the more severe father figure of his original trial strips, Quino updated the stereotype of the breadwinning male, adjusting it to reflect the aspirations advanced by *Primera Plana*. The magazine featured an image of the executive man who represented modern virility, depicting its male readers as members of a successful and sophisticated select group who participated in the growing consumer culture. (See, for example, the representations depicted in ads from *Primera Plana* shown in figures 1.5–1.6.)

FIGURES 1.5, 1.6, AND 1.7 Ads featured in *Primera Plana* (Buenos Aires), September 29, 1964, 13, and October 27, 1964, 27; and Quino, "Mafalda," *Primera Plana* (Buenos Aires), November 17, 1964, 60 (panel 3). © Joaquín Salvador Lavado (Quino).

In the 1960s, this representation could resonate with an increasing number of male breadwinners, as employment in the service economy experienced its most rapid period of growth and advertising and other new services emerged.[37] At the same time, being a white-collar worker took on a new significance in cultural expressions that portrayed the alienation of the middle class, as in the novel *La tregua* by the Uruguayan writer Mario Benedetti or the play *La fiaca* by the Argentine playwright Ricardo Talesnik. The comic strip reflected this, revealing that *Primera Plana*'s modern man was more aspiration than reality. Mafalda's father represented the distance separating the glamorous executive from the real, everyday existence of a middle-class white-collar worker. The mundane daily routines, the overcrowded office, the difficulties making ends meet, and Mafalda's persistent questioning illustrated how far her father was from a modern executive, a successful breadwinner, and the voice of authority in the home. These impossibilities were symbolically underscored when Mafalda referred to her father as a "flower-pot executive," alluding to his hobby of tending potted plants and his relentless but hopeless battle against ants, or in a strip in which we see him enjoying a moment of hedonistic pleasure, drinking coffee and lighting a cigarette, almost convinced that he is that modern executive, only to be brought abruptly back to reality as he steps outside his apartment building in the following panel.[38]

Thus, the comic strip that had been born as a device to sell consumer goods turned into a critique of the fallacy that lay behind the enticing promises of modern advertising. Middle-class readers could grasp—and laugh at—the irony in the contrast between the magazine's images and the comic strip's portrayal. That perception required an empathetic reflection on their own position as members of a class defined by the social, cultural, and political contradictions and impossibilities that pierced it, and whose group cohesion was, at the same time, strengthened by the act of laughter as readers recognized themselves in the storylines.

The magazine also extolled the "new father" promoted by psychological trends in parenting, which called on men to cultivate a more affectionate, understanding, and informal relationship with their children.[39] It was an emerging model that stigmatized "traditional" authoritarian fathers—who were also occasionally portrayed in the comic strip—and was associated with a middle class open to change. Mafalda's interactions with her father illustrated this shift in authority within the family. When his wise-beyond-her-years daughter demanded answers about the state of the world or used the threat of nuclear war to extort candies from him, the father was rendered speechless. But he rarely responded in anger. His reactions were more of surprise and bewilderment.

Even thrown off balance by his daughter's quips and questions, it never entered this perplexed father's mind to use physical violence against her, although he could raise his voice at her in exasperation.

In short, *Mafalda* presented a believable portrait of a "typical family"—as the *Buenos Aires Herald* described it in 1967—based on the hegemonic nuclear model characterized by a married couple and no more than two children, clearly defined traditional gender roles, and loving relationships.[40] But in contrast to other contemporary cultural products that depicted "typical" families—such as the popular soap opera *La familia Falcón*—Quino chose to focus on problematizing their core characteristics. The character of Mafalda embodied the new generations that were successfully upsetting the adults' material, cultural, and political world. The comic strip as a whole offered a unique representation of the anxieties and conflicts caused by modernization, as both an aspiration and a historical process. It addressed the middle class with particular force, at a time in which the values on which it had built its respectability were being undermined by changes that were believed to be as irreversible as they were perplexing and endless. Quino drew on the contradictions brought on by the sociocultural mutations that had forged the middle class and now permeated it. Most notably, instead of painting a prosperous and successful image of the middle class, Mafalda's child/youth perspective exposed the frustrations, difficulties, and even impossibilities that the process of sociocultural modernization entailed for middle-class men and women alike: the limitations faced by breadwinners, the dissatisfaction felt by mothers and homemakers, and the challenges to the family order posed by the new generations. Paradoxically, *Mafalda* offered a representation that succeeded in exorcising the anger that had surfaced in intellectual and progressive spaces against their own class.

BLURRING THE LINE BETWEEN PUBLIC AND PRIVATE

As the main focus of *Primera Plana* was politics, Quino incorporated political issues into the strip from the start. At first this was implicit. In the second strip we see Mafalda drawing and, as she is finishing, her pencil breaks. Furious, she screams, "These things only happen in this country!!" By equating a minor pencil malfunction with a national problem, the punch line played with the absurdity of the comparison but also invited readers to laugh at a common critical attitude that tended to blame the country for any difficulty faced. Some weeks later, on October 27, the comic strip touched on politics again. The three-panel strip showed Mafalda disrupting the household peace as she creeps up on her parents who are reading the paper and commenting on China's nuclear development. Their reaction when she screams "BOOM!"—making them

FIGURE 1.8 Quino, "Mafalda," *Primera Plana* (Buenos Aires), October 27, 1964, 16.
© Joaquín Salvador Lavado (Quino).

jump out of their chairs in terror—evokes the prevailing fear of nuclear war, which Mafalda highlights with her closing quip: "Mass hysteria!" (figure 1.8).[41]

In this strip, irony operates disruptively by turning the generational order upside down and breaking the link between peaceful family life and national security contained in the discourse of the Cold War. In an inversion of generational roles, it is the little girl who scares the grown-ups, undermining the idea of the home as an unassailable fortress in the international order. The comic effect produced by these inversions was magnified by the paradoxical contradiction between the character's young age and the maturity of her reasoning, which allowed her to diagnose her parents as suffering from "mass hysteria," a term that would have evidenced readers' familiarity with psychoanalysis. Mafalda stirred the ghosts that scared her parents and by doing so she mocked adults in general. Some even saw this as a dig at those responsible for spreading these fears, that is, the forces laying the groundwork for the demonization of grassroots and left-wing organizations, which such forces considered subversive elements that threatened Western Christian civilization.[42]

In this sense, the comic strip forced readers to reflect but it did not steer them explicitly in any direction. This made it easier for them to exercise their freedom, in Carlo Ginzburg's terms, to interpret the comic strip.[43] As we will see in chapter 2, *Mafalda*'s significance will be based, to a great extent, on its polysemic nature, which became more and more important.

Only after this reference to international affairs did the strip venture into Argentine politics. The country faced growing social and political unrest, compounded by an increasingly weakened democracy, a stream of military interventions, and the threat of a structural economic and social crisis that evidenced the historical exclusion of the rural and urban working classes. This state of affairs had triggered a wave of political activity among students, new social movements—including some led by progressive priests—and left-wing organizations, whose discussions over how to achieve revolutionary change had spawned the first guerrilla groups. It was in this context that in 1964, the Radical Party leader Arturo Illia won the presidency with only 25 percent of the votes, in an election that had low voter turnout and a high number of blank votes. This outcome revealed how the exclusion of Peronist candidates had weakened the system. As noted earlier, a ban on Peronism was first imposed in 1955 when the military toppled Perón's government, and it was later reaffirmed in 1962, after President Frondizi was overthrown in reaction to his decision to hold unrestricted provincial elections, which had resulted in a Peronist victory.

Once in office, Illia failed both to improve the feeble support that had been barely enough to secure him the election, and to restrain the military groups that were influencing public opinion against him. *Primera Plana* contributed actively to those efforts. It supported a military faction known as the "blues"—which supposedly sought an electoral solution with the inclusion of Peronists—against the "reds," who wanted to exclude Peronists completely. The magazine was also engaged in a campaign to discredit Illia, which had begun almost immediately after his inauguration.[44] In October 1964, it featured a survey that gauged public sentiment toward the president, presenting the results in a way that raised the specter of a coup d'état. While the middle class saw the president as "kind, measured, and fatherly" and his continuity as head of the government was accepted by the majority, the overall image was of a weak and ineffectual president.[45] As in other media, this was used to underscore the strong patriarchal authority represented by General Juan Carlos Onganía, who was the chief force behind the preparations for a military coup.

The cartoon echoed that criticism in a strip that showed Mafalda starting to doze off upon hearing her father begin his bedtime story by likening the benevolent king of the fairytale to the president of Argentina.[46] The readers of *Primera Plana* did not need to stretch their imaginations to grasp the implicit commentary on Illia's dull personality. As the magazine's political opinion pieces repeatedly told them, the president's governing style (his excessive calmness, inability to act fast, and tendency to hesitate) and family life (his provincial marriage to an unstylish homemaker) worked against his efforts to maintain law and order. He was shown in an unfavorable light and contrasted with the modern efficiency and strong leadership that was needed to deal with the country's instability. This image would later be symbolized by the cartoonist Landrú in a caricature in which the president was turned into a turtle. Humor again revealed its political force and, to a certain extent, with such digs it fueled pro-coup sentiment. Quino would later regret having contributed to the president's image as sluggish and inefficient, although by then it was the prevailing view.

In this sense, *Mafalda* painted an accurate portrait of a middle class terrified by the threat of communist China—although here the pranks played by Mafalda on her parents allowed for the possibility of mocking such fears—and receptive to the pro-coup campaign. Interestingly enough, this position did not preclude the rapid ideological shift that shortly after led to Mafalda being unanimously held up as a spokesperson for progressive, intellectual, and pro–Third World elements within the middle class. In any case, these strips were an early indication of the place politics would have in the cartoon: the focus on global conflicts (which made it possible to elude any concrete references to party politics and the partisan allegiances that divided Argentine society) and the linking of everyday life and politics. This established one of *Mafalda*'s most characteristic and oft-employed comic devices: the blurring of lines between the public and the private, a separation that was an essential element in the construction of bourgeois modernity and the idea of the social contract.[47]

This disruption of the public/private division was more powerful because the comic strip's humor turned generational roles on their heads by having as its main character a child who reasoned like an adult. That ambiguity was sometimes charged by the anxieties generated by children and adolescents, at a time when psychology insisted that their playful exploration, spontaneity, and autonomy should not be repressed. Parents faced these new guidelines with trepidation and in putting them into practice were unable to react with the speed and ease that day-to-day interactions required.

The use of this device during the early period of the cartoon is best exemplified by a series of strips in which Mafalda pleads with her father to buy a television set for the family, mirroring a common scene in many households at the time. He refuses to give in, arguing that he does not want his daughter to turn into a "jingle-singing dummy." Having tried different approaches, Mafalda finally resorts to "guerrilla" tactics, jumping out at her father amidst a jungle of potted plants he was placidly tending (figure 1.9).

This parody came shortly after the government had captured a group of young militants from the People's Guerrilla Army (Ejército Guerrillero del Pueblo), who had been operating in the province of Salta, and it suggested a connection between Mafalda and the guerrilla youth. The strip alluded in general to the rebellious attitudes of the new generations both in the family and in politics. Its subversive message emerged in contrast to the ideas of the National Security Doctrine that were being increasingly voiced by various actors in response to the rise in social and political unrest. Not coincidentally, this was one

FIGURE 1.9 Quino, "Mafalda," *El Mundo* (Buenos Aires), March 24, 1965, 8, reproduced in Quino, *Mafalda inédita*. © Joaquín Salvador Lavado (Quino).

of the strips excluded from the first *Mafalda* compilation, which came out in book format a year and a half later.[48]

The comic strip thus highlighted a fluid relationship between the problematization of everyday life and the adoption of tangible political and ideological positions. *Mafalda* went on to express a concrete "political" voice and ideological stance, although that stance was not immediately defined.

In short, the conceptual humor used in *Mafalda* from the start (the clever confusions, the meanings left open to readers' interpretation, the allusions that made readers feel like they were in on the joke, the drawings that played with perspective to underscore contradictions) called attention to the conflicts produced by social, cultural, and political shifts within the middle class. The strip played with the tensions that surfaced with the modernization of the middle class and exposed the gaps between the expectations and the realities of individuals whose identities were being reconfigured at a time of rapid sociocultural change. This unmasking was effected by a character who combined tenderness and a merciless logic typical of children with the critical wit of an adult, or, rather, of a rebellious youth.

"SO . . . WE'RE, LIKE, MIDDLE CLASS?"

Quino quickly made the middle-class nature of these problems evident and by doing so he problematized middle-class identity. Social identities are always constructed in relation to others, and in the case of the middle class its very name presupposes a middle ground between two extremes. This comparison was the focus of a series of strips in which Mafalda discovers she belongs to a certain class. This realization highlighted the problems raised by the definition of middle class and how such problems were at the root of the construction of its identity. In the first strip of the series, published in December 1964, Mafalda asks her father,

"Are we rich or poor?" When her father replies, "We're neither rich nor poor . . . we're, like, middle class," Mafalda comes back with, "Like? We're *like* middle class? So . . . does that mean we're supposed to *like* being middle class?"[49]

In this way, the strip put the dissatisfaction of the middle class at the heart of its identity, and that identity was, in turn, a foundational element of *Mafalda*. This view of a discontented middle class with ambitions above its station followed a long tradition of narratives that, since the early twentieth century, had turned the terms *nouveau riche* and *social climber* into key categories for understanding Argentine society in general and this social segment in particular. In the 1960s, Germani's scientific sociology was being challenged by a "sociopolitical" trend in the social sciences that drew on that tradition and reproached the middle class for its social-climbing attitude. This trend identified with left-wing and Peronist ideas, and its critical view of the middle class was illustrated by the phrase *medio pelo*, a pejorative term that translates as "second rate" (and calls to mind *clase media*, Spanish for "middle class"). The term— coined by leading sociopolitical proponent Arturo Jauretche in his best-selling critical essay—was used to describe people in the middle class (especially the lower middle class) who were trying to work their way up the social ladder but only succeeded in imitating the upper classes.[50]

The following week, in a strip that played on the different connotations of *medio* (figure 1.10), the Spanish word for "middle" (but also meaning "somewhat" or "kind of"), Mafalda is angered again as she realizes what place she occupies in society, dubbing the middle class "clase mediaestúpida" (kind-of-stupid class). The main character asks her mother why they do not own a car and her mother explains that it is because they are middle class. When she hears this answer, after a pause, Mafalda comes back with her conclusion— "kind-of-stupid class, of course"—thus caustically voicing what many adults thought. While many adults could relate to the phrase in itself, it had a particular effect when expressed through the brutally honest logic of a child uninhibitedly and wittily discovering her own social standing. That position was defined by the impossibility of accessing the level of consumption and living standards that the members of the middle class aspired to, while seeing how easily it was enjoyed by others. In this sense, the drawing underscored the idea that others played a decisive role in the definition of the middle class's own identity—Mafalda and her mother are shown walking down the sidewalk from where they see cars (those others) drive by on the street. This strip was the first to be staged in an urban setting. The sketches in the background suggest an anonymous metropolis and a mass society. As we move from one panel to the next, the others appear farther and farther away or increasingly blurry—that

FIGURE 1.10 Quino, "Mafalda," *Primera Plana* (Buenos Aires), December 8, 1964, 20.
© Joaquín Salvador Lavado (Quino).

is, as it becomes clearer to the characters that their place in society, however much they aspire to it, is preventing them from accessing the goods they desire.

This effect was underscored by a perspective that gave depth to the cartoon and by the contrast between background and foreground. The background is drawn in sketchy outlines with little detail. Mafalda and her mother, instead, stand out in greater detail and are drawn with more elaborate and darker strokes. Thus, while in the previous strip (in which Mafalda wondered if belonging to the middle class was a good thing) it was left to the reader to infer the meaning, in this strip the meaning was highlighted.

The greater detail in this second strip emphasizes Mafalda's anger as it dawns on her that belonging to the middle class means there are others above her, more powerful and with a higher standard of living. However, this explicitly angry statement is softened by showing the figures from behind, a device Quino used very rarely. By hiding the character's faces—the main expressive element in his drawings—in almost every panel, he left it up to the reader to imagine their expressions. This device serves to recapture the cartoon's complexity. The solution was accompanied by unique timing. In the third panel the action is suspended, opening a space for reflection, only to be contrasted immediately with Mafalda's unreflective anger. Again, the idea was humorous because it played on the incongruence of the main character's biological age and her intellectual maturity, which was evidenced by her shrewd revelation of the distance between the middle class's aspirations and its reality. However, this resolution did not define the meaning that the discontent and dissatisfaction had. The strip thus allowed readers to add that meaning based on their own ideological position and social experience.

In another strip featured in the same issue, Mafalda watches her parents happily going about their activities at home (cooking, shaving) and exclaims,

"So being middle class does come with certain guarantees of happiness after all." But immediately her satisfied expression fades as she asks herself, "Or could it be that I'm being raised by two witless fools?"[51] Here, instead of anger we have indulgence, which soon gives way to skepticism: Mafalda's features stress the joy of discovering that middle-class existence offers some measure of happiness, tellingly anchored by everyday life and gendered roles in the family, only to have that confidence instantly corroded by irony when she doubts her elders' judgment and their supposed domestic bliss.

Shortly after, Quino incorporated a new character, Felipe, who served further to associate the comic strip with the middle class. Felipe was a boy who lived in the same apartment building as Mafalda and whose family mirrored hers in its makeup and traditional gendered roles. When the two friends meet (figure 1.11), he is introduced as Mafalda's social and generational equal. "Ours is a horizontal and Christian generation," she tells him, echoing the stock phrase *civilización occidental y cristiana* (Western Christian civilization).[52] The word "horizontal" was a pun on the horizontal property regime, which is a form of condominium typical among Argentina's middle-class homeowners, and thus served as a marker of their social class. But with this phrase Mafalda was also parodying a prevailing Cold War discourse, so that the humor in Quino's wordplay was achieved by distorting the government's anticommunist rhetoric. It was an allusion that also called on readers to interpret the irony for themselves.

FIGURE 1.11 Quino, "Mafalda," *Primera Plana* (Buenos Aires), January 19, 1965, 46.
© Joaquín Salvador Lavado (Quino).

As this example shows, from the moment in which it was expressly assumed, the identity of the middle class was problematized and linked to a conceptual and ironic form of humor situated at the intersection of the everyday and the political. If irony in Western society has been historically associated with the subjective "I" and the foundational nature of a self-awareness striving to assert itself, the ruptures registered by the ironies in *Mafalda* can be considered foundational elements of a middle class that self-reflectively viewed its own inconsistencies as part of its identity.[53]

A DENSE AND HETEROGENEOUS CLASS

On March 9, 1965, *Mafalda* left *Primera Plana* without warning. The comic strip had become very popular and when the magazine made a copyright claim over the strips it had featured, Quino protected his interests by pulling out. The strip's success meant that in just one week it was picked up by the daily newspaper *El Mundo* at the suggestion of Quino's friend Miguel Brascó.

Mafalda's new home had been founded by the publishing house Editorial Haynes in 1928 as a "modern, convenient, concise, serious, and informative" morning paper. Its target readers were ordinary people, which were still an emerging readership in the early twentieth century, and with that in mind it had introduced the tabloid format to facilitate reading on trains and buses. Almost four decades later, *El Mundo* maintained its original profile. It was compact, easy to read, and straightforward. Sports and entertainment news featured prominently in its pages, along with accounts of modern life that were probably meant to emulate the literary sketches of Buenos Aires life penned by the prominent writer Roberto Arlt and published in the paper until his death in 1942.[54] According to a 1962 survey, the newspaper ranked fourth among readers of Buenos Aires morning papers. Its audience was clearly very different from the readership of *Primera Plana*, as it was more diverse and less educated. Only 30 percent of respondents who read *El Mundo* had gone beyond primary school, compared to the high percentage of readers of *La Nación*, the traditional newspaper read by the country's elite, who had completed secondary or higher education (84 percent).[55]

It was, however, not surprising that *El Mundo* had opened its doors to *Mafalda*. The newspaper had always given Argentine cartoonists a prominent space in its pages, publishing popular comic strips such as Dante Quintero's *Patoruzú*, starting in 1935. In 1960, the newspaper had begun distributing Landrú's groundbreaking humor magazine *Tía Vicenta* as one of its supplements. Although shortly after Quino joined the newspaper his supplement became an independent magazine, Landrú continued to publish a one-panel strip on the front page of *El Mundo*, where he commented humorously on its domestic politics coverage. A quarter of the two-page space devoted by the newspaper to entertainment was taken up by a variety of comic strips, including the US cartoon *Nancy*, which featured a character that bore a striking resemblance to Mafalda.[56] But like Landrú's, Quino's strips appeared separately, in his case on the editorial page.

With the move to *El Mundo* Quino continued to touch on some of the main themes that had characterized his cartoon in its first home, including generational clashes and the redefinitions of the feminine ideal.[57] But he did have to alter his production. The new daily frequency demanded a faster pace and an adjustment to the immediacy of media coverage, and while he found the evening deadlines highly stressful, he welcomed the chance to address current events.[58] This resulted in greater complexity in the storylines, which was expressed through the incorporation of new characters, the strip's expansion into social and urban settings, and a greater attention to political issues. It also entailed a shift in structure: if until then the cartoon had followed a tradition of family-centered comics, it now connected that tradition—without abandoning it—to one focused on the world of children.[59] The cast of characters that emerged contributed to building an image of a heterogeneous middle class crisscrossed by ideological and cultural differences.

In its third week in *El Mundo*, Quino introduced Manolito.[60] The son of a small neighborhood shopkeeper, this new character echoed the widespread stock figure of the "crude Galician" immigrant. The comic strip thus took up one of the derogatory stereotypes expressing the social fears triggered in the past by the immigrants who had shaped a rapidly changing society.[61] But at the same time it turned that stereotype on its head. As the magazine *Dinamis* explained in 1969, Manolito was "the tenacious son of the corner grocer, oblivious to anything not related with commercial success, who dreams of owning a chain of supermarkets."[62] He represented the capitalist spirit of the small independent entrepreneur. Money and work were the backbone of the system of morals held by the boy, who was a replica of his father in both appearance and ideas. The twist on the negative stereotype is illustrated in a strip featured in the compilation published in late 1966 (figure 1.12), in which Mafalda mocks Manolito's sound logic in comparing his parents' experience as immigrants in a foreign country (Argentina) with that of Argentines leaving the country to look for work abroad, who were the focus of Mafalda's concern. By failing to see the parallelism and arrogantly telling Manolito that Argentina is not a foreign country, Mafalda exposes her own ignorance.

While Quino did not expand on this inversion of the stereotype in future strips, he layered atop the old pejorative characterization references to innovative business concepts typical of developmentalism, placing the negative attitude toward immigrants beside one recognizing their work ethic and role in shaping a rich and modern nation built on a large middle class. Although in the

FIGURE 1.12 Quino, *Mafalda 1*, strip 4. © Joaquín Salvador Lavado (Quino).

1960s the tensions caused by these "social climbers"—who had arrived in the early twentieth century in waves of transatlantic immigration—were history, the figure of the neighborhood grocer or baker was still current. In fact, Manolito's father had likely been inspired by Julián Delgado's own father, a baker. But the fears the immigrants had formerly triggered were now reproduced through other figures, such as the "nouveaux riches" (businessmen, executives, shop owners), who had only recently moved up the social ladder and had in turn given way to new stereotypes. Landrú, for example, had created a caricature that revolved around a mature "executive" whose every action revealed his parvenu status—from putting on airs to conspicuous consumerism to the repeated use of catchphrases in English (which was quickly becoming identified with business culture).[63]

In creating Manolito, Quino had resorted to a new device. As a caricature that evoked a social type long crystallized in Argentine society, the character established a convention or "prototype" in the comic strip—that is, a simplification that becomes fixed through repetition. Such simplifications, according to the art historian Ernst Gombrich, are required by our perception in order to organize the construction of reality. We need universals that will help us distinguish the essential features in others and, at the same time, model our own selves. They are forms of recognition that allow for an economy of effort, dispensing with the need for close examination.[64] The social importance of the prototype—embodied in caricature—is key for understanding the phenomenon of *Mafalda*. The incorporation of Manolito triggered a host of preconceived notions—an accumulated social knowledge—directly and effectively associated with the perception of the immigrant. But Quino used this prototype in a unique way. On the one hand, he drew Manolito with the basic features attributed to the popular stereotype of the crude Galician. On the other, he disrupted that stereotype by connecting it to a more recent and contemporary prototype: the business executive. In this way, Quino used different layers of parody to provide a critical view of economic modernization and developmentalism.

While it is likely that Quino did this intuitively, it resulted in great complexity. Manolito parodied the typical attitudes and practices of the business world, with its inventories (he called his sandals an "IBM computer" and counted his stock on his toes), advertising campaigns (he painted crudely handwritten signs on the neighborhood walls), marketing strategies (by turning a jam ruined by a tipped oil can into a new "marble jam" product), and public relations (offering free candy to his friends in exchange for advertising his store). These ironies exposed the distance between the high modernizing pretensions of businessmen and the primitive or backward state of their companies and their mentalities. But, at the same time, they revealed the incongruence between the limited size of many businesses (and the sacrifices involved in running them) and the zealous capitalist rationale of their owners. The crudeness of the stereotype was distorted by the endearing spirit shown by Manolito, a boy whose profit-oriented motivation was offset by his increasingly evident naïveté and loyalty, expressed symbolically through his friendship with the other characters.[65] Moreover, his character straddled the world of carefree full-time schoolchildren and that of working children who had to help their parents make a living.

In short, the figure of the crude Galician, a stereotype that was somewhat obsolete—not because Buenos Aires lacked grocers with Galician roots but because the type had crystallized in a bygone society—was brought up to date by parodying the prototype of the "executive," that is, a caricature of an emerging phenomenon. This possibility of using multiple references to what amounted to a family of related prototypes connected with the social climber or parvenu makes it easier to see, in contrast, the innovation involved in the construction of the character of Mafalda, whose figure did not correspond to any socially crystallized image.

Soon after adding Manolito, Quino introduced Susanita as Mafalda's opposite. The contrast was evident in the new character's girlish earrings and blond hair, and the doll she carried with her. She was the exact replica of her mother and represented the traditional female model. Her interests and expectations revolved around marriage, motherhood, and social status. Mafalda's father, who only days before had wished his daughter could be friends with a girl her own age, fell flat on his back when he heard Susanita declare she wanted to be a mom when she grew up. His reaction highlighted the ideological distance separating the home lives of the two girls. The family of the intellectually precocious little girl wanted her to succeed outside the home.

In the same series of strips that introduced Susanita, Mafalda's new friend asks her who she loved more, her mom or her dad, repeating a question she had recently heard from an elderly aunt. The reader had to imagine the answer, as the next panel only showed Susanita, no longer with Mafalda and wearing her doll on her head, running in tears to her mom. A few days later, Mafalda exclaimed, "This girl makes me feel like an old woman!" In that way, the image of the little girl who played at being a mother was associated to the past. The main character voiced the generational clash between the new female aspirations of self-realization and the traditional aspirations of motherhood.[66] The social meaning of this characterization was evident for contemporary readers of the cartoon. *Dinamis* defined Susanita as "domestic and envious, a fervent gossip, a girl who dreams only of 'getting married and becoming a mother' when she grows up, a committed reactionary . . . a typical exponent of the *fat ladies*, whose greatest aspiration is to be perfectly mediocre."[67] The term "fat ladies" alluded to another creation by Landrú, who in *Tía Vicenta* and *El Mundo* brought to life a character (*la señora gorda*) who exhibited the prejudices of the affluent ladies of Barrio Norte, a neighborhood initially associated with Buenos Aires' wealthiest and later with the upper middle class.[68]

Like Manolito, then, Susanita brought a crystallized social prototype to the comic strip, drawing on more recent elements. Her character also evoked the representations of the middle class by Jauretche and other proponents of the "sociopolitical" sociology, such as Viñas and Juan José Sebreli. In line with Jauretche's *medio pelo* characterization, these representations mocked feminine domesticity, with its moralism (which was "hypocritical," "repressive," "dull," and "mediocre"); its pretentious but tasteless aesthetics of pianos in the sitting room, garden gnomes, and plastic ornaments; and its reactionary elitism that rejected any form of popular expression.[69] Thus, Susanita reflected both the negative representations of the middle class by the sociopolitical approach and the critical view of traditional women—devoted to the home and the family—who resisted the modernization of family relations promoted by Germani's scientific sociology.[70] She was, therefore, another example of how the cast of *Mafalda* dialogued with both scientific sociology and sociopolitical interpretations of the middle class.

But the play of oppositions was not limited to Susanita and Mafalda. In fact, the comic strip developed the characters' personalities through a series of contrasts, giving them their identities and also casting them in a mold.[71] Quino was able to use these characterizations—which at a certain point took on a life of their own—as a comedic strategy. The caricatures were funny because they spoke to recognizable mind-sets, but also because they referred back to the characters themselves and their interactions in the strip. Quino had composed a new representation using social types that were widely recognizable and had enormous symbolic power and which could be fully fleshed out by readers.

Felipe, the character most like Mafalda, shared her pessimistic view and scathing commentary on world affairs, and he was at odds with Susanita, who found nothing wrong in the world as long as people could be either parents or children—a statement that took on special significance in light of the heated debates over the birth-control pill involving the Catholic Church. She in turn clashed with Manolito, reflecting the tensions that existed between a middle class concerned with social status and distinction and a middle class formed by immigrants who worked hard to achieve economic prosperity.[72] Quino highlighted their differences in the very first strip that featured them together. After Susanita shows off her talking doll and, like a proud mom, asks Manolito if he has ever seen such a smart baby, Manolito responds by bringing out his own toy: a little man in a top hat and tails who speaks in dollar signs instead of words.[73] The logic of economics was thus set against a sentimental logic. The constant conflicts that would engage these two characters throughout the cartoon's history placed humor in the fluid line between these two logics, revealing the material side of Susanita's sentimentality and the tenderness beneath Manolito's capitalist spirit and work ethic.

With this opposition between Manolito and Susanita the comic strip established a representation of the middle class defined by antagonisms. The driving force of the storyline shifted away from the perspective of a middle-class little girl wise beyond her years to the ideological rifts and economic, social, and political conflicts of the middle class. The differences between the characters did not arise from structural variables, such as occupation, income, or housing, but from cultural and ideological dimensions. As the La Rioja newspaper *El Independiente* would observe some time later, "Mafalda and her friends are a device Quino uses to deploy a unique range of characters who, because of their origins, on the one hand, and their actions or reflections, on the other, constitute a rich sample of an equally wide variety of levels of society."[74] In this way, the world created by Quino formed a multifaceted prism organized around the cultural and ideological contrasts of the characters and how these were translated in the everyday.

These clashes between the characters did not, however, affect the sense of generational belonging that had been introduced as a central theme with Felipe, the first friend to join Mafalda's gang. A series of strips in which the kids fashion spaceships out of soda siphons shows how the construction of that dimension worked. As semiologist Oscar Steinberg has explained, in this series

Quino used an absurd humor that suspended the moral logic of the comic. Completely immersed in their fantasy world—as they are propelled by the force of the siphon bottles and imagine they are really traveling in space—the kids are the very image of childhood innocence. The make-believe spaceships represented the new generation that would surpass the "old, discredited generation." The game was cut short by adult intervention in the person of Mafalda's mom. But the power of her authority was offset when generational roles were again symbolically inverted, as Mafalda's father was tempted to try the siphon spaceships, while the kids reverted to mature reflection.[75]

In early 1966, the cast of characters was expanded yet again with the addition of Miguelito, a somewhat younger boy who did not represent any established social prototype. Drawn with hair resembling banana leaves, he embodied a cynical hedonist who maintained a harmonious relationship with all the other characters in the strip.[76]

With each new character the comic strip gained complexity, and this had a number of effects. First, the new characters made it easier for Quino to produce a daily strip and widened the scope for communication with readers. While not deliberate, the incorporation of Manolito and Susanita opened up the comic strip to the public of a mainstream newspaper. Second, the new additions impacted the main character. Gradually, starting with the introduction of Felipe, Mafalda's facial expressions softened, her figure became shapelier, and her androgyny less marked. She also became less aggressive. But her biting wit and irony became more pronounced. Third, more circumstantial characters were added (neighborhood women, door-to-door salesmen, grandparent figures in the square) and more space was devoted to them. Last, the drawings became more elaborate, with more finely detailed expressions and greater movement, along with more perspectives and angles, and they were often used as the humor-triggering device.[77]

Simultaneously, the strip intensified its political allusions, although maintaining their connection to everyday life. The newspaper had a clear division of labor when it came to the issues addressed by its cartoonists, with Landrú dealing with day-to-day national politics on the front page and Quino commenting on major global concerns in the inside pages. *Mafalda* touched on great moral issues, such as war, inequality, and injustice, through references to current events. According to Quino, his was a humanist humor, and he always tried to "go beyond current affairs to find the essence of human beings, because that's what ultimately matters—human beings." That was how he conceived politics, a subject he had been passionate about since childhood, having grown up in a household where the Spanish Civil War and the fate of the Republican partisans were a daily concern. In fact, in creating Mafalda he had drawn inspiration from his communist grandmother. However, he never joined a specific political party or group.[78]

It was from that perspective that the comic strip built a choral depiction of the ideology of the middle class, combining the political and cultural. Mafalda was at the center of that composition, representing the intellectual and progressive segment of the middle class. Her character—in contrast to Susanita and Manolito—embodied a novel caricature. This construction quickly took shape in *El Mundo* with the first politically centered strips featured in the newspaper. At this point, Mafalda positions herself in the world. In one strip, upon finding her place on a globe, she comes up with her own explanation for the international order: the countries of the South were underdeveloped because in their "upside down" position they could not stop their ideas from "spilling" out from them. This reasoning was expressed graphically in a symbolic inversion of the image, with all the panels drawn upside down. The strip was not making a statement about cultural domination per se (as it would do in 1971). Rather, Mafalda's reasoning implied an intellectual play on the idea—which evoked the inverted map drawn by the Uruguayan artist Joaquín Torres García in 1943—that global powers defined the categories with which we perceive the world and determined where the "top" and "bottom" of the world order were. With this image, *Mafalda* abandoned Cold War dichotomies and took on the defense of the Third World.[79] For the main character, the construction of this ideological space was based on her rejection of the two opposing sides. She exposed Western power—with her persistent questions on the Vietnam War—but she also distanced herself from the East. Her position was best illustrated with the sandwich metaphor that she used to explain where she stood: "Having capitalism on one side and communism on the other really kills me! It's like being in a sandwich! . . . And everyone knows what happens to sandwiches!" As she finishes saying this, Manolito saunters into the room eating a sandwich. In the following panel we see him standing alone with a shoe flying toward his head and a dialogue balloon coming from outside the panel that reads, "Imperialist pig!" The ending was thus paradigmatic: in Mafalda's reasoning, eating a sandwich became associated with an imperialist power, which in turn was embodied by Manolito, who represented capitalism.[80]

Some time later, in an interview published in the *Buenos Aires Herald*, Quino identified with Mafalda's political stance. He explained that he did not feel represented by any political leader and that he was not particularly convinced by either capitalism or communism. "I feel, as Mafalda says, that we're sandwiched between two giants."[81] However, the comic strip's position with respect to communism was not always necessarily negative. In many cases there was a certain ambiguity, which worked as a humorous device open to the reader's interpretation. This happened, for example, in a strip that featured a recurring theme in the cartoon and one of Mafalda's defining characteristics: her hatred of soup and her ongoing battle against it. In this strip, Mafalda is as usual complaining bitterly about having to eat her soup; her mom tries to convince her by saying that kids who do not eat their soup "stay little forever," prompting Mafalda to think, "How peaceful the world would be today if Marx hadn't eaten his soup!" By imagining a Marx frozen in childhood and portraying his ideas as disruptive, it was left up to the readers to decide if Marxism was good or bad.

As part of the socialist world but also of Latin America, Cuba was a sensitive subject. The Caribbean island is first mentioned in a strip in which Felipe brings Mafalda a flower only to find that, because of her father's plant hobby, his friend was surrounded by flowers. "It's like bringing Fidel Castro a lump of sugar," he mutters to himself as he retreats dejected. While this comparison to Fidel Castro did not involve a value judgment, this was not the case in a later installment, where we see Mafalda learning her ABCs. When she comes to the letter *F* and reads "That boy is Fidel," Susanita shouts out in alarm, "That boy is undemocratic!" But because the epithet was voiced by Susanita, who embodied the traditionalist and reactionary middle class, it was open to multiple interpretations. This ambiguity is absent from a later strip in which Mafalda declares that "soup is to childhood what communism is to democracy."[82] As she felt that soup was unjustly forced on her by her mother, this comparison linked authoritarian imposition to communism. However, this view contrasted with the strip that came immediately before it, which showed Felipe teaching Mafalda to play chess. He explains how "the king can capture what's in front of it, what's behind, to the side, . . . anywhere! It can move in any direction and take what's there. Pawns, instead, can only capture . . ." Here, as Mafalda hears the fate of the pawns (in Spanish, *peones*, which is also the word for "laborer"), she cuts her friend off, angrily declaring, "And they wonder why communism is spreading!" This punch line assumed, then, that communism was associated with the defense of the weak and the poor—the *peones*. Also polysemic was a strip in which Mafalda wishes that the Cuban leader would praise soup so that the Argentine government would ban it ("Why doesn't that cretin Fidel Castro say that soup is good?"). The humor here arose from Mafalda drawing on the Cold War discourse to devise a scheme to combat adult authority in her war against soup. In this reading, the adjective "cretin" was softened by the implicit nod to Castro, although, as we will see in chapter 4, this strip was not well received in Cuba.

In sum, by adopting a Third World stance, *Mafalda* voiced a position that distanced itself equally from the two opposing forces in the Cold War, whose discourses saturated public opinion. The often polysemic references to communism and the Cuban Revolution made sense in that context and required the reader's active participation to complete their meaning.[83]

Over the following weeks, in a series of strips in which the characters play government, *Mafalda* brought up the issue of ethics in politics in a tone of denunciation. The series began by reflecting on who should elect the government and how. Manolito's refusal to let Mafalda play the role of president served to comment ironically on the place women occupied in Argentine society: they could engage in politics provided they held no power, and any alteration of that state of affairs could only be believable in a game. The irony conveyed here lay bare the fact that while women had enjoyed full political rights since 1947, in reality they were not taken seriously in politics (and increasingly less so with the moves to push Peronism out of politics).[84] Mafalda embodied the aspirations of the new generation of university women whose participation in the student movement and political activism was growing. In the same series, the characters went on to discuss how power should be exercised. Through allusions to news covered by *El Mundo*—for example, the armed forces' intervention in government affairs, the incompetence of government officials (we see Mafalda putting legislative bills to sleep in a crib), and pressures from economic lobbies—the strips denounced "bad" politics and the lack of an ethics directed toward the common good.[85]

Mafalda denounced a harsh reality that was far from the high moral standards that politics were supposed to represent. This was reinforced by her defense of a Third World position that stood for those excluded from the international order. Her voice was seen as the expression of the humanist conscience of the new politically committed generation. According to the *Buenos Aires Herald*, "Quino's dreadful niece punctures a failed planet" and repudiates all forms of authoritarian behavior (by the government, parents, or schools). Shortly after, *Claudia*—a magazine for modern middle-class women—similarly described Mafalda as the "spokesperson for all nonconformism in humanity." "It was eerie," the piece said, because Quino merely "used a mold that we ourselves have cast."[86] Critics thus saw Mafalda—whose voice was heard the loudest in the cartoon's ideological chorus—as expressing the views of the intellectual middle class. In the past, while there had certainly been middle-class intellectuals, the progressive identity had been comparatively insignificant. Mafalda gave substance to that identity and in doing so contributed to its self-perception. The cartoon's humor required shared codes and presupposed a common identity that reflected, and at the same time created, a middle-class *we* that was sensitive to social injustices and committed to the denunciation of "bad" politics.

In 1966, with the coup d'état led by Onganía *Mafalda* took on new meaning, becoming a symbol of the opposition to the dictatorship. In the same edition in which the headlines of *El Mundo* reported that a coup had been staged and that Onganía had taken over the government, readers found a dismayed Mafalda wondering what had happened to what she had been taught in school (figure 1.13).

FIGURE 1.13 Quino, "Mafalda," *El Mundo* (Buenos Aires), June 29, 1966, 14. © Joaquín Salvador Lavado (Quino).

It was up to the readers to complete Mafalda's unfinished reflection, in the understanding that common sense provided the answer. Future political activists still in high school at that time remember feeling the same way as Mafalda. The high-school curriculum included a civics class in which students were taught democratic values. But school-board authorities were declaring their support for the dictatorial government and calling on citizens to recognize it. According to Carlos Martínez—who was a high-school student at the time of Illia's ousting and would later join the People's Revolutionary Army (Ejército Revolucionario del Pueblo, or ERP)—these contradictions marked his political development.[87]

That panel on the coup d'état symbolized the comic strip's opposition to the dictatorship from the start. It made sense that *El Mundo* would publish it, as it had been one of the few newspapers that had stood by President Illia throughout the political crisis and had tried to prevent the worst possible outcome.[88] The first resistance to the coup came from university student groups who occupied the Universidad de Buenos Aires campus, joined by faculty and academics. The brutal repression that followed is known as "The Night of the Long Sticks" (La Noche de los Bastones Largos), a term coined by the journalist Sergio Morero, a close friend of Quino who was covering the incidents for *Primera Plana*. The cartoonist himself was directly affected. His wife, Alicia Colombo, a chemistry researcher and professor at the University of Buenos Aires's School of Science, resigned in protest against the dictatorship.[89] The intellectual or progressive middle class led the growing opposition to the new regime, which began cracking down on spaces and activities associated with their identity, taking over university governments, staging morality campaigns to ban cultural events and modern fashions, and expanding censorship. Mafalda thus headed her own class's denunciation of the dictatorship.[90] In a retrospective look at *Mafalda* published in 1973, the Argentine newspaper *Acción* explained that the comic strip reached adulthood the day this panel—which exposed the contradiction between the principles inculcated by adults and institutions and the political and social reality—appeared in print: "From then on, Quino would use *Mafalda* to channel sensitive issues silenced by censorship."[91] Censorship had been institutionalized in the previous decades in the Cold War context, but it was expanded under the traditionalist and integrationist ideology of the Onganía dictatorship.[92]

 Mafalda was able to capture like never before the opinion of vast sectors that quickly rejected the authoritarian government. Under the dictatorship, the humor in *Mafalda* proved particularly malleable, allowing the audience to grasp its implied messages and turning it into a symbol of the opposition. Readers had been trained to understand the strip's double meanings and subtext as well as the feedback between everyday events and politics and Quino's subtle allusions. Soup—Mafalda's nemesis—came to symbolize the struggle against the dictatorship, representing "the authoritarian governments we were forced to swallow day after day," in Quino's words. These strategies made it easy to avoid censorship.[93]

 For the media, Mafalda had come to epitomize antiestablishment youth. As *El Mundo* explained in 1966, "Mafalda is what you would call a committed little girl. And because she's concerned with what happens around her—to the point that the grown-ups she interacts with cannot keep up with her—Mafalda is disruptive, unsettling, surprising, shocking, aggravating, nauseating, unpleasant; at the same time, she makes us laugh, because Quino is, after all, a cartoonist."[94]

 In this context, the first *Mafalda* book came out in late 1966. The cover featured Mafalda nursing a sick globe—an apt image for the times. The idea for the compilation—which due to *Primera Plana*'s copyright claims was limited to the cartoon's run in *El Mundo*—had come to Quino after he became aware that readers were cutting out the strips to put them up on their office walls and shop windows and even to make their own collections. With this publication in book format, the comic strip became a lasting object in the most established form in Western culture. The publishing house, Jorge Álvarez Editores, was associated with the most radical cultural and political ideas and was being targeted by government censorship. The book was a huge success. In the first three months, 40,000 copies were sold in the city of Buenos Aires alone, and within a year that number had climbed to 130,000.[95]

But the comic strip's readership exceeded by far the number of copies sold. It had become a national sensation. In 1966, *Mafalda* had debuted in *Córdoba*, the second-largest newspaper of the province of the same name, which had been founded in 1928 and featured full coverage of national and international news, a large culture section, and a page devoted to women and family issues. Quino was introduced to *Córdoba* readers as a cartoonist who had "a unique relationship with his audience, one that demands their active engagement. He does not just reflect on certain aspects of reality," he calls on readers to "join him in critically examining the essential structures of our existence."[96]

As the editors highlighted, *Córdoba* readers could see their concerns reflected in the comic strip. Córdoba was a highly urbanized and heavily industrialized province with a growing working class, but it also had a solid middle class and was home to one of the most prestigious universities in the country, attracting many students from across the region who were increasingly politicized.[97] As *Mafalda* also touched on issues that went beyond the immediate context to examine universal problems, the strips were still current even though they had appeared in *El Mundo* some time earlier. The first strip chosen by *Córdoba* focused on Mafalda's battle with her father for a television set. The sarcasm of this "extraordinary *enfant terrible*" contrasted sharply with the view of childhood portrayed in *Donald Duck* and the *Flintstones*, the other cartoons featured in the paper's funny pages. But there were other aspects that set Quino's cartoon apart. It was the only one not syndicated by large corporations (mostly from the United States) that operated globally.[98] For distribution, Quino relied instead on personal contacts and a network of Buenos Aires press agents who represented provincial newspapers. These agents began offering their clients the rights to publish *Mafalda* and arranged for delivery of the originals (which at that time still included metal printing plates).[99]

The comic strip spread rapidly across the country. In 1967, in addition to *Córdoba*, it was published in the newspapers *El Litoral* (Santa Fe), *El Intran-*

sigente (Salta), and, some time later, *Noticias* (Tucumán). And it was not just large cities that fell under the spell of *Mafalda*, as even a newspaper from a small town such as Esperanza, in the province of Santa Fe, saw the comic strip as responding to a public need.[100] A year later, *Mafalda* crossed the border to Uruguay, where it was featured on the pages of the Montevideo newspaper *BP-Color*, and traveled across the Atlantic to appear in an Italian compilation that would launch its global fame, as I examine in chapter 3. This international projection had been possible because, in the words of *Dinamis*, Quino had painted his village and, by doing so, he had shed light on the human condition.[101] *Mafalda* had truly arrived.

THE IDENTITY OF THE MIDDLE CLASS

Behind the heterogeneity it portrayed, *Mafalda* presupposed a cohesive identity. The children all lived in the same neighborhood and went to the same school. To create the strip's setting, the cartoonist had turned to his own neighborhood of San Telmo for inspiration, although it was not a typically middle-class area. Quino took up a poetic tradition dating back to the 1930s, in which the neighborhood was associated with a haven and contrasted with the decadent downtown. But he redefined that traditional image by inserting the neighborhood into an anonymous and massive metropolis.[102] The tension between the two scales—the populous city and the neighborhood close to home—was resolved by rendering urban elements from the perspective of the sidewalk and the square. This perspective allowed Quino to depict the neighborhood as a place where children could play safely in the street and personal ties were forged, but also as a site of intersections. The street was the space where a host of characters and social sectors met, and the contrasts generated by that convergence revealed the singularities of the middle class.

The inclusion of the school completed the focus on the neighborhood. The school portrayed in *Mafalda* drew on a belief rooted in the nineteenth century whereby the institution was a leveling ground where all children were considered equal and any profound differences were neutralized. Mafalda and all her friends went to public school, where both middle- and lower-class children converged in classrooms and courtyards and were made equal by discipline and the mandatory white tunic that was their uniform. However, this view was tempered by the criticism of authority and the standardization of learning. As a child, Quino had unsuccessfully resisted schooling, and Felipe—his sometime alter ego in the strip—embodied the apathy caused by the institution. The insistence on perfect penmanship, the stock phrases used to teach kids to read and write, and the principals who likened the "temple of knowledge" to a "second home" were all features that portrayed schools as assembly lines that produced uncreative, unthinking, indifferent beings.

The neighborhood and the school were thus incorporated as emblematic institutions where class identity was forged. Friendship crystallized these common ties, which were firm and solid in spite of the differences that existed. Affective bonds were so important in *Mafalda* that they even overrode the characters' defining personality traits and demanded loyalty and sacrifices from them. In one strip, for example, Manolito felt that because of their friendship he had to be honest with Mafalda, so he confessed his shady sales tactics. That same sentiment moved Mafalda to talk Felipe out of the idea of wearing a space helmet to avoid contagion when visiting a sick Manolito; she did so by reminding him that good friends stood by each other no matter what. The strength of these bonds, which withstood their ongoing differences, showed the metaphorical significance of friendship.

Theirs was a self-contained child universe. While the inclusion of Manolito as a representative of children who had to work to help out their parents served to underscore the differences in the life experiences of the other kids in the gang, Quino rarely brought them into contact with other working-class children. He explained that his creative process was based on observation and that made it difficult for him to portray a social universe he was not familiar with. This resulted in a homogenization of the space of the middle class that was nonetheless problematized through constant references to social inequality and injustice, but also with occasional glimpses at children in other social environments. For example, figures such as a shoeshine boy in the street or a baby out for a walk with his uniformed nanny prompted reflections on social class and childhood.[103]

In this sense, the inclusion of circumstantial characters often enabled a comparison between the protagonists and others situated above and below the middle class. For example, Mafalda's father meets a man at the beach who mistakes him for someone he knows, until the father reveals he works as a clerk at an insurance agency. At that point, the other man—a doctor—explains the confusion by declaring that "in bathing trunks, we all look the same." Yet the strip graphically exposes the fallacy of that equality in the next panel by making the doctor grow bigger and placing him on a podium, while Mafalda's father becomes smaller. The drawing thus reproduced the perspective of someone positioned at a lower level.[104]

This baring of class differences was especially powerful in representations of someone in a social position below that of the middle-class characters. In these cases, the humor in *Mafalda* exposed, in a problematic way, the ideological differences dividing the middle class. On the one hand, Mafalda would adopt a discourse of guilt that softened the acknowledgment of her own class privilege. On the other, Susanita would smugly recognize the class differences in her favor. The humorous effect often emerged from the contrast between Mafalda's naïveté and Susanita's cynicism, prompting a reflection on the limits of progressive postures and the duplicity of a society (and a middle class) that held itself up as equal while at the same time accepting social differences. In this way, the image of an inclusive and egalitarian society was doubly corroded by the two extremes.

This is illustrated eloquently in an early strip (from 1965; figure 1.14) where Mafalda proudly shows Susanita her new black doll, and Susanita is unable to hide her racism, rushing off to wash her finger after barely touching the doll, even as she declares that she is not a racist. This exchange served to contrast the different positions held by the two characters with respect to race, while at the same time criticizing the hypocrisy of the egalitarianism of the middle class.

FIGURE 1.14 Quino, "Mafalda," *El Mundo* (Buenos Aires), August 22, 1965, 8. © Joaquín Salvador Lavado (Quino).

The "negrito" (literally, "little black one") in the strip represented the social and symbolic exclusion of Argentina's dark-skinned population in a society that took pride in its white, European origins. But, at the same time, the doll brought to mind the country's popular masses in general, whose irruption into political life with Perón in 1945 had earned them the derogatory label *cabecitas negras*, coined by the middle and upper classes. Susanita's reaction echoed the fears that had been portrayed by Julio Cortázar in his short story "Casa tomada" (1951) and by Germán Rozenmacher in "Cabecita negra" (1962).[105] Susanita, a typical "fat lady," was unable to hide the disgust and fear she felt at having crossed class barriers and touched the Other. Her attitude belied her words: Susanita could not openly admit to racism, but her racism was too strong to be concealed. Mafalda, in contrast, represented the moral conscience forged by the egalitarian mandate that called for social inclusion and held public and mandatory schooling as a way of providing better opportunities for everyone, and she expressed a feeling of guilt for her own class's racism. From this position Mafalda challenged her friend's cynicism. The strip echoed two positions dividing the middle class since the overthrow of Perón and which, by 1965, had become two distinct political identities: a progressive one that tried to understand Peronism; and one pejoratively dubbed "gorilla" in Argentine political jargon, which could not hide its rejection of the masses and popular culture, its anti-Peronism, and its racism—even if the last could not be openly admitted.

Quino's humor, then, played with the bonds that structured the middle class and demanded that the different ideological positions within the class and their effects on everyday life be acknowledged. But such differences did not preclude the existence of a common identity, the sense of belonging to the same class, defined by its social standing and shared experience. Because the comic strip increasingly portrayed this social sector as a cohesive but diverse whole, it could easily be viewed as a representation of all of society, were it not for the constant allusions to those situated above and below the middle class. *Mafalda*'s humor thus became a complex prism capable of portraying the contradictions of Argentina's middle class, not only those emerging as a result of the process of social modernization but also those created by a weakening democracy and the rise of authoritarianism. In doing so Quino was able to transcend current issues and turn the intellectually precocious little girl into a moral voice that exposed the great problems faced by humanity: inequality, injustice, and authoritarianism. If, in Gilles Deleuze's terms, humor and irony in modern societies are the essential forms of thinking through which we internalize laws by testing them against ideal principles, *Mafalda* underscored the insurmountable distance between social, cultural, and political rules and the principles that should ideally govern society.[106] The caustic irony in the comic strip, however, was offset by the tenderness inspired by the young age of the characters who delivered the biting messages, thus allowing readers to identify with the *we* represented by the strip: the middle class, Argentine society, and humankind embodied in the new generations.

CHAPTER 2

Controversial *Mafalda*
From Radicalization
to State Terrorism (1968–1976)

"I'm afraid if I let Mafalda out of the comic strip, I'll have no control over her." These were the words a journalist overheard Quino tell someone over the telephone in 1968.[1] The journalist did not know, or chose not to say, who Quino was talking to or what they were discussing, but Quino's comment is a fitting introduction to this chapter. The pages that follow will show how the character broke away from her creator and took on a life of her own, as various actors from across the political spectrum vied to have her in their corner defending their views. This phenomenon had actually begun some time earlier, on the day of the Onganía coup, when Mafalda jumped out of the page and became an antiauthoritarian symbol. But the cartoon had not yet broken away from Quino. Two years later, the cartoonist's fears turned out to be justified. With the country's growing political radicalization, it became increasingly hard for him to have any say over the ideological connotations of his work. The cartoon fueled passionate debates over politics and its characters were used with different intentions to voice political opinions. These, in turn, sparked heated disputes over what the comic strip could be used for, who could use it, and what meanings could be ascribed to it.

Graphic humor in Argentina had always touched on politics. The genre had been used to create identities, define adversaries, establish loyalties, and devise strategies. But in the 1970s two factors converged to make the link between humor and politics highly problematic. On the one hand, politics became more complicated as violence spread across Argentine society and the vilification of opponents led to increasingly life-threatening clashes. On the other, discussions among intellectuals and artists over the need to assume a political commitment and participate in social movements and left-wing organizations forced humorists to look more closely at their work and ponder its political meaning.[2] I examine these dilemmas in this chapter with the aim of understanding how the ideological climate permeated humor during those years and, more specifically, how *Mafalda* was interpreted and used politically between 1968 and 1976, that is, during the period of rising political radicalization leading up to the last coup d'état. I posit that studying the discussions prompted by the comic strip provides insight into this historical process. In line with Henri Bergson, I argue that in order to examine the relationship between humor and politics "we must put [laughter] back into its natural environment, which is society, and above all we must determine the utility of its function," that is, what I refer to here as its social and political uses and significations, which are certainly not univocal.[3]

My analysis looks at how radicalization, violence, and political repression disrupted the social, cultural, and political coordinates that had marked the emergence of *Mafalda* and in doing so modified the comic strip's social significance. This context generated a pressing awareness of the political weight of cultural production. Alongside those who were critical of comics because they saw them as having an alienating effect on readers, there was a new demand for ideological transparency in cultural products. This approach to reading clashed with Quino's comedic strategy. The irony in *Mafalda* required an ambiguity that would let readers work out for themselves if there were any messages or moral connotations. Also, during this period the comic strip's structural makeup was ultimately rendered anachronistic. In the Argentina of the 1970s portraying a heterogeneous middle class united despite its differences became impossible as it was tragically and violently torn apart. And the same could be said about society as a whole.

The chapter is divided into five sections. The first part looks at how the comic strip changed with its move to the magazine *Siete Días* in 1968. In the second part I explore the controversies that erupted around *Mafalda* as political radicalization grew. This entails, in a third part, reconstructing how the comic strip touched on the issue of revolutionary artists through its problematization of the political role of humor and discussing how it dealt with everyday life by addressing economic stability, inflation, and the rising cost of living. In the fourth part I describe *Mafalda*'s farewell to its readers in 1973, positing that it symbolized the end of a political period. Finally, I review the new discussions that emerged and how the cartoon was used by military intelligence services.

In December 1967, *El Mundo*—*Mafalda*'s home since early 1965—finally suc-
cumbed to financial problems it had been facing for some time and shut its
doors permanently. A month later, Quino received a letter from Jorge B., a
reader who said he felt adrift with the newspaper's demise. He wanted to know
what would happen to his favorite characters—"Will Mafalda still have a baby
brother?"—and he told the cartoonist that he and a friend had even considered "popping over to your house" to inquire, but were "shy." He signed off
with a "Say hi to Mafalda and the rest of the gang." This letter playfully illustrates the intimate relationship readers had forged with the comic strip's characters, to the point that they viewed them as actual flesh-and-blood friends and
wondered about their fate. They could imagine the baby brother—announced
in the last strips—being born outside the frames.

These strikingly lifelike characters were the result of a carefully crafted
universe. Quino paid close attention to every detail to make it more real. "I
look at dresses and shoes in shop windows and wonder if they would look right
[on Mafalda] . . . I've even bought books she might read . . . to see what she was
learning," he confessed.[4] His readers were just as obsessive and were constantly
on the lookout for inaccuracies to point out to him. For example, when the strip
showed the kids doing penmanship exercises at school he was flooded with letters telling him teachers no longer did that. But the characters were not just real
in the eyes of the readers. The media saw them that way, too. In late 1967, the
Buenos Aires Herald had conveyed that image convincingly with a photomon-
tage of Quino with Mafalda on his lap (figure 2.1).[5] A year later, *Confirmado*, a
major political magazine, described Mafalda as a "(near) living doll, the most
in-touch-with-reality cartoon character that Argentina has ever known."[6]

Despite the comic strip's popularity and the support from journalist
friends who put the word out that *Mafalda* was looking for a new home, it was
not easy for Quino to find a new publisher. He met with *Crónica* and *Clarín*,
two of the country's top newspapers, but failed to reach an agreement with
either. It was not until mid-1968, six months after *El Mundo* closed, that *Mafalda* appeared in *Siete Días*.[7] This magazine, published by Editorial Abril, had
only been out a year. It was a weekly publication in the style of *Life* magazine
and one of the first in Argentina to venture into photojournalism, featuring
high-quality photos with short but daring captions.[8] With a weekly print run
of 150,000 copies, it targeted a wide readership, mainly men, who, in contrast
to *Primera Plana* readers, were not portrayed as belonging to a political, economic, or cultural elite.[9]

FIGURE 2.1 Andrew Graham-Yooll, "Mafalda: The Star with No Illusions," *Buenos Aires Herald*, October 1, 1967, 8. Mafalda cartoon © Joaquín Salvador Lavado (Quino).

Editorial Abril was a great fit for *Mafalda*, as the publishing house had found success through its representation of Disney (with comics such as *Mickey Mouse* and *Donald Duck*) and the cartoon characters it brought to Argentina from Italy, which were featured in magazines such as *Salgari*. The original idea to focus on comics had come from its founder, César Civita, an Italian immigrant who had come to Argentina fleeing fascism and who had built one of the country's most innovative print media companies. It combined ingenious market and mass-media strategies with cultural innovation, harboring intellectuals and artists who had been relegated by Peronism or had fled from Europe to Argentina during the war. Civita's efforts created a stimulating social network and fostered major cultural and economic ventures. This explains, for example, how Gino Germani could write an advice column with his friend and fellow sociologist Enrique Butelman in a women's magazine that was illustrated by the avant-garde German-Argentine photographer Grete Stern, or how the company came to publish authors such as Bronisław Malinowski or Margaret Mead and feature drawings by Saul Steinberg, who had inspired Quino and the new wave of cartoonists.[10]

Mafalda thus joined a publishing house with which it shared a similar background, where the market met the media and the intellectual community, and the cartoonist's connections were instrumental in securing a publishing deal. Quino had friends in Editorial Abril, including Norberto Firpo, who would later become editor in chief of *Siete Días*, and Sergio Morero, who would be the magazine's editorial secretary, and their relationship made the negotiations easier. Quino began delivering material for a humor section under an exclusivity agreement, but three months later the magazine started featuring *Mafalda* and Quino's humor page was moved to *Panorama*, Editorial Abril's political magazine.[11]

In 1968, the publishing house was still very active. It was among the leading players in various market niches, with successes such as *Claudia*, the magazine for the "modern woman," and *Nocturno*, a *fotonovela* (the photo-comic melodramas so popular at that time).[12] By then, however, Editorial Abril was in a difficult position, as the historian Eugenia Scarzanella has explained. It had taken in intellectuals committed to social change and was not immune to censorship, with rival magazines writing editorials against it. But it also sought to get on the government's good side in the hope of benefiting from industrial development measures that would allow it to open its own paper mill. This would free the publishing house from paper supply restrictions, which governments had used over the years to put pressure on the press.[13]

These contradictions were particularly evident in *Siete Días*. The magazine had a streamlined design and its contents combined coverage of political and social news with lighter general-interest pieces, including new fashion trends and modern living. This double focus was a perfect match for *Mafalda*'s portrayal of both politics and everyday life, although certain sales gimmicks by the magazine—such as photographs of bikini-clad women featured on the cover to attract male readers, or the moral advice column penned by a priest that was meant to appease their wives—went against the comic strip's philosophy. Civita initially put at the helm his right-hand man, Raúl Burzaco, who took a moderate position in politics—equally distant from both fascism and communism—and had a difficult relationship with the union of journalists.[14] This also contrasted with the views of many of the young journalists on staff, who were leaning to the left and were poised to take more committed stands, although not all in the same way nor with the same degree of intensity.

On July 2, 1968, the magazine presented *Mafalda* to its readers. The main character was featured on the cover aiming a spray can at a globe (figure 2.2). The label on the can had a dove and the word "peace," so that Mafalda appeared to be spraying the world with peace. Inside the magazine, a letter supposedly

FIGURE 2.2 *Siete Días* (Buenos Aires), July 2, 1968, cover. © Joaquín Salvador Lavado (Quino).

written by the intellectually precocious little girl—in a somewhat uncharacteristically sweet tone—introduced the gang and saluted the United Nations.

With this presentation, which tempered Mafalda's more acerbic side, some readers may have thought that Quino was adjusting the character's ideology. But a week later, when the strip began its run in the magazine, there was no doubt that both it and the character would maintain the features they had become famous for.[15] Quino could not have made any real changes even if he had wanted, because by then there was a solid pact between the readers and the comic strip that could not be broken by the illustrator.

The cartoon's followers were no longer limited to newspaper or magazine readers. By 1968, the first two *Mafalda* books were out, with sales reaching record numbers. The comic strip was also being featured daily in newspapers across the country, bringing the estimated readership to two million. These readers expected to find "their" *Mafalda* in *Siete Días*.[16] Moreover, there was not much room for innovation, as Quino was constrained by the makeup and characteristics he had already given the comic strip. As we saw in chapter 1, his creative work was not guided by an agenda, political or otherwise; it was rather an intuitive process that relied on his keen observation of everyday life and close attention to current events, as well as his ability to use production demands to his advantage, introducing new characters and adding complexity to the storylines. This does not mean that he was unaffected by the new production conditions in *Siete Días* or the sociopolitical environment.

The move to *Siete Días* took *Mafalda* to another level. The magazine's glossy paper enhanced the drawings and the four weekly strips took up a whole page. They were often featured on one of the coveted odd-numbered pages and would later be moved to the last page, an even more important spot. This evidenced how much the magazine's editorial staff valued the strip and its creator. Some months earlier, when Quino had first published his humor page in *Siete Días*, the magazine had proudly introduced the cartoonist to its readers as "a character straight out of his own comic strips: tall, skinny, otherworldly, disheveled, electrified by flashes of energy, like a cartoon." According to the magazine, he was too modest to accept his status as "one of the leading humorists in the country and [the fact] that Mafalda's birth in 1962 was—and is—a milestone in Argentine journalism."[17]

The weekly frequency was liberating, as it released Quino from the highly demanding pace of producing a daily strip, which had led him to declare he felt shackled by *Mafalda*. Each issue of the magazine was prepared a fortnight before it came out, and that meant the strip could not deal with the latest political developments. To get around this, Quino came up with a new feature: he created small vignettes that he submitted right before the magazine went to press and could be overprinted on the upper margin of the page with the comic strips he had delivered fifteen days earlier. The vignettes provided a paratext that enriched and added more layers to the strip, so much so that they now emerge as the most creative aspect of this stage. The characters seem to leap out of the frame as if they are addressing the readers directly, which they actually did in many vignettes. These vignettes often dealt with current events but also referred to more philosophical issues or established a connection with readers through nods and by letting them in on the joke.

One vignette shows Mafalda literally winking at the readers while she reflects, "If you think I'm thinking what you think I'm thinking, you're way off base."[18] In this way, Quino played with the psychological traits that had defined his characters. It also allowed him to give readers a glimpse into the comic strip's production process, with references to himself, his friends, the editor of the magazine, and his cast of beloved characters. For example, a vignette could feature Snoopy with Mafalda wondering about foreign intervention in the page's affairs (figure 2.3), in allusion to imperialism, and a few weeks later Felipe would appear on another vignette asking, "Who sent us this infiltrator?" to which Charles Schultz's famous dog answered, "Don't worry, it wasn't the CIA."[19] Changes in the title fonts and the style of the illustrator's signature, as well as the background they were printed on, were used as additional humorous devices. Readers could thus agree with Mafalda when she mocked the flowery title contributed by Susanita, which contrasted with the main character's pessimistic view of the state of the world, and laugh knowingly at the dark cloud obscuring her creator's signature in another vignette.[20] In short, the margin had become a playful and lively space that refreshed the humor in *Mafalda* with absurd and tender touches, and it provided material for a series of individual books released in 1970 and 1971.[21]

FIGURE 2.3 Quino, "Mafalda," *Siete Días* (Buenos Aires), May 11, 1970, 38. © Joaquín Salvador Lavado (Quino).

The comic strip itself continued to gain complexity. Mafalda's little brother, Guille, was born when the strip moved to *Siete Días*, although he had been conceived in *El Mundo*. When the paper closed and before the comic strip was picked up by the magazine, Quino let his audience in on what he had planned for this new member of the family, as he had already involved them in the character's production process, announcing his sex and sharing with them his ideas and possible names for him. Through him, the cartoonist was able to forge a unique connection with readers. In many senses, Guille was like no other character, in particular because Quino gave him a trait none of the others had: he allowed him to grow.[22]

Guille, in fact, condensed the strip's greatest innovations, in both style and content. His character represented the counterculture of the new generations. He was a disruptive presence in the adult world. As chance would have it, the character was born shortly after the May 1968 protests in France. Quino had been in Paris when students took to the streets, and he was struck by the violence of the clashes, which heralded the radicalization that was spreading across the planet and which *Siete Días* covered in detail. The magazine also focused on the growing unrest in Latin America, where student marches were brutally repressed, leaving several students dead in Montevideo and many more in Mexico City, in the Tlatelolco massacre. It also devoted large feature stories to the student protests in Argentina. In keeping with its aim of striking a balance between left and right, the editorial line alternated between deploring the violence, giving voice to the students, and denouncing repression in accounts that highlighted the challenge posed by university students around the world. According to the magazine, the protests revealed a nonconformism that was a core characteristic of the new generations.[23]

This context influenced the character's development and the new readings that Quino enabled. In the first strip featuring Mafalda and her baby brother, we see Guille screaming his head off after she takes his pacifier away, and Mafalda remarking, "If the masses learned to use their lungs like that, dictators would be in real trouble!" A few strips later, Guille's pacifier again served as a device to illustrate characteristics of the younger generation. Upon seeing her brother spit his pacifier up in the air with force and catch it again expertly in his mouth, Mafalda reflects, "It looks like this generation is off to a good start." With this she was acknowledging that not only was her brother's generation different from hers, it was a generation she had great hopes for.[24]

With Guille, Quino put a fresh spin on the comedic strategy he used to reflect ironically on the interaction between the public and the private spheres and expose underlying moral and ideological issues. In particular, the new character served to give a new twist to the comic strip's take on generational clashes. On the one hand, Guille brought back the contradictory feelings aroused by children at a time when more and more parents were adopting the new nurturing paradigm that valued the child's autonomy, freedom, and critical ability. In doing so, the comic strip spoke to middle-class mothers and fathers who were changing their parenting style, as illustrated by the increasing popularity of singer-songwriter María Elena Walsh, who with her poetic and playful children's songs put herself at her audience's level. These modern parents attended educational talks and were obsessed with finding the right way to deal with "those little monsters," whose unruliness, defiance, and awkward questions they were now expected to celebrate or at the very least tolerate.[25] The first strip that showed Guille with this father addressed this issue. In it, while the father gazes lovingly at the baby in his crib, we see him from the baby's perspective, where he appears as a distorted figure that makes the baby squeal with laughter (figure 2.4). The implication was that the new generations laughed out loud at their parents. The humor was in the readers' recognition of these perceptions, which often echoed their own experiences. But by achieving this humorous effect through drawings alone—without the use of words—the implied mockery was softened.

FIGURE 2.4 Quino, "Mafalda," *Siete Días* (Buenos Aires), August 5, 1968, 31. © Joaquín Salvador Lavado (Quino).

On the other hand, Guille allowed Quino to call attention to the generational gaps between young people and children. In the strip that followed Guille's first interaction with his dad, Mafalda explicitly contrasts her baby brother's defiant attitude to her own, as she asks her father if when she had started laughing at him she had been more discreet about it.[26] In this way, the strip showed that both young characters laughed at their father but also that they did so differently. This reflected the differences in life experiences between the youth who had entered the public sphere in the early sixties, represented by Mafalda, and those who had done so at the end of that decade, represented by her baby brother. In that short span, cultural and political radicalization had advanced rapidly, with the younger generation embracing rock music, the developmentalist confidence giving way to an awareness of underdevelopment, and the admiration for Cuba turning into militant conviction. This caused great generational rifts that did not go unnoticed by both generations. In this new stage of the comic strip, Quino worked with those distances, which became wider as counterculture grew.

When Guille arrived on the scene, bringing his total disregard for the adult world, Mafalda repositioned herself in her confrontation with her parents. She could now be seen overcome by compassionate tenderness, devoid of cynicism, in an attitude that contrasted with her usual style. As Claire Latxague has suggested, the little girl went from mocking her mother to occasionally show-ing female solidarity—for example, when Mafalda finds her mother slaving over housework and asks her what she would like to be if she could be truly alive (figure 2.5), or when she wakes abruptly from a dream in which she sees her mom chained to the washing machine, and tiptoes to her room to give her a kiss.[27]

FIGURE 2.5 Quino, "Mafalda," *Siete Días* (Buenos Aires), no. 90 (January 27, 1969), 27. © Joaquín Salvador Lavado (Quino).

The same compassion was present when Mafalda helped her father with his morning routine and, in a reversal of roles, sent him off to work reflect-ing, "There are things the poor guy just can't manage on his own yet."[28] The new baby character instead embodied a challenging force that completely un-dermined the foundations of authority. This attitude was highlighted in many strips. For example, the father was portrayed in a tender but somewhat ridicu-lous light as he tried to entertain Guille, talking gibberish and rolling around on the floor, while his son looked at him with a mature puzzled expression.[29]

In short, with Guille Quino heightened the tension between cynicism and childhood innocence. The fact that he was a baby magnified the contrast between the tenderness inspired by small children and the irony conveyed by his facial expressions and, later, his baby talk. This disparity was especially ef-fective in strips that showed the bewildered reactions of the adults to the inces-sant but endearing questions of the children—those same questions that were applauded by modern parenting theories. And it was especially powerful in light of the dismal fate that awaited Argentina's younger generations, who were already being persecuted by the government for their antiestablishment stance. One strip, for example, shows Guille in a typical "why" phase—a stage com-monly touched on by child-rearing experts at the time—speaking more and more loudly as his sister's answers fail to satisfy him. It ends with Mafalda concluding that "at only a year and a half, he's already a candidate for tear gas"—a clear reference to the plight of protesters.[30]

Again, the comic strip's increasing complexity was reflected in the drawings themselves, which became more intricate. Quino used more perspective and shades of gray to add depth to each panel and sketched the characters from different angles and with a wider range of facial expressions. The four strips per page also allowed for more elaborate and longer storylines, as the strips were often linked with a running narrative. In this period, Quino also frequently used different stylistic references and jokes that incorporated other genres. For instance, he drew strips in the style of traditional children's fairy tales or police procedurals, and he even parodied himself. In one strip Mafalda is seen dreaming of what looks like one of Quino's humor pages, where an Uncle Sam–type figure—with a slightly different profile meant to redefine the stereotype—is putting the Statue of Liberty up for sale. When Mafalda asks him about the statue's missing flame, he tells her it lights up when you hold her down, thus prompting a reflection on the relationship between capitalism and freedom.[31] In the coming years, Quino would resort to this device often, playing with popular symbols and slogans but altering them to create new meanings that were often left open for the reader to complete.

The comic strip also ventured more into the street, and the surroundings were rendered in greater detail—cracks in building walls as characters turned the corner, changing traffic lights as they crossed the street, and high-rises silhouetted in the distance. New minor characters were drawn in to provide a wider social background. These often included long-haired youth in miniskirts and loose-fitting clothes, giving a glimpse of the rising counterculture that was also reflected in the characters' tastes. Mafalda's love of the Beatles, for example, quickly became another point of contention with the more conventional Manolito. Among the unnamed circumstantial characters that passed through the strips and interacted briefly with Mafalda and her friends there were also clerks on their way to work, tax collectors, old wrinkled grannies, and bossy mothers. These incorporations opened the strip up to the outside world from a child's perspective. The kids took it all in from their own unique angle and turned the adult's view on its head.

Finally, the invitation to read between the lines, which had been a signature comic device since the start, took on new meaning under the Onganía dictatorship, which banned political activities, took over university governments, jailed opponents, repressed students, and posted morality guards on plazas and beaches. As part of the government's war on communism and its efforts to control cultural expression and impose its brand of decency, books were seized, dances were raided, and movies were censored on a daily basis.[32] The idea of the "enemy within," constructed by the government as a figure that posed a threat to Western and Christian values and the national essence, saturated public opinion. Discourses and representations linked fears of disruption of the status quo with the dread caused by changing gender roles and attitudes toward sex. These images brought back traditional family-centered views that assumed a direct and immediate connection between society and family and saw the loss of family values as leading to political subversion, and at the same time demanded a return to such values to restore the "traditional order."[33]

The prevailing climate heightened the antiauthoritarian tone of the comic strip, which had become a symbol and instrument of the resistance to the Onganía regime. In 1968, for example, an article in *Siete Días* used *Mafalda* to wrap up a detailed account of the overthrow of Arturo Illia, reproducing the famous strip published the day of the 1966 coup. To remove any doubts as to the panel's meaning, the journalist explained that Mafalda was mourning the demise of "the National Constitution, Parliament, the three branches of government, and representative democracy."[34] *Mafalda* was used in a number of ways to denounce the repressive state of affairs in the country. The magazine *Revista Extra*, for example, criticized and mocked censorship saying that Quino "shamelessly" insisted on drawing Mafalda's little brother with no clothes on and, even though he was only a baby, "a naked body is still a naked body" and who knew what mental associations could be triggered by such images.[35]

This only served to fuel *Mafalda*'s popularity. According to the Latin American magazine *Visión*, the comic strip represented an "explosive charge" that was a thorn in the side of pro-government sectors in a country under military rule. The first Mafalda posters were launched in 1968 by Jorge Álvarez Editores, which selected the character following a survey of Argentina's top idols in which respondents also chose the Beatles, Robert Kennedy, and Jane Fonda.[36] By then, for many young people *Mafalda* was among the cultural objects that symbolized—and supported—their own identity. Some time later, Horacio, a contributor to the Uruguayan communist weekly *El Popular* (probably Horacio Buscaglia, a young artist and author known for his irreverent and experimental style), paraphrased the exchanges that the comic strip prompted among his friends: "'Did you read about the fly dropping its view on the world? . . . No . . . the one that really got me was when Mafalda calls her father the Nobel Laureate of indoor gardening. . . . Miguelito is fabulous . . . Guille and Felipe really crack me up. . . .'" This illustrates how in young adult circles reading *Mafalda* was very much a part of socializing processes, evidencing a social and political sense of belonging.[37]

But besides the pleasure of sharing the strip's humor with their peers, there was also an individual reading that operated at a more subjective level on these readers' rejection of the system. The comic book artist and writer Guillermo Saccomanno—who at the time was not yet eighteen years old and worked as an office boy at an ad agency—recalls reading *Mafalda* on the subway and laughing out loud. This attracted the "irritated, annoyed, and peeved looks that the middle class typically casts on idiots who can't behave in polite society." One very formal-looking man even told him outright to behave, indignantly raising his voice at him demanding that he tell him what was so funny. He recalls thinking it was "precisely that discomfort of middle-class subway riders, with their ordinary miseries and frustrations, packed in a train car like prisoners on their way to a concentration camp: that was what I was laughing at with Quino."[38]

As the comic strip triggered these rebellious feelings, it was also used intentionally to further political and social action. A reader recalls, for example, that in 1969 some of his coworkers had pasted a strip on the factory wall that featured Manolito declaring, "You can't amass a fortune without hurting others."[39] This did not prevent the strip from being just as popular with young people from very different walks of life, such as the teachers at a private school in the typically middle-class neighborhood of Caballito who had chosen Mafalda as a symbol of their ideal schoolgirl: a "witty, refined, precociously intelligent" girl, in the words of a former student.[40]

In any case, *Mafalda* opened up a space for unrestraint, irony, and satire, which carried a powerful political charge in the face of that period's moralist crusades, such as those led by the infamous Buenos Aires federal police chief Luis Margaride, known for his involvement in repressive actions. The comic strip was at the peak of its popularity and *Siete Días* used it to boost sales, offering a free *Mafalda* calendar with its holiday issue.[41] Each new *Mafalda* book was launched at unique events designed to create an impact. These were staged by Jorge Álvarez's press agent, Pirí Lugones, a charismatic and intelligent woman who would go on to join the Montoneros armed group and become one of the more than thirty thousand disappeared. In late 1968, for example, *Mafalda 4* came out, with an initial print run of seventy thousand that was expected to sell out quickly. The launch was a huge affair organized as an outdoor party with drinks served to the public. The venue, a Buenos Aires square (Plaza Lavalle), was festooned with balloons for the occasion, and Alba Lampón, a friend of Quino's, remembers Lugones's magnetic presence as she mingled among the guests, handing out flyers to passersby.[42]

In 1968, the social and political role of comic strips was a subject of much discussion in Argentina. In October of that year David Lipszyc, a major promoter of the genre, and Oscar Masotta, one of the first to study cultural industries, organized an International Comics Convention at the Torcuato Di Tella Institute, which had great media impact and was a success among the public. The event was meant to emulate similar exhibits held at the Louvre in Paris and the Tate Gallery in London. *Tarzan* illustrator Burne Hogarth was the international guest of honor. The exhibit featured original works by Al Capp (*Li'l Abner*), George McManus (*Bringing Up Father*), and Roy Crane (*Captain Easy* and *Wash Tubbs*), along with leading Argentine cartoonists (Alberto Breccia, Eduardo Ferro, Guillermo Divito, Lino Palacio, Quino, Hugo Pratt, Oscar Blotta, García Ferré, Solano López, and José Salinas), and movie screenings (*Superman*, *El Zorro*, Héctor Oesterheld's famous science fiction comic *El Eternauta*, and many others). *Mafalda* was a major attraction, as evidenced by the press release announcing that "Charles Schulz's *Peanuts* and Quino's *Mafalda* will be examined and discussed in particular." *Mafalda* was the only Argentine comic included among the keynote presentations.

According to Lipszyc and Masotta, the idea for the convention was prompted by a growing interest among intellectuals in mass culture, and comic books in particular. It began with Masotta, who, seeing the interest the genre had in Europe and the United States, had decided to take on the challenge of initiating a debate on the subject in Argentina. The organizers also sought to support publishers, foster copyright protection, and defend freedom of speech, as well as compete with large corporations by helping to distribute Latin American comics around the world.[43] Masotta was convinced of the cultural value of comics and joined forces with others against critics who looked down on the genre as a lesser and reactionary art form. "Neither are all comic strips conservative nor are they limited to American war comics, nor is the best current work found in the United States," he argued. Aware that comics had both harsh detractors and avid fans, he hoped to "create the instruments that would one day allow us to judge the offending [genre] up close."[44] This entailed recognizing the linguistic, technical, and artistic value of comics, which he believed had the potential for revolutionary political meaning.[45] This interpretation was at odds with a vast and varied literature that, in line with the country's growing radicalization and politicization, denounced the ideological manipulation of mass media by imperialist forces and the ruling classes.[46]

In the context of 1968, these discussions were inextricably linked to the issue of revolutionary commitment. The repressive measures adopted by the Onganía regime to neutralize social protest had radicalized young people in the country's universities and high schools, and also at the grassroots level in neighborhoods and small churches where the Movement of Priests for the Third World was active. Che Guevara's death in 1967 had a similar impact, as his demise amplified the revolutionary mystique that surrounded him, re-kindling the militant commitment of social and political activists who wished to continue his legacy and prompting new debates over the question of tak-ing up arms. This gave renewed force to proponents of armed struggle on the left. New guerrilla organizations, such as the Peronist Armed Forces (Fuerzas Armadas Peronistas), appeared on the scene, and the Workers' Revolutionary Party (Partido Revolucionario de los Trabajadores, or PRT) formed an armed wing that would become one of the country's leading guerrilla groups. The Revolutionary Armed Forces (Fuerzas Armadas Revolucionarias, or FAR), which had originated to support Che Guevara in Argentina, adopted urban guerrilla tactics and joined the efforts of left-wing Peronist activists to raise awareness among the masses and encourage them to take action.

The emergence of these armed groups resonated strongly among artists, intellectuals, and writers, who were asking themselves whether they should play a role in the struggles for social change under way at the grassroots level. Around the same time as the International Comics Convention, a group of avant-garde artists took up these causes by launching a series of artistic and political interventions under the Tucumán Arde (Tucumán Is Burning) cam-paign. This included exhibits, performances, and actions in public spaces and trade union facilities in which they denounced the dismal working conditions of rural laborers. It was the culmination of a process of radicalization that had led these artists to break with the established art world and stage actions such as dyeing the waters of fountains across Buenos Aires red as a tribute to Che Guevara on the first anniversary of his death.[47]

Artists in general were engaged in a debate over their political responsi-bility, questioning whether art should "educate" the masses and whether artists needed to sacrifice their individual creativity to further social aims and turn art into a political instrument. As Ana Longoni and Mariano Mestman explain in their study of these vanguard artists, such dilemmas produced a shift in how they viewed their own artistic production and activities. They now conceived their works as actions rather than objects and went from portraying political violence to performing artistic acts of political violence. In the words of the painter León Ferrari, a "work of art will only be such if the impact it has within the space in which the artist moves is in a certain sense equivalent to the impact a terrorist attack has in a country that is being liberated."[48] It was not just the Tucumán Arde artists who struggled with this dilemma. More than a clear-cut opposition between those in favor of political commitment in art and those who rejected it, there was a wide range of positions among those who accepted it but were unsure as to how it should be expressed and what it entailed for their work. Some even believed that creative freedom itself would show them the way to express their social awareness and that there was no need to condemn certain artistic styles.[49]

Quino echoed this ongoing debate in a series of strips that focused on artists and social and political commitment. In the first strip, Mafalda characteristically bursts in on her father, who is enjoying a quiet moment. But this time she does so to the tune of "The Good Guys Are Getting Fed Up," a protest song she has written. "We love people dearly, so it makes us sick to our stomach to see them pierced by bullets or scorched by napalm," she sings. In the following strip, she asks Manolito if he thinks protest songs could in some way change the world, and then reflects on this herself. She notes that when Guille cried he immediately got what he wanted, which was for his mother to feed him. So she reasons that no guitar was necessary for his protests to succeed. The bluntness of Mafalda's lyrics would suggest the song was meant to be ironic, considering Quino's penchant for subtlety. The series, however, seems to be dominated by a genuine concern for the issue and a need to share the questions it raised: Were gains achieved with songs or through the strength of the popular movement (represented by Guille's cries)? What role should artists play? What should Quino himself do with his humor? These were dilemmas that troubled him and would plague him over the coming years.[50]

Quino's doubts set him apart from some of his colleagues and friends, such as Héctor Oesterheld, who had taken more firm stands. Oesterheld—a writer of graphic novels who had become famous not only for the critically acclaimed *El Eternauta* (1957), but also for *Sargento Kirk* (1953) and *Mort Cinder* (1962)—had put his creativity at the service of the revolution, using his work to convey direct political messages. In 1968, just three months after the death of Che Guevara, he wrote *Vida del Che*, a biographical comic of the revolutionary hero, illustrated by Alberto and Enrique Breccia.[51] A year later he published a new version of *El Eternauta*, in which he turned the main character into a leader of the masses, thus reflecting his own shift toward the revolutionary left.[52]

As political unrest in the country intensified, Quino followed events closely. He echoed them by incorporating the political and ideological jargon popular among university students, sprinkling the characters' dialogues with such expressions. Thus, the kids talked about "school alienation," and Mafalda wondered if Guille was becoming "bourgeoisified" when she saw him sleeping peacefully in his cot. In this context, the comic strip acknowledged the existence of censorship and repression directly, addressing these issues through different characters and situations.[53] Neither repression nor censorship were new. Censorship was, in fact, a part of everyday life in the press rooms where journalists had spent their formative years. Quino has described many times how, when he moved to Buenos Aires in the mid-1950s, he had been told that there were certain subjects he could not touch on in his humor: sex, the military, and the Church.[54] Over the following decades, censorship became stricter. Additional regulations were adopted to control news content, publishing, and television. After the 1966 coup, censors were given greater power and more government agencies had mandates that enabled them to implement measures to restrict the circulation of publications that "undermined the national way of life or the cultural norms of the community."[55]

This environment had made Quino an expert in "self-censorship and circumventing controls." While the decision not to include certain strips in his first compilation, *Mafalda 1*, was in some cases for aesthetic reasons, in others it was because of political references—most notably, the strip in which Mafalda plays at being a guerrilla among the jungle of her father's house plants.[56] These decisions posed an ethical dilemma for Quino, which he addressed in a vignette published in October 1968. The vignette showed Mafalda sticking her tongue out in front of the mirror. Susanita explains to Felipe why her friend is examining her tongue: she is afraid it would not be sharp enough to let her speak her mind. This reminded readers of an article on the relationship between journalism and government that had been published some weeks earlier in the magazine.[57] But the vignette also spoke to Quino's fellow cartoonists and journalists, who faced this dilemma on a daily basis.[58]

In this way, the comic strip spoke out against censorship, in line with the position adopted by *Siete Días*, but also against repression, which the magazine clearly opposed through numerous photo essays.[59] Guille, as the representative of the new rebellious generations, was at the center of many of the strips that touched on this subject. In November 1968, with student unrest constantly in the news, the baby of the family could be seen grounded in his playpen, behind bars, like the activists arrested in the streets and thrown in jail. Mafalda came to her brother's defense: "I told mom that locking you up like this is an outrage! And I warned her about trampling on your individual freedom! I even reminded her of the Universal Declaration of Human Rights! But it turns out none of that has anything to do with you taking dirt from dad's plants and eating it, Guille." Once again the strip resorted to the strategy of resignifying political phenomena through the experiences of children. The illustrator set a mother's commonsensical disciplinary efforts against the arbitrary actions of a repressive police force.[60] With this strip Quino was taking a stand. By then he had become so well known that, in December 1968, he was among the intellectuals asked to give their opinions on the year's turbulent events. In his response, Quino asked for "a bit more freedom for political humor" in the coming year.[61]

While continuing to deal with everyday life, the comic strip incorporated more direct references and nods to social struggles, strikes, and repression. These references did not always come immediately after a specific event; rather, they entailed a reflection modulated by the political and social context. For example, Quino produced a long series of strips on repression that show how he gradually developed his position with respect to the country's political radicalization and the actions of the armed forces. Even though they were not published one after the other and Quino did not connect them intentionally, there is a unity to these strips, and they help provide an understanding of certain sociopolitical developments.

One of the first strips in this series, published in October 1968, shows Miguelito—the youngest member of the gang before Guille's arrival—asking a policeman if he was going to arrest him for not washing his hands, as his mom had threatened. In response, the policeman looks at the boy angrily and tells him to inform his mother that the police have more important "things" to take care of.[62] This scene was anchored in a long-standing representation of the policeman as the neighborhood watchman, one who protects the community and participates in its daily life.[63]

This relationship changed in a later strip, published in April 1969, which alluded to the student demonstrators in Tucumán, Santa Fe, and Rosario who were defying the police and taking center stage in political events (figure 2.6).[64] In this strip, Miguelito asks the policeman *not* to guard his house because he imagines himself in the future, as a university student, necessarily clashing with the police in "some strife." "How, then, could I bring myself to throw rocks at the man who protected my house?" he tells the policeman. Although the characters could still see police officers as one of them and the confrontation imagined by Miguelito was not a serious one, his concern heralded the aggravation of such conflicts that was to come.[65]

FIGURE 2.6 Quino, "Mafalda," *Siete Días* (Buenos Aires), April 14, 1969, 33. © Joaquín Salvador Lavado (Quino).

Less than two months later, *Mafalda* returned to this subject after the May 1969 worker and student uprising in Córdoba. The protests (which would be known as the Cordobazo) were sparked by the combative trade unions of the General Labor Confederation (Confederación General del Trabajo, or CGT) and garnered significant support from many sectors of the population. The situation quickly escalated into a civil insurrection as protesters seized control of the city. As they successfully resisted police repression, the Onganía government sent in the army to crush the revolt. This shift from police to military forces indicated a new level of repression, which was illustrated in a strip published in June. In the first panel, Mafalda is seen overhearing two men on the street talking about how development was coming slowly but surely. As the strip progresses, she first comes across a policeman with a small billy club and then a soldier with a much larger truncheon. Countering the assessment by the two men in the first panel, Mafalda reflects that in some cases growth was actually coming hard and fast—in reference to the regime's strategy of furthering economic development by stepping up repression, an allusion that readers could not have failed to grasp.[66] Two weeks later, a vignette also echoed the fast pace of the changing political scenario. Felipe notices that a different font has been used for the title, remarking, "Looks like there's been some changes," to which Mafalda replies, "*More* changes?"[67]

Over the following weeks, Quino continued to use a range of humor devices to critically depict the rising repression. This was the case with the strip described earlier in which Mafalda realizes that Guille's string of innocent questions, insistently fired, would make her little brother a perfect target for police repression. Another strip in the same issue has Mafalda refusing the bowl of soup her mother brings her and threatening to throw a tantrum, because, as she tells Raquel, she is "losing all respect for high-handedness."[68] Soup was again presented as a metaphor for the unfair imposition of authority and Mafalda as a symbol of antiauthoritarianism. A few months later, the contrast between Miguelito's naïveté and Mafalda's wisdom served to underscore a similar message. The strip features the two friends and a neighborhood policeman, but this time the kids only address each other. Pointing to the officer's baton, Mafalda shrewdly reveals to Miguelito the police's true role as an instrument of ideological repression (figure 2.7). The humor lay in the partial concealment of her explanation behind tree branches, as this played with the idea that Mafalda was exposing a semihidden truth. After a suspension produced by two uncaptioned panels, in the last panel her full message was finally revealed to readers when the baffled policeman ponders Mafalda's damning description of his baton as "an ideology-denting stick." In this way, Quino reworked the cartoon's earlier representation of the police, turning it on its head: from guardian of the kids' homes to repressor of ideas. In the prevailing context, this strip resonated with readers and highlighted the main character's role as a moral voice.

FIGURE 2.7 Quino, "Mafalda," *Siete Días* (Buenos Aires), October 13, 1969, 53. © Joaquín Salvador Lavado (Quino).

Thus, the characters no longer engaged with police officers, as Miguelito had done just a few months earlier. But they were not yet so estranged that they could not approach a policeman to mock him. What is more, the officer was slow to react and did not fully understand the meaning of the accusation. The situation and the pace of the strip were reminiscent of devices used by Charles Chaplin. Quino proposed a scene in which humor was used to defy power through a combination of irony and tenderness. The children—the new generations—escaped unscathed from their clever acts of defiance. The stable, neighborly background removed any conflict from the scene. But the strip had an undeniably dangerous side to it: repressive forces could be outwitted. Especially when the government came against young people—as was the case with the protests in cities across the country who were experimenting, but also refusing to be subdued by police batons or even firearms.

This disruptive element could not go unnoticed by readers. The magazine—like other media—had been closely following the daily confrontations, which were illustrated vividly by the images featured in its photo essays, often without any accompanying text (see figures 2.8–2.10). They showed the strength of worker and student protests and the savageness with which they were repressed. The magazine's editorial line called attention to the government's deterioration and its increasing isolation as it was faced with difficulties from various fronts.[69] In his own way, Quino had composed a denunciation of repression in the framework of political radicalization. This context gave new meaning to the generational dimension in *Mafalda*. In the pages of the women's magazine *Claudia*, the journalist Adriana Civita described how the comic strip revealed that the "enemy" that challenged adults was, in fact, "the source of our deepest affection: our children." Civita called Mafalda a "little know-it-all monster" who was read by two million Argentines and represented "the bright children of today, the skepticism with which kids regard adults and life. She represents the fears and hopes of youngsters as they contemplate the future, and also exposes the childish side of adults . . . millions of beings who want to fix all the world's problems and fail, so they translate all their impotence into irony and aggressiveness."[70] While the journalist portrayed the new generation in a sympathetic and understanding light, Argentina's political and social elite was starting to fear the increasing radicalization of the country's youth.

FIGURES 2.8, 2.9, AND 2.10 "El desafío cordobés," *Siete Días* (Buenos Aires), special edition, June 2, 1969, n.p., and "Mayo: De corceles y de aceros," *Siete Días* (Buenos Aires), June 8, 1969, no. 108, 14–20.

The strips that touched on repression and the "ideology-denting stick" were not the only examples that reflected the swift spread of political commitment and radicalization. On February 16, 1970, Quino introduced a new character: Libertad. As with Miguelito, she arrived during the summer, while Mafalda was on holiday with her family; the absence of the other kids in the gang meant that the storyline had to be supplemented with new figures. This character was a tiny girl whose height and name symbolized the place of freedom, her namesake, in Argentina. Quino made this connection explicit soon after Libertad's first appearance (figure 2.11). The two girls meet at the beach and Mafalda introduces her new sunburned friend to her parents. When her father hears her name, he says "Libertad? You're *so* tiny"; her mother adds, "And *so* burnt!" To which Mafalda retorts, "I brought a friend, not a political pamphlet!" Libertad's name heralded a linear character, easily grasped by readers, who stood for intellectual and politicized middle-class youth.

FIGURE 2.11 Quino, "Mafalda," *Siete Días* (Buenos Aires), no. 146 (February 23, 1970). © Joaquín Salvador Lavado (Quino).

Again, as with Mafalda, Quino intuitively chooses a female character to channel the progressive middle class. In doing so the comic strip implicitly echoed the disruptions caused by feminist demands, both globally and locally. In 1970, the Argentine Feminist Union (Unión Feminista Argentina) was formed, whose acronym, UFA, is also a slang interjection used as an exclamation of annoyance, in the manner of "argh." The union gathered women in "awareness-raising" groups, staged marches and performances, and distributed pamphlets denouncing women's oppression.[71] The media who participated in the new wave of journalism perceived the enormous news potential of the women's movement and sought to profit from it. By giving voice to representatives of various positions, it stirred up controversies, and editorials often combined a certain empathy with women's causes with a touch of misogyny. Two years earlier, for example, *Siete Días* had published a special women's issue, which included an entire page by Quino with four *Mafalda* strips on the situation of women. The page was headed by the comic strip's title crossed out by Susanita and replaced with her own name, thus symbolizing the complexity of women's views. The first of these strips dealt with the limitations women faced in politics. This issue had already come up when the gang played government and Manolito scoffed at Mafalda's presidential aspirations. Mafalda's comeback then had been, "Why not innovate? After all, we're only playing!" Her response was symptomatic of an emerging feminist awareness and of second-wave organizations because it evidenced women's demands for equality but also a certain naturalization of self-imposed restrictions, which only a few years later would not be overlooked by someone who, like Quino, was so committed to denouncing such inequalities.[72]

In a new installment touching on the subject of women in politics we see a similar naturalization of the unequal status of women, as Mafalda asks herself why a woman could never be president and comes to the typically sexist conclusion that women are incapable of keeping secrets and thus could not be trusted with confidential government information. This conclusion—which was not included in the 2004 English edition in deference to changing norms—contrasted with the following two strips, in which Mafalda reflects on how, throughout the history of humanity, women have been relegated to "cleaning the house instead of running it." In fact, these and other strips were later incorporated by feminists into their struggles.[73] While she never mentioned feminism, Libertad's mother was the stereotype of the intellectual woman. In contrast to the other mothers in the strip, she dressed in jeans, smoked, had a university degree, and worked translating the works of Jean-Paul Sartre, although she did so from home (figure 2.12). Libertad's father was a socialist sympathizer, but he was not a member of any political party or movement.[74]

The definition of Libertad's character took on meaning in the context of the growing visibility of guerrilla groups. In June 1969, the FAR had placed bombs in a chain of supermarkets owned by Nelson Rockefeller, to protest his visit to Argentina. The trade union leader Augusto Timoteo Vandor was killed, and the ERP was organizing its first armed action, which it planned to stage in February 1970.[75] On May 29, 1970, the Montoneros made themselves known by kidnapping and killing General Pedro Eugenio Aramburu. This action, linked to the Peronist resistance, was meant as a trial and execution; it carried great symbolic power and had a huge media impact. It sought to show the weakness of the armed forces and the fearlessness of the nascent

FIGURE 2.12 Quino, "Mafalda," *Siete Días* (Buenos Aires), no. 162 (June 15–21, 1970), 38. © Joaquín Salvador Lavado (Quino).

guerrilla organization. It succeeded in eroding Onganía's government, as his failure to deal with widespread social unrest was compounded by his inability to stop the rise of guerrilla groups.[76] But radicalization was not limited to these organizations. In an interview published by *Siete Días*, the Catalonian singer-songwriter Joan Manuel Serrat—who was very popular in Argentina—told the journalist that while "guitars don't shoot bullets," there might come a time when everyone would have to put down their guitar and pick up a rifle.[77] In this context, guerrilla groups renewed their call to intellectuals to actively join their ranks, which entailed putting their creativity, knowledge, and works at the service of political causes. This meant that they were expected to relinquish their intellectual freedom and, if necessary, even interrupt their work to take up arms. This demand resonated with the words of Che Guevara, who had stopped practicing medicine to give himself entirely to the revolution. This created a deep rift between intellectuals and artists who wished to remain independent and those who assumed a social and political commitment. In the early 1970s it was still possible for those who had chosen different paths to find some common ground, but in the coming years those paths would veer further apart. Thus, writers and journalists like Rodolfo Walsh and Francisco "Paco" Urondo, who had joined armed groups, could still gather in the same press rooms and circles of newsmen as other colleagues or friends, such as Quino, who chose not to go down that route.

Libertad's character illustrated the ideological dilemmas of a segment of Argentina's intellectual left, which is important for understanding the growing polarization and political violence. She represented a progressive, disillusioned, and caustic middle class that had discovered the impossibility of a libertarian utopia. Because of the concerns she voiced, but also because of what she did not say, she spoke to vast segments of the country's young people who were immersed in discussions over the Cuban Revolution, the political organizations they should join, and whether or not to take up arms or the right time to do so. Libertad expressed these issues rather elusively, echoing a more open affiliation in which readers who identified broadly with the left or with socialism could see themselves more comfortably.

In this sense, the introduction of this new character was preceded by a drop in the references made by Mafalda to the dichotomist views of the Cold War and even to Third Worldism. It is symptomatic that the Cuban Revolution and Fidel Castro were rarely mentioned in the comic strip at a time when these featured prominently in the debates and culture of left-wing youth. This general lack of references during this time made the one isolated instance in which Cuba was mentioned all the more significant. On June 7, 1971, the vignette showed a blank-faced Mafalda saying: "A Fidel in the hand is worth more than an intellectual in the bush!"[78] This remark was an allusion not only to the popular saying "A bird in the hand is worth two in the bush" but also to the arrest, two weeks earlier, of the Cuban writer Heberto Padilla on charges of counterrevolutionary activities. This could be interpreted in two ways: Mafalda could be saying that Fidel was worth more than any intellectual, but it could also be an ironic commentary on the Cuban leader's actions against independent intellectuals. The ambiguity could also be read as a pun that was merely meant to lighten or ease a heated debate that, as Claudia Gilman has argued, has divided Latin American intellectuals forever.[79] However, it was not a light matter for Quino, who, around that time, insisted that he did not like to "spell things out for people." It was for this reason that he fell out with Oesterheld, who believed that art—Picasso's art—had no value if it was not understood by ordinary people. They argued bitterly over the matter, and to this day Quino is saddened by the memory—his friend and fellow comic book artist was disappeared in 1977, never to be seen again.[80]

These discussions intensified when Onganía's government finally fell in June 8, 1970, under the weight of widespread social protests. But the situation did not improve under the new government. Roberto M. Levingston, who succeeded Onganía, continued along the same lines as his predecessor and refused to call an election. The armed groups stepped up their actions. In July of that year, for example, the FAR took control of the town of Garín in the province of Buenos Aires, in an action commanded by the organization's top leaders Carlos Olmedo, Juan Julio Roqué, and Roberto Quieto—all of whom would later join Montoneros. The renowned writer, poet, and journalist Paco Urondo is also believed to have participated in this action.[81] In December, the organization staged a new action, this time in La Plata, robbing a branch of Banco Comercial with the aim of "confiscating" the bank's money to use it to fund its own activities. According to the local newspaper *El Día*, the guerrillas acted with "extraordinary boldness and determination." While the guerrillas were able to control the situation rapidly, two policemen were wounded. Before leaving the bank they left a message that included a photocopy of a caricature by Quino that had been featured in *Panorama* a week earlier (figure 2.13).[82] Over the words "Black has the advantage and it can call checkmate whenever it pleases," the drawing showed a chessboard where the black pieces were depicted as rich men and the white pieces as working-class people, or, as the La Plata paper described them, "well-off and needy sectors." Under the drawing the guerrillas had left a printed statement explaining their actions.[83]

FIGURE 2.13 Quino, "Ajedrez," reproduced in "Un grupo de extremistas," *El Día* (Buenos Aires), December 16, 1970, 8. © Joaquín Salvador Lavado (Quino).

At the center of the debates among politicized intellectuals and artists was the question of how to achieve social change and whether armed struggle was the right path. But one thing they all agreed on was that change was inevitable and that their involvement was necessary. These shared convictions allowed the writer Tomás Eloy Martínez to declare—upon taking the helm of *Panorama* in November 1970—that all those who worked for the magazine knew that the transformation of society was an inexorable law of history and that they were all committed to ensuring that in Argentina change would be brought about democratically and with equality.[84] This position became firmer in the magazine's subsequent issues, as Salvador Allende was elected president of Chile (becoming the first democratically elected socialist in Latin America), the Tupamaros guerrilla group gained popular support in Uruguay, and growing social unrest in Argentina made revolutionary change seem increasingly attainable. In an exclusive interview for the magazine, Julio Cortázar had discussed the great turbulence in Latin America with Paco Urondo. According to Cortázar, who had been in Chile and was convinced that the only way forward for Latin America was socialism, the common denominator in the continent was social inequality. It was precisely that social inequality—also highlighted by Tomás Eloy Martínez—that Quino had portrayed in the chess board cartoon that was used by the armed group of which Urondo was a clandestine member. Quino later explained in *Panorama* that the drawing had been meant merely as a social commentary, in the manner of the famous tango "Cambalache," written by Enrique Santos Discépolo in the 1930s, which described the troubles of the world in the twentieth century. It was not intended "to incite people to violence, or to steal; it wasn't even meant to be identified with any political ideology in particular; it just illustrated a reality that humanity discovered ages before I did."[85]

Interviewed by Oscar Giardinelli, Quino said he realized that what he hoped for was not real—"what they teach you when you're little: to be good, to aspire to social justice, to refrain from fighting . . . history shows that it's not that easy. Right now that depresses me." When Giardinelli asked him what he thought of violence, he said: "I don't like it, of course, but I understand it when I read about it . . . I was in Paris during the May turmoil and I was intrigued; I intellectualized violence and it's brought me a lot of pain." The journalist then brought up the incident of the chess caricature: "It bothered me greatly. I felt used. If I knew what their beliefs were I would be able to decide if I agree with them, but as it is . . ." (A year later he would add: "It's as if I'd gone to the site of one of their heists and sprayed on the wall: 'This heist is an ad for Don Manolo's Grocery Store.'") When Giardinelli asked him his opinion on irony, the cartoonist answered that it was a weapon he would use to attack rather than to defend himself. "Who would you attack?" the journalist asked. "People who are intent on hurting. There are a lot of people whose aim is to hurt. Not hurt me specifically, but others, the many. Of course there are people like that—for example, weapon manufacturers. Their mission is to hurt."[86] Thus, like the Tucumán Arde artists, Quino had come to understand—albeit differently and through great efforts—the use of violence. He certainly did not embrace armed struggle and the only weapon he was prepared to use was irony.

As the country became more and more radicalized, it was not just Quino who was called on to explain where he stood. Readers also argued among themselves over how *Mafalda* should be interpreted, what social sector it represented, whom it spoke to, and what political effects it had. These arguments sometimes assumed that Mafalda channeled the illustrator—as Quino himself had admitted on occasion—in a symbiosis that fused creator and character and rendered the cartoon almost human. At the same time, the political influence of comics was becoming a subject of discussion, most notably with the study conducted in Chile by Ariel Dorfman and Armand Mattelart in the context of Allende's democratically elected socialist government. These two politically committed researchers with solid academic training posited that Disney cartoons were a vehicle for bourgeois capitalist ideology and an ingredient in the "colonization strategies" deployed by the United States in Latin America. They presented their research in the book *How to Read Donald Duck*, published in Chile in 1971 and a year later in Argentina.[87] Their ideas were part of wider discussions that were taking place across Latin America, engaging Argentine intellectuals such as Héctor Schmucler who were pioneering studies on social communications and ideological domination.[88]

In March 1971, Oscar Steinberg—who was among the first to take a semiotic approach to comics in Argentina—published a critique of *Mafalda* in the magazine *Los Libros* (which focused on structuralism and whose target audience was young intellectuals). After recognizing the value of Quino's artwork and its place in a great tradition of graphic production, Steinberg found fault with the content of his comic strips, as it rested on a "rational and safe view of History" that used simplifications and consolidated stereotypes such as that of the crude Galician immigrant. This characterization made sense from a social point of view because, according to Steinberg, "in most installments, the strip channels a conceptual joke, on the shoulders of a nod to an explicit opinion shared by its (liberal middle-class) audience. *Mafalda* captures its readers with the illusion of an exercise in nonconformist reading, based on an ideology that rejects the establishment." By calling it an "illusion" Steinberg criticized both the self-satisfied audience who fancied itself critical and Quino's creation, which offered "a repertoire of human types determined, very pedagogically, by an environment comfortably dominated by commonsensical social characterizations."[89]

Not much later, *Clarín* featured an essay that painted a scathing picture both of the strip and of Quino. It described Mafalda and her family and friends as "typical Buenos Aires exponents of the petit-bourgeois neighborhood mentality," who were, as befitted their social class, "representatives of a pathetic reformism that leads nowhere." What was presented as a message was, in fact, not a message at all but merely reflected "the nihilism, weariness, political apathy, and skeptical protestations of the middle sectors and petite bourgeoisie of the city of Buenos Aires." The essay concluded by predicting that "the marriage between Quino and his dwarfs would eventually fall victim to routine and alienation, and they will grow old peacefully and die, like the rest of us."[90] This prophecy also presupposed a direct correspondence between the characters, on the one hand, and Quino's voice or the opinions of the readers, on the other.

These bitter discussions and the image of an aged Mafalda reflected the difficulty of keeping the storylines current and the characters fresh. This was no easy feat with characters who had long ago acquired canonical status and had been created under a different state of affairs, one in which it was still possible for a middle class divided along ideological lines to live together in harmony.[91] In the new context of the early 1970s, Argentine society seemed hopelessly fraught with rifts that would soon be made unbridgeable by spiraling violence.

The main interpretative approaches suggested by *How to Read Donald Duck* failed to take in the complexities of *Mafalda*. By assuming—and expecting—a direct relationship between the cartoonist, his work, and the readers, they obscured the hiatus between the comic strip's contents and reality. Moreover, these approaches matched the prevailing climate of ideological polarization. While Argentina was no stranger to intolerance in politics, as evidenced by past attempts to eradicate Peronism, in the early 1970s that intolerance reached new heights. That atmosphere of exclusion brought back the anger directed at the middle class and the one-dimensional representations typical of the sociopolitical-interpretative trend in sociology that a decade earlier had questioned the middle class, although now instead of criticizing its anti-Peronism, it reproached it for its lack of political commitment.

Quino's position on violence became more complex as radicalization advanced. In March 1971, the military junta that had brought General Roberto Levingston to power withdrew its support when a new uprising in Córdoba, known as the Viborazo, heightened social protests. The new president, General Alejandro A. Lanusse, changed the government's strategy. In a move to stem social unrest, he lifted the electoral ban on Peronism and allowed for greater political participation. But at the same time the military government cracked down hard on social activists and left-wing armed groups. In addition to institutionalizing torture, it began killing and forcefully disappearing militants. *Mafalda* followed these developments closely. Once again, soup was used as a metaphor for authoritarianism. On April 5, 1971, less than two weeks after General Lanusse came to power, a strip (figure 2.14) shows a grim-faced Mafalda offering resistance to a bowl of soup her mother has put in front of her, mimicking the stilted rhetoric used by the military in her plea: "If anyone were to deliberately rebel against drinking, eating, swallowing, gobbling, and/ or sipping this crap, would you beat them?"[92]

FIGURE 2.14 Quino, "Mafalda," *Siete Días*, no. 207 (May 3, 1971). © Joaquín Salvador Lavado (Quino).

This rhetorical question required no answer. On the contrary, the humorous effect worked because readers could identify the style of official bans in Mafalda's words and thus associate it with authoritarian repression. Some weeks later, when the possibility of elections was being discussed, readers could see Mafalda looking up a word in the dictionary: "DEMOCRACY (from the Greek *demos*, 'common people,' and *kratos*, 'rule'): government by the people." The following panels show the girl laughing hysterically long into the night. The irony conveyed in this strip resonated with readers who met the announcements of a return to democracy with disbelief. The following strip, featured on the same page, continued in this vein. Mafalda is greeted by her youngest friend, who declares that he is the "brand new Miguelito!" as he was tired of his old self and "decided to stage a coup and topple my former personality!" After a brief pause, Mafalda asks him, "What does this mean? What are we going to have to put up with from you now?"[93] A few weeks later, the main character again took on authoritarianism. Standing on her chair, with a bowl of chicken soup on the table before her, Mafalda screams at her mother in a trembling voice: "What did chickens ever do to you? Nothing! What are they guilty of? Nothing! Your hands, mother, are stained with the broth of the innocent!!!"[94]

The comic strip's political significance was not limited to touching on the country's advancing political radicalization. It also commented on the economic downturn and other developments that were deeply affecting everyday life. Inflation went from 22 percent in 1970 to 39 percent in 1971, soaring to 64 percent in 1972. This was further aggravated by a steady drop in real wages. Civil servants, for example, saw their income reduced by 13 percent between 1970 and 1972, while construction workers suffered a 10 percent cut in their wages.[95] Households were hit the hardest, as families faced increasing economic difficulties that forced them to lower their standard of living and consume less and less. The media focused on what this meant for a middle class that until recently had enjoyed the benefits of modernization. *Siete Días*, for example, featured a report on how much it cost a "typical middle-class family" to "live decently," based on information provided by heads of household and housewives, and found that they had to supplement their income with odd jobs and find clever ways to feed their families with less money.[96]

The hardships suffered by the middle class threw into sharp relief the irony that had characterized *Mafalda* from the start, when it exposed the false promise of modernization even in the heyday of the modernizing discourse. As the downturn shattered the illusion of economic well-being, the comic strip turned the middle class's loss of status into a central issue. In a strip from the mid-1970s, for example, Mafalda was pictured staring at a hole in her shoe. In the following panel we see her bringing the shoe to her mom, who then takes it to her husband, who responds by telling her about the car payments they still owe. The last panel shows the little girl sitting on the curb with her broken shoe. Below this, in another strip, Felipe meets up with his friend, and when he asks her how she is doing, she says, "Here I am, with a hole in my shoe until my father gets paid next week." And to Felipe's stream of questions— What would happen if her dad didn't get paid? Didn't they have any savings? Was that her only pair of shoes? Could he be of any help?—Mafalda angrily tells him, "You can help by taking your interview with the middle class and stuffing it!" But it was not just an interview *with* the middle class. It was an interview *by* the middle class, for which these difficulties merited questions that revealed they had not yet naturalized such problems, as had working-class children used to living in poverty. The last strip in this installment addressed the possibility of relativizing those difficulties. An uncharacteristically pious Mafalda starts praying to God to "straighten up the state of affairs" (in allusion to the economic problems of her class), only to realize she can reverse the terms of her appeal—"Or should I say the affairs of the state?"—thus highlighting the government's responsibility. This device of expressing the personal through the public, and vice versa (a foundational element in *Mafalda*), acquired full political meaning here: the problem involved the state.[97] The following week's installment offered a view of the problem from the perspective of the other members of the gang. When Manolito comforts his friend by reassuring her it was normal for employers to be late with wages, but at the same time is outraged when a customer asks to buy something from his father's store on credit, he reveals how much he was looking out for his own interest. Susanita showed her perverse duplicity when, after telling Mafalda not to dramatize, she gives her friend the telephone number of Emaus, a well-known charity. Miguelito, instead, angrily tells her that when he grew up he would scalp his boss if he did not pay him on time, but immediately forgets all his rage when a bird, symbolically, lands on his head. The series closed a week later with Mafalda's father being paid at work and the fleeting joy his paycheck brings him, which lasts until his daughter shows him the list of school supplies she needs.[98]

"I don't love my inflation. Do you?"—in that way a 1971 vignette summarized a then-widespread feeling among Argentines. Shortly after, Mafalda's mother gave a new twist to the problem. In a strip that echoed Mafalda's unending fit of laughter after reading the definition of democracy, Raquel unpacks her groceries in hysterics as she recalls how much each item has gone up. In the last frame, her daughter highlights the contrast with the past by exclaiming, "It was better back when she flew into a healthy rage!"[99] Other strips contained similar references to the economic crisis: Manolito imagining his customers asking for credit, word games with the expression "tighten one's belt," allusions to the beef shortage or currency devaluation.[100] *Panorama* highlighted just how much these references reflected the prevailing mood in the country when it chose Mafalda's father as its 1971 personality of the year, as a representation of the "Argentine Everyman," featuring him on the cover of the magazine against a backdrop of handwritten annotations of household expenses. According to Tomás Eloy Martínez, other candidates had been considered, including the Chilean writer Pablo Neruda and the politician and future president María Estela Martínez de Perón, but they had finally chosen this "antihero" character who not only had withstood price inflation and wage deflation but also suffered censorship, political exclusion, and unemployment. The idea was for that "Argentine Everyman" to stand for the essence of what it meant to be Argentine.[101]

The strip also addressed the fast-paced changes that the younger generations were experiencing in the early 1970s. Of all the characters, Guille continued to offer the best opportunities for humorous effect, with his rejection of authority, his cynical naïveté, and his scathing remarks delivered in baby talk. That role—which at one point he shared with the next youngest character, Miguelito—was eloquently captured in a sequence that showed Mafalda's baby brother hitting a long-haired, gangly youth on the back of the head with a toy truck, after she pointed him out as one of the grown-ups who would rob them of their future. However, even with the inclusion of such incidental characters, *Mafalda* failed to fully portray the radical nature of the cultural and political clashes that were reflected in youth styles during those years. Neither the arguments between Manolito and Mafalda over the Beatles nor the miniskirts sported by Felipe's crush, Muriel (a sensual girl with an air of Brigitte Bardot), could bridge the gap that separated the comic strip from what young people were experiencing then—from rock concerts to drugs—and that were baffling and frightening adults.

In this aspect, the strip's social and cultural commentary lagged behind that of a new crop of cartoonists, who nonetheless looked up to Quino as an inspiration. In 1971, these humorists were just starting to make their mark, most notably in the magazine *Hortensia*, which had recently begun its run in the province of Córdoba. The magazine covered the tumultuous political and cultural scene of the 1970s in a caustic satirical style, crossing the line into moral and political incorrectness. Along with *Satiricón* and other magazines that came out around this time, *Hortensia* thematized, with a heavy dose of irony, the features of politicized, countercultural youth. Like *Mafalda*, the humor in these publications was intended for middle-class readers, who could identify with the satirized subjects, and called for an exercise in introspection.[102]

Mafalda's popularity, however, was not affected by its failure to reflect the most convulsive expressions of youth culture. In 1970, the sixth book of *Mafalda* strips sold 200,000 copies in just three days, and the unauthorized use of its characters to promote all sorts of products was becoming increasingly hard to control, according to Quino himself.[103] More important still, this disconnection with emerging youth cultures did not prevent the strip from providing a way to access cultural changes for many readers who were only then catching up with fashion, language, and aesthetics that had been new a decade earlier. This massification spoke to other social sectors, more humble or marginal, but also to younger readers.[104]

In the early 1970s the strip became popular among preteens and small children. The writer Rodrigo Fresán, born in 1963, recalls that Quino was a friend of the family and he would brag about that relationship at school, even convincing the cartoonist to let him take his fingerprints so he could show his friends. He also remembers identifying with Felipe, and how Muriel was "if not the first sex symbol of our generation, at least the object of our romantic passions."[105] Fresán was not the only young reader who felt a close connection with the characters, as reflected in many interviews and written accounts. Many saw in *Mafalda* the possibility of objectifying their own differences with the adult world. Miguel Rep, for example, now a well-known cartoonist himself and a friend of Quino's, remembers how as a kid a friend at school described a sequence in which Mafalda refused to eat her soup and embarked on a "passionate harangue about her incorruptible ethics," which ended abruptly when her mother tempted her with "pancakes." "I don't know why, but that really cracked us up. Mafalda was one of us, up against the clever and dominating adult world," Rep recalls.[106] Young readers in the early 1970s also felt that with *Mafalda* they were being admitted into a political and moral universe that was the domain of grown-ups—even if they did not fully understand it—and the fact that that initiation was done through humor made it all the more attractive. It was exciting and challenging to try to decipher the jargon used by their parents and the nods to events in the adult world, and when they succeeded in understanding, it was satisfying to learn about serious issues. Of course, *Mafalda* also appealed to these readers on a more superficial level, but no less important in terms of the strip's intergenerational transmission. This included the many *Mafalda* products sold in the first half of the 1970s—from plastic dolls to soaps shaped like the characters (see figures 2.15–18).[107]

FAREWELL TO A LOST WORLD

New debates involving *Mafalda* emerged in the prevailing climate of ideological polarization. In 1971, the daily *La Nación* featured a full-page article on the comic strip that described the main character as the "voice of vast segments of society's middle class" and asked two university experts to comment on Mafalda's social effects. These experts in the field of psychology agreed that while the intellectually precocious little girl exhibited social awareness and a perceptive mind, she did not offer a "healthy" image because her "lucid thinking" did not lead to action. For that reason, having a child like Mafalda was a terrifying prospect.[108] In other media, the comic strip sparked more passionate reactions. According to the magazine *Grandes Chicos*, the character of Mafalda "embodied any and all rebelliousness found in and around Buenos Aires" and "objectified the guilty conscience of legions of people." In its words, Mafalda "never aspired to be anything more than a critique of the system, but [a critique] from within," and she expressed the view held by many intellectuals "who

FIGURES 2.15, 2.16, 2.17, AND 2.18 Jenning's brand Mafalda and Manolito soaps and Rayito de Sol brand Mafalda doll, ca. 1970, courtesy of Antonio Torres, Club del Cómic, Buenos Aires. Plastic Mafalda doll, ca. 1970, courtesy of the Pérez Carrara family, Montevideo.

perceptively understand that only a change will help Argentine society, and who, without putting themselves above society, adopt a clear critical stance that is worth heeding."[109] While the comic strip had become more complex in response to developments in Argentine politics, the frameworks used to analyze it had been simplified. The view that assumed a transparent correlation between fiction and reality had become widespread, and in Mafalda's case the implications were more significant because of the sociopolitical importance attributed to her character.

The fact that Mafalda was criticized for her moderate stance—which the newspaper *La Nación* equated with "inaction"—reveals the extent of radicalization and the importance placed on social commitment in Argentine society by late 1971. Around this time, *Siete Días* claimed to have polled three hundred young men and women on Perón's possible return from exile and found that it was "no longer a source of irritation for the large middle class that rejected him fifteen years ago," both echoing a prevailing sentiment and also revealing where the magazine's sympathies lay.[110]

A strong criticism directed at the middle class permeated every review of *Mafalda* at this juncture. But with such questioning, critics ultimately hoped that the middle class would be spurred into action and reveal its worth. Tomás Eloy Martínez—who a year earlier had sang the praises of the "Argentine Everyman"—described the middle class as a "rotten" majority, a "domesticated and consumerist" sector opposed to change, which had found in Onganía a government that represented its views on politics, education, and sex. He argued that the middle class had only lent its support to the "epic feat" of May 1969 (in reference to the Cordobazo) because it felt that authoritarianism had become a nuisance. But while he denounced the opportunistic nature of the middle class, he acknowledged that in some situations the "bourgeoisie" could come to realize that the only solution was to "turn society inside out like a glove."[111] In a similar vein, a review featured in *Siete Días* of Ricardo Monti's recently premiered *Historia tendenciosa de la clase media* (A Biased History of the Middle Class) noted that the play "challenged the civic responsibility of the audience" from a "neo-Peronist or left-wing" perspective.[112]

In just a few months, political events had further radicalized the left and exacerbated the repressive violence of the armed forces. Once again, *Mafalda* addressed the current state of affairs. In July 1972, after a break of almost three months, which he spent in Europe, Quino resumed production of *Mafalda* with a strip that shows Guille asking his sister about an antiriot water-cannon truck. She answers that "it's in case any violence has been sown" explaining that as a farming method it may seem counterintuitive but they use those trucks "to nip it in the bud, watering it before it sprouts."[113] Two weeks later, on August 22, 1972, sixteen guerrillas who were serving time in Rawson Penitentiary (in the southern province of Chubut) were killed by government forces after an attempted prison break. In an account published in *Panorama*, Tomás Eloy Martínez reported that the guerrillas were unarmed and had been executed in cold blood near the city of Trelew after surrendering, despite government claims that they had weapons and had tried to escape again. His denunciation of the Trelew Massacre (as it came to be known) cost him his job. Twenty years later, as the ultra-right was again gaining ground in Argentina, he recalled Mafalda's tirade against her mother and her accusation that her hands were "stained with the broth of the innocent."[114] While in his recollection of those events the journalist had the timing of the strip wrong (it had actually been published a year earlier), what was still vivid in his mind all those years later was how the strip's recurring use of soup as a metaphor for authoritarianism had resonated with him when he exposed the Trelew Massacre.[115] A week after the killings, readers could see a solitary and dismayed Mafalda asking herself, "Is today also Saint Martyr of the Stomach Day?," as a bowl of soup advances toward her. In the following installment, in another reference to this growing authoritarianism, Mafalda looks directly at readers from a vignette and asks, "Are cannons the hair rollers of freedom?"[116] Earlier, Mafalda had seen some workmen with jackhammers drilling the pavement and had asked them what confession they were trying to extract from "that poor street." Similarly, Miguelito, with a characteristic mixture of malice and innocence, had tried to convince his friends to let him be the cop in a game they were playing by telling them, "I even have a pin I can use for torturing."[117]

How are we to interpret these allusions? First, it is important to bear in mind that humor does not work without the audience that triggers its comedic potential. Central to Quino's humor was its political and social meaning. In this sense, in 1971 the cartoonists Alberto Bróccoli and Carlos Trillo argued that *Mafalda* was "for many people their main source of political and social commentary of the week. Our middle class is comforted when they see someone worrying about the world, the country, mankind, diseases. And, in *Mafalda*, they see their own anxieties reflected."[118] A letter to the editor of *Siete Días* confirmed this view: a group of students explained that the comic strip was their weekly dose of "critical and original wit." According to another reader, Alberto Mazzei, writing from Corrientes, Quino's "page is my weekly laugh (and that of thousands of readers). There are a great many of us who need that therapy to lift some of the gloom of our days, to counter the deluge of crimes, bans, depreciations, attacks, and other similar events."[119]

The reference to the therapeutic qualities of laughter brings us to a line of inquiry that is essential for understanding humor in times of repression. In Freud's seminal study on humor, he discovered its liberating power and the pleasure of saving energy that would otherwise be spent on repressing the unconscious. A decade later he returned to this subject. He distinguished jokes and the comic (which he had analyzed in his initial study) from humor, which has something of "grandeur" and "elevation." The grandeur lay in the possibility of refusing to suffer and in asserting the ego's invulnerability in the face of the "traumas of the external world"; the elevation was in the briefness of that parenthesis produced by laughter, after which pain again torments the individual. Hence, Freud concluded that "humor is not resigned; it is rebellious." It is part of the methods deployed to evade the compulsion to suffer. Quino's ironies were thus a productive way of resisting the pain caused by reality, a stubborn rejection of the traumas of the external world, by confronting them.[120]

Quino was conscious of the political and social role of humor. Asked to comment on the subject in a 1971 interview, he referred to humorists as a "relief valve." They made it easier for the public—who had undergone "a process of intellectualization"—to "pass judgment on the irritating aspects of humanity."[121] A year later, in a conversation with the writer and journalist Osvaldo Soriano, he elaborated, beginning by criticizing his earlier work: "Now I know what I want to say. Back then I didn't give a damn about politics." Soriano asked him if his more recent works were therefore essentially political. He replied that he was unsure if they were political, because he considered them ineffectual, at least on their own. "What I do doesn't change anything," he said. "But my drawings, together with plays, movies, songs, books, they all form a body of work that may help bring about change. I have my doubts, though. My drawings are political, but with respect to human situations, not so much to political situations per se." Soriano then asked him if he was a humanist and if being a humanist was a political stance. Quino replied, "It's rather a political view of the human condition, not of certain regimes." And drawing on ideas expressed by his fellow humorist Landrú, he returned to the metaphor of the relief valve, whereby laughter eliminated the irritation that triggered it and thus had a pacifying effect. He illustrated his point with what was happening in Spain, where a few months earlier he had witnessed how people "laugh with the aggressiveness of humor and that helps them put up with everything that's going on." Soriano insisted that Quino's humor had a "tremendous fury against certain forms of politics, against a system of life." But the illustrator confessed that the fury was "directed against the human condition. The exploitation of man by man is inherent to human nature and has developed over the course of five thousand years. I don't see how that can change. That is why I believe that humor is no good; but it's all I've got. At least I enjoy drawing; I don't enjoy thinking. . . . My problem is that I have no political ideas. I would be happy if I could believe in something. Some people say I'm a Marxist, but I have never read Marx. I'm ashamed to admit it, but it's the truth. I don't believe in anything . . . human beings are the only creatures that harm themselves."[122]

Despite these claims, the character of Libertad expressed increasingly radicalized views. In 1972, in a strip where the kids were shown playing "cowboys and Indians" (clearly influenced by US television shows and comic strips), Libertad tells Felipe, "Since we're already armed, why don't we drop all this nonsense and play social revolution instead?" Her suggestion mirrored the path taken by many young people who were becoming socially and politically active. But it also represented a call to stop living in a world of fantasy and start addressing national problems. It is Libertad's only allusion to armed struggle, but it is significant. It was the most burning issue in the ideological debates that had challenged Quino directly. In contrast, the previous panel had shown Susanita asking herself, "Once guerrilla warfare is over, will we have guerrilla *peacefare*?" Susanita thus spoke for certain segments of the middle class who viewed the rise of the armed left with fear.[123]

Shortly after, the ideological clash between Libertad and Susanita was made explicit in a strip in which Libertad asks Susanita if she is for or against private property, to which Susanita answers, "It depends . . . Whose private property are we talking about?" as she holds on tightly to the building blocks she is playing with.[124] In one of the very last strips before the characters bid farewell to the readers, Libertad argues with Mafalda over the value of money. She first accuses Manolito of caring only about money, telling him, "The world is in the state it's in thanks to you and capitalists like you!" Mafalda steps in to back her up, explaining to Manolito that there are more important things in life than money. But Libertad calls her a "reactionary" because her point of view implies that since money cannot buy happiness it does not matter that poor people have no money.[125] In this way, the strip reflected the differences between the progressive segments of the middle class, with Mafalda representing the liberal middle class with its critical but pacifist and democratic stance, and Libertad echoing the anticapitalist and revolutionary positions held by more radical sectors. The comic strip thus portrayed the ideological differences that marked a middle class committed to social change. However, the radicalized left was increasingly unable to distinguish those differences and it brought back the univocal views of the middle class that saw it only as vacillating, moralist, and snobbish. These views ran counter to *Mafalda's* portrayal of a heterogeneous middle class, characterized by ideological and cultural differences that could coexist within the same identity.

For many in 1973, Peronism seemed to offer the only way out of the country's political and social crisis. In his speeches, Perón promised to bring together different social sectors—including the middle class—and called on them to unite as Argentines, rising above what separated them. This tempered the reproaches against the middle class. In that context and as a result of the strip's established popularity at home and the success it was having abroad, Mafalda was again seen as a "defiant" little girl who expressed the rebelliousness of the new generations. Or, as *Le Monde* put it, a "subversive little girl who might become dangerous if she is allowed to speak too much," a description reproduced by the local press. In Argentina, the strip's insubordinate tone nonetheless contrasted with the more savage style of a new brand of humor that was experiencing a boom, as evidenced by the type and number of magazines sold (three million in 1971 and three times that many in 1974, according to Mara Burkart) and *Clarín's* "nationalization" of the funnies, as Florencia Levín called the newspaper's 1973 decision to devote a whole page exclusively to comic strips by Argentine cartoonists.[126]

This more ferocious style of humor was in tune with the growing violence that characterized the country's political life. The prospect of elections did nothing to halt the confrontation between those who believed they were on the brink of revolution and those who resorted to death squads to prevent it. *Mafalda* did not fit into that picture.[127] The country—and not just its middle class—was facing a rift that countered the comic strip's portrayal of society. *Mafalda's* caustic depiction of humanity, Argentine society, and the middle class did not mean that differences could not be overcome and that reconciliation was not possible. In the summer of 1973, for example, the characters viewed their country's future with great skepticism. A vignette echoed the German poet and philosopher Friedrich Schiller with the reflection "Freedom exists only in the land of dreams." Another vignette played with several election-related words, gradually distorting them.[128] At the same time, there was a shift in the long-standing opposition between Mafalda and Susanita. They squabbled, they invaded each other's space, but even in their quarrels they emerged from their differences united.

This capacity for reconciling opposite views clashed, however, with the violent turn in Argentine society. The empathetic view of a middle class united despite its differences had come to an end. Heterogeneity had given way to insurmountable barriers. Quino had long become weary with a creation he felt trapped in. But underneath that tedium was the realization that the kind of world in which Susanita and Mafalda could be friends and see each other as inhabiting the same universe no longer existed. Shortly before bidding readers goodbye, the two appeared with their backs turned, as in the first reflection on the middle class (figure 2.19). In this strip, Mafalda and Susanita now wondered how they could be friends when they were so different, sometimes not being able to stand each other. The strip ended with the two hugging and concluding that it was better to put up with someone you knew than to tolerate a stranger.[129] This prompted the question of what it took to forge a *we* rooted in different worldviews at a time of mounting political strife. The space of conflict was invaded by tenderness.

FIGURE 2.19 Quino, "Mafalda," *Siete Días*, no. 301 (February 19, 1973). © Joaquín Salvador Lavado (Quino).

Quino used that same duality in another of *Mafalda*'s last panels. Following the electoral victory of the Peronist party on March 11, 1973, a strip showed a smiling Mafalda dreaming of a world flooded with demonstrators, and Susanita irrupting in the dream, visibly upset by her friend's attitude. This dream represented the utopia of a nonconformist personality that had by then become anachronistic. The storyline and characters created in the early sixties—their features now canonized—could no longer keep up with the times.

On June 25, 1973, Mafalda said her last goodbye. In that same edition, *Siete Días* published photographs of the Ezeiza massacre, which had occurred five days earlier when a mass demonstration organized to welcome Perón on his return from exile ended in a bloodbath, announcing the fate that would soon tragically befall Argentina.[130]

MAFALDA AMID POLARIZATION AND POLITICAL VIOLENCE

In 1973, Quino stopped producing new strips, but *Mafalda* remained relevant. The animated cartoon produced by Daniel Mallo (which had premiered in

1973) was televised and the strips were still featured in newspapers across the country.[131] New editions of the books continued to be published, and the panel with the policeman and the "ideology-denting stick" had been turned into a poster that was sold in newsstands (figure 2.20). With this poster, Mafalda's denunciation was no longer veiled, as in the past. The little girl now unabashedly assumed a moralizing role. The poster became immensely popular. It graced the walls—in both homes and workplaces—of Argentines who opposed repression, many of whom had experienced firsthand the force of those truncheons.

FIGURE 2.20 Quino, "El palito de abollar ideologías" poster. The imprint reads: "Copyright 1973 by Quino—Manolo's Inc. Producciones®." © Joaquín Salvador Lavado (Quino).

Mafalda was still a household name, and the comic strip continued to spark debates. In late 1973, Pablo Hernández, a twenty-three-year-old sociology student from a Peronist family, called Mafalda a petit bourgeois with a reactionary ideology.[132] His provocative remark—intended to rile fellow students—took to extremes a critical view of the strip that had been expressed in the past but, according to Hernández when he voiced it, rejected by everyone. He, however, was thoroughly convinced of his analysis of the character and set out to expose the ideological content of the strip. In 1975, he published *Para leer a Mafalda* (How to Read Mafalda). Elaborating on previous interpretations, Hernández argued that, under the guise of progressivism, Quino's creation conveyed a way of thinking typical of a "liberal middle class" that flirted with the left but ignored Peronism and the working class and was part of the distortion strategy of the ruling classes and imperialism.[133] He directly assimilated the opinions voiced by the characters and the comic strip's storyline to Quino's ideology and the views of the middle class. He combined furious recriminations against the characters (which were actually meant for the middle class) with scholarly arguments (including references to Dorfman and Mattelart, Arturo Jauretche, Juan José Hernández Arregui, and C. Wright Mills) to show that Mafalda and her friends embodied the "deviationism" and "individualism" of the middle class and its tendency to "overestimate free will" and seek change only to the extent that the general state of affairs remains the same. The middle class played into the "liberal hoax," in line with its lack of "national conscience," "solidarity," and "popular sentiment," expressed most significantly in its disregard for Peronism. This interpretation rested on a series of "unmaskings." Mafalda's father, for example, was criticized because "his ideology and that of his coworkers prevents them from joining together to try to improve the current state of things through the only means possible: the strength of a collective movement." Hernández viewed the strip in which the main character turned the globe on its head so that the South was on top as "subliminally reactionary" because its critique was limited to expressing views without questioning power (and it was the countries of the North that had the power to trace maps). He further argued that the idea contained a "fallacy": "Turning the map upside down does not solve anything"; the solution will come when "imperialism relinquishes its power and transfers it to the oppressed." Moreover, "the individual will of a single person can bring no situation to an end. That can only be achieved with the awakening of the conscience of the people."[134]

Upon the publisher's suggestion, the prologue was written by Rubén Bortnik, a revisionist associated with the left, and the result was somewhat critical of Hernández's interpretation. First, Bortnik noted that the middle class comprised various strata and that such heterogeneity was expressed ideologically, because the lower-income strata could, in certain circumstances, be assimilated into the working class. But he did not deny the individualism of "those in the middle" nor their fluctuating sympathies, as the middle class was conservative when there was stability and during a crisis "fancies itself revolutionary." Second, Bortnik pointed out the multiclass nature of Peronism, which explained its own contradictions.

Hernández himself tempered his criticism of the middle class and presented it as a way of contributing to identify its limitations and show the need for unity among all sectors fighting US imperialism. Mafalda, however, had "the ideology that our US masters want her to have," and so she must be judged. But he was hopeful that the middle class would eventually join the struggle for national and social liberation. Once the Argentine people triumphed in that struggle, Mafalda would "only be a bad memory," but in the meantime she had to be exposed as "another example of pedagogical colonization."[135] This conclusion drew on and expanded the strong criticisms of *Mafalda* that had peaked in 1972. Hernández's analysis was more pronounced to the extent that it failed to see that fiction was not a mirror image of reality and ignored the difference between humor and ideology.

The book sold out in only four months, amid much controversy. In January 1976, Jorge H. Giertz wrote in the magazine *Cuestionario* that Hernández had read *Mafalda* "much too seriously, or, perhaps, he was misled." The author forgot that "Quino is not Frantz Fanon; if he were, he would have written a study on colonialism instead of a comic strip." And he added that it would be "absurd" to have "Mafalda thinking like Rosa Luxemburg." Giertz concluded that the scenario on which Hernández based his criticism had become anachronistic, as Argentina was "now at risk of turning into a country of 'night visitors,'" in allusion to the death squads that operated in the shadows.[136] In contrast, on a program broadcast by the National Library around this time, a radio commentator praised the analysis but from a different ideological stance. According to this commentator, Hernández's book revealed a scenario dominated by studies conducted "under subversive methods and principles by overwhelmed and denatured" sociologists who championed certain foreign doctrines that had spread in recent times, "fueled by the indiscipline, confusion, and need for change that affects the masses." From that approach, he congratulated Hernández on having discovered that behind an "innocent product for mass entertainment there were elements working to destroy the true essence of the people." He concluded by giving Quino the right to reply and recalling the words of Martín Fierro, the eponymous hero of Argentina's classic epic poem depicting gaucho life, when he cautioned Argentines not to fight among themselves, because if they did they would be destroyed by outsiders.[137]

This commentator's analysis reflects an ideological position that combined a prevailing nationalism with the war against subversion that had been declared by the government. In July 1974, Perón died and was succeeded by his widow, María Estela Martínez de Perón, who in October 1975 gave the armed forces authorization to "wipe out" subversion in the country. The repressive measures implemented by the armed forces to carry out her orders were supplemented by the actions of the infamous paramilitary organization known as the Triple A (Argentine Anticommunist Alliance), which had begun operating before Perón's death, murdering hundreds of political activists. The bullet-riddled bodies that were dumped in the streets by the hundreds were a testament to the impunity with which the death squads operated, and the practice of disappearing militants and political opponents soon became commonplace. In February 1976, *Crisis*, a magazine directed by the Uruguayan writer Eduardo Galeano, reported the disappearance of one of its contributors, Luis Sabini Fernández. In the same issue, it published the first part of a celebrated essay on the history of printed humor, written by Jorge B. Rivera, who saw in Quino the progressive ideology of a sector of the middle class and in *Mafalda* his most popular creation.[138] As the armed forces became more and more powerful, the rhetoric of the "war against subversion" became louder and louder, and it was directed at the middle class in an effort to secure its support for repressive government action.

The far right's ideological offensive was not new, as it had been developing for a long time. In previous years it had taken on a unique tone with publications such as *El Caudillo*, a magazine that had organized courses, honed a class-based discourse, and even attempted to co-opt humor.[139] The last page of the magazine generally featured a running caricature spoofing Peronism. On March 1, 1973, the caricature was replaced by "The Joke of the Week," with a drawing by Quino (previously featured in *Panorama*) of two cavemen facing each other ready to fight, thus suggesting a reflection on the conflict that divided Argentine society, a reflection that was completely out of tune with the furious invectives hurled by the magazine at the opponents it demonized as "infiltrated" enemies.[140]

This was not the only time the right tried to appropriate Quino's work for its own purposes. In April 1975, an unauthorized variation of the ideology-denting stick appeared on posters pasted around the city of Buenos Aires (figure 2.21). In this version, it was Manolito who pointed at the stick and said, "See, Mafalda?! Thanks to this stick you can go to school today." The poster, which inverted the original meaning of the famous panel, was the brainchild of the government's intelligence services. According to Quino, it revealed an attempt to alter and co-opt a symbol of the antiauthoritarian spirit and of the resistance against political repression. It was also intended to further the efforts of the far right and the armed forces to gain social support and to legitimize the coup in the eyes of the population.[141]

The *Buenos Aires Herald* reported on this use of the poster, featuring both versions side by side and explaining that Quino—a "true humanist liberal"— had been used by both extremes of the political spectrum, in reference to both the altered panel and the chess caricature used in the 1970 action by the FAR. A month later, as Argentina's independence day approached, the poster covered

FIGURE 2.21 Bootleg version of the poster "El palito de abollar ideologías," reproduced in "Quino," *Buenos Aires Herald*, April 5, 1975, 6. The newspaper also included the original poster next to this version. Copy courtesy of Andrew Graham-Yooll.

the faces of several schools in Buenos Aires. According to the anarchist magazine *Educación Popular*, it was a tabloid-sized poster in color. The reporter observed that in the 1960s *Mafalda* had highlighted problems and contradictions that affected Argentine society and "our middle classes." With the ideology-denting stick poster, the comic strip "makes us feel and reflect on the need to defend democratic freedoms." By substituting Manolito for Mafalda, he said, the altered version brought into play "those sectors of the commercial petite bourgeoisie whose members, driven by [the immigrant's] dream of 'making their fortune in America,' can only respond individually when they feel threatened by the ruling classes, at the expense of their peers, and always with the hope of 'moving up in the world.'"[142] In August, this article was reproduced in a small town in the province of Buenos Aires by the newspaper *Alberdi*, which was known for its critical thinking and literary content. Its director, Joaquín Álvarez, was arrested shortly after by the armed forces.[143]

With this poster, the intelligence services sought to spur the public into demanding order and security, and it focused in particular on a segment of the middle class that was the political and ideological opposite of Mafalda and Libertad. But there was also a threatening undertone, as the poster was signed by a fake organization ("Agrupación Cerezas al marasQUINO," or MarrasQUINO Cherries Organization) that mimicked the products sold by the fictional grocery store and incorporated the illustrator's name, thus making an attempt at humor (through a play on words) as a means of intimidation.

There were also more direct threats. Quino recalls that the minister of social development at the time, José López Rega, approached him to ask for his authorization to use *Mafalda* in a press campaign. Quino said no and some days later a group of armed men tried to enter his house by force, breaking down the door. Nobody was home, but it served as a warning. Quino knew he was in danger and decided to leave the country.[144]

In Argentina there was no longer room for a *we* founded on caustic ironies offset by tenderness. Neither was there room for antiestablishment kids or youth who stretched to the limit the tension between harsh reality and ideal principles. For them, there was no longer any room for laughter.

CHAPTER 3

Global *Mafalda*
Circulation, Appropriations, and Resignifications

Mafalda is Latin America's best-selling and most internationally celebrated comic strip. It has been translated into more than twenty languages, including Danish, Japanese, Korean, and Chinese. Its characters are easily recognizable in many countries and they are regularly featured on everything from T-shirts and mugs to magazines and posters. It even has millions of followers on Facebook.

When Mafalda turned fifty, in 2014, both the cartoon and Quino were honored with numerous prizes and tributes. The cartoonist received the medal of the Legion of Honor in France and the Prince of Asturias Award from Spain, and both countries put up a replica of the Mafalda statue that stands in a Buenos Aires plaza. Special Mafalda exhibits were held in several countries around the world, including France, Italy, Costa Rica, Brazil, and Chile. The character's fiftieth anniversary was covered by leading media outlets, not only in Latin American and Europe but also in places as distant from its origins as China. The "birthday" was celebrated in countless blogs penned by anonymous admirers from all over the globe.

How was such a geographical expansion possible? And what meanings did the comic strip acquire for each newly conquered audience? This chapter will try to answer those questions with the aim of addressing two issues that go beyond the comic strip itself. The first issue has to do with understanding Latin America's place in the ideological and cultural climate of the 1960s and 1970s. This entails taking into account the asymmetrical and hierarchical nature of global relations and the leading role played by the continent—an active and even groundbreaking role that contrasts with the one-directional views that have traditionally seen the region as lagging behind or as a passive recipient of modernizing and countercultural trends originating in Europe or the United States. The second issue has to do with the approach chosen to examine a phenomenon as changing and elusive as the circulation and social uses of a comic strip. In this sense, I propose bypassing taxonomical discussions over the concepts of transnational history, global history, or connected history—which reflect an embryonic stage of the research on the issue—to delve directly into the interaction among the various actors, processes, and scales involved in this phenomenon and how they influenced each other.[1]

When Quino created *Mafalda* he never imagined that such a typical exponent of the culture and people of Buenos Aires would be of interest anywhere outside Argentina, with the exception perhaps of Uruguay. The comic strip did, in fact, cross the border into that neighboring country almost immediately, and before long it was being featured in *Época,* a newspaper of the capital, Montevideo, edited by the writer Eduardo Galeano. The books were sold and advertised by distributors in Uruguay shortly after they were published in Argentina, and in 1967 the comic strip was picked up by another Montevideo newspaper, *BP Color*.[2] Given the shared history and close relationship between the two countries, however, the comic strip's presence in Uruguay, while important in terms of sales, was not exactly indicative of foreign interest. But *Mafalda*'s appeal to international readers was undeniable once it crossed the Atlantic and disembarked in Italy. Its inclusion in a compilation in 1968 and the release a year later of a book devoted entirely to the comic strip opened the doors to the European market and launched its global success. By 1970 it was being featured daily in the Roman newspaper *Paese Sera*, and that same year a *Mafalda* book was published in Spain. In 1971, it appeared in the popular French daily *France-Soir* and in the German magazine *Pardon*. These were followed by newspapers in Australia, Denmark, Norway, and Sweden. At the same time, the publishing house Ediciones de la Flor—which in 1970 took over the series of *Mafalda* strip compilations that were published as booklets—had syndicated it to printed media throughout Latin America, so that by 1972 it was featured in sixty magazines and newspapers across the continent.[3] By then, the comic strip had also been published in book format in Portugal (1970), Germany and Finland (1971), and France (1973).

I argue that this international success can be explained by the context in which it occurred, which was characterized by two processes. The first process involves the growth of global exchange, which can be traced back to the expansion of European imperialism but whose scale increased significantly after World War II. These exchanges became particularly intense in the 1960s as more ideas, fashions, and products circulated through new forms of transnational contacts, furthered by technological developments in communications and cultural industries.[4] The second process has to do with the utopian imagination of the 1960s and 1970s and the hopes that were pinned on the poor regions of the world. In the 1960s, in particular, the course of history appeared to hinge on the fate of liberation movements in the so-called Third World that seemed capable of bringing down the old world order and building a more just and equal society. In that context, Latin America was especially appealing. This new interest in the region is illustrated by such trends as the Latin American literary boom, the many artists and intellectuals from central countries who visited the continent, and the May 1968 protesters who, in places like Paris, donned Che Guevara's signature beret.[5]

These historical processes were conditions of possibility for the global success of *Mafalda*. However, they do not in themselves explain why, among the countless cultural productions that originated in Latin American countries, certain products spread beyond the region. Understanding this phenomenon thus requires determining exactly how these circulations occurred and what their effects were. In that sense, I posit that the dissemination of *Mafalda* was enabled by a confluence of actors and interests in favorable contexts and through contingent connections and unique appropriations in each social space and historical moment. To illustrate this, in the following pages I distinguish and reconstruct three different—but equally important—scenarios, according to the dissemination and popularity achieved by the comic strip in each context: Italy, Spain, and Mexico.

ITALY: A *BAMBINA CONTESTATARIA* MAKING HER WAY IN THE WORLD

In 1968, *Il libro dei bambini terribili per adulti masochisti* (*The Book of Enfants Terribles for Masochistic Adults*) featured the first *Mafalda* strips to come out in book format outside Argentina. It was published by Feltrinelli, a Milan-based publishing house whose owner, Giangiacomo Feltrinelli, was a wealthy heir who dressed in hippie shirts and believed that the New Left in Italy should look to Cuba and Latin America for inspiration. With his publishing business, Feltrinelli hoped to bring together readers of the traditional left (intellectuals and workers) with those who were embracing the new styles of the youth movement.[6] With a nod to readers, the compilation was aimed at the "masochistic" parents of the title, mothers and fathers baffled by their own children—their enfants terribles—who dominated them. Born during the baby boom of postwar Europe, these young couples had grown up in unprecedented economic prosperity, and by the late 1960s they were raising their own children. The Italian "miracle"—the country's accelerated, unequal, and unregulated industrial development—had caused profound alterations in family relations and life-styles. The young people who came of age in that prosperity experienced a child-hood like that of no other generation before them, and as parents they were open to the psychological productions of the time and new forms of child-rearing.[7]

The book featured classic literary texts, pedagogical and sociological es-says, and humorous pieces, which were meant to appeal to these mothers and fathers. In the introduction it was taken for granted that their "thumb-sucking" and "bed-wetting" charges would take these parents by storm, thus posing the novel challenge of understanding these "rebellious," "iconoclastic," "sensual," and "cynical" children. In the book's final pages, in a text that spoofed the psy-chological tests and surveys typical of the 1960s, readers were asked to share their children's "first guerrilla action." In doing so it linked family to politics, and by using the politicized language of the 1960s it succeeded in resonating with its intended audience.[8] The joke was meant as a playful allusion to the prevailing climate. When the book came off the presses in 1968, Italy was being shaken to its foundations by a wave of demonstrations staged by students who were calling for a complete transformation of university structures, demanding a new role for themselves in society, and standing up against repression.[9] Their defiance targeted all forms of authority, including the family. These antiestab-lishment youth, influenced by hippie and countercultural trends, eschewed the modernizing promises of the older generations and defied the values held by their parents. These generational conflicts were at the center of the compila-tion and *Mafalda* occupied a major place in it.[10]

The book was a sensation as soon as it hit bookstores. Mafalda was fea-tured on the cover against a hot pink background, in a choice of colors typical of the pop style of the 1960s (figure 3.1). Inside, a whole section dealt with the comic strip, spanning more than thirty pages under the title "Mafalda, the Antiestablishment Girl." In the strips chosen, the little girl with a young-adult attitude took a firm stand against soup—which symbolized authoritarianism—and in doing so rejected the model her parents conformed to. When her father tried to coax her into eating her soup by telling her it would help her grow *"come la mamma . . . come me . . ."* (like your mom, like me), Mafalda cried out, *"Cosí, oltre la minestra . . . anche questo!"* (So, soup and to top it off . . . *THAT!*). The following strips continued along the same lines, with the intellectualized little girl exasperating her parents and teacher. The scenes depicted showed the adults' bewilderment and stress in dealing with such defiance. The politi-cal strips selected for the book focused on international conflicts seen from a generational perspective. For example, in one of these strips Mafalda tells Felipe that whenever she asked the grown-ups what was happening in Vietnam they replied with some cockamamie story involving a stork. This called to mind the typical explanation given by parents when asked where babies came from and the implication was that adults resorted to fables when faced with uncomfortable questions from their children. This choice of strip highlighted a cause (the opposition to the Vietnam War) embraced by young people around the globe, not just in Italy, which set them against US policies and prompted mass demonstrations. But with the reference to the stork it also connected politics with sexuality, as it alluded indirectly to a political reading of sex associated with counterculture and feminism that challenged existing "taboos." The comic strip was also present in the book's table of contents, as it was illustrated with an image of Mafalda's father looking frazzled. There was no doubt that the publishers had chosen the main character to represent all enfants terribles.

FIGURE 3.1 Cover of Marcelo Ravoni and Valerio Riva, *Il libro dei bambini terribili per adulti masochisti.* Mafalda cartoon © Joaquín Salvador Lavado (Quino).

The compilation also featured an essay by Umberto Eco in which he analyzed the character Franti, the "bad boy" from Edmondo de Amicis's famous novel *Cuore*, a fragment of which was included in the book. Eco argued that Franti evoked François Rabelais's roguish character Panurge, a figure who subverted the status quo from within. In that reading, laughter was an instrument used by those who innovated by questioning. In this essay, which heralded Eco's later work on laughter and the human condition, the philosopher highlighted the subversive power of laughter when it came from a child.[11]

The book was the product of an expanding publishing industry. Marcelo Ravoni—who along with Valerio Riva edited the volume—was an Argentine translator with links to the group that published the communist newspaper *La Hora*. He was also a close friend of the well-known Argentine poet Juan Gelman, and he had settled in Milan with his wife, Coleta, some years earlier.[12] Since moving to Italy, they had been working as readers and translators for the publishers Feltrinelli, Franco María Ricci, and Bompiani, whose efforts were aimed at breathing new life into the business by capturing a culturally progressive and even radicalized public.[13] Ravoni wanted to break out on his own and looked for comparative advantages he could use in such a competitive market, and, in particular, Argentine authors who could be of interest to European readers. As a fan of comics himself, he tried to contact Quino, but it was Alicia Colombo—Quino's wife and agent—who eventually replied. That was the beginning of a working relationship that lasted four decades. In 1970, Ravoni founded an agency called Quipos—an allusion to the Incaic *quipu* notation system but also to Quino's name—that published more than fifty books in addition to producing magazines, albums, and television programs.[14] His publishing savvy, expansive personality, and hard-working nature quickly turned him into a key actor in the efforts to further the flow of cultural exchange between Latin America and Europe.[15]

The connection between *Mafalda* (for which Ravoni had just secured the publishing rights) and Umberto Eco (whom the Argentine publisher knew from his work in the business) was also decisive. In 1965, having joined the avant-garde literary movement Gruppo '63 and in the framework of the discussion about the old canon of left-wing culture, Eco had published *Apocalittici e integrati*, a collection of essays in which he confronted that canon from two angles. He criticized the cultural policies of the Italian communist tradition, which prioritized realist aesthetics and favored the circulation of cultural productions mediated by political organizations (cultural centers, book clubs, partisan media) over individual consumption mediated by cultural industries.[16] But he also disagreed with Marxist intellectuals who saw cultural industries as merely a cog in the machinery of the ruling classes, in line with the powerful analysis introduced by Max Horkheimer and Theodor Adorno. Eco recognized that the masses had become a part of social life. He argued that they consumed "bourgeois cultural models believing them to be the independent expression of their own class," while bourgeois culture looked down on that industrial production. He used the comic strip genre to illustrate his argument. He maintained that the "persuasive effectiveness" of comics—with millions of copies sold annually worldwide—lay in the production of a mythological repertoire that had the "co-participation of the people" but was established from above. However, he acknowledged that the "system of production" of the cultural industry allowed for the emergence of artists who could transform consumers in a critical and liberating way. This was the case with *Peanuts*, in which he identified a "critical and social vein."[17]

The heated debates triggered by Eco's book were still resonating in 1968. His critics had reproached him for his scarce attention to the media's economic dimension, his interest in analyzing the culture industry, and his positive assessment of some of its products. From that angle, *Mafalda* represented a valuable addition to the discussion. It showed the critical potential of a comic strip that embodied the generational conflicts affecting the world. Eco quickly realized this. In 1969, he was instrumental in the publication of the first European book devoted exclusively to *Mafalda*, as he secured a favorable contract for the author through his conversations with Valentino Bompiani, for whose publishing house Eco directed a small collection.[18] The book came out that same year with a prologue—written by Eco but initially unsigned—that was decisive in establishing the success of the comic strip (see figure 3.2).

The title of the book, *Mafalda, la contestataria*, with its qualifier *contestataria* (antiestablishment), connected the comic strip directly with Italy's political and social climate. It was released in the winter of 1969, when labor struggles rekindled the atmosphere of protest in the country. In his prologue, Eco deftly placed the strip in that context. He explained that Mafalda was not just "a new cartoon character: she is perhaps the character of the 1970s. If we have described her as antiestablishment, it was not with the aim of jumping on the nonconformist bandwagon. Mafalda is truly a 'fierce' heroine who rejects the present state of the world." More so than *Peanuts*, the strip proved Eco's view on comics, and even on the role of humor, with respect to the social order. By comparing the two, Eco was able to highlight their different origins and the political significance of Mafalda's birthplace. Quino's character had been born in a Latin American country rife with social contrasts, thus making *Mafalda* more relatable than the US cartoon. Charlie Brown was a kid from an afflu-

FIGURE 3.2 Cover of Quino, *Mafalda, la contestataria*. Mafalda cartoon © Joaquín Salvador Lavado (Quino).

ent society desperately trying to fit in and be accepted by his peers. Although in *Peanuts* the kids supposedly tried to emulate their elders, adults were completely excluded from their world. In contrast, according to Eco, Mafalda was "in constant dialectical confrontation with the adult world, a world she neither likes nor respects, and which she sees as hostile and puts down and rejects, claiming her right to remain a child who does not want to be held accountable for a universe that has been adulterated by parents."[19]

From this perspective, Eco imagined that *Mafalda* had read Che Guevara, although he acknowledged that her political views were somewhat "muddled" because she did not understand what was happening in Vietnam and was baffled by poverty. "She only knows one thing for certain: she is not satisfied" with the state of the world. In his closing reflection, Eco returned to the controversy that his earlier book had sparked. Calling Quino's character the "heroine of our times" was no exaggeration. He argued that nobody could deny the social relevance of comics as a testimony of the times. In Mafalda's case, she "reflects the tendencies of a restless youth, which paradoxically take the form of child dissent, of a psychological eczema in reaction to mass media, of moral hives brought on by the logic of a divided country, of an intellectual asthma caused by the nuclear mushroom cloud. As our children prepare to become—by our own choice—a legion of Mafaldas, it would be wise to treat Mafalda with the respect a real person deserves."[20]

Reading *Mafalda*, one could agree with Eco's interpretation. Adding new strips to those published in *Il libro dei bambini*, this compilation focused on the generational clash. The book began with a series of strips that featured Mafalda and friends in school. These were followed by scenes in which the characters engaged in water fights, in a series of absurd comedy. As noted in previous chapters, the everyday world of both children and family was linked to social and political problems, further blurring the typically bourgeois separation between public and private life. With long series of strips on bureaucracy, nuclear weapons, the Vietnam War, and the space race, it was certainly easier for the comic to speak to European readers and involve them in the production of meaning. To achieve that effect, the Italian edition also logically excluded strips that touched on more specifically Argentine issues, with local nods that would be lost on a foreign readership. For example, it included a series in which Mafalda and friends started school but left out a strip in that series that had them playing children's games, with Manolito shouting "Revolution!" and calling everyone to jump in the tanks—an allusion to Argentina's frequent coup attempts.[21]

Regardless of the strips selected, the Italian edition had to be translated. Translation is always a complex operation, but more so with humor, due to the genre's constant use of often untranslatable puns and wordplay and the implicit cultural assumptions shared by readers. Translating humor thus involves a transculturation effected on the text rather than on the image or the size or arrangement of the speech balloons. Marcelo Ravoni adapted linguistic and iconographic aspects, taking into account the target colloquialisms, cultural frameworks, and contexts he imagined for Italy.[22] These interventions at times involved ideological aspects. In such cases, two operations can be distinguished. First, Ravoni used formulas that nationalized the issues reflected in the strip. A clear example is the issue of national identity, which a strip included in the book touched on. National unification was fairly recent in Italy and in the 1960s patriotic discourse was still associated with fascism, so Ravoni translated Mafalda's "Viva la patria" as "Viva la Repubblica," substituting the republic for the fatherland. Similarly, he translated the threatening text "Ahorcaremos a los vendepatrias" (Hang the traitors), written on a wall in one of the strips, which reflected Argentina's ideological debates, as "Giustizi per i lavoratori" (Justice for workers). Second, Ravoni's modifications updated the ideological references to make them more comprehensible or appropriate to the radicalized post-1968 context. For example, in the Spanish version of the above strip there was also a threatening graffiti that read "Fidel al paredón" (Execute Fidel), which was replaced with "Boia chi molla" (He who abandons the struggle is an executioner), a motto used by Mussolini for traitors and taken up again by the Italian far right in the 1960s.[23] Ravoni also made small changes intended to make the text more familiar to European readers. In this way, José de San Martín was replaced with Simón Bolívar, in the understanding that he was more widely known in Europe than Argentina's national hero.[24]

Over the following decades, this analysis by Umberto Eco—who would only be revealed as the author of the prologue sometime later—was taken up in news articles, essays, and interpretation in different places around the world. For example, in a piece featured in the newspaper *La Stampa* right after the book came out, the reviewer welcomed the new cartoon about a gang of "inconvenient" kids, and to illustrate his point he reproduced the strip with the stork and the Vietnam War that linked sexuality and politics, and he discussed how the concept of femininity was challenged by the contrast between Mafalda and Susanita. He placed the strip within the space of both comics and ideology when he described Mafalda as "not neurotic like Charlie Brown nor passionate à la Cohn-Bendit." This characterization was intended for the progressive middle class that could share such antiestablishment views but rejected the virulence of the clashes breaking out across Italy and other European countries. This position took on special meaning for the "classic" left, whose leadership was being challenged by the style of the new protests.[25] In this sense, Darío Natoli, writing in the communist newspaper *L'Unità*, praised the comic strip but avoided associating it with protesting youth, while at the same time stressing that as a Latin American, Mafalda confronted those in power and expressed a desire for change.[26]

The book was released when protests were peaking and part of the Italian left was advocating methods of struggle used by liberation movements in Latin America and Asia.[27] Political unrest fueled the cultural changes already under way, with debates on issues such as the family and sexual morality emerging along with new feminist organizations.[28] This intense activity called for an aggiornamento in the cultural strategy of the traditional left. In 1967, the communist daily *Paese Sera* set out to do just that. Founded in 1948, it featured such intellectuals as Norberto Bobbio, Umberto Eco, and Arturo Gismondi among its staff. Humor was already part of its editorial style, but with the paper's efforts to update its content and approach it became more prominent. It promoted an Italian comic strip (Bonvi's popular *Sturmtruppen*) and later incorporated others which were for the most part distributed through US syndication. Some, like *Blondie* or *Gli Antenati* (*The Flintstones*), naturalized the values of capitalist society, but others, like *Peanuts* and Johnny Hart's *B.C.*, were considered alternative.[29]

In 1970, *Paese Sera* added *Mafalda* to the mix. Among the features it highlighted in its presentation of the Argentine comic, the paper noted that in the strips political dissent was linked to the daily rebellions sparked by gender and generational redefinitions. It promised an antiauthoritarian cartoon, where soup represented dictatorial oppression and there were repeated references to injustices in the global status quo and the need for a new world order, symbolized by a map of the world drawn upside down. It also pointed out the comic's cynical depiction of religion, as in a strip where Mafalda complained she was "getting a busy signal from God" when she called to ask him to right the wrongs of the world. Quino was introduced as an Argentine but above all as "a citizen of the wider world of protest against injustice, stupidity, abuse, and tedium." Building on Eco's analysis, the introductory article also explained that Mafalda was no Dennis the Menace or Charlie Brown, as the former was apolitical and the latter longed to be accepted by society. It also acknowledged the comic strip's limitations, noting the main character's bewilderment at the existence of poverty. Mafalda's failure to understand the cause of poverty was not a minor detail that could go unnoticed by the paper's communist readers, as evidenced by the editors' need to address them directly on the subject: "You, readers, will surely know why poverty exists. But we mustn't forget that Mafalda's parents live among Argentine colonels." This somewhat forced explanation (which blamed ignorance on censorship) should not obscure the fact that the comparison with the US comics featured on the same page was meant to minimize those alleged ideological limitations. In fact, the very first *Mafalda* strip published by the daily showed the various ways in which the comic touched on everyday aspects of bourgeois life, when Mafalda, with her naive but biting wit, asked her mom, "Do we lead a decent life?," and when her mother answered that "of course" they did, she came back with a new question: "But exactly where is it we're leading it to?"[30]

Mafalda was introduced to the Italian public when comics were experiencing a boom in that country. Eco's *Apocalittici e integrati* had elevated the genre by highlighting both its sociological and its aesthetic value. That book triggered discussions that made the genre attractive to cultured readers. For example, the magazine *linus*—whose name paid tribute to *Peanuts*—had been a source of intellectual debates and high-quality cartoons since 1965. Encouraged by the publishing house Rizzoli, its pages featured the leading foreign comic strips (*Peanuts, Krazy Kat, The Wizard of Id*) alongside local cartoonists who were modernizing the genre in Italy, including Guido Crepax and his famous *Valentina*, Enzo Lunari, and Francesco Tullio Altan. Comics were thus linked to social criticism and youth rebelliousness, and, according to Daniele Barbieri, this created a comics-based consciousness.[31] To compete with *linus*, in 1972 the publishing house Mondadori launched *Il Mago*. Its editors in chief—first Mario Spagnol and later Carlo Fruttero and Franco Lucentini—aimed for something different from their established competitor. They wanted something bigger and brighter and chose not to feature any political articles or pieces on current events, producing instead a magazine focused exclusively on comics.

Mafalda occupied a central place in *Il Mago*'s offering, and the cartoon was selected for the cover of the magazine's inaugural issue. As can be seen on the cover (figure 3.3), the Argentine comic strip allowed the magazine to incorporate political and cultural dissent while linking other products of the genre from various origins, times, and styles. In the following numbers, the magazine featured classic strips (*Dick Tracy*, *Felix the Cat*) and US comics that were revolutionizing the genre (*B.C.*, *The Wizard of Id*) with Italian products (*Il Mago* by Beppy Zancan, *Anita* by Guido Crepax, *Ivan Timbrovic* by Massimo Cavezzali), comics from other European countries (such as *Asterix* by René Goscinny and Albert Uderzo), and works by Latin American cartoon writers and artists (Quino, Guillermo Mordillo, Héctor G. Oesterheld, and Alberto Breccia).[32] With this lineup and at an affordable price (half the cost of a regular comic book), the magazine could satisfy the expectations of readers who were discovering the genre, as well as those who were interested in cult comic strips. A young-adult and adolescent readership was drawn to its pages, where *Mafalda* forged a new generational connection.

Quino's creation had earned a place in Italian culture. The intelligentsia could express its anti-US sentiment by contrasting it to *Peanuts*, while at the same time celebrating a character like Mafalda who had been born to protest in a Third World country. In 1973, Il Salone Internazionale dei Comics, held in Lucca, gave *Mafalda* a place of honor alongside *Pinocchio*.[33] The toy industry had begun producing dolls of Mafalda and her friends. This was initially done without permission, but Quino's authorization was later obtained. *Mafalda* had become so popular that, according to a journalist's account at the time in the Argentine newspaper *La Opinión*, many Argentines visiting Rome "have been surprised by Italian children coming up to them with a Mafalda doll, wanting to know if people have heard of Mafalda in Argentina. Some of these *bambini* don't believe [these visitors] when they say Mafalda is also Argentine like them. For thousands of fans, Mafalda has a French air about her." This mistaken notion, the journalist explained, was due to the fact that many

FIGURE 3.3 Cover of *Il Mago*, no. 1, Mondadori, 1972. Mafalda cartoon © Joaquín Salvador Lavado (Quino).

Italians associated Latin America with "huts," "physical squalor," and "archaic" imagery, but it also had to do with the issues addressed in the comic strip, the same issues that concerned the European urban middle class (political conflicts, inflation, the media, cultural changes, tensions between parents and children).[34] The account was accurate. *Mafalda*'s success, boosted among intellectuals because of its Latin American origin, had to do with the global nature of the middle-class problems depicted in the strip, which European readers recognized as their own.

In sum, in Italy Quino's comic strip spoke to a diverse audience: concerned parents of enfants terribles, young people willing to fight against the injustices of the world and stand up to their elders, and men and women who identified with the strip's issues because they were middle class. But in order for the comic strip to effectively engage these readers—and many others—an editorial intervention was necessary. This required editors willing to promote it, publishing houses that would agree to publish it, intellectuals who could give it prestige, and journalists interested in reviewing it. These conditions were not found in Italy alone. That country was the launching pad for new markets. Following its debut in Italy, the comic strip was released in book format almost simultaneously in Portugal, Finland, and Germany—where it was also published in the monthly magazine *Pardon*—and featured in newspapers in Australia, Sweden, Denmark, and Norway. In France, Edition Spéciale had begun publishing the comic strip in book format in 1971; *France Soir*, a popular and sensationalist paper with a print run of 1.5 million copies, started carrying it daily; and, shortly after, a boutique in Paris was offering *Mafalda* merchandise.[35] But it was in Spain where *Mafalda* became particularly popular, and the following section reconstructs the comic strip's incursion into that market.

SPAIN, A SYMBOL OF ANTIAUTHORITARIANISM FROM THE SOUTH

In her memoir, the renowned Spanish editor Esther Tusquets admitted candidly that her publishing house, Lumen, got off to a good start because of two strokes of good luck: *Apocalípticos e integrados*, the first Spanish edition of Eco's book, published in 1968, and *Mafalda*, released in 1970. These two works—connected once again—became her first best-sellers, bringing Lumen prestige and sales. The publishing house was part of a surge in cultural activity that in the mid-1960s saw new entrepreneurs reviving a field dominated by the obscurantist atmosphere of Francoist Spain.[36]

The efforts of these entrepreneurs contributed to the reemergence of Spain's publishing industry, which had been hit hard by exile and the Franco regime. This rebirth was fueled by economic growth in Europe, the Spanish government's developmental policies, and an increasing number of readers open to works that opposed the country's Catholic obscurantism. Barcelona was the nerve center of this renaissance, driven by Carlos Barral, Jorge Herralde, and Esther Tusquets herself. This group of publishers, friends since childhood, shifted the industry's focus toward Spanish America's literary production. This was instrumental in the role Spain played in furthering the Latin American boom, as it contributed to the intercontinental visibility, unity, and success of the movement's authors.[37] Esther Tusquets concentrated on creating original collections, such as her unprecedented children's book collection featuring leading authors, and other collections that combined photography with literary texts. As she forged fluid relations with authors and artists, the publishing house's catalog incorporated works by Juan José Cela, Mario Vargas Llosa, Pablo Neruda, and young avant-garde talents such as Pere Gimferrer, Juan Benet, and Oriol Maspons.

Expanding the publishing business in Francoist Spain was not easy. Mass culture permeated everyday life but the censorship and power wielded by the Falange retained its hold on cultural life. The "prior censorship" system was still in place, which meant that publishers had to submit all original works to a government office in Madrid to be approved, cut, or rejected altogether. When publishers succeeded in obtaining approval, they enjoyed the possibility of influencing cultural activities and cultivating a readership of young artists and students who eagerly awaited their production. That readership was expanding along with the improvement of living conditions for important segments of the middle class that were benefiting from the country's economic development.[38] Society as a whole was convulsed by the conflicts of a country that, weighed down by authoritarianism and Catholic moralism, had thrown itself into hedonism and capitalist consumerism—consuming everything from television sets and cars to shows. This in turn fueled demands for political freedoms. By then there was a student movement that could successfully defy the Falange's domination, staging mass protests and clashing fiercely with the government, and a labor movement that challenged the regime's corporatist trade unions.[39]

Mafalda's arrival in 1970 coincided with a boom in political cartoons in Spain. Satire and irony had managed to slip through the cracks of censorship, creating a more relaxed space. Cartoonists such as Josep Escobar—who had been prosecuted for treason—developed a socially conscious satirical style that first took a popular approach to post–Civil War poverty and, later, in the 1960s, lampooned modernization in the *costumbrismo* tradition, with characters like Petra, who stood up against everyday oppression. The famous magazine *La Codorniz*, while not openly opposing Francoism, evidenced the growing popularity of comics with print runs of 250,000 copies, featuring quality works by renowned cartoonists such as Miguel Gila, Forges, Julio Cebrián, Máximo San Juan, and Chumy Chúmez. Many of these also graced the pages of the new magazines that took a courageously critical stance in the 1960s and early 1970s.[40] At the same time, the publication of *Apocalípticos e integrados*, essays by Luis Gasca and Terenci Moix, and the magazine *BANG!* established the status of comic strips as intellectual products.[41]

This context favored the circulation of foreign productions, with Latin American works featuring prominently. In fact, *Mafalda* was first distributed in Spain by Miguel García, whose Visor bookstore in Madrid was a space where intellectuals could find new works from abroad. Jorge Álvarez—*Mafalda*'s Buenos Aires publisher and the first to release it in book format—introduced García to the strip during one of his visits to Madrid. García, in turn, brought it to Esther Tusquets, who was instantly taken. In 1969, at the Frankfurt Book Fair, Marcelo Ravoni offered *Mafalda*'s publishing rights to Carlos Barral, of the Seix Barral publishing house. As Barral was not interested in the genre, his wife suggested that Lumen might want to publish it. Esther Tusquets immediately agreed to purchase the rights, but she did not imagine then that *Mafalda* would turn out to be such a commercial success.[42]

Meanwhile, the government was responding to the political use of humor with an iron fist. In 1966, new regulations had dismantled the system of prior censorship, replacing it with a harsher policy. If a book was confiscated or partially censured after it was in print, publishers could lose everything they had invested.[43] This new policy affected *Mafalda* as well. While the comic strip did not suffer any alterations, censors required that an "Adult Readers Only" warning be included on the cover. However, while it limited its readership to certain age groups, this rating also made it easier to associate the comic strip with cultural products that merited the censors' attention and were therefore more attractive to progressive readers. In any case, according to Miguel García, *Mafalda*'s subtle humor flew under the radar of censorship: "Only we understood it." In a public used to reading between the lines, the comic strip's ironies reaffirmed the *we* in opposition to the dictatorship.[44]

Mafalda was an instant success. Lumen initially printed three or four thousand copies of the first book, according to Tusquets's memoir. She recalls, "To our great surprise sales shot up immediately and they're still going strong . . . millions of copies have been sold in Spain."[45] In 1971, *Mafalda* was among the top books recommended by *La Vanguardia*, a nonpartisan Barcelona newspaper. That same year it was one of the greatest attractions at the Seville Book Fair, and over the following months the comic made the top-ten best-seller lists in both Madrid and Barcelona.[46] It also received good reviews from critics. The magazine *Triunfo*, associated with the resistance to Francoism, welcomed the character's "innocent perceptiveness." It noted that, in contrast to Charlie Brown, Mafalda doubted "everything," an attitude explained by where she came from, as the character lived in "a country whose real problems are framed by the geography of underdevelopment."[47] In 1972, according to the magazine *Cambio 16*, the comic strip was achieving "phenomenon" status because of the issues it touched on. To prove its point, it conducted a "sociological analysis" that involved quantifying the problems mentioned in the second and third volumes of *Mafalda*. The most frequent problems included relations among kids (19 percent), global issues (14 percent), and the place of children in society (13 percent). But the magazine concluded that the decisive element in the comic's success were its characters, who combined a naive view with criticism that "demystified" norms.[48]

In 1972, a visit by Quino to Spain boosted the public's interest in *Mafalda*. The illustrator was scheduled to give a press conference in Barcelona along with the cartoonists Jaume Perich and Cesc. But at the last minute authorization for the event was denied and the huge crowd waiting in the conference room was cleared out. Ana María Moix, a well-known writer and one of the authors published by Lumen, recounted the incident in the press. She was careful not to mention censorship—which reveals the importance it still had—but she obviously expected the Spanish public to read between the lines as she explained that they knew "these things" happened and that Quino, being "a man of few words, well-mannered and prudent, merely remarked that, coming as he did from a country like Argentina, . . . 'well, what can I say?'" Nonetheless, the book signing went as planned, although, as a precaution, it was not announced over the venue's loudspeakers.[49]

The comic strip quickly attracted the interest of academia. In 1973, Oriol Coll Garcés, a student at the University of Barcelona, wrote his thesis on it. In line with Eco, he argued that *Mafalda* showed the critical potential of comics, despite the unquestionably oppressive effects of the genre. He considered that, like *Peanuts*, it had a critical and corrosive tone, but in contrast to the US cartoon, *Mafalda*, being from the Third World, made the "latent violence" seem "closer, more immediate." This did not prevent him from seeing it as portraying a "typical middle-class world with a typical middle-class ('liberal-democratic') mentality," and he concluded that the "reformist progressive ideology" could prove useful for raising "critical awareness" in the average reader targeted by the comic.[50] In any case, *Mafalda* had already been assimilated into intellectual, artistic, and show business circles. Around that time, a *La Vanguardia* journalist cited the comic strip when analyzing laughter in the family, a popular actress mentioned the "anti-soup" girl to illustrate her own eating habits, and a gossip writer paraphrased a "macabre and politicized" joke in *Mafalda* to mock Princess Grace of Monaco.[51]

In 1973, *Mafalda* found new readers. The main character graced the cover of the first issue of *El Globo*, the magazine that launched Spain's comic strip boom (figure 3.4). Like the Italian magazine *linus,* the editors combined cult comics with information on the genre.[52] They featured classic cartoons from the United States and Europe in an attempt to win over comic strip fans, while introducing Spanish-language products, including from Latin America. Quino's *Mafalda* was the centerpiece of the magazine's offering: a Spanish-language creation, recognized for its aesthetic quality, and with an international readership.[53] The magazine even introduced itself to the public through *Mafalda*. As with *Il Mago*, the main character dominated the cover, where she was shown with her arms wide open in a welcoming gesture.

Mafalda also "penned" the editorial, speaking directly to readers: "It is my pleasure to introduce this new magazine to you. It is an honor for me, as this is the first-ever Spanish-language publication of its kind." With this strat-

FIGURE 3.4 Cover of *El Globo*, no. 1 (March 1973). Mafalda cartoon © Joaquín Salvador Lavado (Quino).

egy, borrowed from foreign magazines, *El Globo* not only brought the latest global trends to Spain but also sought to build a Spanish-language canon in the genre. In this setup, Mafalda emerged as a bridge between the local and the universal, and by addressing her audience with *vosotros*—the second-person plural pronoun typically used in Spain—she spoke a variety of Spanish that was not her usual Buenos Aires (*Porteño*) Spanish and differed widely from the varieties of Spanish spoken in Latin America.[54] This identification thus effected a "Spaniardization" that distanced the comic strip from its own identity. It did not, however, entail hiding its origin or modifying the language in the strips themselves, which retained the same slang that characterized them—in the words of the magazine, "an incisive *Porteño* vocabulary [from the mouth of an] irreverent, precocious, defiant" little girl.[55]

Readers could also find Mafalda in letters to the editors and even in the ads featured in the magazine. It was almost as if she had been chosen to be the magazine's mascot, as one reader called her. The political reason behind this decision was expressed openly: the comic addressed major global issues such as violence, racism, and hunger (according to Quino himself) and it did so (as the editors noted) guided by a little girl who opposed the "sexual discrimination" of mass culture and "broke with clichés," in line with youth protests, the crisis of traditional teachings, and "the downfall of the authoritarian father/ state conception."[56] The formula must have been crystal clear for Spanish audiences, who, used to reading between the lines after decades of censorship, were familiar with fossilized, monarchical, and patriarchal conceptions, so that Mafalda appeared as an opponent of the regime. By then, the book *Diez años con Mafalda*, an anthology edited by Esteban Busquets, was topping best-seller lists, where it would remain for the next ten years.[57] In the words of Esther Tusquets, "it had beaten every record."[58]

Mafalda forged a significant bond with readers in Spain as soon as it arrived. In 1972, the Spanish magazine *Cambio 16* described how the strip was passed "from hand to hand" among an increasingly wide readership with concerns similar to those expressed by its characters. It became a part of the objects, records, and authors that characterized the lifestyle—and the sense of belonging—of young progressives and intellectuals. The comic strip could even lend a hand in affairs of the heart. In an autobiographical account, the journalist José Alejandro Vara recalls that when he was a university student "if you didn't have a couple of *Mafalda* comic books on your nightstand you didn't get any action. It was like the latest Paco Ibáñez record or a Bob Dylan poster. It was a *must* in the 'Hindu-style' decorated attics of those pale and wretched 'lefties' of our youth." Just a few pages of the scathing dialogues by Mafalda, "that 'pocket-sized terrorist,' as [the musician] Víctor Manuel calls her, . . . and a relationship was instantly forged, with lofty exchanges leading inevitably to dialogues down below."[59]

In the Spain of the early 1970s, cultural products from Latin America were being consumed not only by local audiences but also by exiles from the Southern Cone. In 1973, the coups d'état in Uruguay and Chile turned Spain into the leading destination for Latin Americans forced to flee their countries. As Silvina Jensen has explained, the following year economic instability and the killings perpetrated by paramilitary gangs created a new wave of Argentine exiles. Franco's death in 1975 opened up an even more favorable context for the arrival of political immigrants. In 1976, the flow of political exiles from Argentina peaked with the coup.[60]

Spain quickly turned into a forum for denouncing state terrorism. The newspapers *El País* and *La Vanguardia* reported the human rights abuses committed in Argentina and informed of the disappearance of artists and intellectuals and the activities of the exile community. By the early 1980s, according to various estimates, Spain had welcomed some 75,000 to 130,000 Latin Americans, including 45,000 to 60,000 Argentines, the vast majority of them (70 percent) aged 35 or under. The flow of immigrants had intensified during the 1970s, doubling over the course of the decade. As Jensen highlights, there were two leading strategies among these exiles: those who tended to assimilate prioritized the forging of ties with people born in Spain, while those who chose to isolate themselves—in an exile marked by nostalgia—favored the reconstruction of relations with Argentina.[61]

Mafalda, like other Latin American artistic expressions, could facilitate links with the country of exile. In this sense, the strip operated as a cultural mediator. In the words of Eduardo Blaustein, it was "the best object of cultural exchange." In casual conversations between Spanish nationals and Argentine exiles, questions about the meaning of the slang terms used in the strips furthered the understanding of one another's culture, thus giving way to greater empathy. Blaustein recalls that the comic strip's characters could be seen painted on graffiti murals in different neighborhoods of Barcelona (Horta, Hospital, Poble Sec) voicing a range of popular demands—anything from daycare centers and trees to nuclear disarmament.[62] But *Mafalda* could also be part of the cultural artifacts that allowed exiles to remain outside Spanish culture and lock themselves within their own culture. Between these two extremes there were, of course, many other experiences.

One thing is certain, however: *Mafalda* occupied a unique place in the cultural scene of 1970s Spain, energized by a host of exiled artists, writers, and journalists from the Southern Cone. Many of them—the actor Héctor Alterio, the singer Nacha Guevara, and the writers Eduardo Galeano and Mario Benedetti—became icons of a Latin American identity that connected the initial association with the exoticism of the literary boom with a second era marked by the exile experience. Quino's creation linked those two different moments of the influx of Latin American culture to Spain. The comic strip had become popular in Spain after the literary boom but before the arrival of the great flow of exiles and cultural productions from the Southern Cone.

In this sense, *Mafalda* occupied a space in the junction between Latin American culture and universal culture. As Miguel García recalls, "Mafalda surprised us all. She bewitched us all. She had brilliant quips. In the 1970s, the comic strip's readers were adults under forty. Later even children read it. A lot of parents named their daughters Mafalda. People loved Mafalda. Spaniards loved her. Both men and women. Many young people. Exiles too, of course. They were huge promoters of the comic. Mafalda is a character that everybody knows. When *10 años con Mafalda* came out, thousands and thousands of copies of the book were sold, with sales continuing over the years."[63]

By then, the cartoon's international popularity was gaining unprecedented proportions. The Mafalda Boutique in Paris carried dolls, key chains, shirts, and posters that were purchased by fans who had appropriated the strip as a symbol of their identity, but also by the public in general, who found the drawings charming. Quino received new honors, crowning *Mafalda*'s success. In 1977, he was awarded first prize in the Twenty-Third International Humor Salon in Bordighera, Italy. As the Madrid newspaper *El País* reported, the prize "was shared with Mafalda."[64] That same year, Quino—who had always refused to put his creations at the service of a specific cause—gave the United Nations Children's Fund (UNICEF) permission to use the comic strip for a children's rights campaign. His decision could be seen as a logical conclusion of the cartoon's development. After all, Mafalda imagined that she would grow up to be an interpreter at the United Nations and the strip was associated with the younger generations, the defense of the most vulnerable sectors of society, and the struggle against injustice. This 1978 campaign, which raised millions of dollars, confirmed *Mafalda*'s universal status but, at the same time, strengthened the strip's Third World and Latin American identity, which was the target of UNICEF's institutional message.

MEXICO: ANTI-IMPERIALISM, REBELLION, AND THE LATIN AMERICAN BOOM

In the late 1960s, *Mafalda* was sold in Mexico through the distribution channels of small Latin American publishing houses. The cartoon's Argentine publishers sent their catalogs by mail, traveled to Mexico to offer the books in person, went through arduous customs procedures to bring them into the country, and had to wait months to receive payments, but *Mafalda* eventually found its way into bookstores. Mexican intellectual circles, always interested in what was happening elsewhere in Latin America, were closely following the tumultuous developments in Argentina.[65] In that context, the audience for Quino's production was still small enough that readers saw themselves as connoisseurs who were part of a select fellowship. A decade later that had changed and *Mafalda*'s widespread popularity was undeniable. The cartoon was featured in a supplement to the Mexican newspaper *Excélsior*, its books were published in the country, and it could be found in theatrical productions, art, and toy shops.

Mafalda could not hope for a more receptive country. Mexico had a long tradition of production and consumption of comics. The golden age of the genre dated back to the 1930s and '40s when magazine print runs reached almost thirty million copies a month, with comics such as *Pepín* and *Chamaco*. These comic books targeted a working-class readership that had grown with the expansion of school enrollment.[66] In the 1950s, publishing houses suffered a crisis as they failed to keep up with the times and were no match for the powerful US syndicates that supplied material to Mexico's newspapers, which in many cases published a weekly magazine in color. In the 1960s, however, local production made a comeback with monthly magazines that featured fresh content and new cartoonists who spoke to popular local tastes, and they were able to offer a steady stream of comic books and new titles that appealed to the country's increasing number of high-school students.[67]

While US comics continued to dominate the market, this renaissance gave readers the alternative that Carlos Monsiváis had called for in 1963. That year, in a pioneering essay, the Mexican writer and critic had argued that comics lacked an ethical purpose of their own. Their ideological content, he argued, was defined by the US Comics Code Authority, a regulating body established by the Comics Magazine Association of America, which acted as a de facto censor for comic books, with restrictions such as prohibiting the portrayal of bad guys as attractive or the praising of criminal acts. Monsiváis considered that *La Familia Burrón*, a popular Mexican comic strip, expressed the mythologies of the middle class in the poor neighborhoods. This cartoon convinced him that a socially aware line of comic strips was possible. In 1965, Eduardo del Río García proved him right. That year this political cartoonist, who went by the penname Rius, began publishing his famous comic strip *Los Supermachos*. With a weekly readership of 200,000 and an award from the World Comic Conference in Milan, the strip established a new form of graphic humor. In 1968, when Rius lost the rights to his strip—something that was not uncommon as a result of abusive clauses in agreements—he created *Los agachados*, which gained great significance in the climate of student protests. This comic reached its peak popularity in the early 1970s when it was featured in the magazine *Kalimán*, with a weekly print run of 2.5 million.[68]

Mexico's student movement erupted in 1968. Young people rose up against the political power of the Institutional Revolutionary Party (Partido Revolucionario Institucional, or PRI) that had governed the country for the past four decades. Its long hold on power had created a state that was based on the centralization of power and the suppression of any dissent, but which also had the capacity to unify Mexican society through the development of public policies in a range of areas (most notably health, education, and culture) and a nationalist ideology that fed on popular traditions. In the 1960s, this form of domination had begun to fray at the edges.

The government's distributive policies had brought changes to society. On the one hand, economic growth had furthered the emergence of a middle class with greater buying power whose youth were open to the cultural influence of the United States and had begun to defy their parents' authority. The expansion of the media and cultural industries invigorated the youth market. Rock music, dancing, fashion, and other cultural trends such as comics were increasingly popular among young people, many of whom, as they reached high-school age were more independent and able to move freely in their cities.[69] On the other, the government's policies had highlighted existing inequalities and heightened the perception of the social dislocations caused by these transformations. Access to secondary education had spread across the social spectrum and enrollment experienced a massive expansion, with members of the working and lower classes seeing it as their ticket to upward social mobility. This growth laid bare the difficulties in infrastructure, teaching staff, and curricula and revealed the limitations in future career and job opportunities.[70]

In July 1968, high-school and university students staged demonstrations in streets and campuses and were brutally repressed. Over the following months, intellectuals and various social sectors that opposed the government joined the students in a widespread revolt that culminated in a bloodbath on October 2, when the army cracked down on protesters on the Plaza de las Tres Culturas in the Tlatelolco neighborhood of Mexico City. The experience of daily struggle had a profound effect on the students and others who participated in this rebellion against patriarchal power.[71] The defeat of the protests boosted the importance of the cultural expressions that symbolized the identity of the rebellious students—Che Guevara's image, long hair, rock music, Rius's humor. The new cohorts of students who were enrolling in large numbers in secondary schools and universities (in higher education alone, enrollment went from 250,000 in 1970 to 500,000 in 1976) were shaped by this tradition of struggle.[72] Left-wing ideas were thus linked to the appropriation of a rock and hippie culture and feminist demands voiced by activists who were aware that they played a role that was instrumental but also subordinated to the male leadership of the protests that had shaken Mexican society. In this sense, young people were united in their social and political criticism but evidenced rifts when it came to the changes that were affecting family relations and sexuality. Student struggles were thus pierced by class and gender tensions.[73]

This climate heightened local interest in developments in other Latin American countries. The coups d'état in Uruguay and Chile had cut short a historical rise in popular movements and turned Argentina into the focal point of the battle between the revolutionary left and the repressive forces of the state. Mexican newspapers reported daily on that country's spiraling violence, escalating repression, and war on culture. In 1975, cultural pages and columns expressed their solidarity with Southern Cone writers and artists who were being persecuted, including the Argentine singer-songwriter Mercedes Sosa and the Uruguayan writer Eduardo Galeano and the magazine he published in Argentina, *Crisis*.[74] Mexico took them in. As with Republicans fleeing Franco after the Spanish Civil War, more and more Argentine and other Southern Cone exiles were driven to Mexico by the threats and killings perpetrated by the military and paramilitary forces waging a "war against subversion." They joined the thousands of Chileans and Uruguayans who had been forced to leave their countries after the coups and had a growing presence in neighborhoods, cafés, and bookstores in the Mexican capital. While no precise data is available, immigration from the Southern Cone went from being so insignificant that it was not reflected in demographic statistics to becoming one of the leading migration phenomena of the 1970s.[75]

In 1975, Mexican public opinion was not just focused on the critical situation in Latin America, as preparations for the United Nations World Conference on Women were under way. This event, which would be held in June of that year in Mexico City, put media attention on the status of women, with discussions on a range of issues, including working conditions, the double burden, political participation, and gender disparities.[76] These were not minor matters in Mexican society, where women and family relations were undergoing profound changes. Just a decade earlier, birthrates had seen a sharp reduction (from 1965 to 1968), and that drop, combined with government birth-control policies, had strongly affected cities. Many young women were openly or discreetly venturing into greater sexual freedom, outside the confines of marriage, and challenging the traditional feminine model based on sacrifice and suffering. Family relations—between husbands and wives and parents and children—were under debate, as evidenced in articles, reviews, ads, and the media in general. Children were the focus of discussions in newspaper and magazine sections devoted to them, and their unquestionable importance is also illustrated by the concerns of educators, specialists, and parents, as well as the proliferation of toys and children's shows.[77]

Pierced as it was by sociocultural transformations, the expansion of education and the media, political radicalization, and the Latin Americanization of culture, Mexican society was an ideal audience for *Mafalda*. Mexico's traditional newspaper *Excélsior* seized the opportunity. In early 1975, a review of a compilation of drawings published by Quino under the title *Yo que usted* served as an excuse to praise Mafalda and the strip: "Everyone knows the irreverent little girl who is popular with kids and grown-ups, with her clever comebacks, her daunting questions, her categorical judgments, her messages to humanity." The article finished by underlining the universal nature of the character's concerns—hunger, birth control, changing social mores, "family life today," "sociopolitical chaos"—which made the comic strip "a success because it is a universal type."[78]

On June 1, 1975, a full-page ad in *Excélsior* announced to its readers that the newspaper was bringing "Quino's World Famous Comic Strip" to its pages. For the ad, the newspaper's editors had chosen two strips with ironic takes on freedom of the press and bad governments, and these strips flanked the cover of the latest *Mafalda* book, which showed the main character facing a globe populated by demonstrators.[79] Without further introduction, *Mafalda* joined the many cartoons that were published in color in *Excélsior*'s Sunday funnies.

The newspaper featured Quino's comic strip on the last page, a prominent space in the supplement. Each issue had numerous cartoons distributed by US syndicates, in addition to a single Mexican comic strip, the popular *Chicharrín y el sargento pistolas*, produced by Armando Guerrero Edwards for the newspaper since 1936.[80] *Mafalda* fans must have been surprised when they saw Quino's creation in full color. This intervention had been done almost mechanically, with each figure featured in a single color, which varied in each case, over a background also in color. The idea was to match the style of the supplement—where all the cartoons were in color—but it ruined the fine lines of Quino's drawings and even made it difficult to understand the strips.

Although the content of the first strips published was not altered, in future issues the editors would occasionally make changes to the text. They often normalized the second-person singular form *vos* typical of Buenos Aires speech, replacing it with the form *tú* used in Mexico and much of the Spanish-speaking world.[81] There is no discernible pattern in these alterations that could reveal what motivated them, but in the newspaper's files there are enough examples to suggest that it was a common practice. The editing process for the comic strips may not have followed a style guide, or it may have been carried out by more than one person, which would explain its inconsistency.[82]

The first strips featured in *Excélsior* addressed the issue of television in society and in the education of children. Mafalda's father's refusal to accept television—a typical attitude when the strips were created and television was still a new and expanding technology in Argentina—may have sounded somewhat anachronistic to Mexican audiences in the 1970s, but it served to illustrate an ideological stance that characterized intellectual and progressive circles and their wariness of cultural industries.

The topics covered by the strips chosen were ideal. The cartoon raised issues that could be of interest to a significant sector of parents and children in Mexico who, like their peers in Argentina and Europe, were witnessing major transformations to everyday life and the family. For some—the more intellectual—*Mafalda* represented the existence of an alternative cultural production in Latin America, in the framework of advancing US cultural industries and the continent's "Americanization." In that context, which affected Mexico in particular, Quino's creation expressed a criticism of the "system" from within Latin America. As Antonio Soria recalled in 2012 in *La Jornada*, *Mafalda* was received by a wide audience that celebrated its origin ("Finally a non-gringo comic strip") and its "contrarian spirit," that is, its rebelliousness.[83] In *Mafalda*, that Latin Americanism had the peculiarity of offering a modern image, both because of Quino's drawing style and because of its themes and characters. That characteristic set it apart from most productions associated with the Latin American boom of the 1960s, which involved a reworking of popular traditions, as was the case with folk music and magical realism. In this sense, the comic strip took on an "exceptional" meaning for many readers.

The *Mafalda* books came out in Mexico almost as soon as the comic strip began its run in *Excélsior*. As in Italy and Spain, the difficulties involved in its publication reveal how cultural production is affected by the economic, social, and political developments of a specific time, but, at the same time, they show the contingent intertwining of long-term historical processes. In Mexico, the comic strip was published by Nueva Imagen, a publishing house founded in 1976 by the Mexican entrepreneur Sealtiel Alatriste in association with the Argentine Guillermo Schavelzon. Each partner brought a specific contribution to the venture. Sealtiel Alatriste was familiar with the intellectual and publishing scene in Mexico. He had a bachelor's degree in literature from the National Autonomous University of Mexico (Universidad Nacional Autónoma de México, or UNAM) and a master's in philosophy from the University of Cambridge. His father had been a renowned editor and cartoonist, but he had no experience in the publishing world himself, despite having owned a bookstore.[84] His Argentine partner, however, had been in the business for almost a decade. He had begun in the publishing house Jorge Álvarez Editores and had gone on to establish Galerna, with a catalog that included such titles as Osvaldo Bayer's *La Patagonia Rebelde* and the magazine *Los Libros*. But he had only recently moved to Mexico, having fled his home country as a result of the threats he had received for his publishing work. He had chosen that destination because he admired Mexico's publishing tradition, having visited the country before to offer his catalog. When his exile began, however, he only had one contact and friend: fellow Argentine Noé Jitrik, a prominent writer and literary critic who had settled there two years earlier when his family had come under threat from paramilitary groups prior to the coup.[85]

When they started planning their catalog, they contacted Quino to request the rights to publish *Mafalda*, but they only secured a contract after another Mexican publishing house that was in talks with Quino passed. As had happened with Esther Tusquets in Spain, *Mafalda*'s success exceeded their expectations. In their case, a decisive factor was a distribution strategy involving two companies that operated nationwide—one had nearly one hundred branches along the Pacific coast and the other worked with newspaper outlets. This strategy meant that their publications reached small magazine stores but also Sanborns, a large chain that offered a range of products and, according to Schavelzon, sold 40 percent of the books marketed in Mexico.[86]

Comic books became one of the leading products offered by Nueva Imagen in its catalog. In addition to Quino, the publishing house included the Chilean José Palomo and the Argentine Roberto Fontanarrosa. These cartoonists joined prominent authors from other genres, such as Julio Cortázar and Mario Benedetti, and intellectuals such as Umberto Eco, Ariel Dorfman, and Néstor García Canclini. There are no figures available for the number of *Mafalda* books sold in Mexico, but the two publishers remember how popular the character was. The success of the comic strip launched their business. Alatriste estimates that thousands of collections were sold annually. He recalls that when they first published the comic strip, its audience was formed by young adults, but it immediately expanded to include high-school and university students, and later even children. In 1977, a representative of the Spanish company Romagnosa began marketing Mafalda toys, following attempts by other companies to manufacture similar dolls without authorization, as reported in the press by Alicia Colombo.[87] This reveals that Mafalda's popularity had grown so much that there were companies willing to invest in merchandising. (See figures 3.5 and 3.6.)

However, these appropriations were not necessarily motivated by economic considerations alone, as political and ideological reasons also came into play. In 1979, the theater troupe Los Infantilotes staged a play in Galería Gandhi inspired by *Mafalda*. According to a description featured in the theater section of the newspaper *La Onda* after the play had been shown in a number of venues over the course of three months, "the famous character created by Quino proves that children's theater can have left-leaning ideological nods."[88] The troupe was part of Mexico's intense theater scene, which was fueled by socially committed groups engaged in artistic experimentation. While no copies of the play have survived, its author and director, Jorge Belauzarán, explained in an account from that time that the idea was to use the character "as an ideological device" to show how children saw the troubled world of their parents,

FIGURES 3.5 AND 3.6 Dolls produced in Spain under copyright and probably marketed in Latin America, ca. 1980. Courtesy of Antonio Torres, Club del Cómic, Buenos Aires. © Joaquín Salvador Lavado (Quino).

and to counter "mainstream productions and advertisements whose content is limited to magicians, elves, princes, witches, dragons, Cinderellas, and silly TV clowns that only serve to mediatize children without stimulating their imagination and sensitivity, merely pushing them to buy the candy sold by multinational corporations that is bad for their health."[89]

As summarized by a review featured in *Conjunto*, the theater magazine published by Casa de las Américas, the troupe's aim was to give children a play that was not just fun but also offered other ideological choices.[90] Anticipating criticism regarding Mafalda's adult attitude, the reviewer explained that the play was not meant only as "a story with a child character" but as an invitation to both children and adults to enjoy the show together.

The play was not authorized by Quino, who on a visit to Mexico met with troupe members and asked them to stop staging it. He explained to them that the characters were not made for the theater, that they belonged on the page, and that putting them on stage shattered the "image" he had built for a comic strip format. On a different occasion, the cartoonist recalled how he had seen a *Peanuts* play in London in 1968 and had found it dreadful. That experience had convinced him of the difficulty of adapting comic strips for a different medium. The members of Los Infantilotes explained that they had not asked the publishing house for permission because they assumed it would refuse it to protect Quino's own interests and that they had not made any money off the play. On the contrary, they had used their own money to cover the costs of staging it and had barely broken even. Although the director and his troupe apologized to the cartoonist and promised to cancel the play, they did argue that Quino's decision was unfair. They claimed that while Quino denied them permission, he was unable to do the same with those who manufactured *Mafalda* merchandise without his authorization, because he could not identify them.[91] Their argument questioned the possibility of successfully controlling how the characters were used and by whom, but it also disputed Quino's criteria.

Three weeks later, a representative of Los Infantilotes announced that they would not cancel the play, despite Quino's request. To justify their decision, they cited the many letters of support they had received and the "need to bring the character to members of the lower classes who lack the means to buy the books." They thus put cultural and political principles and the opinion of readers above the wishes of the cartoonist.[92] This reveals that in Mexico, too, Quino's creation had, to a certain extent, taken on a life of its own. Members of a theater troupe had appropriated the comic strip to the point of believing they were entitled to do anything they wanted with the characters regardless of the wishes of its creator. They did so in the belief that they understood—and shared—the cartoon's intrinsic political meaning and that the content was more important than Quino's copyright.

This dispute over the uses of *Mafalda* did not mean that Quino himself was not influential. Far from it. The author had a large following and his annual conferences and book presentations attracted large audiences. There was, moreover, a certain intimate identification between creation and creator, giving him an aura that endeared him to the public. As a journalist put it, "Quino's appearance is that of an absentminded professor, with his disheveled and thinning hair and his glasses sitting crookedly on his nose. He wears an ordinary brown-colored corduroy suit and a tie he obviously dons as a necessary concession to formality . . . He acts and moves as if he were another character from that children's world, straightforward and without complications, who every day confronts the rough realities of the adult world with wit and cleverness as his only resources."[93] As with movie stars and the fictional characters they play, the public conflated Quino's characters with the image they had of the author.

In 1981, the UNICEF Mexico Office honored the cartoonist with a medal and an award for his support to the organization.[94] UNICEF had raised millions of dollars with the *Mafalda* campaign, thus confirming the popularity of the comic strip, but also its connection with children and its universal nature.

Commenting on the award, *Excélsior* described Mafalda as a "fierce little girl who uses her candid wit to judge man's conflicts and put systems on trial." The journalist went on to say that Quino's universe had displaced "Donald Duck, Mickey Mouse, Woody Woodpecker, and all those other insipid and empty US cartoons" in every Spanish-speaking country. The journalist's assertion was not that preposterous, despite possible evidence to the contrary in the very newspaper where the article was featured, where *Mafalda* was surrounded by US comics. Viewed as an alternative to productions from the North, the cartoon's ideological significance was real, as was its antidictatorial component.

In 1980, Quino was again publishing material in an Argentine newspaper (*Clarín*) and had returned to his country for short stays, but he was very careful with the political opinions he voiced. He defined himself as a "bitter sniper" and when asked if he was worried about being censored by the Argentine government—which according to the *Excélsior* reporter was "known for being right-wing and 'tough'"—he explained, "I have always lived in countries with military governments. That's how I've learned just how far I can go." His answer did not deny that censorship existed—rather, it assumed it did—but it underscored his ability to know the limits and the possibilities of what he could say in that context.[95]

FIGURE 3.7 Quino giving a talk at Gandhi bookstore, ca. 1977, holding a record of the Music for UNICEF Concert, which featured artists such as ABBA, Elton John, and Olivia Newton-John. Photograph from the archive of the newspaper *Excélsior* (Mexico).

However, for his readers, Quino's work spoke for itself. And *Mafalda* could become a symbol of the opposition to the dictatorship. Jorge Tovar, a Mexican artist who was a great admirer of Quino, made that representation explicit in four works he exhibited in the Salón de la Plástica Mexicana.[96] He drew Mafalda confronting a general who looks like a gorilla (figure 3.8). Mafalda and her friend Felipe are separated from the officer by funerary urns adorned with skulls. The distance between them was heightened by the use of a different caricature style for each and by the depth of perspective. Quino's characters appear to be situated outside the frame and approaching the picture with a typical children's attitude, with Mafalda standing on Felipe's back so she can reach in. The space between them symbolized the gap that separated what each represented: the military and the people. The difference in size also evoked the meaning of the action that was re-created: a tiny Mafalda grabbing the huge gorilla by the lapels. The dialogue balloons stressed the meaning conveyed by the image. The gorilla screams angrily, "Ban everything! Including Mafalda! !@#$%^&* comic strip!" Mafalda insults the gorilla, calling him a "murderer," and tells Felipe that she wants to "punch him hard." A worried Felipe exclaims, "Watch your mouth! Be careful, they've had people killed for less than that . . ." His warning completed the denunciation, as it alluded (along with the skull-painted urns) to the absent: the victims killed by the dictatorship. It also denoted the fear spread by the dictatorship, which was taken to new levels with the practice of disappearing opponents to erase all traces of its crimes.

FIGURE 3.8 Untitled work by Mexican artist Jorge Tovar, ca. 1981. He included Quino's name along with his signature as an homage to the cartoonist.

Tovar's view is not difficult to understand. The disappearances in Argentina had been denounced very early on in Mexico. In 1976, ninety days after the coup, the Latin American Solidarity Committee (Comité de Solidaridad Latinoamericano) issued a report denouncing the regime's crimes: 24,000 disappeared persons, 17,000 political prisoners, 1,000 executions, and 800 people who had died under torture. The organizations that gathered exiles—the Committee for Solidarity with the Argentine People (Comité de Solidaridad con el Pueblo Argentino) and the Argentine Solidarity Committee (Comité Argentino de Solidaridad)—continued denouncing these crimes with demonstrations, marches, and solidarity events. Every March 24, on the anniversary of the 1976 coup, they staged a demonstration in front of the Argentine embassy, with demonstrators carrying pictures of the disappeared. Mexico became one of the leading platforms for denouncing the military dictatorship, as these initiatives were supported by the government, intellectuals, artists, and the press, where many exiles were working.[97]

As in Spain, in Mexico *Mafalda* contributed to forge an empathetic connection between nationals and Argentines. The Argentine journalist Carlos Ulanovsky, who was living in exile in the Mexican capital, recalls that when people from both countries met there were certain conversation "openers," including the political situation, soccer, the tango legend Carlos Gardel, and *Mafalda*. He remembers, for example, how the waitress at the coffee shop he frequented daily would often greet him with questions regarding the meaning of typical Argentine sayings or terms she picked up in the comic strip. *Mafalda* had become popular among a vast Mexican public who, far from being put off by foreign expressions, had made the comic strip their own, as its universal meaning enabled multiple appropriations. This anecdote, like the numerous press reviews, shows that many readers viewed the cartoon as part of a Latin American identity that transcended Argentina and that in the 1960s and '70s was increasingly meaningful for the left across the continent.

In this way, the comic strip of the Argentine middle class—the social sector that had promoted the Europeanized images of that country that were often used to look down on the rest of Latin America—was now, paradoxically, considered representative of Latin America and was seen as feeding a continental identity. According to Martín Zamor, a literature student at UNAM in the late 1970s, he and his politicized friends were willing to overlook any political "ambiguities" in *Mafalda* because the comic represented the power of Latin America against US culture. As he remembers it, even the idiomatic expressions so specific to Buenos Aires, whose meaning often eluded him, added to its attraction. It was a bridge to the country of Julio Cortázar and Jorge Luis Borges and a link to the many Argentines they knew. But this was certainly not the only reading of the comic strip. Mabel Domínguez, who discovered *Mafalda* when she was still a little girl in the late 1970s, remembers the pleasure she felt in seeing how the kids in the cartoon challenged their parents like she would have liked to.[98] For Argentine exiles, instead, the cartoon's use of local expressions and references brought them back to the country they had been forced to leave. Mario García had not been a fan of the comic strip before leaving Argentina, but he rediscovered it during a weekend outing with Mexican friends. "I couldn't stop reading it. Far from home, it had a different appeal. It was strange. A kind of humorous nostalgia." Rosana Muñoz was only four years old when she moved to Mexico in 1976 and she discovered *Mafalda* on a shelf in her house when she was about ten.[99] The comic strip allowed her to imagine the streets, squares, and schools of the city she was born in, of which she had very few memories. This experience resonated with my own discovery of Mafalda as a thirteen-year-old living in Quito, far from my native Río de la Plata. The sharp, direct, and ironic dialogues captivated me. In my case they evoked the much smaller city of Montevideo, which nonetheless has much in common with the large metropolis of Buenos Aires, and whose differences were blurred in the distance and the contrast with the unhurried and quieter style of the Andean city.

It would be impossible to describe the many different appropriations of the comic strip that were born in social interactions and in the subjective experience of individual reading. By the early 1980s, *Mafalda* had attracted new readers from different parts of Mexico and from various generations. According to the publishers, it was sold throughout the country and had reached a teenage audience. At the time, Antonio Soria of *La Jornada* described a "Mafalda boom" that was sweeping the country. The characters had turned into icons of a certain ethics and aesthetics and were featured in posters, keychains, and stickers, among other objects. In the words of the journalist, they expressed "the spirit of a generation that spoke and thought like Mafalda et al., who listened to the same music she did, lived in an apartment very similar to hers; who were concerned over much the same issues she was."[100] Favored by the expansion of education, the homogenization of middle-class consumption, the 1968 cultural and political radicalization, and the Southern Cone exiles, *Mafalda* had come to Mexico to stay.

In the years since, the comic strip's popularity has continued to grow worldwide. This growth was boosted by the awards received by Quino and the global circulation of the cartoon in new formats, such as a 1981 movie produced by Daniel Mallo in Argentina, which would be followed years later in 1995 by a Cuban film version directed by Juan Padrón. *Mafalda* has also expanded into other markets and its readership has increased steadily with each new edition (anthologies, unpublished strips, full collections), tributes, prizes, and even an ebook launched recently in Spanish and English.[101]

Mafalda is proof that Latin American cultural productions played a leading role in the processing of the disruptions produced by modernization among various social sectors, in particular the middle class and workers, around the world. This underscores the simultaneity of these disruptions that contributed to redefine everyday life, family values, and gender roles. And, at the same time, it evidences the way in which such processes were driven by actors and dynamics on a transnational scale involving different social sectors in each country with different significations, effects, and temporalities. It reveals a more or less global readership that could laugh at itself with a conceptual humor that worked with the ruptures caused by modernization. The universal references to injustices, inequalities, and wars brought into play universal values in which very diverse issues and sociocultural realities could be projected.

This context was even more favorable as it operated on a certain change of direction in cultural exchanges, repositioning the "South" with respect to the "North" in the 1960s and 1970s, giving Latin America a new place, based on the utopian hopes pinned on the construction of a new world order originating in the Third World. This view does not entail ignoring the inequalities in the global balance of power. In fact, it is those inequalities that explain why the Latin American productions that achieved transnational circulation were comparatively few. In that sense, the study of *Mafalda* can be approached through the examination of the concrete actors, the contingent connections, and the unique appropriations in each social space and historical moment. These actors and dynamics reveal that the importance of the global scale did not entail a displacement of nation-states, whose political processes, markets, and regulatory frameworks are decisive for understanding the expansion and social meanings of global cultural production.

This perspective shows the special value of small ventures, in which professional and economic needs were intertwined with the aesthetic choices, personal interests, and political aims of an educated, active, and politically committed middle class. These ventures gradually created a cultural market of political antiestablishment products that contributed to shape identities with global entity in a process that fed on and fueled the circulation of individuals.

Mafalda allows us to identify what has been referred to as a progressive, antiestablishment, or left-wing sensitivity on a global scale. I use the term "sensitivity" to denote an imprecise cultural configuration, at times somewhat ethereal, at the intersection of the ideological, the aesthetic, and the emotional. *Mafalda*—and similar phenomena—offers an especially rich example for understanding this kind of sensitivity. The comic strip's malleability was determined by the emerging nature of the phenomena it catalyzed, in part because it referred to universal themes such as war, injustice, and inequality, which facilitated its translation into different perceptions, diagnostics, and political intentions, but also because Quino worked those processes through humor and irony, that is, discursive structures whose meaning needs to be completed by the very subjects addressed. In sum, there were multiple—even contradictory—appropriations, but their communicating vessels made them part of a shared sensitivity that emerged at the intersection of the ruptures produced by the processes of modernization, political radicalization, and cultural antiestablishment.

CHAPTER 4

An Antiestablishment Voice in Turbulent Times

This chapter shifts the focus back to Argentina to look at a violent and still unresolved past that began on March 24, 1976, with the coup d'état that deposed María Estela Martínez de Perón. The coup intensified a process launched under the democratically elected government, which had fostered the actions of paramilitary groups and given the army full authority to "wipe out subversion." What distinguishes the military regime that came to power with this coup from previous dictatorships is its intent on exterminating all opposition and the savageness with which it pursued its goal. With that aim, it introduced and systematically applied a series of clandestine and illegal methods that began with the abduction of militants and social activists, who were then tortured, murdered, and finally disappeared. To lend authority and legitimacy to the regime, the juntas drew on the National Security Doctrine. It was only in 1982, with Argentina's defeat in the Malvinas/Falklands War against Great Britain, that the dictatorship was completely isolated and discredited and the country began its return to democratic rule. The election the following year of Raúl Alfonsín—the first president under the newly restored democracy—opened up a new period marked by the investigation of human rights violations against a backdrop of economic crisis. This chapter spans the thirteen years from the 1976 coup to the end of the Alfonsín administration in 1989, when the legacy of the dictatorship threatened to bring down a frail democracy and the country took a sharp neoliberal turn under the presidency of Carlos Saúl Menem.

The discussion of state terrorism is now, as it was then, at the center of Argentina's political, intellectual, and judicial life. The efforts to expose its methods and understand its nature and causes have produced partial results. From the *Nunca más* (*Never Again*) report issued by the National Commission on the Disappearance of Persons (Nunca más: Informe de la Comisión Nacional sobre la Desaparición de Personas—CONADEP) in 1984, and the trials held then and resumed more recently, we know how the violence and disappearances were perpetrated by the state. We also know what the ideological foundations of the war against subversion were, which linked the defense of Western Christian civilization to the threats against the "national" way of life and the pillars of the political, social, and family orders. Repressive policies were accompanied by an economic program that set out to dismantle the welfare state and promote neoliberal policies.[1] The insight gained has in turn posed new questions. As in other countries in which the state systematically committed crimes against humanity on a massive scale, a major issue that has demanded attention is the relationship between culture and politics under authoritarian rule and how the horror of those crimes became part of everyday life.

What can *Mafalda* tell us about these issues? As noted in the introduction, by actively engaging its target audience in the construction of meaning, humor provides a powerful lens for observing social phenomena. I draw on earlier studies on the subject that posit that humor under the dictatorship did not operate unilaterally, nor was its meaning uniform.[2] But more specifically, I am interested in exploring the significance of humor during that period through a detailed reconstruction of the social and political uses of *Mafalda*. My aim is to explore how censorship and repression affected cultural dynamics and subjectivities during the dictatorship and how the meanings ascribed to the comic strip changed in the context of brutal authoritarianism and later, when the full extent of the human rights abuses committed came to light with the restoration of democracy.

Quino had stopped producing new strips in 1973, when the humor in *Mafalda* had become anachronistic as Argentine society—and not just its middle class—was increasingly unable to settle its political differences peacefully and polarization grew with each new violent death. Despite Quino's decision to discontinue the cartoon, *Mafalda* would not remain on the sidelines of the disputes that tore the country viciously apart. With the coup, the comic strip was swept into the dictatorial terror that followed, and in 1983 it joined the efforts aimed at defending democracy.

THE PALLOTTINE MASSACRE

Mafalda's continued social and political significance beyond its run is illustrated by a violent episode involving Pallottine priests and seminarians that happened shortly after the coup, on July 4, 1976. This Catholic order founded by the Roman priest Vincenzo Pallotti in 1837 had a small congregation in Argentina, formed by Irish and German immigrants in the nineteenth century. In 1973, following the changes in the Catholic Church in the 1960s, some of the Pallottine priests and seminarians of the Buenos Aires Parish of San Patricio began to advocate for change in both society and the Church. Among them was the parish priest Alfredo Kelly, who also headed the seminary. Although the higher-ranking and senior members, Alfredo Leaden and Pedro Eduardo Dufau, were more conservative, the parish had attracted progressive seminarians. These included Emilio Barletti, a former member of the Peronist Youth who was part of the group Christians for Liberation (Cristianos para la Liberación), and Salvador Barbeito, a Peronist sympathizer who had no previous history of activism.[3] While none of the seminarians were part of the Movement of Priests for the Third World, they welcomed the postconciliar transformations in the Church and made a preferential option for the poor. Their views and the more relaxed atmosphere at the parish had attracted young members to the congregation, and it had become a space for discussion about the changes in the Church as well as other social and political issues. The 1976 coup alarmed them, as they were aware of the brutal repression suffered by anyone who opposed the regime. Nonetheless, Father Kelly spoke out against the dictatorship. In particular, he denounced residents of the parish's upscale neighborhood of Belgrano who had attended auctions of property obtained illegally from people kidnapped and disappeared by the regime, which, he said, made them complicit in the crime of disappearance. Following that denunciation, Kelly had received anonymous threats, including a letter calling the priests in his congregation communists, and had noticed a strange car parked permanently at the corner of the priests' lodgings.[4] On July 1, Kelly wrote in his diary that he "realized the gravity of the slander against" him and was "aware of the threat to [his] life," but had prayed to God to give him strength to keep fighting and face the possibility of death.[5]

Despite the looming danger, the priests and seminarians went about their daily activities without altering their routine. On July 3, Father Dufau officiated a wedding in the Santo Domingo Parish, while Kelly and Leaden were officiating another wedding in San Patricio. Barletti and Barbeito had returned to the Belgrano lodgings late after going to the movies with fellow seminarian Roberto Capalozza, who decided to stay at his parents' house that night.[6] The following morning, as the Church was still closed at eight o'clock when mass was supposed to begin, Rolando Savino, a sixteen-year-old organ player, let himself in through a window thinking that the priests had overslept. He found the lights on and when he went upstairs he discovered the slain bodies of the three priests and two seminarians. According to the journalist Eduardo Gabriel Kimel—who conducted a thorough investigation of the crimes based on eyewitness reports, newspaper accounts, and evidence from the unfinished police inquiries—the boy found a gruesome scene: "The five bodies were on the floor, one next to the other, face down, and they were riddled with bullets. The image was unmistakable: they had been executed."[7]

The police report indicates that there was a lot of blood on the floor and 9 mm bullet casings from at least five different guns, and that all the rooms in the house were in disarray. The killers also left messages on the walls and floors, accusing the victims of being "lefties," "indoctrinators of virginal minds" and "members of the MSTM" (the Movement of Priests for the Third World). The report also described some items found in the house, including something that looked like a hand grenade and the famous "ideology-denting stick" poster featuring Mafalda, along with other posters with messages such as "the open veins of Latin America" (in reference to Eduardo Galeano's book on the history of imperialism in Latin America) and "Victory to Indochina." There was also a handwritten sign with antidictatorial messages, allegedly made by the Third World priest Carlos Mugica, assassinated by a Triple A death squad in 1974. Kimel's investigation revealed that the Pallottine priests and seminarians were murdered by a police task force and that the motive was revenge for a bomb that had killed eighteen policemen in a building of the Federal Police (the SEG) two days earlier.[8] One of the messages left by the killers at the scene of the crime leaves little room for doubt as to their identity and motive: "This is for our brothers in arms blown up in the Federal SEG. Victory will be ours. Long Live the Fatherland."[9]

One of the crime scene photos in the case file shows the Mafalda poster draped over one of the bodies (figure 4.1).[10] How should the presence of that poster be interpreted? The photograph offers a first clue. The way the poster is placed reveals it was deliberate, as it was spread carefully over the body closest to the door, so that it was immediately visible as one entered the room.

The repressive forces were all too aware of the symbolic importance of this poster, which featured one of their own and Mafalda's critical assessment. As noted in chapter 2, the image had become so popular that it had transcended the comic strip and was used as a statement on repression; but it had also been co-opted by the security services themselves who had altered its meaning and turned Manolito into a supporter of the "ideology-denting stick" because it brought the order that allowed him and his friend to go to school. The aim of that first appropriation had been to garner social support for repression. Now, by placing it over the body of one of their victims, the repressive forces

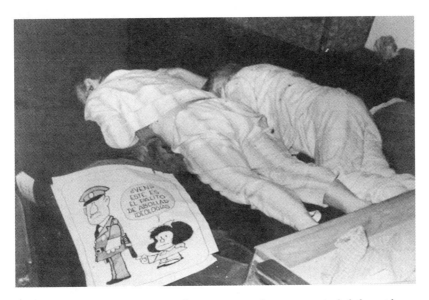

FIGURE 4.1 Photograph of the slain Pallottine priests and seminarians, included as evidence in the 1977 criminal court case file (no. 7970, archive of Secretaría 23, Juzgado Criminal y Correccional Federal 12).

appropriated it in yet another, very different way. Acknowledging its original antiauthoritarian meaning, they used it in an act of heinous revenge as a macabre joke. It was aimed at those who had been amused by the little girl and her denunciation of the police batons, with the intention of showing them that the power of the repressive forces was capable of much more than just denting ideologies—it could kill with impunity. It expressed the power of co-opting the enemy's humor to wield it as a perverse instrument of terror.

The murderers had ripped the poster off one of the walls in the house. As Capalozza said when I interviewed him, it was a poster commonly found in many homes. This is not surprising considering that it was sold everywhere in Argentina, from newsstands in downtown Buenos Aires to train stations in remote towns, and although it is impossible to know how many were sold, the numbers were probably in the tens of thousands. The poster conveyed a strong message that underscored the power of weapons and the vulnerability of ideas, and it spoke to many individuals with a wide range of political and ideological views who opposed authoritarianism. This was not the only *Mafalda* item at the parish house. According to Capalozza there were also books; while the priests and seminarians "weren't huge fans" of the cartoon, they "liked to comment on the strips." Visibly moved by the memory of what happened, he remembers that Barbeito most enjoyed the comic strip, and it was on his body that the killers had placed the poster.[11]

There was no mention of the poster in the press. Quino, who was living in Milan at the time, only learned of it many years later.[12] The messages found on the scene were also kept out of most press accounts. Mentioning them would have meant exposing as a lie the official version, which blamed the killings on a "group of extremists."[13] The police press statement even said the acronym MSTM stood for Movimiento Sindicalista de Trabajadores Montoneros (Trade Unionist Movement of Montonero Workers), in an effort to associate the crime with the Montoneros guerrilla group. The editor in chief of the *Buenos Aires Herald*, Roberto Cox, received threatening calls because he had printed the messages left by the killers.[14] His editorial also exposed the repercussions of the act of revenge within the repressive forces, which had led to the resignation of the police commissioner, General Arturo Corbetta, after only fifteen days on the job. According to Cox, Corbetta had vowed that "both forms of terrorism" would be dealt with through legal channels. That would have meant abandoning the system of kidnappings, torture, and clandestine disappearances that was being implemented with the approval of the armed forces.[15]

In the days before and after the San Patricio massacre, many more bodies turned up in Buenos Aires and around the country, in some cases with signs left on their bodies identifying them as extremists. That same day seven unidentified bodies were found in Villa Lugano, Buenos Aires, and several political prisoners were killed as they were transferred from Salta to Córdoba.[16] The macabre staging of the crime scene thus contained a message aimed at those within the armed forces who opposed the clandestine methods of repression used by their peers, showing them the risk of leaving bullet-ridden corpses strewn across the city for all to see and identifying themselves as the authors of such crimes. If they were free to crack down on the opposition using any methods they chose without exposing themselves and their crimes, they would not risk being held accountable in the future, regardless of how brutal they were. But, as Emilio Mignone notes, the killings were also meant as a threat against the Church, as they showed that repression would not stop at the door of a place of worship.[17]

More than four decades later, the court case is still open, and the Mafalda poster can be found among the hundreds of pages that make up the case file. It is impossible to know if the wrinkles and tears were caused by the many people who handled the file over the years, or if they were made when the killers ripped it off the wall to place on the body. The murderers used the poster as part of their revenge and threats, but in doing so they also turned it into evidence that could be used in the investigation. At the time nobody tried to lift fingerprints from it, and today the effort would be useless, as the original fingerprints are unrecoverable. The poster, however, preserved along with the sign written by Carlos Mugica, makes us wonder again—and investigate— what happened that night in San Patricio Parish and what happened during those dark years in which humor was turned into a weapon used by the state to terrorize the population.

PUBLISHING AND READING *MAFALDA* DURING THE DICTATORSHIP

On February 16, 1977, Daniel Jorge Divinsky and his wife, Ana María Teresa Miler, were arrested in the offices of their publishing house Ediciones de la Flor. Three weeks later, his father, José Divinsky, and her mother, Elisa Miler, sent a letter to the de facto president informing him of their arrest and that they were still in custody with no formal charges filed against them.[18] As other parents had done before them, they wanted to leave a record of their children's arrest and prevent the government from claiming ignorance if the couple disappeared. Unlike many other parents, they were fortunate, because their son and daughter were ultimately neither tortured nor disappeared.

Divinsky and Miler had been detained after publishing a censored children's book, entitled *Cinco Dedos*, which contained a popular fable about how the weak were made strong through unity. Censorship laws had become stricter in the 1960s, as the rhetoric of the Cold War intensified. The Broadcasting Act (adopted in 1957 and regulated in 1965) stipulated a number of limitations on freedom of speech (protecting national symbols and institutions and banning erotic material and anything that portrayed the triumph of evil over good), and in 1961 a movie rating system was introduced. During the Onganía dictatorship, two laws were passed that further restricted freedom of expression: the National Defense Act in 1966, and the Defense against Communism Act (Law 17,401) in 1967, which were said to protect "vital national interests" that were supposedly under threat and whose defense justified any means. These regulations created a censorship system characterized by vagueness and the existence of multiple control bodies. The state emerged as the judge of all cultural expression, subordinating it to certain moral values and ways of life that were presented as essential, invariable, and defining of the nation. In contrast to the censorship system in Francoist Spain, books were censored after they were published, thus entailing a greater economic risk. This encouraged self-censorship.[19]

Founded in 1967 by Divinsky and Miler, Ediciones de la Flor had an open, original, and provocative style from the start. The directors were not political activists but considered themselves "generically progressive" and were willing to challenge the status quo.[20] The name had been suggested by its future press agent, Pirí Lugones—Jorge Álvarez's brilliant cultural agent who would later join the Montoneros guerrilla group. She thought the publishing duo wanted *una flor de editorial*, literally "a flower of a publishing house," which in Argentina is equivalent to saying "a tremendous publishing house." The publisher also later associated its name with the "flower power" culture. It gradually built an eclectic catalog, including work by Argentine writers such as Leopoldo Marechal, León Rozitchner, Bernardo Verbitsky, and David Viñas, and foreign authors such as Vinicius de Moraes, Ezra Pound, and Boris Vian. To celebrate its second anniversary and its thirtieth title, Pirí organized an event at the zoo, sending out invitations that read, "Don't let the animals outnumber us."[21]

By 1970, the press was pretty much established. As had been the case with Lumen in Spain and Nueva Imagen in Mexico, the qualitative leap, according to Divinsky, came with *Mafalda*, which they started publishing as of its sixth volume.[22] The comic strip provided a profit margin that allowed them to significantly expand the number of titles they published. Their countercultural approach was in line with the cultural and political radicalization of that period. A typical advertising flyer would invite readers to "Snatch a book today," echoing a common practice among students, to whom they offered works such as *Sur Marcuse* by Jean-Michel Palmier, or *Grapefruit* by Yoko Ono (with an introduction by John Lennon). In 1973, they launched a series of activist books, including *Operación masacre* by Rodolfo Walsh, and tempted potential readers with scripts from a movie censored by the military. They also presented a series they dubbed "books for pleasure and for thinking," an expression that served as an apt slogan for the press.[23]

This approach made Ediciones de la Flor a perfect target for censorship. By 1973, new regulations allowed government bodies to intercept private mail, and in 1974 the Anti-Subversive Act (Law 20,840) stipulated a jail sentence for "anyone who by any means advocates disruption of the institutional order" and established that "editors, publishers, and radio or television directors who spread such messages shall be sentenced to two to five years in jail."[24] Censorship was applied directly and openly, but it also operated obliquely through Catholic and far-right organizations, most notably the League of Mothers (Liga de Madres) and the League of Family Men (Liga de Padres de Familia).[25] In 1974, a committee formed by the Argentine Book Chamber (Cámara Argentina del Libro), among others, called for an end to censorship and denounced that it affected more than 500 books by Argentine and foreign authors and 237 publishing companies from the country and abroad.[26] Editorial de la Flor suffered several attacks, with accusations against popular novels, and had to defend itself in court, winning a number of trials.[27]

Following the 1976 coup, the military government deployed new controls and regulations in its battle against the cultural enemy, targeting artistic and literary products and the media. In March, Law 21,272 was passed, stipulating the death penalty for anyone who used violence against the repressive forces and up to ten years in prison for anyone who offended their "dignity." The censorship apparatus involved numerous offices, advisers, and resources in a strategy organized by the intelligence services in coordination with various state bodies and civil society. These measures took on a new meaning against the backdrop of the systematic practice of disappearance. However, many who were targeted by repression were unaware of the existence of such a systematic plan to disappear dissidents.

The initial failure to realize the radically new nature of the regime instituted by the coup explains why, at first, many confronted it as they had done with previous institutional breakdowns, which were not rare in Argentina. Editorial de la Flor tried to continue with the same strategy it had used thus far to avoid censorship. The theme of the Frankfurt Book Fair held in October 1976 was Latin America, and Divinsky attended the event as he had done in previous years. There he saw the renowned Argentine writer Osvaldo Bayer, who tried to convince him not to return to Argentina because he feared for his safety. Bayer told Divinsky that he had decided to leave when an officer from the intelligence service (Secretaría de Inteligencia del Estado, or SIDE) who owed him a favor contacted him to warn him to leave the country within forty-eight hours because the police would be coming after him and many like him, and as an example of the "advancing subversion" he had waved a book published by Ediciones de la Flor at him. The book was the *Cinco Dedos* fable. It had been written by a West Berlin group and published in the children's book collection Little Flower Books (Libros de la florcita), directed by Amelia Hannois. It told the story of the fingers of a green hand (an allusion to the military) chasing the fingers of a red hand (the left) and how the red fingers came together in a raised fist to beat the green fingers. In January 1977, the publishing house included the book, along with others by the Argentine poet and short-story writer Silvina Ocampo, the Brazilian author Clarice Lispector, and the Paraguayan novelist Augusto Roa Bastos, in an ad in the newspaper *La Opinión*, urging parents to "Make the Magi less magical and truly Wise Men this year," in reference to the traditional holiday celebration in which children received gifts.[28]

A month later, on February 8, 1977, a government decree banned the children's book, claiming it "trained children for subversive activities." Divinsky recalls that he did what he had done in similar cases in the past: he filed a complaint against the decree. In the complaint, addressed to de facto president General Jorge Rafael Videla, he argued that the moral of the story was that there is "strength in unity" and that it encouraged children to "overcome senseless discord."[29] On February 16, the police raided the publishing house's offices and arrested the owners. According to Divinsky, the ban had been requested by a Neuquén colonel whose wife had purchased the book for their children and was outraged that the red hand defeated the green hand, as green was the color of military fatigues. Despite being triggered by a chance incident, Divinsky realized then that the measure was a sign that censorship and repression had changed for the worse. The anecdote reveals that censorship operated not only through the many agents of censorship, aided by official and unofficial contacts and informants, but also through the actions of the armed forces. Around the same time, the army's high command issued a special report calling for the establishment of an integrated system to combat the allegedly subversive actions of the media. Moreover, numerous works were banned and the heads of several major publishing houses, including Eudeba, Centro Editor de América Latina, Siglo XXI, Granica, Guadalupe (which published a Latin American Bible), and Fausto, received threats or were charged by the police. Municipal libraries were purged and texts were pulled from school curricula.[30]

Divinsky and Miler's arrest was reported in the press. The newspapers *La Prensa* and *La Nación* reproduced letters from Claude Gallimard and other French publishers asking for their release and an open letter by a group of Argentine writers asking the National Writers Association (Sociedad Argentina de Escritores) to intervene on their behalf.[31] The publishing house was well known and respected and an international solidarity campaign was quickly launched, organized by the journalist Rogelio García Lupo. A month after the arrest, when the publishers' parents appealed to Videla, they attached the letters they had received from foreign supporters. Peter Weidhaas, director of the Frankfurt Book Fair, played a decisive role in their release. He sent the publishers an official invitation to the upcoming edition of the fair and plane tickets so they could travel.[32] The combination of national and international appeals was successful and the publishers were able to leave the country unharmed.

While in prison and as he was being moved from one holding cell to another, Daniel Divinsky had a peculiar experience. When he was being led to a physical examination, naked and with his head down by order of the guards, he heard someone behind him saying, "There he is! The guy who does Mafalda." He was left standing in a hallway and while he was waiting to be examined a prison guard came up to him and said, "After we finish up here, can you draw a little Mafalda for the boys?"[33] They had obviously mistaken *Mafalda*'s publisher for its creator, but the point is that a member of the very same forces that had used the cartoon as part of their revenge and to threaten opponents did not hesitate to express his admiration for a prisoner's work and to use his power over him to extort a drawing. The comic strip was so popular that its audience had gone far beyond the ideological niche that had originally embraced it. The comic strip's polysemy, which was based on diverse characters with a range of often opposing views, made it possible for many different readers to identify with it, and that resulted in such paradoxes.

This was not the only paradox. Editorial de la Flor continued operating during the dictatorship. In fact, according to Divinsky, "it survived thanks to Quino and [Roberto] Fontanarrosa, who remained faithful to it, and to Elisa Miler, who took over its operations." The *Mafalda* books, a symbol of anti-authoritarianism, were not censored in Argentina. But, as we will see, the film adaption that came out in 1981 did not escape censorship completely.[34]

Before delving further into the issue of censorship, what do we know of *Mafalda*'s circulation in Argentina during those years? In December 1973, the newspaper *Río Negro* had stopped carrying it, and in February 1974 *Córdoba* had followed suit.[35] The books continued to sell—according to Daniel Divinsky, they were available throughout the dictatorship—but there is no information as to whether any new editions came out or if sales were limited to the tens of thousands of books printed prior to the coup. Neither are there any figures for the volume of sales. In 1980, Juan Sasturain attested to the ongoing popularity of the comic strip, which could be found in newsstands around the country and was enjoyed by a young readership. The 1982 report by the National Copyright Bureau includes a new *Mafalda* edition.[36] There is no doubt that *Mafalda* was taken up by younger generations who read from different perspectives. According to the journalist Leila Guerriero, during the dictatorship the comic was "a very inconvenient Trojan horse" because it was "filled with political allusions that remained relevant for a long time." She notes that the kids who were reading it then could be moved by their natural curiosity to ask their parents about human rights, Fidel Castro, or the right of the people to determine their fate, all issues touched on by *Mafalda*. And that could be "dangerous." In the words of Guerriero, raising those questions "for those of us who grew up during the last government of Perón and the 1976 military dictatorship, who went to school when we couldn't even wear our hair down and had to bury banned books in our backyards, who lived through the euphoria of the 1978 World Cup while our parents had friends whose name couldn't be said out loud, [those questions] helped us know who they were, and who we were, and what they were doing to us."[37]

Drawing on my interviews, I have attempted to reconstruct the situations in which *Mafalda* was read and discovered by new audiences during the dictatorship. For many readers of the comic, the possibility of returning to the books meant keeping alive—and even reliving—the cultural, political, and affective experiences they had had in the still-recent past. For example, Manuel Díaz, a sociology student in the early 1970s, remembers how he kept the *Mafalda* books close by, on his night table and bookshelves, and would often pick them up to reread them. He liked it when friends came over and found them as they rummaged through his books, because it gave him the opportunity of revisiting the characters and the strips with them. And when they did that, they were transported back to moments they had shared in places that had been obliterated by repression, and with other friends whose fate they did not know.[38] It was the reality of life under the dictatorship that gave new meaning to the experience of reading *Mafalda* and contributed to its ongoing relevance. Daniel Rey Piuma, a seventeen-year-old Uruguayan who had been an active member of the Revolutionary Student Front (Frente Estudiantil Revolucionario, or FER) in 1973 and had infiltrated the Uruguayan navy's secret service, found a different meaning in the comic. Inspired by one of the characters, he chose "Felipe" as his alias. He did it because "Felipe is the most innocent of them all. He's a believer, he believes in the goodness of men." The explanation makes sense in view of Rey Piuma's undercover work, as he secretly photographed political activists who were tortured in the detention centers of the Uruguayan navy and the bodies of Argentine disappeared persons thrown into the sea that washed up on Uruguay's shores. He was able to smuggle hundreds of negatives out of the country, sewn into the seams of his clothes, which he later handed over to the Inter-American Court of Human Rights as evidence.[39]

The cartoon could also acquire affective meaning for someone who had never read the strip and was still too young to understand it, as was the case with M. V., a Uruguayan girl who was only four years old when her father, an undergraduate student of mathematics, was arrested for being a member of the Communist Party. While in prison, he wrote her a letter trying to explain why he was there, and in the letter he pasted a panel from the comic strip in which Mafalda kisses her father while he is about to shave, and he leaves the spot where she kisses him unshaven, not wanting to "erase" the kiss.

There were also less intense connections to the comic strip. María Rinifort, whose parents were psychoanalysts and lived in the upscale neighborhood of Belgrano, discovered *Mafalda* when she was seven, in 1975, at the home of a friend of the family during visits when the grown-ups were deep in conversation and she slipped away to the room of the kids of the house, who were older and had books she had never seen. She would read half a book at a time, not understanding the political references but entertained by the stories. Later, when that family had to leave the country, her parents started buying the comic strip for her. Reading *Mafalda* made her feel different from her classmates, whose reading choices went no further than romance comic books in the style of *Young Love*.[40] The comic thus had strong meaning even for those who did not have a connection to it through their experiences of political activism.

In many cases, new readers "inherited" *Mafalda* from their elders, not only their parents but their older siblings. Mario Amado—who currently sells books and magazines—remembers that his "mother was a typical middle-class woman. She wasn't concerned with social issues. . . . But my sister showed me one of the little books from Ediciones de la Flor, and they opened up a whole new world for me."[41] In other cases, it was the parents who introduced their kids to the comic strip. As Leila Guerriero recalls, many responded willingly to the questions their children raised after reading *Mafalda*. They saw it as an opportunity to tell them about the country they had lost and that their children had not known. There were also parents who reacted negatively because they thought that through silence or censorship they were protecting their kids. Miguel Rep, currently a well-known cartoonist, recalls that he had discovered *Mafalda* when he was in grade school in the early 1970s. Some years later his father made him take down the "ideology-denting stick" poster he had put up in the room where he drew. His father thought the poster could be incriminating because it was seen by the police as a political pamphlet. That did not stop Rep from reading the comic; on the contrary, *Mafalda* was a constant presence in his life throughout the years. He and his friends would get hold of "those marvelous hard-bound little books, with their matte-laminated covers, published by Ediciones de la Flor. We loved everything about them: the author's dedications, the epigraphs ('"*I swear I didn't die*," Paul McCartney!'), the imprints. . . . We read and reread them. We loved examining every little detail. The memories! Like that long wait in Almagro, going up to that apartment that was just like the one Libertad and her parents lived in; the *Mafalda 5* with the light-blue cover, how it transported us!"[42] His words reveal the intimate relationship—both affective, aesthetic, and social—between the reader and the comic strip and its author.

Mafalda was a material object in which aesthetic and political marks of the 1960s and '70s lived on explicitly, openly, and directly, marks that were moreover linked to personal and collective moments that had great significance for many young people and adults. In that sense, *Mafalda* was part of the intergenerational process of preserving and conveying a sensitivity that permeated and cut across the many different—and sometimes opposing—approaches to reading it. But the comic also took on new meanings that were not connected with past experiences. For the military regime, the label "subversive" was not restricted to activists or militants who, with or without arms, opposed the political establishment in organized groups. It also included anyone who was in any way in favor of social change and who posed a threat to the intangible "national essence." According to the military rhetoric, the components of that essence were the Catholic Church, the family, and the traditions of the "Nation," conceived as a homogeneous and immutable entity.[43] Once in power, the armed forces set their sights fully on culture, which they saw as a major battlefield. The comic strip, then, did not just evoke the past as memory, it also represented a specific cultural configuration that countered the dictatorial model and could be found, purchased, and read by anyone in the country.

Mafalda fell through the gaps left by censorship and repression, which allowed for cultural products that blatantly subverted the status quo to continue to circulate. We cannot know for certain why it was able to do so. But it was perhaps due to the very inconsistencies of the censorship system, which made it possible for works (like *Mafalda*) that reproduced content that had run uncensored in the press some time earlier to fly under the authorities' censorship radar. It could also be argued that the enormous popularity of the comic made it easier for censors to tolerate, or that the scarce attention it had in the press between 1976 and 1980 (when the movie version came out) allowed it to circulate unnoticed in book format. The fact that it received limited press coverage may suggest that the media was aware of how disruptive *Mafalda* was. Whereas before the March 1976 coup *Mafalda* and Quino were often featured in newspapers and magazines with long articles that celebrated both comic and artist, during the dictatorship there was hardly any mention of either. In Quino's case, his international acclaim meant that, if necessary, the media could justify to the authorities the few news items they featured on him—for example, the newspaper *La Nación*'s brief report in 1977 of the first prize awarded to the cartoonist in the Twenty-Third International Humor Salon in Bordighera, Italy.[44]

As noted earlier, an essential element of the armed forces' systematic and widespread practice of eliminating opponents through kidnapping, torture, murder, and disappearance was its clandestine nature—it left no trace of its repressive actions. This created a protective shield for the perpetrators and exacerbated the isolation and fear of those who thought they could be targeted.

According to the investigation conducted by the National Commission on the Disappearance of Persons after democracy was restored, 77 percent of all reported disappearances occurred between the day of the coup, March 24, 1976, and the end of 1977.[45] By 1978, the leaderships of the Montoneros and ERP guerrilla groups had been decimated, and the leaders who had managed to survive were in exile. After achieving this victory, the armed forces set out to restructure society with a strategy based on social discipline and the logic of the market and efficiency, which in the long term would lead to a transition toward an elected government with the participation of the armed forces. With that aim, the military commanders implemented an economic program designed by the minister of the economy, José A. Martínez de Hoz, which favored capital and foreign investment and attempted to control inflation. Major sectors of society supported the military government, and that support peaked in 1978, when Argentina hosted that year's FIFA World Cup and the regime exploited nationalist sentiment, which was expressed through pro-government slogans generated by the media. The widespread support garnered that year, together with the Malvinas/Falklands War, created a scenario that brought the regime closer to fascism. However, it failed to channel that support to sustain its long-term project, which caved under the weight of internal disputes in the military high command, criticism of its economic interventions, and its increasingly discredited image in the international community.[46]

By 1980, the symptoms of that failure were more or less evident. The regime's economic policies had had notably destructive effects on the population, deteriorating the living conditions of workers, civil servants, and agricultural producers. In 1979, after hearing accounts from relatives of the disappeared and inspecting facilities that were reported to be clandestine detention centers, the Inter-American Commission on Human Rights of the Organization of American States (OAS) accused the military dictatorship of human rights abuses. Some months later, a letter signed by 6,700 people was published as a paid ad in a newspaper demanding the repeal of the law that established presumption of death for disappeared persons. At the same time, media controls were relaxed. Miguel Paulino Tato, one of the most notorious censors, was removed from his position as head of the Film Rating Body (Ente de Calificación Cinematográfica); the comedian Tato Bores, who specialized in political humor and had been previously banned, returned to television screens; and some exiled artists were allowed to return to the country. New self-published magazines with small print runs started to shake the media out of its prevailing stupor, offering readers styles and content that to a greater or lesser extent countered official productions.[47]

In that context, humor was an especially ductile instrument for mobilizing public opinion against authoritarianism. Its liminal, open, and polysemic nature made it an ideal means for creating critical spaces, as did its "defensive function," which, according to Freud, helped individuals fend off suffering.[48] In 1980, the magazine *Hum®*, which had begun its run two years earlier, launched a powerful opposition to the dictatorship and channeled a cultural and political alternative. As Mara Burkart has explained, the magazine operated within the shifting lines that separated the official from the "other," allowing it to sidestep censorship and challenge it. That is, *Hum®* used to its advantage the interstices left by the "dominant culture" and did so precisely to criticize it. In that way, it brought back a "social polyphony," worked to erode the legitimacy of the armed forces, and tried to hinder the regime's cultural and political projects. It spotted the cracks in government censorship and controls that had enabled the circulation of *Mafalda* and used them to express novel subjectivities and, in the medium term, question the "domestication of state terrorism," in the words of Burkart.[49]

It was in that context that in March 1980 Quino returned to Argentine newspapers as a contributor for *Clarín*. After his move to Milan in 1976, some magazines in Argentina had continued to feature material by the cartoonist, although rejecting some of his work from time to time due to its content, and while he had visited the country occasionally during the dictatorship, the media largely ignored him. This changed when *Clarín*—the newspaper that years earlier had "nationalized" its humor when it began featuring Argentine cartoonists in its comic section—gave Quino and his stories a whole page in its Sunday supplement. Quino recalls the mixed feelings he had about the cartoon at this time and how upset he was when he realized how similar Mafalda was to Nancy (which he saw as a joke played on him by his subconscious).[50] Over the following months, people started talking about Quino and *Mafalda* again. That year, *La buena mesa*, a collection of restaurant-centered cartoons by Quino, was reviewed in the press, and the following year *Mafalda* prompted one of the period's first intellectual controversies in cultural media.[51] In September 1981, when a film version of *Mafalda* produced by Daniel Mallo was set to premiere and Quino had been announced as the winner of the Quadragano D'Oro prize awarded in the Homo Ridens Graffiti contest in Italy, the humor magazine *Superhumor* devoted a whole section to the comic strip artist's most famous cartoon.[52] Mafalda came to life again on the pages of a popular publication. And she did so with a bang, as she was reintroduced to readers as a "miniskirted chick with grand ideas."[53] One of the contributors, the critic Juan Sasturain, himself a cartoonist, gave her a similar welcome in an article entitled "Little Mafalda Turns 17 and She's Smoking Hot," an adjective that also alluded to the politically charged moment. The magazine thus inaugurated a trend that imagined Mafalda as an adult and which would accompany the comic strip in the coming years as its meanings were brought up to date.

Sasturain's article reveals how his contemporaries processed historical time, with an awareness of political breaking points but without denying the continuity between past and present. The piece began by citing a 1972 interview with Quino published in *La Opinión*, which had been conducted by the Argentine writer Osvaldo Soriano, who had been censored by the dictatorship and was living in exile. It also brought back the debate that had surrounded the comic in the 1970s, namely, whether it was politically committed. That connection with the past, however, was offset by a more distanced perspective achieved in three ways. The first had to do with the passage of time itself. Sasturain highlighted the fact that almost a decade had gone by since Quino had stopped creating new *Mafalda* strips, and how that decision had been, in the cartoonist's own words, "a liberating act," because the character had taken on a life of its own and had become a source of tension. According to Sasturain, as the comic was used more and more as a vehicle to voice a range of opinions, it had moved increasingly away from its creator. The second was the new vantage point afforded by time. Sasturain saw the comic strip from a different historical moment that allowed him to perceive how anachronistic it had become in the 1970s. Mafalda, he said, had been born at a time in which there was a margin for hope, because "criticism and dissent were still possible," and despite the pain and the contradictions, "the bloodshed was yet to come." After that, "reality became unmanageable" and "Quino felt he could no longer—he couldn't, it wasn't that they wouldn't let him—deal with the noise coming in from the street."[54] The third way distance was achieved was through an attempt to balance critical studies. Sasturain distinguished local analyses from international ones. The Argentine studies, he said, focused on examining the comic's ideological aspects, and with that approach they discussed how critical *Mafalda* was. In contrast, foreign readings, such as those by Umberto Eco and David William Foster, took the comic strip's critical stance at face value, and from there they sought to understand its significance. Eco discovered Latin America and Foster recognized in *Mafalda* "a body of cultural texts well worth preserving."[55]

Sasturain analyzed the covers of the ten *Mafalda* books and found a cycle that began with a concerned Mafalda nursing a fevered and bandaged globe and ended, in the last installment, with the main character smiling broadly next to a healthy globe populated by demonstrators (figures 4.2 and 4.3). In his view, the covers reflected—more than the strips themselves—Quino's effort to

FIGURES 4.2 AND 4.3 Covers of Quino, *Mafalda 1* and *Mafalda 10*. © Joaquín Salvador Lavado (Quino).

"preserve an image of universalist humanism," even in the face of a reality that moved in the opposite direction. They also showed the cartoonist's willingness to cater to a readership predisposed to consume such messages in what were special circumstances.[56]

According to Sasturain, previous studies had been wrong because they had viewed the comic strip as merely an expression of a liberal middle class at a given point in time. In doing so they had failed to understand *Mafalda*'s lasting relevance, which survived even as the social sector it had represented appeared to be exhausted. What these studies had not realized, in his opinion, was that the cartoon was a "uniquely perfect work" that would see a resurgence in popularity in the more liberal years to come.[57] Oscar Steimberg, one of the authors criticized by Sasturain, responded shortly after in the pages of *Superhumor* that his and other previous studies were not limited to a purely ideological analysis and that understanding such a work entailed not only looking at how it was presented, rather one also had to "consider its subject matter, its drawings, its readers, and its political and social context." He noted that the lasting relevance of the comic strip was explained by the traits of its "harsh" but "brave" characters, and he closed his response by challenging Sasturain: "Could there be anyone more interested in seeing the world populated by demonstrators and covered in flags than the members of that middle class that, tragically, had started to dwindle as their character began to fade?"[58]

Even with their differences, the two critics agreed on *Mafalda*'s relevance and its significance in the context of the dictatorship. That relevance was further highlighted in the special section of *Superhumor* devoted to Quino with a sidebar showing the number of readers the comic strip had in Argentina and around the world. According to Marcelo Ravoni, by 1973 two and a half million books, in six different languages, had been sold outside the country. While precise figures for Argentina were not available, it was estimated that it had sold in the millions. This matched the view of the two critics, who spoke of "legions of readers," and coincided with the data from Ediciones de la Flor, which reported that every year it put on the market 10,000 new issues for each of the ten volumes, that is, an annual total of 100,000. With such estimates, the expectations surrounding the release of the film adaptation of *Mafalda* were not surprising.[59]

FROM AUTHORITARIAN CONSENSUS TO THE RETURN OF DEMOCRACY

On December 1, 1981, the entertainment sections of all the leading newspapers in Argentina announced the premiere of the *Mafalda* movie (*Mafalda, la película*). The film was produced by Daniel Mallo, based on television episodes broadcast in 1973, also produced by him. (See figure 4.4.) It was directed by

Carlos Márquez and the animation was done by Catú (Jorge Martín). The initial production was thus almost a decade old. According to Quino, his involvement had been limited to listening to the voices his characters would have, a process that took six months. None of the voices had satisfied him.

FIGURE 4.4 Advertisement for the *Mafalda* movie featured in the newspaper *La Nación* (Buenos Aires), December 3, 1981, 3. © Joaquín Salvador Lavado (Quino).

The media promoted the movie with images of the characters and highlighted its suitability for audiences of all ages. This was not surprising, given that the film softened the more controversial aspects of the comic strip. Voiced by the actress Susana Klein, who had recorded the episodes in 1973, the character of Mafalda sounded high-pitched, sickly sweet, and artificial. It clashed with the character's personality. The voice erased all traces of the mature little girl who cursed and had become an unsettling "little monster."

In the film's opening scene, a sweetened Mafalda floats among multicolored flowers and butterflies, celebrating spring. Her family and friends are then introduced, with the exception of Guille and Libertad, who were not included in the film because their characters expressed the cultural and political radicalization of the 1960s. The production had worked with the earliest version of the comic strip. These introductions were followed by a selection of colored strips that were animated and shown in a disconnected sequence of scenes with no structuring narrative. The animation merely put the strips in motion and made the image the accessory of the text. It broke the rhythm set by the succession of frames in the original printed version, to the point of ruining the humorous effects.

A catchy soundtrack helped erase the cartoon's edgier aspects. All that remained of the social commentary were a few mild references to the "poor" in

Susanita's stigmatizing view as she clashed with Mafalda. Gone were the digs at repression, as well as the constant cross-referencing between the public and the private, a prominent feature of the comic strip that undermined the rigid division between the two spheres. The film's peace-and-love version of *Mafalda* was reinforced by the image chosen for the film's ending, which showed the gang gathered around a Christmas tree singing carols, similarly to the scene in *A Charlie Brown Christmas*, although there is no evidence that the producers were aware of that film.

The elimination of *Mafalda*'s "subversive" connotations was in line, first, with the escalating repression of the 1970s and, later, the post-coup context. The script had in fact been submitted for approval to the National Film Bureau in 1978, which considered the character of Mafalda "critical and not very constructive," but nonetheless raised no "major objections" to the script. The only exception was a bit in which Susanita spoke badly of charity organizations that were active in censorship committees. According to Susanita, who planned to join them when she grew up, these organizations held benefit banquets that served sumptuous dishes to raise funds to buy rice and beans "and all that junk" the poor eat. It is surprising that the censors objected to these lines but were not bothered by the references to Mao (including the bit where Mafalda says that if the 700 million people in China kicked together at once they would impact the world), or by Mafalda imitating a guerrilla in the jungle to scare her father into buying her a television set, or by Felipe when he told Mafalda his father must be a socialist because while he was teaching him the game of chess he explained that pawns (in Spanish *peones*, the word for rural laborers) always went before the king or queen. In the end, the producers of the movie ignored these objections and kept Susanita's reference to charity organizations. But upon watching the movie, a second censorship operation can be observed. The origin of this censorship is unknown, but in the strip where Mafalda resorts to guerrilla tactics the word *guerrilla* is silenced, and the whole chess scene with Felipe's socialist remark has been eliminated.[60]

It is interesting to compare the response in Argentina with the alarm the comic strip had raised in Chile, which was under military rule since the September 11, 1973 coup. In July 1975, some Chilean press outlets had criticized the state channel's decision to broadcast *Mafalda* instead of *The Pink Panther* during its prime time slot, after the news. They argued that the comic was an "exponent of Marxist intellectualism." Colonel Héctor Orozco, the government representative to the channel and Augusto Pinochet's communications adviser, explained that he knew the comic strip had left-wing leanings but there was "nothing to fear, as all the episodes aired were especially selected by a team from the military psychology division."[61] Thus, the Chilean dictatorship's official television network absurdly enough included the cartoon in its programming, despite the fact that its directors considered it had a communist message and, therefore, censored it.

In sum, the dictatorship did not stop the sale of the *Mafalda* books, but it did object to and act on some scenes in the movie, which itself presented a sugarcoated version of the comic strip, whose popularity was difficult to ignore. In any case, *Mafalda*'s continued circulation gives us insight into the cultural dynamics under the dictatorship and the important role played by such gaps during those years, revealing that power can never be absolute when it comes to culture, as there are always black holes created by the inefficiencies and contradictions of the regime, as well as individuals who know how to take advantage of those pockets of freedom, inhabiting and appropriating them as spaces for their own purposes.

Moreover, and despite the film's watered-down tone and the cuts, the screening became an opportunity for a political reading that questioned the dictatorship. Among those who seized this opportunity was, again, Sasturain. In the pages of *Clarín*, he commented on the absence of Libertad and Guille and, in remembering them, he brought to mind the radicalized readers of the early 1970s: "This movie comes out when the party is over, and when, of the legions of guests, many are gone and others are hard to find, and when we can barely remember what was being celebrated." The allusion to the decimation the country had seen was made explicit when he explained that production for the movie had begun in 1972, before Perón's last presidency and before the darkest period began, and that it was premiering almost a decade later, in 1981, when "the dictatorship is gasping for air, having reached the bottom of the pit, if it indeed has a bottom . . ." The dark image conveyed by his words and the ellipses took on an undeniably political meaning, which Sasturain reinforced when he noted that Mafalda's maturity was absent from the movie and for that reason it would disappoint the numerous readers that the comic strip had attracted in the early 1970s. The movie tricked them.[62] His review thus used the movie to criticize the dictatorship and build a *we*—formed by the readers of 1972—capable of coming together again to reject that trick.

In contrast, all other reviews in mainstream media did not touch directly on the political, making only implicit allusions, in line with their usual bland approach. *La Prensa* attributed Libertad's absence to an effort "to preserve consistency and relevance," a euphemism for the reinterpretations of the character during the dictatorship. Another review in *Clarín* provided a view that acknowledged the generation of the 1960s and its failures, including university studies that were frustrated and "political cycles [that were] cut short," in what was perhaps an allusion to the dictatorship.[63]

The view was situated somewhere between the realization of the defeat of the 1960s generation, the efforts to revive its spirit, and the acknowledgment of its value in terms of its cultural contributions and "concerns," which, in this case, were expressed by *Mafalda*. The reviews were more straightforward in their evaluation of the movie's production. They were unanimous in their praise of Quino and *Mafalda*'s "caustic humor" but noted the film's limitations and faults: the animation, the voices, the lack of boldness. *Mafalda*'s "cruel humor" had been lost, they said.[64] The negative reviews did not stop the public from flocking to movie theaters to reconnect with the cartoon. The film was shown simultaneously in the city of Buenos Aires and in more than thirty cities around the country. In the capital, the movie was in theaters for more than a month. No data is available for the first two weeks, but we know that in its third week it was the fourth most-watched movie (along with *Lady and the Tramp*), with 4,600 moviegoers.[65]

In 1981, then, Quino and *Mafalda* were again making headlines in Argentina. That year, the cartoonist, whose production had been published in several languages (including Japanese, Greek, Romanian, and Finnish), was awarded the Grand Prix de l'Humour Noir in France, and with a new book out (*Ni arte ni parte*) he was one of the most renowned Argentine authors in his field.[66] The movie was an excuse to celebrate him, and it also gave the comic strip new political meaning, as it once again prompted discussions and reflections in Argentine society.

While *Mafalda* was still showing in theaters, Lieutenant General Leopoldo Galtieri became de facto president by decision of the army's commanders. The previous dictator, General Roberto Viola, had further weakened the already declining regime. The measures adopted in previous months in an effort to curb inflation and stop capital flight had only made the economic crisis worse and drawn criticism from business associations—a first for the dictatorship. Viola's government had also failed in its political aims, as its call for a dialogue to secure continuity for military rule met with little enthusiasm from politicians and upset his military peers. In that context, the leading political parties—including the Radical Civic Union (Unión Cívica Radical) and the *Justicialista* Party (the largest component of the Peronist movement)—joined together in a multiparty group to demand elections and a transition to democratic rule. This group said nothing, however, about repression and the disappeared. Meanwhile, the country's human rights organizations were growing stronger and staging increasingly larger demonstrations.[67]

On February 1982, *Río Negro*, the most important newspaper in Patagonia, began publishing a daily *Mafalda* strip.[68] In the 1960s, the company that owned the newspaper had spoken out against violence on both the right and the left, and in 1976 it had reported on the disappearances, along with the *Buenos Aires Herald*.[69] In 1982, Julio Rajneri—the newspaper's director since 1967 and a supporter of the future democratic president Raúl Alfonsín—secured the rights to publish the comic strip and Quino's humor page. Carlos Torrengo, one of the paper's journalists at the time, recalls that "Mafalda matched the newspaper's ideology: freedom, development, social mobility, and justice."[70] This retrospective assessment is accurate. The addition of *Mafalda* was in line with the demands for democracy that were gaining ground among certain sectors of public opinion in a society that also could identify with the economic and social issues the comic touched on.[71]

In 1982, the effects of the economic crisis could be felt in the rising cost of living and a resurgence in labor activity. In March 1982, the most critical sectors of the General Labor Confederation (Confederación General del Trabajo, or CGT), under the leadership of Lorenzo Miguel and Saúl Ubaldini, staged a demonstration in the capital's Plaza de Mayo. The military regime cracked down on protesters, but it also sought to distract from economic issues and stem further unrest by stoking nationalist sentiment. Acting on the country's sovereignty claims over the Malvinas/Falkland Islands in the South Atlantic Ocean, on April 2, it invaded the islands and declared war on the United Kingdom. This move succeeded in gaining support for the regime from a range of social and political actors, as well as much of society, which backed the war effort enthusiastically. The British prime minister, Margaret Thatcher, however, launched a strong offensive to recover the islands. Moreover, the military junta had miscalculated the diplomatic response it had counted on, in particular, from the United States, which early on in the conflict sided with the United Kingdom, providing material support for its operations. Neither the lack of international support nor Argentina's inferior military power convinced the regime to abandon its sovereignty claims. After British troops disembarked on the islands and the fighting intensified, it was soon evident that the British had the advantage and the Argentine military was improvising. Within three months Argentina had surrendered.[72] Faced with a crushing defeat and an outraged populace that felt cheated by false media reports and the government's triumphalist rhetoric, Galtieri was forced to resign.

But few had been against the initial decision to go to war. Raúl Alfonsín was one of those few, along with the newspaper *Río Negro*. Alfonsín's opposition to the war turned him into a persuasive candidate to lead the transition to democracy and face the problems posed by a declining military government, a society that was waking up to the horrors of repression, and a country in crisis. The latest economic measures adopted by the dictatorship (absorption of corporate debts by the state, oil concessions, deficit increases) had aggravated a deep-rooted crisis and left Argentine society greatly impoverished. In October 1983, Alfonsín won the presidential elections after a campaign in which he championed democracy, promising to bring the perpetrators of state terrorism to trial, return the country to the rule of law, and reactivate the economy. On December 10, the day of his inauguration, the country celebrated the restoration of democracy, and a brief period of euphoric confidence followed, as hopes were pinned on the new democratic government's ability to bring much-needed change.[73]

However, it was a shaky optimism, tempered by awareness of the dictatorship's horrors. In the ideological climate that emerged, *Mafalda* found new relevance. The discussions prompted by the comic strip in the past took a back seat as the focus shifted to human rights. The figure of the political militant was overshadowed by state terror and the void left by the disappeared. A large part of public opinion—of which the middle class was central but not exclusive—embraced the celebration of democracy, the defense of human rights, and political mobilization. As the comic strip echoed these views, its popularity spread across society, like it had two decades earlier, but this time it did so in an unprecedented way. Three elements combined to seal this success: Quino's reflections on *Mafalda*, new readings of the strip during this period, and the novel ways and formats in which it circulated.

RIDING HIGH: A POLITICAL COMMITMENT TO DEMOCRACY

"Was the humor produced during the dictatorship effective?" "Was it fearful? Did it censor itself?" "Can critical humor weaken democracy?" In 1984, the Fifth Argentine Humor and Comics Biennial put these questions to Quino and all the other cartoonists who were invited to contribute to its catalog. In his answer, Quino acknowledged that the magazine *Hum®* had played a role in the efforts to end the dictatorship, but he did not believe that humor was capable of building "democratic awareness" on its own. He thought that "together with theater, cinema, literature, and—why not?—politics, it can contribute to the struggle against repression and obscurantism." Asked about the changes that the recent elections would bring, he confessed, "I'm not yet used to the idea of a freedom that we can't spoil." He admitted that he was keenly aware of his own responsibility, but he believed "an intelligent people should not allow critical humor, or anyone, to weaken a democracy that has been gained at such a high cost in blood and suffering."[74]

Quino went on to acknowledge his own responsibility in the role that humor had played in creating the pro-coup climate that enabled General Onganía's rise to power in 1966: "Our ignorance of how the democratic game was played and the very instability of democracy [in Argentina] turned us unwittingly into one of the best allies of the enemy."[75] For that reason he became actively committed to defending democracy, and that commitment put his most popular character on the first line of defense. "Mafalda: A Plea for Peace and Freedom" was how a headline in early 1984 described her. The title headed a full-page piece on the cartoon featured in the newspaper *Tiempo Argentino*, whose editor in chief, Raúl Burzaco, had been César Civita's right-hand man at *Siete Días*. Presented as a mock interview with Mafalda, the anonymous journalist made the character speak for herself, with imagined answers based on situations or expressions drawn directly from the comic strip. According to the pretend interviewer, Mafalda was "brilliant in her responses, cheerful, realistic; she has all the ingredients necessary to be apolitical, a pacifist, an advocate for the rights of man."[76]

The return to democracy had put the spotlight back on Quino and *Mafalda*. In the early months of 1984 a retrospective exhibit of Quino's work was held at the Fundación San Telmo in Buenos Aires, and in November the exhibit traveled to Mendoza, his native city. Quino also agreed to draw the characters again. As he had done with UNICEF in the past, he now lent Mafalda for health-related events and campaigns conducted by organizations including the Argentine League of Dental Health, the International Amblyopia Conference in Montevideo, and the Red Cross in Spain. A year later, in 1985, Quino provided a design for a campaign organized by the Public Health Secretariat to prevent respiratory diseases in children. He did not think that this collaboration with the Alfonsín administration turned him into a "radical" (an allusion to the governing Radical Party). It was just a way of helping his country, he said.[77]

By then, the cartoonist had joined his characters in becoming part of people's lives. He would receive letters from ladies who reproached him for his pessimism, but he also met readers who wanted to share their positive connection with him. At the 1985 Buenos Aires Book Fair, for example, as he was signing books he was approached by fans from three generations who told him *Mafalda* had brought them together. This intergenerational transmission was also expressed by the place he had been given in *Comiqueando*, a magazine published by comic fans in their early twenties who shared a love of the genre with their readers.[78] *Mafalda*'s visibility was also boosted by news and awards outside Argentina, which were covered by international press agencies and featured in the local media, always eager to celebrate a fellow countryman who found global fame.[79]

Another element that contributed to *Mafalda*'s renewed political significance was Quino's contacts, beginning in 1984, with Cuba. The Caribbean island was home to Quino's friend Jorge Timossi, a journalist who had founded the news agency *Prensa Latina* and had been the inspiration for Mafalda's friend Felipe. During Quino's first trip to Cuba, when he was invited to participate in the Latin American Film Festival in Havana, he also struck a friendship with the well-known Cuban illustrator Juan Padrón. The two later worked together from 1985 to 1987 on the production of *Quinoscopios,* a short film based on Quino's cartoons, and in 1993 they again collaborated in a new animated version of *Mafalda*. But more important, that first visit marked the beginning of a fluid relationship between the cartoonist and Cuba, which Quino had not had when the Cuban Revolution held a magnetic fascination for the Latin American left. While it did not prevent Quino from looking at Cuba with a critical eye, that relationship influenced the comic strip ideologically in a way that would be particularly significant in the coming years.

In 1985, Quino voiced his ideological views with uncharacteristic candidness in an interview by the Madrid newspaper *El País*, after he discovered that Mafalda had been used by fascist Falange groups in Spain to illustrate a series of stickers. He was outraged and declared that he identified fully with the left and that his family had been on the side of the Republicans in the Spanish Civil War. He recalled his childhood and how "during the war, every city that was conquered by Franco would bring my family to tears. I remember my mother knitting socks for Spanish refugees. So I can't understand why they would use my characters for an ideology that is the complete opposite of what I believe in."[80] According to *El País*, Quino had recalled how a decade earlier "parallel" services of the armed forces in Argentina had inverted the meaning of the "ideology-denting stick" poster to extol repression, and how he was unable to react then because many of his friends had been disappeared and life had become impossible. But in the new democratic context he could defend himself publicly and planned to bring an action against the state. In line with his idea that humor could be used as a weapon, he created a vignette that was published in *El País*. At the center of the vignette was the most radical character in the *Mafalda* universe, Libertad, looking at the unauthorized drawing of Guille holding a Falange flag and thinking, "Wow, it looks like the right doesn't find any of its own characters funny!"[81] The interview was featured in many other newspapers around the world and, of course, in Argentina, where the opposition to Francoist elements could easily be projected onto the situation at home and strengthen Quino's connection with antidictatorial voices.[82]

The country faced a difficult moment, with the promises of democracy fading as the economy showed no signs of recovery. Unemployment rates were still alarming, but the most evident indicator of the government's failure was inflation. This context fueled social discontent, and as poverty expanded the government had to implement emergency food distribution programs. CONADEP, the truth commission set up by the Alfonsín government, had completed its investigation and published its findings in the *Nunca Más* report, and the trial of the top military commanders exposed the crimes committed by the regime. The photographer Eduardo Longoni remembers how he was in tears when he took a picture of the moment the sentences were read. He could have never imagined just a few years earlier, when he feared for his life, that he would live to see justice done.[83] But as satisfying as these developments were, nobody could ignore the fact that the intelligence services were still very much active. Their hand was evident in the attacks perpetrated against political clubs and the efforts to hinder the trials. Pressure from the military to put a stop to the proceedings was mounting, and in December 1986 Congress passed the Full Stop Law, which set a term of sixty days to bring any actions against perpetrators of human rights abuses. The law was categorically rejected by human rights organizations, which nonetheless moved quickly to file as many actions as possible before the deadline. As a result, in early 1987, the courts issued more than three hundred summons to military officers. The armed forces responded with an insurrection led by Lieutenant Colonel Aldo Rico in April 1987, during the Easter holiday. The president called on the country to defend democracy and people took to the streets to protest, while the government negotiated with the rebels. The rebels surrendered and a month later the government passed the Due Obedience Law, which further limited the possibilities of holding military perpetrators accountable for human rights abuses, establishing that most were not responsible for their acts because they were obeying orders from their superiors. It became clear to the public that this was a term of the negotiated surrender.

Many feared for the fate of democracy, and this threat gave many sectors of society reason to pause. This included intellectuals, who had learned to fully value the importance of democratic rule after years of dictatorship. In this sense, and in line with his critical view of his own role, however small, in the discrediting and ousting of Arturo Illia, Quino stepped up his commitment to the defense of democracy. On April 17, when Aldo Rico had still not surrendered and just after Raúl Alfonsín had spoken in Congress against the insurrection, Quino sent the president a three-panel strip with Mafalda telling him, "We all

FIGURES 4.5, 4.6, AND 4.7 Three-panel strip sent by Quino to President Raúl Alfonsín during the Easter Week military uprising of 1987, reproduced in Quino, *Toda Mafalda*, 41–43. © Joaquín Salvador Lavado (Quino).

have your back" and cheering for democracy, justice, freedom, and life. (See figures 4.5, 4.6, and 4.7.)

Preserving the frail democracy while furthering the cause of justice for victims of human rights abuses became a major dilemma for these social sectors. Mafalda and friends had always championed democracy and human rights, even during Argentina's most radicalized years. But in the new context of regained democracy and as the country started to come to terms with its dictatorial past, the comic strip's defense of such values cemented its significance as a cultural icon. *Mafalda*'s association with the democratic creed—at that time embraced by Argentines across the social spectrum, including the intellectual middle class—heightened the cartoon's symbolic standing.

In 1988 the comic strip hit a milestone, as Quino had drawn his first Mafalda twenty-five years earlier, and this birthday contributed to consolidate the cartoon's fame. The anniversary was celebrated around the world, with numerous awards and acknowledgments for both the cartoonist and his creation. In 1987, *Quinoscopios* had won best prize in the short film category at the Eighth International Imagination and Fiction Film Festival in Madrid. The following year, Quino was named Distinguished Son of the City of Mendoza and was given the keys to the city, and at the Third International Comic-Salon Erlangen, West Germany, *Mafalda* was awarded the Max Moritz Prize for best comic strip published in an international newspaper.[84] Shortly after, a Buenos Aires theater, Teatro San Martín, held an exhibit of his unpublished strips. The event coincided with the publication of *Mafalda inédita*, a compilation of previously unreleased *Mafalda* material accompanied by a detailed historical account of the context in which the strips were created.[85]

The numerous articles featured in the media in Argentina and around the world during this period took stock of the cartoon's history and at the same time highlighted its current relevance. One of these articles, penned by Norma Morandini and published in the Spanish weekly *Cambio 16*, sang the strip's praises, noting its resignifications but also linking it with a trend that looked nostalgically back to the recent past. The "intellectualized little girl," who was playfully compared to tango icon Carlos Gardel, prompted Morandini to reflect that the era that had created the cartoon had come to an end. It was a pessimistic view of a present in which "utopias are slain by generous salaries, consumerism leads young people to believe there is no future, drugs stigmatize them, [and] AIDS has killed sexual liberation." Latin America had gone from offering a promising future to being "an impoverished continent." After listing the differences between the present and the past, Morandini asked readers to imagine what Mafalda would be like in 1988. Sergio Penchatsky, an Argentine photographer, pictured her as a psychologist, "sporting round glasses and a miniskirt, with vacuous ideas peppering her intellectual chatter." Pea Acedo, a Spanish cohort of the "antiestablishment generation," saw her as "a liberal conservative, like so many who participated in the May 1968 protests in France and are now yuppies." The psychologist Raquel Ferrario, instead, explained, "It's hard for us to imagine her at twenty-five, because we are all Mafalda, it was the child in us that grew. The illusions of the 1970s stayed with her." But she went on to add that she pictured Mafalda studying in the university and "making her way in a difficult Argentina." But Quino weighed in and abruptly shut down Morandini's game. After recalling that readers believed the inspiration for Mafalda had come from an Italian princess who had died in Auschwitz, Quino concluded that "Mafalda wouldn't have reached adulthood. She'd probably be among Argentina's thirty-thousand disappeared."[86]

Back in Argentina, in the pages of the magazine *Página/12*, Eduardo Blaustein also wondered what Mafalda and friends would be up to in 1988. In doing so, he projected onto each character the historical processes that the country had suffered in its darkest decade. He pictured Susanita married to a rich businessman and enjoying steamy escapades with a lover. Manolito could have succeeded in one of the currency speculation (or "financial cycling") schemes common in Argentina, but the journalist thought a more likely scenario was that the crisis would have forced him to close down his grocery store. Of the most radical character, he said that unless she had been able to escape to Yale on a scholarship, it was "terrifying to think what could have happened to Libertad and her progressive parents." As for Mafalda, she must have been "baffled in her antiestablishment routine," eventually caving to "the onslaught of the modern age." Echoing the images of the *Cambio 16* story, he imagined Mafalda as "a typical complicated chick in shades, a pragmatic, deftly flinging cynical remarks." The article ended with Quino's version of the fate his famous character would have met among the disappeared. The *Página/12* journalist noted, however, that ever the "prudent, kind, rational man, who often reminds us that Mafalda was not born to change the world," Quino's exact words were that "she'd *probably* be" among the disappeared.[87] But Mafalda's association with the antiestablishment youth of the 1960s had become such a fixed part of the character that it seemed almost inevitable that she would have met the same tragic fate as many of that generation.

More generally, the consolidation of *Mafalda*'s fame at the cartoon's twenty-fifth anniversary was linked in these articles to discussions and stock-taking regarding the 1960s and 1970s. This included the contradictory meanings that had characterized the era and the disagreements they now prompted in an Argentina marked by an economic and political crisis, in which military uprisings reawakened the fear that had prevailed under the dictatorship. That fear was heightened as awareness grew of the extent of the tragedy that had befallen that generation. These journalists reexamined the comic strip from a retrospective approach. Theirs was a subjective construction, based on the urgencies of the present, but tainted with the marks left by an era they had experienced.

In contrast, the intention behind the publication of *Mafalda inédita* was quite different. The book targeted devoted readers, who, as with any classics whose value has grown over time, are interested in any material that, for whatever reason, the author had previously not considered fit to print. Memory was at the book's heart, as it inevitably awakened the subjective meaning that *Mafalda* had for all those who purchased and read it, because it was part of their life experience. However, their personal memories notwithstanding, the book invited readers to participate in a historical exercise. Every section was preceded by an introduction in which, by way of explanation and assessment, Quino and the other editors described the history of *Mafalda*: its milestones, characters, and the political, social, and economic events that served as backdrop and which the author had followed daily as part of his newspaper work. This effort involved recalling all the details that readers needed to properly contextualize each drawing and humorous take. "Mafalda is a child of her era. The era of the Beatles, Che Guevara, the decolonization of Africa," Quino reflected in *Página/12*.

The retrospective exhibit at Teatro San Martín was visited by thousands of people of all ages. As Carlos Ulanovsky noted, there was a whole new generation of teenagers who were not *Mafalda*'s initially intended audience but whose enthusiasm for it spawned a "Mafaldamania," with some of the most ardent fans confessing they preferred Mafalda to the latest teenage idols and wished they had a friend just like her. A member of this fandom, fifteen-year-old Emilio Divinsky, had obtained his father's permission to organize a contest for *Mafalda* experts at the last Buenos Aires Book Fair. He received more than 3,500 answers to his questionnaire, which included questions such as the name of the doorman of the building where the main character lived.

For Ediciones de la Flor, the comic strip was still a best-seller. By then it had overcome any controversies or disputes over its meaning and it was considered "the leading political and social reading material of several generations." Mafalda had been "a little girl who had gradually become the conscience of a society that experienced history from a place of anguish."[88] Having attained mythical status, *Mafalda* helped process the ruptures that divided Argentine society, and she emerged with force—almost like a talisman—in defense of democracy and human rights. Quino had refused to use his humor to comment on the tragedy that had affected, and even killed, so many of his friends. In the past he had explained that he could not address the issue of the disappearances and that it only emerged unintentionally, in a drawing he made in Milan, in which a body disappears after a car accident.[89] After publishing it, he was disturbed when he noticed what lay under the surface of that frame, because when the disappearances began in Argentina he had even stopped making jokes about prisoners—a classic subject in the genre. In 1988 he again explained his position: "I always have problems with the people at Amnesty [International] because I've never agreed to do anything for them. If you put something like torture or the disappeared in cartoons, you risk giving the impression that it's not so bad. And you can't be so careless with such a delicate matter."[90] He did, however, agree to bring Mafalda back to life to defend democracy. On the fifth anniversary of the return of democratic rule, he designed a poster for the Ministry of Foreign Affairs in which he featured Mafalda, and when he sent a copy of his book of unpublished strips to Raúl Alfonsín, he dedicated it "to the president who was capable of showing us that everything they taught us at school could really be true!" In this way, Quino reached backward, evoking Mafalda's dismayed reaction to the Onganía coup in 1966 and the incongruity with what she had learned in school, and used it to exorcize the past with new symbolic force.

But the hopes pinned on democracy by large sectors of Argentine society were shattered, buried under the rubble of economic, social, and political crisis. By 1989 it was clear that the Alfonsín government had failed to curb inflation, stop wages from falling, and prevent the deterioration of living conditions that had begun during the dictatorship. Workers had started to protest again with a new wave of strikes, and small-business owners and independent professionals tried unsuccessfully to stay afloat.[91] Pressure from military quarters continued, with a new uprising in late 1988 under the command of Colonel Mohamed Alí Seineldín, who demanded amnesty and vindication for the armed forces. Although the uprising was quelled, it evidenced the government's weakness. A month later, a group of armed left-wing militants raided the military barracks at La Tablada and further complicated a difficult political situation. In May 1989, the government of Raúl Alfonsín came abruptly to an end when Carlos Saúl Menem, the candidate of the opposition Peronist Party, won the presidential elections. Alfonsín, faced with hyperinflation and riots, stepped down before completing his term.

The new government lost no time in pardoning the military officers who had been sentenced for their involvement in the repression during the dictatorship, as well as the guerrillas who had also been convicted. A year later Menem extended the pardon to the junta members and the leaders of the Montoneros. Quino was in Italy at the time for *Mafalda*'s anniversary celebration and expressed his concern in an interview in the magazine *L'Espresso*, describing Menem's decision as "the democracy-denting pardon." With that he gave a new twist to the metaphor he had coined decades earlier.[92] In the context of the return to democracy, the "ideology-denting stick" took the form of a pardon that freed the perpetrators of human rights abuses and, therefore, continued the legacy of those who twenty years earlier had used it to repress ideas. This perspective connected the pre- and postdictatorship scenarios through the demands for justice and democracy. As we will see in chapter 5, the rise of neoliberalism would shape the new meanings ascribed to *Mafalda* as it became a symbol of an era that called for a return to political commitment, collective action, and social struggle as a way of combating individualism, capitalism, and the end of history.

Mafalda, the Myth

Mafalda's status as a global celebrity is at the center of the cartoon's past twenty-five years. With each new anniversary, the comic strip's popularity grew and, at the same time, its social and symbolic meanings evolved. It is not my intention to examine here the many interventions—events, publications, exhibits, interpretations—that surrounded its international rise to fame. That would be impossible. My aim, rather, is to understand the strip's continued significance and the main meanings it carried both in and outside Argentina from the late 1980s to the early 2010s. What immediately stands out is the contrast between the character of Mafalda, who is still very much alive to the public as evidenced by the many celebrations in honor of her fiftieth birthday, and the fact that the strip has not had a single new installment for decades. This sustained interest can be explained in part by the cartoon's flexibility, which has allowed for constant reappropriation.

Above all, however, *Mafalda*'s persistence is explained by the mythic status it has achieved. The historian Mircea Eliade noted that a myth refers to "a story that is a most precious possession," which serves as an exemplary model for human behavior and contains the significant meanings of a social group's existence. Myths express, heighten, and codify beliefs; safeguard moral principles; and offer practical rules for individuals to follow. In his 1963 book *Myth and Reality*, Eliade called attention to the connection between myths and mass media. Citing Umberto Eco's first essay on Superman, Eliade argued that comic strips channeled the "secret longings of modern man," who, frustrated, "dreams of one day proving himself an 'exceptional person,' a 'Hero.'"[1]

I argue that *Mafalda* gave rise to the social and cultural creation of a myth. The comic—and the story of its beginnings—entered the realm of social memory, and it did so in such a way that it expressed a primordial time that condensed "feats" (behaviors, virtues, moralities), a style of remembering defined by nostalgia and actualization, to the point of generating a game that brought the characters to life and inserted them in an origin story and in communal rituals and spaces. I posit that those images, accounts, and practices constituted a myth for a unique social group. This group was formed by different subjects with their own identities that were gaining a global presence: the middle and working classes fractured by the advance of neoliberalism, the young generations of the 1960s, and the generations that, in the years that followed, took up the struggle against injustice and the efforts to build a better world. I use these rather vague concepts because, as a myth, the comic strip channeled a certain sensitivity, a sense of belonging based on loosely structured aesthetic, moral, and political elements, rather than a precise ideology or political position. That was where its strength lay. *Mafalda* expressed—and expresses—a "committed," "progressive," "rebellious," and "antiestablishment" sensitivity that encapsulates different positions woven together with almost invisible threads. These positions gain substance in their contrast with "others," those who, for example, at the beginning of this period in the late 1980s, celebrated the fall of the Soviet bloc and forecasted the end of history and of social utopias.

Mafalda, in sum, reveals how a mass culture product can become an image, object, and practice that connects the present to the past, mobilizing—in Maurice Halbwachs's terms—a social construction, a selection, in which different groups and actors participate based on their present values and interests.[2] As I argue in this chapter, that was possible through the involvement of multiple actors (Quino himself, publishers, journalists, entrepreneurs) who put into circulation concrete productions featuring Mafalda (editions, exhibits, interpretations); at the same time, those productions were appropriated by a range of subjects in different parts of the world.

RENEWED GLOBAL SUCCESS IN A NEOLIBERAL CONTEXT

As we saw in chapter 4, *Mafalda*'s twenty-fifth birthday in 1988 was celebrated around the globe. Tributes in Argentina, Spain, and Italy were held almost back to back and their coverage by international press agencies made an impact on audiences in different parts of the world. The multiple echoes in the news—with articles marking the anniversary, stories describing the events, and pieces chronicling the history of the cartoon—formed an upward spiral in which each new event magnified the next. *Mafalda* became an obligatory headline as newspapers and magazines tried to outdo each other, boosting the cartoon's media appeal and, as a result, its symbolic significance. The strip's history contributed to that heightened appeal and significance and so did its larger-than-life main character, who had been part of colorful and even glamorous anecdotes but who also had struck a chord with readers, attaining political and cultural value.

The fact that the cartoon lacked a precise date of birth—having instead been crafted in a process that took several months—allowed for a certain elasticity that made it easier to hold multiple celebrations that stretched out over the course of the year and beyond. In this way, the publication of the *Mafalda inédita* compilation and the retrospective exhibit that had been the highlights of the commemoration in Argentina could be replicated the following year in Italy and Spain. In 1989, with the twentieth anniversary of the May 1968 protests not far behind and as the French Revolution reached its two-hundred-year mark, Europe experienced a memory and retrospective boom.

Commemorations are always an opportunity for taking stock of the past and making projections about the future. In this case, with the added magic that round-number anniversaries have, they took center stage in public discussions and political debates. Controversies arose over the legacy of the revolutionary past—that is, its political meaning in the present. The issue was particularly complex with respect to the rebellious 1968 generation. On the one hand, the historical status of that generation was still not quite crystallized. On the other, European societies were going through political and social processes hostile to the causes that students and workers had fought for twenty years earlier. This commemoration erupted in a divided ideological scenario, marked by the crisis of Eastern Bloc socialism (with the fall of the Berlin Wall that year) and the rise of the right. On one side were those who were preparing to criticize the fabrication of a "sacrosanct generation" and, with it, "nostalgic" and "melancholic" events that would extol the "adventures of the left."[3] And on the other were those who wanted to vindicate the "spirit" of '68 by celebrating collective action, the ideals of social justice, equality, and antiauthoritarianism, and the utopian imagination.

The twenty-fifth anniversary of *Mafalda* was commemorated in that context. As it had in Argentina, the game of imagining what could have become of the characters prompted projections and assessments regarding that 1960s generation. In Spain, where the media began covering the anniversary early on, the issue was intertwined with discussions about Argentina. It was in a Spanish magazine that Quino had said that if he imagined Mafalda as a young woman he saw her as meeting the same fate as the thousands of disappeared in Argentina. His statements made a great impact and were picked up by many newspapers and magazines. The original piece, featured in the Madrid magazine *Cambio 16* and penned by Norma Morandini, had highlighted certain traits of the character: "A feminist before her time, critical of television, concerned with the environment, the fate of Humanity, and the yellow scare, Mafalda was from a typical middle-class family and could have been born in Madrid, Buenos Aires, or Rome." The Argentine journalist nostalgically remembered a strip in which the "intellectualized little girl" realized that "if you don't hurry up and change the world, it will be the world that changes you." The same acerbic tone was found in accounts by Morandini's interviewees in Spain, who projected onto Mafalda the criticism aimed at the 1968 rebels.[4]

The anniversary of the comic strip, with the story of its origins repeated ad infinitum, triggered the memories of those who had been young in the 1960s. It recaptured a time when a better future seemed certain, a future in which the collective and the individual came together and the political and the personal converged. Those memories were tinged with nostalgia. For many, remembering their youth also meant acknowledging failure to bring about radical political change. The lasting success of the comic strip—which continued to sell as it had when it was "at its best," that is, "when that Argentine little girl was still considered a true rebel"—allowed readers to feel they were coming together in their condemnation of the prevailing neoliberal order. Echoing that sentiment, an article published in the Spanish newspaper *ABC*, for example, concluded, "We hope that, even if only in Quino's memory, that little girl . . . is still thinking that the Beatles could have been the world's best presidents."[5]

It was impossible to bring back that past. Not even Mafalda could come back to life, as Quino repeated again and again. That was why it was so compelling to imagine how she would be as an adult. The continuity between the fictional universe created by the cartoonist and real, everyday life was broken. Readers could no longer demand that the characters take a stand on political affairs. The comic strip was thus sheltered from the controversies that such views had prompted in the past. While not fully expressed at first, that rupture eventually helped perpetuate more timeless meanings and others that emerged in the comic strip's constant aggiornamento through new appropriations and resignifications. The new terms under which *Mafalda* was read enabled it to evoke the meanings attributed to the period in which it was created and produced daily—the 1960s—and to contrast the comic strip's own history with the subjective biographies of the readers.

In this sense, *Mafalda inédita* represented an innovation, as it allowed readers to rekindle the joy of discovering new strips and reliving the social experience of collective reading. They brought back a sense of community among readers who were intimately familiar with the comic strip and would therefore be interested in a cult book, but who also shared an ideological space that made reading it special. *Mafalda* could thus be linked to other cultural expressions inherited from the 1960s that symbolized a leftist, progressive feeling that could be harnessed into opposition against the rise of neoliberalism. These connections were highlighted by journalists. In one article published in the Madrid newspaper *El País*, the reporter noted that the book featured a drawing of Mafalda that had originally been meant for a record (*El Sur también existe*) by the Catalan singer-songwriter Joan Manuel Serrat with poems by the Uruguayan writer Mario Benedetti, both major cultural references for the left in Latin America and Spain.[6] While Serrat had opted not to include Quino's drawing—a decision that the cartoonist jokingly attributed to "differences between a Catalan and an Andalusian" (in reference to his family's Spanish roots)—the collaboration nonetheless revealed a shared sensitivity based on artistic and ideological empathies. Not coincidentally, when *La Vanguardia*, one of Catalonia's leading newspapers, revamped its format and content in 1989, it decided to feature *Mafalda* regularly on the back cover of its magazine.[7]

The stocktaking prompted by the anniversary was not limited to politics. Comparisons with the past also involved looking at the living conditions of the middle and working classes. According to Horacio Eichelbaum, an Argentine journalist living in Spain, the reason behind the comic strip's continued popularity in Europe was that it was precisely the "European middle classes [that were] still persevering in that struggle between ambitions and the limits of reality." The middle classes in the European Community were indeed suffering the effects of deindustrialization. Unemployment had more than doubled between 1970 and 1980, from 4.2 to 9.2 percent, and by 1990 it had climbed to 11 percent. There was also greater income inequality among the employed population, and working conditions had deteriorated.[8]

In Italy, the publishing house Bompiani released *Mafalda 25*, its own compilation of previously unreleased strips. For Italian readers, Mafalda was the "poster child for the antiestablishment." The comic strip had continued to be featured in the Roman daily *Il Messaggero*, and its main character had been described by another newspaper as a "little feminist witch" born at the height of the women's movement.[9] When *Mafalda 25* was published, the press reprinted statements by Quino, who recalled that his creation was a product of the era of the Beatles, Che Guevara, and the decolonization of Africa, but that all of that was now meaningless, as "today people are only interested in making the most money they can in the shortest time possible. There's no space for the illusions of children, and my eyes are now always less innocent, less naive. That's why I could never draw her again."[10]

As international press agencies covered the celebrations held around the world, media in Latin America picked up their dispatches and invariably highlighted the cartoon's success in Europe. It made for good copy, but it was also a source of pride for Latin Americans. In Mexico, *Mafalda*'s popularity had fueled the swift growth of Nueva Imagen. But in the 1980s the publisher was unable to withstand the strong devaluation of the Mexican peso, and when it filed for bankruptcy, it sold the comic strip's publishing rights to Tusquets, which is still publishing the *Mafalda* books today.[11] As a result of Nueva Imagen's financial troubles, *Mafalda inédita* was sold in Mexico in the Ediciones de la Flor edition. In 1988, it was presented to great acclaim by Quino himself at the Guadalajara Book Fair. According to the magazine *Plural*, in Mexico, like in other countries, *Mafalda* was "enjoyed by diverse readers who identify with [the main character's] antiestablishment attitude in school and at home, and in her judgments and assessments of the state of the world." The ideological significance of this was underscored at the end of the article by Quino himself, who was quoted expressing his political views openly (something he had carefully avoided doing in the past, but would return to increasingly in the future): "I think capitalism is shit; to me it's the worst system of all, but socialist countries are backtracking a bit with their orthodoxy. . . . With leaders like Che Guevara, Ho Chi-Minh, Mao, and Pope John XXIII gone, I'm not sure where things are going."[12]

In addition to making the news with this new publication, in various Latin American countries *Mafalda* expanded its readership among the working classes through cheap pirated editions that were circulated through informal channels. For many of these readers, the issues portrayed in the strip of economic hardship and skepticism in the face of political change had probably always been a part of their lives.

In sum, *Mafalda* gained new currency in multiple ways. But the coverage in the press reveals that, in particular, the comic strip rekindled a sensitivity that had seemed defeated by the pragmatic harshness of neoliberal adjustment programs and the rhetoric of individualism. It was thus possible to turn it into a living legacy of resistance. The story had all the ingredients for a myth. By reading *Mafalda*, people could give meaning to the present by re-creating collective events, intertwined with their own memories. For this reason, the account of how it was created and developed could be featured again and again in the media without saturating audiences. In the following years the story of its origins, that lost time, would be re-created in various spheres.

"MAFALDA'S WORLD"

The twenty-fifth anniversary of the comic strip fueled a rising movement that gained speed, propelled in part by its own momentum. But the height of the celebrations was yet to come. In 1992, *Mafalda* featured prominently in Spain's commemorations of the five hundredth anniversary of the voyage of Columbus to the Americas, as the state agency hosting the events organized a Mafalda exhibit in Madrid as part of the celebrations. Mafalda's World—or "Mafaldaland," as *El País* dubbed it—occupied a vast venue that included a large tent with dolls representing the comic strip's characters designed by the *fallero* artist Manolo Martín in the style of the *ninots*, the typical puppets used in the Falles festival in Valencia. Quino oversaw every detail that went into re-creating the universe of Mafalda and her friends, which, according to a news account, promised kids in Spain that they "could go to school with Susanita, Libertad, and Felipe, pop into Manolito's grocery store to buy something, and play with Guille's toys." The characters would be brought to life through "dozens of television monitors, movie screenings, and panels" that would narrate their adventures and "delightful animatronics [that would] imitate their movements."[13]

The five hundredth anniversary was a controversial affair that sparked bitter discussions on both sides of the Atlantic. The differences lay in defining what should be commemorated and how. It was a debate that engaged indigenous peoples directly, but also Latin America's political and intellectual elite, and it involved two conflicting paradigms. According to the first, the Spanish conquest was seen as the origin of the destruction of the peoples of the Americas, and as such it had to be condemned and the resistance celebrated. The second prioritized the notion of "cultural encounter" or "meeting of two cultures." In Latin America this view was criticized because it failed to take into account the Spanish empire's interests and vastly greater power.[14] This notion was, however, a solution for those in Spain who needed to find a way to commemorate what had been—and for many still was—the country's greatest glory, without at the same time celebrating an extermination.

Why involve *Mafalda* in this discussion? In Spain, the comic strip had been appropriated in two ways: it had been "Hispanicized," but it had also been associated with Latin American identity. In both senses, *Mafalda* had served as a bridge between Spaniards and Latin Americans, who were bonded by their shared pride in the cartoon. These connections had been strengthened in 1991 when Quino applied for Spanish citizenship. His decision had been announced in *El País* under the headline "Mafalda Is Now Spanish." The comic strip was hugely popular in the country. As of 1992, annual sales of the *Mafalda* books in Spain stood at 100,000 copies (including editions in Spanish, Catalan, Galician, and Basque). At the same time, the comic strip continued to gain global visibility. It had been translated into Danish, Swedish, Norwegian, and Finnish, it was featured in over thirty newspapers in Scandinavia, and pirate editions had been spotted in China. So by invoking *Mafalda*, Spain was also showcasing a world-famous production that embodied Iberian American identity.[15] As the organizers argued, "Few things evidence the link between Iberian America and Spain as clearly as *Mafalda*." They also claimed it was a "symbol of the 1960s that has transcended" and gained a universal dimension. Quino himself explained that his cartoon had been chosen because it was the most widely known Spanish comic.[16] The decision to include *Mafalda* in the five hundredth anniversary probably arose during the long planning process for Seville Expo '92, which was the epicenter of the commemorations.[17] Still, the choice was not an obvious one and the organizers resorted to additional arguments to support it, including pointing out coincidences in the calendar of celebrations. In the comic strip, Mafalda had been born on March 15, 1962, which meant that on the five hundredth anniversary she would be turning thirty.

A one-panel strip drawn by Quino was chosen for the exhibit and animated in a short film by the Cuban illustrator Juan Padrón (figure 5.1). It showed a feathered Mafalda meeting Christopher Columbus, who is offering her soup, her well-known nemesis. Politically, the strip evoked the "discovery" as a cultural encounter.[18] But Mafalda's reaction to the soup offered by the smiling Genovese navigator was one of disgust. The drawing, originally created in 1990 for a week-long event organized by the Madrid City Council to celebrate Argentine culture, was a perfect response to the dilemma posed by the commemoration. It showed the "meeting of two cultures," but in doing so it highlighted the imposition of power and the rejection by the native population. Also, by featuring Mafalda the scene made it easier to empathize with a progressive sensitivity. Quino's statements to the press contributed to that interpretation. Despite being a skeptic, he declared that the only future possible lay with socialism.[19]

FIGURE 5.1 Caricature drawn by Quino in 1990 for Argentine Culture Week, organized by the Madrid Mayor's Office. Juan Padrón later animated the caricature and it was shown as part of the five hundredth anniversary of the voyage of Columbus to the Americas. Reproduced in Quino, *Toda Mafalda*, 640. © Joaquín Salvador Lavado (Quino).

In the exhibit itself, there was no trace of the five hundredth anniversary except for that image of Mafalda and Columbus. It was almost as if the organizers forgot what was being commemorated. Instead, the focus of the exhibit was, as the title announced, Mafalda's world. In re-creating that world, they tried to contemplate different generations of readers: the adults who had grown up with *Mafalda* and the kids who were attracted by the cartoon characters. The exhibit first took visitors through the origins of the comic strip, with drawings and explanatory texts on display and animations of *Mafalda* and other comics playing on a number of monitors. This was followed by a room devoted to "The Era of Mafalda," with a historical audiovisual installation of the 1960s and 1970s presented by an animatronic Quino voiced by the Argentine actor Héctor Alterio. The next room focused on the characters, but the heart of the exhibit was the room where everyday scenes were reproduced through moving images and sound—Guille doodling on the wall, for example. Another room was divided into two sections: "Quino without Her," featuring the cartoonist's later work, and "Mafalda without Him," which gave an overview of how the comic strip had been projected outside the page. The exhibit closed with a "Recess" section that was basically a playground for children, with funhouse mirrors, puzzles, hopscotch designs, labyrinths, and swings.[20]

The cost of production ran to 100 million pesetas (books were sold at 1,500 pesetas a copy), but there was no entrance fee. The exhibit had been financed by private sponsors and with the sale of merchandise. In a way, the antiestablishment little girl who opposed the neoliberal order had been put on display through a production whose foundations could very well contradict her philosophy. The curators helped downplay that possible contradiction. In staging the world of the main character and her gang of friends, the exhibit brought back the legacy of the 1960s, with music playing a key role in that effort. It began with the Platters, Louis Armstrong, and Carlos Gardel and was followed by the Beatles, Rolling Stones, and Chico Buarque, a socially committed Brazilian singer-songwriter. In the space devoted to the characters, Argentine children's songs were played. Quino's section was musicalized by Brahms and Chopin and Mafalda's by Joan Manuel Serrat.[21]

The exhibit was a huge success, both with the public and the media. "If Spain is hoping to become the epicenter of the world during 1992, Mafalda has already become the epicenter of Spain and it will remain the epicenter for the next nine weeks." That was how *Cambio 16* announced the exhibit, and it invited readers to visit a "fantastic country" and be part of a "great tribute."[22] Quino and his famous characters were all over the media. *El País* ran a feature story in its Sunday magazine with glossy pictures of the cartoonist posing with his creations.[23] The response from the public was no less spectacular: 38,000 people visited the exhibit in the first two weeks after its inauguration. According to a reporter who gathered impressions, the visitors had different reactions depending on their age and connection to the comic. Children flocked excitedly and were initially disappointed when they saw only pictures and text on display. They were only interested in the dolls. When they finally found them they were eager to share what they thought of them—like a little girl who was surprised at how ugly Felipe was or another one who thought Guille was a girl. Many adults were moved by nostalgia. That was the case with an Argentine couple who had been living in Spain for seven years and a Spanish couple who had lived in Argentina. But there were also visitors in their twenties who approached "the exhibit as if it were an archaeology museum." "It feels a bit old to us," two students who had been introduced to the comic by their older siblings told the reporter. A drawing of Mafalda that invited the smallest visitors to leave a message on the wall prompted the journalist to remark on the irony of the "repressive forces"—embodied by the museum guards—driving away the kids who rushed to christen the spotless wall with their drawings, for in doing so the guards clearly violated the principles of the progressive "advocate of children rights" and freedom. One could also imagine another irony, as some of the parents who brought their kids to the exhibit had probably identified with Mafalda and her concerns when they first read the strips years before, but they were now perhaps feeling closer to the parents of the "intellectualized little girl."[24]

With this exhibit, a new format for disseminating the comic strip emerged. The exhibit staged a concrete, real, and tangible world in which Mafalda fans of all ages could materialize their bond with the cartoon, in a communion that renewed the importance of its origin myth and conveyed it to younger generations. The Madrid exhibit was taken on the road with a series of traveling shows that visited a number of cities inside and outside Argentina like a secular procession. With each new venue, *Mafalda*'s significance as a social phenomenon grew.

Simultaneously with the Madrid exhibit, in 1992, the Spanish publishing house Lumen released two new books: *Todo Mafalda*, a compilation of all the strips plus previously unpublished drawings; and *El mundo de Mafalda*, a year-by-year chronicle of the history of the comic. The compilation was a large hardcover edition, more than seven hundred pages long, and it was meant for a readership that would be sufficiently interested in all things Mafalda to pay for a cult book. A handwritten message by Gabriel García Márquez included in this edition reinforced the strip's connection with Latin American culture, which had begun with the literary boom.

Over time, the "big book"—as many readers interviewed for my research referred to the compilation—became the comic's point of entry for many young people who discovered it at home. The second book, which had the same title as the exhibit, targeted both connoisseurs and beginners. Dozens of pictures, caricatures, and drawings accompanied a flowing sequence of text in three columns where readers could find the historical context for each year but, above all, memories, anecdotes, and reflections. Curated by Marcelo Ravoni—who was still Quino's European agent—and with a Lumen-designed layout based on a project by the renowned Argentine artist and graphic designer Juan Fresán (who had been exiled in Barcelona), the end result was a product that appealed to a progressive sensitivity. The two books complemented each other and contributed to the goal of celebrating the comic strip and telling its story.

COMING FULL CIRCLE: *MAFALDA* IN CUBA

The Madrid exhibit had another consequence. It convinced Quino to give animation a second chance, after seeing Juan Padrón's work with the drawing of Mafalda and Christopher Columbus. The two artists had built a relationship over the course of many years and through chance contacts, deliberate strategies, and inevitable coincidences. As we will see, those ties explain *Mafalda's* resignifications against the backdrop of the collapse of the Eastern Bloc and vaunted end of history.

Mafalda was at the very beginning of that relationship. In 1964, when Quino introduced Felipe, his inspiration had been his friend Jorge Timossi. Timossi had been among Quino's group of friends who met to discuss politics in the late 1950s. The group—which included intellectuals and journalists such as Paco Urondo, Pirí Lugones, Rodolfo Walsh, and Miguel Brascó—had lost touch with Timossi in 1959, when he decided to abandon his job as a chemical engineer and travel across Latin America to pursue his passion, poetry. When he left, Rodolfo Walsh gave him the name of a contact in Rio de Janeiro, because he thought Timossi would be a good fit for a Cuban press agency that was in the works. After the triumph of the Cuban Revolution, Timossi traveled to Havana in the same boat as Gabriel García Márquez to join the staff of the newly founded agency Prensa Latina. Timossi quickly built a career in the news, becoming a renowned journalist. In 1969, while in Algeria, he came across a copy of a *Mafalda* book. "As soon as I saw [Felipe], I said to myself, 'this looks familiar,'" Timossi later recalled. Shortly after, when he traveled to Chile with Fidel Castro for the inauguration of Salvador Allende, he sent Quino a formal unsigned card with the words "Confess, you cretin!" In response, he received a poster of Felipe with a speech bubble that said, "Just my luck I got stuck being me!"[25] Over the following years, Timossi would occasionally call his friend on the phone, so it is quite possible that the journalist was behind Quino's invitation to participate in the Latin American Film Festival in 1984. One of the films participating in that year's festival was the animated movie *Vampires in Havana* by Juan Padrón, who was already a famous cartoonist, and when the organizers asked Padrón to be Quino's host, the two immediately hit it off.

Mafalda's relationship with Cuba was not as simple. Not all of the strips had been well received there. Many Cubans reminded Quino that Mafalda had once called their *comandante* a cretin and demanded an explanation. He patiently explained that the strip in question had come out during the Onganía government, when everything Fidel Castro said was considered bad, so that it was enough for Castro to praise something for it to be banned. Hence Mafalda's annoyance at the Cuban leader's indifference toward soup. It had merely been a humorous device used by Quino to comment sarcastically on a widespread attitude. They also asked him about Mafalda's "Soup is to childhood what communism is to democracy" aphorism. This was not so easily explained, because, as we saw in chapter 1, it was not meant ironically.[26] Castro himself let Quino know he had not been amused. According to Quino, "Fidel is known for his good memory, but every time he sees me he asks: 'Who did you say you were?' He ignores me completely." But the cartoonist did not avoid the issue. He had been informed by the staff of *Dedeté*, a well-known Cuban humor magazine, that, while it was not expressly forbidden, nobody drew caricatures of Castro. In one of his meetings with the Cuban leader, Quino asked him about it. Castro answered, "'I said that? Has anybody ever heard me say that? Draw all the caricatures of me that you want.' And poking me on the chest, he added: 'Just as long as it's not something counterrevolutionary; because in that case, I'll have to throw you in jail.'" Quino did make a caricature, but he could never get it published in Cuba.[27]

Despite these mutual recriminations, Quino's ties with the island grew stronger. In 1985, he was awarded a prize at Cuba's Second International Art Biennial and began to work with Juan Padrón to produce animated versions of his humor pages for *Quinoscopios*.[28] In the ensuing decade, Quino traveled to Cuba at least once a year to work on joint projects with Padrón, in a mutually rewarding and enjoyable collaboration. Padrón learned about the structure and setting of Quino's characters, and Quino, in turn, obtained high-quality animations of his drawings, which at the time (before the widespread use of computers) were very costly. His visits to the island gave him firsthand knowledge of Cuban life. In interviews in the Latin American and European press, he increasingly praised revolutionary Cuba, although he could also be critical of certain aspects.[29] In the eyes of the public, these statements placed him among the intellectuals who supported Cuba. The international circulation of *Quinoscopios*—and the prizes it received—revealed the vitality of Cuba at a critical moment, as the Berlin Wall came down and the Soviet Union began to crumble.[30] Thus, for example, at the film's screening in Buenos Aires, Quino was full of praise and awe for the Cubans he had worked with, who, despite the US embargo and lack of resources and technical equipment, had delivered an extraordinarily high-quality animation that had even enhanced the resolution of his drawings.[31]

In 1992, the two cartoonists obtained financing from Spain's national television network TVE (Televisión Española), which partnered with the Cuban Art and Film Institute (Instituto Cubano del Arte e Industria Cinematográficos) to produce a film version of *Mafalda*. A year later, the shorts had been completed. Unlike the 1981 film, Quino was very much involved in this production. Both he and Padrón decided to focus on the visual and limit the dialogue.[32] They gave the characters voices but made their speech unintelligible, so that viewers could imagine the dialogue without it interfering with the effect of the visual gags. With that in mind, they selected the strips that would not lose their humorous impact without text. They also paid special attention to the timing and how the sequence unfolded, in order to preserve the surprise element of the punch line. By focusing on the comedic aspects and the meaning of each strip, Padrón was able to deliver carefully crafted and effective reconstructions of the cartoon in a different medium.

Their work yielded 104 standalone shorts that were arranged thematically in sequence to create the movie. Social unrest and the police repression of student protesters were among the themes featured. But there were also references to social inequality and the generational clashes triggered by rock music, for example. The different views typically held by each character were highlighted through the use of images instead of words. Overall, in contrast to the saccharine version of the first film, Padrón's animation was well executed, even with respect to the graphic lines, although it lacked a unifying story (perhaps because the standalone segments were seen as easier to sell to television networks).

Quino was pleased and the production was a success. The shorts were widely broadcast and received good reviews. In 1995, for example, they were shown regularly on Colombian television, before the news, and in Spain they were aired on TVE and repeated on regional channels across the country.[33] The film won prizes at international festivals and was shown in special screenings in Latin America and Europe.[34] As had been the case since the twenty-fifth anniversary celebrations, the prizes and awards were covered by international news agencies and featured in the media around the world, producing a ripple effect.[35] In 2000, Fox Kids included the short films in its programming—the cartoon could now engage children everywhere without their parent's mediation.[36]

Later, in 2008, the film was submitted to the VivAmérica Festival in Casa de América, a government agency seated in Madrid that furthers cultural relations between Spanish America and Spain. At that festival, the intimate connection between the comic strip and Cuba was symbolized by an illustration made especially for the occasion by both Quino and Padrón. The drawing showed a vampire sweet-talking Mafalda in typical Cuban Spanish, in a mashup of the two artists' creations.[37] There was no trace of the old recriminations. Cuba had breathed new life into *Mafalda*, and the comic strip had in turn become the island's ambassador, paving the way for it in Europe in lively, creative, and playful strokes.

The Cuban Revolution was even incorporated into the origins of *Mafalda*, by way of Jorge Timossi, and thus became part of the myth. Timossi's story, which he made public through a book of poetry he published with illustrations by Quino, was picked up by international news media. The media loved the anecdotes of this Argentine-turned-Cuban revolutionary, whose friendship with Quino had spawned Felipe, one of Mafalda's endearing friends.[38] The play between fiction and reality was such that it was rumored that whenever Timossi was running late for some high-level government meeting in Cuba, Fidel Castro would ask where "Felipito" was.[39]

Mafalda had moved into the socialist camp. The association was not merely symbolic. In 1995, the strip was picked up by a newspaper in the United States, a market that had resisted the global charms of the intellectualized little girl. It was introduced in the Sunday edition of *Nuevo Herald*, a Spanish-language Miami daily, in the first week of May.[40] Four months later, Quino was demanding that they stop publishing it. He had been interviewed over the telephone for the piece that introduced the comic strip to the paper's readers, and months later when he received a copy he discovered that they had omitted— or "censored?" he wondered—his socialist sympathies and his support for the Cuban government. The Buenos Aires daily *La Nación* reported the cartoonist's displeasure under the headline "Quino's Resounding Support of Castro" ("Quino dio un portazo en apoyo a Castro"). It was a fitting headline. In Cuba, the news was picked up by *Juventud Rebelde*. According to the Cuban Communist Youth's weekly, the US paper had left out a quote by the cartoonist in which he stated that Cuba "continues to give its people many benefits and a dignity found nowhere else in the world." Two days later Quino clarified that he had said "nowhere else in the continent" and not the world. "While I confirm that I wholeheartedly support a political system that protects the health and education of its people . . . I am not such a fanatic nor am I so stupid that I cannot distinguish the differences that logically separate Cuba from countries like Sweden, Switzerland, or England."[41] A decade later, in 2007, Quino signed the rights to *Todo Mafalda* over to the government of Cuba. He announced his decision at the sixteenth edition of the Havana Book Fair—which was dedicated to Argentina—before a large audience that had come to hear him speak. The five thousand copies of his book available at the fair sold out in one day.[42] There was no doubt about it: the creator of the character who had upset Cuban readers by challenging communism from a Third World position now chose socialism, just as the cultural dominance of capitalism appeared to be unshakable.

NOSTALGIAS OF A GENERATION

In 1995, in his book *The Age of Extremes*, Eric Hobsbawm concluded that if humanity continued along the same path the end result would inevitably be darkness, as that was the "alternative to a changed society."[43] At the height of the triumph of neoliberalism, Hobsbawm believed that the magnitude of the crisis was determined by more than just the collapse of the global economy or the demise of the socialist camp. It was a social and moral crisis. His diagnosis was even grimmer: no less than the foundations of modern civilization—shared by liberal capitalism and communism—were at risk, in a crisis "of the historic structures of human relations."[44] This pessimism was not the product of the disturbed view of an obstinate Marxist historian. That atmosphere tainted the views of many across the ideological spectrum who could not resign themselves to seeing the end of an era characterized by faith in humanity and the utopian dream of building a better world.

 Mafalda stirred that sensitivity. As we saw earlier, by the late 1980s the comic strip was being celebrated both for its own history and for evoking the feats of the 1960s generation, with its heroes and utopias. That form of appropriation of the cartoon reached a high point with the commemoration of its thirtieth anniversary in 1994. At a time when politics and culture were saturated by the logic of economic returns and the rhetoric of the end of history, *Mafalda* was part of the cultural resistance to the hegemony of neoliberal capitalism. It was a cultural expression that enabled an opposition on all fronts. It represented a sensitivity that linked ideology, aesthetics, and subjectivity against the neoliberal onslaught.

The anniversary came at a time when the comic strip had gained new visibility. In Italy, it consolidated Quino's intellectual and artistic reputation. The celebrations featured renowned personalities such as Umberto Eco, new book editions with strips organized thematically, and the first complete compilation in Italian, *Il mondo di Mafalda*.[45] These were accompanied by the new political meanings ascribed to the comic strip. In Eco's words, "Mafalda became popular among us because her attitudes toward life are European." Quino, for his part, declared that it was not the anniversary of his cartoon that concerned him but the Italy of Berlusconi and the "hundredth year anniversary" of the right in the world.[46] His statement spoke implicitly to a leftist identity and, at the same time, to the utopian dreams of the 1960s. This could also be seen in popular appropriations. In 1991, for example, a television show called "Mafalda," after the character, promised its audience of nearly six million viewers a "provocative and edgy" take on women workers' issues. The Italian librarian Neva Kohman recalls that many girls in the 1970s saw themselves in Mafalda because of what she represented (a female rebel who could not be made to conform) but, also, because of her struggle against injustice and her love for humanity.[47] According to Quino, "Mafalda wanted to change the world. Today, all young people care about is finding a job.... There are more Manolitos and Susanitas than there are Mafaldas and Felipes."[48]

In 1994, on the cartoon's thirtieth birthday the collective game of imagining the fate of the characters bordered on mania. In Spain, *El País* acknowledged with sarcasm that with the prevailing ideological disillusionment, comics had replaced the heroes that had fallen with the Berlin Wall. But the Madrid paper also used Susanita as an example of the hypocrisy of European societies, which awarded prizes to photographs of poverty-stricken Rwanda while at the same time continuing with their imperialist actions.[49] Quino had given shape to social prototypes that, three decades on, had become metaphors that could be easily adapted to understand the dilemmas posed by the crisis brought on by neoliberalism.[50] As it had before, the comic strip also meant many different things to many different people. At the heart of all those different meanings, however, there was always a constant: a questioning stance that went against the spirit of the times and joined Mafalda in raising the banner of social utopia. As Patricia Kolesnicov noted in *Clarín*, Mafalda expressed "the pride and optimism of a better future imagined in the spring of the sixties."[51] That, according to Quino himself, was at the core of the myth. He often explained bitterly that the comic strip remained current because the problems it denounced remained unsolved. But in the late 1990s he elaborated further: "The world is even worse now than when I was drawing 'Mafalda.' Back then, we had the Beatles, [the opposition to] the Vietnam War, the French May. That's all gone to hell. The reason the character speaks to people today is because they are nostalgic for the ideals of my generation. . . . You could say that we're sixties nostalgics."[52]

In Argentina, the meanings ascribed to "Mafalda" were updated in an especially powerful way. Starting in 1989, the government of Carlos Menem had privatized public utilities and other state-owned companies, laid off thousands of workers from the public sector, and implemented a policy of indiscriminate liberalization of the economy. These measures affected a large part of the working class and significant segments of the middle class, who saw their past material and symbolic standing crumble.[53] A skilled politician, Menem was able to carry out his agenda and successfully hold on to the reins of the Peronist party, even as many of his actions went against that party's historical tenets and major gains. He also engineered a fleeting economic stability through the granting of soft loans and artificial dollar-peso parity, which would eventually lead to the unprecedented crisis of 2001, and fostered a frivolous style of governing in which the worlds of politics and show business were intertwined and scandals were commonplace. These measures combined were undermining the material foundations of the identity of the middle and working classes committed to social inclusion, while at the same time furthering an antagonistic middle-class culture. That middle class was retreating from the city, leaving behind the neighborhood, the square, public schools, and other symbols of its identity that the comic strip had extolled, and trading them in for a culture of suburban gated communities, malls, and private schools.[54]

In that context, *Mafalda* revived the identity of the socially aware working and middle classes already seriously corroded and now under attack by Menem and his policies. The comic strip was again at the center of cultural life with the release of *Toda Mafalda* in 1993, at the same time that a Quino exhibit opened at Centro Cultural Recolecta, a space in Buenos Aires devoted to the arts.[55] *Página/12*, at the time the leading newspaper of the opposition in Argentina, announced the exhibit in an article entitled "Menem and Quino." Penned by Miguel Rep—by then one of the most renowned cartoonists of his generation—the piece stoked the confrontation between those two opposing Argentinas: the "ingenious" Quino, "a refined gentleman," "the very definition of sensitive," versus Menem with his "vulgar arrogance."[56] The event spoke to all those who felt a connection to that sensitive identity. A young man, surprised to see former president Raúl Alfonsín at the event, told a reporter, "All sorts of people are here: big, small, medium, even presidents. . . ." The only one who did not make an appearance was Mafalda, but her presence could still be felt, as she was not far from everyone's mind. This was partly because it was the character's social significance that made that communion possible. She was a symbol of the "melting pot" Argentina, an Argentina proud of its middle class. But she was also there because readers materialized her. They brought with them their copies of the just-published *Toda Mafalda* so that Quino would sign them. The press also evoked Mafalda, and it did so even more symbolically. A *Clarín* journalist described how she had spotted a "mischievous" little girl who was kicking a ball near the entrance of the Centro Cultural and she heard her father call out to her, "Mafalda!" It was obvious to the reporter that the child had been named after the iconic sixties girl.[57]

These were not the only appropriations. Quino was continuously surprised at how his character was used by ideological traditions that were the complete opposite not only of his own beliefs but also of Mafalda's. Around that time, the right-wing Movement for Dignity and Independence (Movimiento por la Dignidad y la Independencia, or MODIN) had used Mafalda's image for an election campaign. The party had been created by Aldo Rico, the former military officer who had led the *Carapintada* insurrections in the late 1980s, and who, after being pardoned by Menem, was trying his hand at electoral politics. The campaign posters, which Quino had stumbled upon by chance, showed Mafalda rolling up her sleeves and saying, "Let's see now! Where do we have to start pushing to move this country forward?" The cartoonist was outraged and immediately demanded that all posters be destroyed. Just as in the past, the comic strip's popularity and polysemy made it an attractive loot that could be co-opted by those who stood in stark opposition to the progressive middle class.[58]

The celebrations for the thirtieth anniversary of the cartoon in 1994 had more than one epicenter. Buenos Aires had kicked them off the previous year and they continued almost uninterruptedly throughout 1994.[59] The book signings and the coverage in the news evidenced the interest that the comic strip had among younger generations. A book signing at the book fair held in the Municipal Exhibit Center attracted more than one hundred kids who joined the hundreds of adults hoping to meet the famous cartoonist and ask him for his autograph, either for themselves or for their children or grandchildren. At the same fair, the Buenos Aires Press Workers' Union invited kids to engage in a conversation with Quino.[60] *Clarín*'s Sunday magazine *Viva*, which featured Quino's current cartoons, did a long piece on *Mafalda* that included interviews with teenage fans. The girls interviewed said they identified with the main character, and they shared their memories with the reporter. Mariana Tuchinsky, a seventeen-year-old high-school student, recalled, for example, that when

"I challenged my parents or refused to finish my soup, they'd tell me: 'What's the matter, Mafalda?'" The boys instead saw themselves as Miguelito, because they felt they were just as scatterbrained and self-centered as he was, or Felipe, because of his rejection of educational institutions. Many companies tapped into this interest among kids and came out with all sorts of Mafalda-inspired products, including chewing gum featuring the cartoon on the wrapper and sold under the slogan "Finally! Gum that makes you think!"[61] *Viva* also sought the opinion of renowned personalities, such as the singer Mercedes Sosa, the writer Ernesto Sábato, and the painter Guillermo Roux, who in evoking *Mafalda* highlighted its universal nature but also its capacity to represent a shared Argentine identity. For others, the comic strip's lasting relevance rested on its ability to express the social processes that cut across Argentine society. Thus Jorge Schvarzer, in *Página/12*, used the comic strip as a symbol of a middle class that had been fractured by successive economic crises. *Mafalda*, he said, recalled the "idyllic world" of equitable distribution of wealth that had come tumbling down. Starting in 1975, with the economic adjustment policies known as the "Rodrigazo" (after the economy minister Celestino Rodrigo), the old distribution model that sought to achieve economic development and social harmony had quickly eroded. Schvarzer argued that over the following years, the backbone of the middle class—formed by public employees and teachers—had descended into poverty, while others made fortunes through financial speculation and by exploiting niche markets. "The fracturing of the middle class was the result of a deliberate redistribution of income that affected all of society and divided this pseudo-class hopelessly in two. Now some buy imported cars and travel to the Polynesian islands while others can't pay their bills." *Mafalda* expressed those ruptures eloquently. Schvarzer imagined an embittered Manolito who had been unable to save his parent's grocery store from bankruptcy; he saw Susanita returning from a trip to Disneyland; and he pictured Mafalda saddened because her father had been forced to sell his beloved car. His article—with the suggestive title "The Middle Class Cut Down the Middle"—described the impoverishment of that social sector and its irreconcilable division. Similarly, an installment of *Matías*—a new comic strip centered on a kid—echoed the famous *Mafalda* strip on the definition of middle class, and in doing so it was symptomatic of the change that class had undergone. Like Mafalda years earlier, Matías asked his mom about their social standing: "Ma . . . are we rich or poor?" And his mom replied, "We're too poor to be rich and too rich to be poor. Do you understand what that means?" "It means we have good meals . . . but bad digestion," he answered.[62]

In another newspaper, Luis Alberto Quevedo remarked on this phenomenon that "Mafalda illustrated the virtues and miseries of a class that was living its best moment at that time," but which has now resigned itself to "vacationing in its own backyard."[63]

In sum, the new anniversary rekindled the comic strip's social and political significance. The appropriations were a way of responding to social processes that affected broad sectors of Argentine society and especially its middle class, which had been pushed out of its symbolic and social positions by neoliberal adjustment policies and economic crises. Having attained mythical status, *Mafalda* offered a powerful device to confront them. It contributed to preserve an identity that was wounded by material pauperization and challenged by a new middle-class culture that disputed its claim over that social sector. The crisis served to stress the importance of the comic strip and, with it, of certain cultural practices, such as going to exhibits, visiting the book fair, and buying books. The act itself of buying the comic strip, and not just the image, was a way for that sector of the middle class to resist the neoliberal order. And while Mafalda merchandise sold well, it was book sales that truly expressed this phenomenon.[64] According to Divinsky, some twenty million copies of the standalone "booklets" had been sold, all 115,000 copies of *Mafalda inédita* (published in 1988), and almost 55,000 copies of *Toda Mafalda*, which had come out a year earlier, with another 15,000 copies planned.[65] But the number of readers exceeded by far the number of books sold. During this period, and as a paradoxical effect of the country's neoliberal policies, numerous papers across Argentina were able to purchase the rights to publish the comic strip.[66]

THE CRISIS HEIGHTENS THE MYTH

Argentina's economic recession deepened in the second half of the 1990s. More and more industries were dismantled, privatized utility companies raised their rates to record highs with the aim of maximizing profits while providing increasingly poor services, and capital concentration and foreign ownership grew, further shrinking productive activities and favoring financial speculation. A large number of small companies were ruined as a result of the crisis but also as they lost competitiveness in the globalized economy. The social repercussions were immediate. The number of people living below the poverty line grew, and unemployment went from 7 percent in 1992 to 19 percent in 1995. Workers from the former state-owned companies who had agreed to "voluntary early retirement" spent their compensation in order to meet their daily needs as they found it hard to find new employment or saw their ventures fail. Moreover, labor flexibilization impacted the living conditions of workers across the board. The specter of casualization loomed over broad segments of the population like never before.[67]

This situation sparked protests across the country. In addition to labor strikes, unemployed workers staged major roadblocks, known as *piquetes*, eventually forming a nationwide *piquetero* movement. Teachers held a permanent demonstration in front of the congressional building, setting up a white tent that represented the color of the smocks they used in school and symbolized their rejection of educational reforms and their opposition to the government's economic adjustment policies and their underlying ideology. Rampant corruption, widespread insecurity, and deteriorated health and education services fueled social discontent. As neoliberal policies faltered, Menem failed in his attempt to amend the constitution so he could run for a third term and his sector was voted out of office. This was followed by a period of instability, during the government of Fernando de la Rúa, elected in 1999 under the Radical Party ticket in alliance with other political forces. The measures adopted by his government (reducing public spending, cutting wages, and maintaining a convertibility plan that pegged the Argentine peso to the US dollar) caused greater social unrest. In October 2001, following a corruption scandal, the government lost the legislative elections. Two months later, when protests peaked and descended into looting and rioting, the government responded by declaring a state of emergency and cracking down on demonstrators indiscriminately, killing thirty-three people. On December 20, the president was forced to step down.[68]

In that context, a caricature in Spain connected *Mafalda* with the social upheaval. On December 21, the Spanish newspaper *El Mundo* featured a vignette in which Mafalda was seen fleeing the "Don Manolo" grocery shop carrying several packages. As he watched her run, Manolito remarked "Not you too, Mafalda?" echoing Julius Caesar when he discovered that Brutus was part of the conspiracy to kill him. The image caused a stir in Argentina two weeks later, when Quino lashed out against the authors of the caricature, saying they had his comic strip all wrong. "Mafalda would have never looted the Don Manolo grocery store. . . . And, what's more, Manolo would've shown up at Mafalda's house with food if she were ever in need of it." Like many times before, Quino was angered to see Mafalda wrongly associated with actions that had nothing to do with the views she represented and which he moreover believed had been orchestrated by right-wing interests. The authors apologized, explaining that they only wanted to show their solidarity with Argentina and in their "European ignorance" had obviously "blundered."[69]

The Spanish caricature, however, is telling. It placed *Mafalda*—the mythical comic strip of the 1960s—in the eye of the political storm that was raging in Argentina. As we saw, the collective game of imagining the fate of the characters had served to catalyze the impact of neoliberal policies on both the middle and working classes. In the new scenario, *Mafalda* took on renewed meanings. The 1960s nostalgia went from channeling the resistance against neoliberalism to feeding the ideological and symbolic rhetoric of a broad range of actors who, over the following years, would bring back social utopian ideas, political activism, and social commitment. That was the strategy deployed by President Néstor Kirchner, who was able to fill the political void left by the crisis and the widespread disillusionment with politicians and win the elections in 2003. Kirchner then sought to garner further support through his defense of human rights and the promotion of welfare state policies.

This climate favored the circulation of *Mafalda*. In the years leading up to the Kirchner administration, the comic strip had been featured occasionally in the media whenever Quino was awarded a new international prize (such as the Iberian American Quevedo Prize for Graphic Humor) or new translations were published (into Korean, for example). In 2003, *Clarín*—which, by then, backed the Kirchner administration—chose *Mafalda* to launch a collection of twenty classic Argentine comics.[70] This new edition contained a selection of strips organized thematically in sections (thoughts, parents, baby brother, friends, school, and questions). The collection came out in installments every fifteen days and was sold at a very affordable price. That, combined with *Clarín*'s position as the leading national newspaper and its powerful publicity and distribution machinery, helped bring the comic strip back to mass audiences.[71] Oscar Steimberg penned the prologue, lending his prestige to the publication. He called on readers to reflect on the genre, how the social and political context had changed with each new publication of *Mafalda*, and the comic strip's complexity (the issues addressed, the different personalities of the characters, the correlations between them and the political views of the middle class, and the relationships forged between them), which contrasted with the transparency of the main character. In that reflection, Steimberg noted that *Mafalda* encouraged readers to delve into their own personal memories and to engage in readings that were private explorations.[72]

That was without a doubt a key element in the resignification of the comic strip. In 2004, Mafalda turned forty and this new anniversary, like the ones before it, was celebrated with an almost continuous stream of tributes, starting at the Guadalajara Book Fair. That year was also Quino's fiftieth as a professional cartoonist and he received a number of awards, including the Hans Christian Andersen Award and Milan's Ambrogino d'Oro. The comic strip was celebrated in exhibits around the world (including Milan, Salamanca, Buenos Aires, Córdoba, and Mar del Plata), by the media (with articles in the papers and television coverage), presentations of new books (such as *¡Qué presente impresentable!*), and new editions in Italy, France, Spain, and Argentina.[73] Ediciones de la Flor also settled a long-outstanding debt in *Mafalda*'s international expansion with the publication of an English edition. According to Daniel Divinsky, publishing houses in the United States had considered that it was not appropriate for kids in their country (perhaps because *Mafalda* was originally meant for adults) and British publishing houses argued that it was too similar to *Peanuts*. According to Quino, a US publishing house had once approached him, but nothing had come of it because it turned out it was only interested in young talent.[74]

The lack of interest in English-speaking markets brings us back to the issue of the relationship between humor and the social context. In this sense, no single factor can be identified as the cause for *Mafalda*'s difficulties in entering the US market. As we saw in chapter 3, the comic strip's global expansion accompanied the Southern Cone exile diaspora and the possibilities it enabled for multiple appropriations of *Mafalda*. Nonetheless, the number of exiles was never a determining factor, as the comic strip was published in countries where immigration from the region was insignificant. The decisive element seems to have been that it was a product that could mobilize publishing networks and, at the same time, appeal to a progressive sensibility in each place.

The key for understanding this is to look at how humor is constructed. In his 1969 prologue, in which he compared Quino's comic strip to *Peanuts*, Umberto Eco argued that Charlie Brown lived in a children's world in which he tried desperately to fit in and from which adults were excluded. Mafalda instead lived in "dialectic confrontation" with the world of adults, which she rejected. The irony in *Mafalda* demands a reader who can navigate a complex composition, one that requires reading at an unhurried pace, and which contrasts with Schultz's economic, but equally effective, gags that allow for a faster tempo.

It could also be argued that *Mafalda* clashed with US politics from the position of the outsider. Andrew Graham-Yooll, the translator of the English edition, grappled with the difficulties involved in "transferring" the humor in *Mafalda* (which relied heavily on wordplay, allusions, and shared codes) from one language to another, while at the same time remaining faithful to the comic strip's meaning, as Quino had requested.[75] In that sense, it is symptomatic that one of the few strips omitted from the US edition was the one in which Mafalda echoed gender stereotypes when she argued that a woman could not be president because women had a tendency to gossip. It was thought that, taken out of context, that joke would attract criticism from a public influenced by a rising awareness of gender inequality.[76] The translation did, however, include the strips with Mafalda's uncomfortable questions about Vietnam, even though they could offend certain segments of public opinion in the United States, because it involved criticism voiced by a Latin American character.

Thus, no single element alone explains why it took so long for Mafalda to enter English-speaking markets; rather it was a combination of factors, including chance circumstances. In any case, it is something of a paradox that *Mafalda* became a global icon without being mediated by the preferred language of globalized exchanges. Moreover, in its rise to international popularity the comic strip actually benefitted from its marginal position, as its origin made it attractive to Europe, where there was great interest in Latin America. This in part explains how a product from a Latin American country came to globally symbolize the modernization of the middle class, the antiestablishment generation, women's struggles, and other phenomena for which US culture had been known in the 1960s and 1970s. While Quino had originally been asked to draw inspiration from US comics such as *Blondie* and *Peanuts*, he had created a product that sidestepped and even challenged that cultural hegemony.

PLACES OF PILGRIMAGE

As *Mafalda* entered the English-speaking market, it was also consolidating its renewed significance in Argentina's public life, at a time in which the country began to improve once again the prospects of the middle class and reclaimed (as a myth) the rebelliousness of the 1960s generation. In 2004, Argentina celebrated Quino's half century as a cartoonist with an exhibit held at the Palais de Glace in Buenos Aires. The "Quino, 50 Years" exhibit became a place of pilgrimage for fans, drawing more than sixty thousand visitors, a record number for the time. It was then taken to Mar del Plata, where it was seen by fifty thousand people, and over the next two years it traveled to Córdoba, Rosario, and other cities across the country.[77] A number of new tributes followed. In 2005, Quino was honored in both Buenos Aires and Mendoza with the title of Distinguished Citizen for his contribution to the arts, and he was appointed Knight of the Order of Isabella the Catholic by the King of Spain.[78]

The tributes to "Mafalda's father," as the media liked to refer to Quino, continued with several permanent spaces dedicated to him and his work. In August 2005, two squares were christened "Mafalda," one in the city of Mendoza and the other in the Colegiales district of the city of Buenos Aires. According to local accounts, the idea for the Buenos Aires square had originated a decade earlier with a group of people from the area who set out to block the construction of low-income housing in a vacant lot and prevent the relocation of families from a nearby shantytown. Although unconfirmed, the story is paradigmatic because it calls to mind popular works of fiction—such as Julio Cortázar's "Casa tomada" and Germán Rozenmacher's "Cabecita negra"—that reflected a middle class living in fear of an invasion of the masses. That exclusionary and violent sentiment typical of the social-distinction dynamics of a middle class that felt dangerously close to the lower classes had a somewhat peculiar twist here: the strategy for repelling the "invasion" involved celebrating the image of the progressive middle class as represented by Mafalda, the character who argued with Susanita, the "fat lady" who was disgusted by having to touch a black doll. It thus used the egalitarian myth for a purpose that subverted it.[79]

Whether accurate or not, there were no echoes of this story when the square was finally built ten years later in August 2005. The inauguration paid tribute to the little girl with a penchant for questioning, who, along with her gang of friends, represented a golden past that the new social climate appeared to be bringing back, and in which it emerged as a model for all generations. The square itself restored that past by evoking the communal culture of the neighborhood. This egalitarian urban spirit was expressed by the children playing together in the square and by the public school that opened across the street from it, which was also named after Mafalda and is currently coveted by middle-class parents in the area. The strips that grace the square were selected by Julieta Colombo, Quino's niece and representative, who had worked as curator in earlier projects. But the cartoonist and his creation were also honored by the people of the neighborhood themselves, who painted a permanent sign that reads, "Your characters touched our hearts and helped us resist. Your lucidity and honesty keeps us smiling even in hard times. For all of that, we promise to make your work known to the next generations, so that they may enjoy it, no matter what the world may bring. That is no small thing."[80] The inauguration, held on a Sunday morning, brought back other icons, as a band playing Beatles songs arrived in a Citroën like the one Mafalda's father cherished. A letter from Quino was read, balloons were released into the sky, and mothers and primary school teachers gave their impressions on the famous cartoon. One of them called Mafalda "the voice of our conscience."[81]

Three years later, in 2008, the comic strip joined subway riders below the streets of Buenos Aires when a fifteen-meter-long mural by the ceramist Teodolina García Cabo was installed in one of the underground passages of the A and D trains. Every day, thousands of people walk through that passage, which connects two stations near the Casa Rosada presidential palace.[82] Under the title "The World According to Mafalda," a series of strips unfolds along the tiled wall, showing the iconic main character typically speaking out against the problems of the world and in favor of children's rights. City officials and colleagues from Quino's generation—including the caricaturist Hermenegildo Sábat and the artist and writer Luis Felipe Noé—were present at the inauguration to celebrate the cartoonist. In its coverage, *Clarín* featured tributes from a new crop of illustrators, who spoke of his lasting influence and relevance. "I grew up with *Mafalda*, it's a part of my family and of my aspirations as an illustrator," graphic designer Pablo Bernasconi explained. "Like everyone in my generation, I learned to read with Mafalda," Liniers, a young cartoonist, confessed.[83] By then, the role the comic strip played as a tool for language acquisition and learning to read had expanded beyond the restricted scope of the family. In schools across Argentina, teachers had begun using the comic strip as reading material. In 2007, Argentina's Ministry of Education and Culture selected *Mafalda* for a collection of one hundred literary works to be distributed in schools.[84] The comic strip had also been included in Spanish courses for foreign students offered in Argentina. Similarly, it was used by Spanish teachers outside Argentina who found in it a fun and easy way to introduce students to colloquial vocabulary.[85]

At the same time, a "World According to Mafalda" exhibit especially curated for children by a Córdoba museum (Museo del Barrilete) received sixty thousand visitors and was later taken on the road to several other cities around the country. It also traveled to Mexico for an annual Guadalajara festival (Festival Creativo Papirolas) that attracts 100,000 visitors each year. The exhibit included games for the kids and was an opportunity for their parents to revisit Argentina's past through a nostalgic encounter with Mafalda's home life. The ochre tones of the displays helped set the mood and made it easy for them to relive their own experiences.

The image of the modern family, which Quino had so vividly painted in his comic strip, was completed with the inclusion of Mafalda and family riding in an actual Citroën and with a re-creation of their apartment. These displays evoked the discreet well-being enjoyed by the middle and working classes in the 1960s, but whose modernity seemed somewhat anachronistic forty years later. The outdated, but also mythical, connotations were all the more evident in a society in which the very notion of "typical family" was being challenged by demands for the legal recognition of diverse families.[86] As a reader recalls today, when she discovered the comic strip fifteen years ago she was struck

FIGURES 5.2, 5.3, AND 5.4 Statue and plaque located on the corner of Chile and Defensa Streets, in the neighborhood of San Telmo. Photos taken by the author, February 2014.

by how different Mafalda's family was from her own, as she had never known her father.[87] Readers in the 1960s who came from families that did not fit the established model must have felt a similar distance; but the difference is that four decades earlier social norms were only starting to be massively challenged.

With the inauguration in 2009 of a Mafalda statue in the Buenos Aires district of San Telmo, fans of the character finally had their mecca. The statue was placed in front of the building where Quino had lived and which he had incorporated into the comic strip as Mafalda's home (see figures 5.2, 5.3, and 5.4). The character literally materialized in the space where she was born. One of the building's dwellers came up with the idea and pitched it to the government of the City of Buenos Aires. The city authorities that green-lighted the initiative (which included a plaque on the building's facade) justified their decision arguing that it was the birthplace of all the characters and their childhood home, and thus echoed, and at the same time strengthened, the vivid materiality of Quino's creation, the sense that it was not just fiction, but real. Javier Irrgang, a sculptor well known for his work in open spaces, was commissioned for the job.[88] A massive statue was initially suggested by the project committee, but the artist thought a more life-size statue would be better, as it would put the character at the same level as her fans. However, he felt that bringing her out of the page and turning her into a three-dimensional figure was a huge challenge, and he asked Quino to oversee the whole creative process so everything would be just right. He had endless details to consult with Quino (Where exactly should he put the bow on her head? What texture should the hair be? What color skin should he give her?). The people in the neighborhood wanted to have her sitting on the curb, as Quino had often drawn her. But the urban planning office did not authorize it for fear that the crowds it was expected to draw would create traffic jams and even accidents. So Mafalda was finally placed on a park bench.[89] When the statue was unveiled, the whole neighborhood came out to welcome Mafalda as one of their own.[90] At the event, Hermenegildo Sábat called for justice for all those "rebel and consistent young people who were Mafalda's friends" and who had no sculptures of their own, and Quino spoke on behalf of "a generation that saw humor persecuted and jailed, [a time] when smiling was a threat and laughing out loud a risk." In this way, the ceremony that inaugurated the main place of worship for Mafalda followers also evoked the absences caused by state terrorism.

As the planners expected, the statue has become a pilgrimage site. Mafalda has since been joined by Manolito and Susanita. The choice of additional characters is significant, because ideologically they were both completely different from Mafalda. The site thus recovers the kaleidoscopic view of a middle

FIGURES 5.5 AND 5.6.
Mafalda items sold in
stores in the area.

class that felt united despite its differences. However, most of the objects, cards, books, and souvenirs that are sold in the many stores that have opened near the site feature Mafalda (figure 5.6). She is the main reason the site has become a tourist destination and is flooded with visitors seven days a week—people from around the city, across the country, and all over the world coming together like a nonreligious congregation.

On a warm summer day in 2014 (before the other characters have been added), I make my way to the site shortly after lunch to experience it for myself and gather impressions for my book. When I arrive some eight people are waiting patiently in line in front of the statue. I tell them about my research and ask if I can interview them. Before I can finish, a woman cries out excitedly in a Portuguese accent, "Interview me! You *have* to talk to me!" She tells me she is a fifty-year-old dentist from Belo Horizonte, Brazil. She has been coming to Buenos Aires every year since 2009 and always pays a visit to her favorite character. She was introduced to the comic strip by an Argentine friend. "Mafalda is very perceptive, very clever. I admire her," she tells me. Behind her is a taxi driver born and bred in a Buenos Aires working-class district. He discovered *Mafalda* in the 1970s. "What got me interested was that political thing the comic strip had," he says. His parents did not like him reading it. They could not stand it. Perhaps, he tells me, because they were of Galician descent and were offended by Manolito's character. By the time I finish talking to him, the line is much longer.

I see grown men and women, young people, boys and girls. They each have their unique story that connects them to the cartoon. They bring no offerings. They have no prayers. They just hug Mafalda. Kiss her. Speak to her. Joke with her. And as they do, Mafalda brings them close to others who, like them, admire her. They share their memories: how old they were when they started reading the comic strip, what it has meant to them. They pose for pictures, alone or in groups. Some send their picture to a friend or sibling who was not able to come with them. An office worker tells me, "Mafalda was an important part of my life. Now I'm bringing my daughters and grandchildren to see her." An Argentine researcher in his thirties has brought along two friends with the same intention. They come all the way from the United States, where he now lives. I realize there are very few teenagers on their own. It seems more like a family affair (there are many fathers and mothers with their children, or grandparents with grandchildren), or an outing with friends, or even as part of a city tour. There are also tourists visiting San Telmo who have no idea who Mafalda is but are attracted by the fuss around the statue and stop to take a picture next to it. The vast majority, however, is not here by chance. It was the statue that brought them here. The people in the neighborhood have forged a different relationship with this Mafalda. Some pat her on the back as they walk by and children stop and give her a peck on the cheek on their way to school.[91] She is alive to them. No other statue in Buenos Aires has that effect.

A FLESH-AND-BLOOD CHARACTER

"I feel funny leaving her like that, all alone." Quino's words—almost a confession, coming unexpectedly at the end of the statue's unveiling ceremony—betray a tenderness we usually reserve for living beings. Quino seems to have sensed that Mafalda has become just that. Anyone reading this book could very well argue that she had stepped out of the frame long ago. And they would be partly right. The character has always had a lifelike quality, which turned her, and the comic strip, into a social phenomenon. Quino himself unintentionally nurtured that quality, which would at one point turn out to be overbearing for him. In interviews and news accounts "Mafaldita"—as he used to call her in the 1960s, using the affective diminutive—would be treated almost as if she were a real person. The same thing happened with the other characters. He had created them, but, as novelists like to say, they had taken on a life of their own, often even in his mind. This did not prevent a symbiosis between creator and creation—"Mafalda is me," as Quino has said—but that phenomenon has been tainted by the autonomy that each of the characters gained.

In the 1990s, the vividness of the characters prompted the social game of imagining them as adults, which highlighted—and still highlights—a key element of the Mafalda myth: the ambiguous nature of the comic strip's condition. I draw again on Mircea Eliade to consider a characteristic of myths that I have not yet mentioned: their supernatural quality. Mythical beings are such precisely because they set themselves apart from human beings, whose existence is governed by the laws of nature, life and death, and by social norms that make them historical beings. As supernatural characters, mythical figures are not subject to the laws of time and space. Perhaps one of the best examples of contemporary mythical figures is Che Guevara, whose image represents the figure of the eternally young and virile hero.

Mafalda is mythical but in a different way. To analyze the supernatural element in the cartoon we can draw on the concept of ambiguity, as defined by Victor Turner, which establishes a threshold, a sort of limbo, that creates a suspension—a symbolic fracture—of the coordinates of normal reality.[92] In this sense, *Mafalda* evolved from social phenomenon into myth when the characters became part of a social game that involved giving real, concrete life to a cultural creation, to fictional beings drawn on paper, so that the cartoons grew and changed like actual living individuals. Moreover, Mafalda was a character born from a grotesque combination—again in Turner's terms—that resulted in a masculine/feminine, child/adult creature. The characters had been stepping out of the frame as early as the 1960s—for example, when the *Buenos Aires Herald* published a picture showing Mafalda sitting on her creator's lap. Later, the accounts surrounding the announced arrival of Mafalda's baby brother, Guille, introduced a playful innovation as speculations about an event that had not yet happened in the comic strip spread to the media. But this phenomenon really kicked off with the vignettes featured on the upper margin of the pages of *Siete Días*, which expanded the jokes in the strips with playful nods to the readers that connected fiction with reality. That blurring of the lines between the cartoon world and real life was perhaps best epitomized by the strip in which the characters bid farewell to their readers. But when Quino decided to stop producing new strips, the readers and the media took the social game of interacting with the characters and bringing them to life to a whole new level. As noted throughout the book, there were multiple spaces and moments in which Mafalda and her gang of friends came alive: for example, the title chosen by the Argentine critic Sasturain for the *Superhumor* article in which he imagined the character coming of age ("Little Mafalda Turns 17 and She's Smoking Hot"), or Mafalda's presence in the Letters to the Editor section of *El Globo* in Spain, where readers addressed her directly, calling her "The best comic book creation of the Spanish-speaking world."[93] This trend was particularly popular during Argentina's democratic restoration.

The stories woven by readers and the media about the post-strip life of the characters reached a new level of malleability at the intersection of three different episodes in 1988. First, the speculations regarding the fate of the characters fell into a nebulous—even dangerous—space, somewhere between ludic and serious, when Quino declared that Mafalda could have been one of Argentina's disappeared. Second, the global dimension of the comic strip's twenty-fifth anniversary boosted the playful component involved in celebrating a cartoon's birthday. Third, new players that were not part of the media or the field of humor joined in on this social game of bringing the characters into the real world. In 1994, *Clarín*'s supplement *Revista Viva* reported that back in 1988 the renowned historian Félix Luna had proposed that Mafalda be declared "Distinguished Citizen" of Buenos Aires. Luna, who was at the time the city's culture secretary, had supposedly argued that she deserved the honor because she "symbolizes the noblest sentiments of many young Argentines who refuse to toe the line of the establishment and strive to change it and enrich it with their fresh ideas." While there is no official evidence that Luna's initiative actually existed—only the anecdote in the news several years later—the fact that it seemed plausible enough to print reveals the liminal space that Mafalda inhabited, straddling life and fiction, reality and fantasy, playfulness and seriousness. *Revista Viva* claimed that many fans thought of Mafalda as a "flesh-and-blood" being. As one fan explained, "Mafalda is more human than many human beings," and she even "has a birth certificate."[94] A *Somos* article published in 1988 recognized the importance of that ambiguity that was part of the essence of the comic strip: "What has Mafalda been up to these past fifteen years? All those books, posters, and exhibits contributed to *partially bring her back* from her (apparently definite) *death*. And many of her admirers are heartened by the fact that it is only an apparent death—those admirers who cannot accept her fifteen years of silence."[95]

Over the following years, Quino grew tired of being asked over and over what had become of Mafalda or what would Mafalda think of every new event that confirmed the catastrophic state of the world. He still answered patiently, but his responses reflected that ambiguity. Sometimes he would play along— for example, when he noted that neoliberalism had wiped out the Felipes and Mafaldas and had left only Susanitas and Manolitos. That tendency to see Mafalda as a real person was also evident when he said he could imagine her as an environmental activist or when he declared that he would never put her in an instant soup commercial because that would be a betrayal ("I would never do that to her!" he said). But he was only willing to go so far. He could draw her again—and in fact he did, for special campaigns or as a gift for friends—but he never drew her as an adult. To him, Mafalda was still that little girl wise beyond her years, with the same features and the same age she had when he stopped drawing her in 1973, no matter how vivid she felt to readers.

That did not stop Quino's colleagues from drawing an adult version for him, thus introducing a new phase in the social game of imagining her life outside the comic strip. In 1984, Italian caricaturists re-created her as a young woman. Mauro Monetti imagined a thin, long-legged grown-up Mafalda sporting a miniskirt walking by a graffitied wall from which the original Mafalda looked on with a knowing smile. Similarly, Bruno D'Alfonso drew a sexy adult version, without showing her face, and a surprised teenage boy exclaiming, "Mafalda? Quino's Mafalda? I almost didn't recognize you!" In her home country, in 1988, a comic strip penned by Eduardo Maicas and Juan Carlos Muñiz and illustrated by Mercado published in *Hum*® magazine staged a meeting between Patoruzú (another famous Argentine cartoon) and an adult Mafalda. In this case the changes had been less dramatic: she had become a bookish young woman with glasses and no sex appeal.[96] With the thirtieth anniversary of the cartoon in 1994 came new adult versions. The popular

Argentine cartoonist Caloi imagined his character Clemente (featured daily in *Clarín*) dreaming that he was marrying his fiancée in the Bombonera stadium, home to Maradona's soccer team, and that Mafalda and Patoruzú were guests at the ceremony. The dream ended with Mafalda as a sensual bikini-clad beauty. The cartoonist and painter Carlos Nine took the sexual theme to extremes with his version of Mafalda as a "cabaret girl" with a revealing outfit and bedroom eyes.[97] This image was in stark contrast to the virginal and saintly Mafalda sketched in 2007 by Uruguayan illustrator Alfredo Sábat against a background of what looks like the interior of a gothic cathedral, which was meant as an allusion to the legacy of Western culture.[98]

In Spain, the game took on a different form and meaning at the ceremony of the Quevedo Prize awarded to Quino in the year 2000. The organizers did not produce a grown-up version of the characters but they did have flesh-and-blood doubles bringing them to life. These performers did not put on a play; rather, honoring a long tradition, they composed living portraits to create a symbolic scene that connected with the people in the audience. The characters ceremoniously stepped out onto a grand stage and Quino, astonished, heard Mafalda's mother ask him, "What do you think of these characters?" The kids who played the character then cried out together, "Thank you, Quino!" The cartoonist hugged them and congratulated them. The children had been selected among students of the Francisco de Quevedo public school in the city of Alcalá de Henares, where the prize is awarded, and they were not familiar with Mafalda.[99] After the ceremony, many criticized the idea. According to *El País*, it evidenced a "penchant for the grotesque" and the "tendency to infantilize the famous strip," which removed all traces of its "anti-establishment and subversive meaning." According to the critic, instead of renewing *Mafalda*'s readership, as had been the intention, the tribute had trivialized the comic strip.[100]

The image of a living, breathing Mafalda was constantly reaffirmed by headlines in Argentina and Spain. Newspaper editors engaged in a friendly competition to outdo each other in creativity. "Stay Strong, Mafalda!"; "Mafalda Now Speaks Korean"; "Quino, Mafalda's Dad, Celebrates His Seventy-Fifth Birthday in Paris"; "The Word Is Out: Mafalda Turns Twenty-Five"; "We'd Love to Have Mafalda at the Prado Museum"—these were some of the many headlines that treated her as if she were a person.[101] When Mafalda was named one of the ten most influential Argentine women of the twentieth century—along with Eva Perón, the poet and singer-songwriter María Elena Walsh, and Hebe de Bonafini, one of the leaders of the Mothers of Plaza de Mayo—Quino exploded, "It's absurd! She's a cartoon. A little girl. Not even a woman."[102] Unable to stop the game, Quino considered countering it with a strip in which he imagined her death. That idea was not new, of course. It had come up even before the cartoonist decided to stop drawing her. In 1971, Alberto Mazzei, a reader from Corrientes, wrote a letter to the magazine *Siete Días* asking if it was true that Quino was thinking of eliminating the character for good. "If it's true," the reader said, "it looks a lot like a crime, a 'humoricide' of sorts." And he included a drawing in which Mafalda's friends were portrayed crying at her funeral.[103] In 1972, while visiting Spain Quino had confessed to the Catalan press, "Sometimes I feel like I'm going to kill Mafalda. As time goes by, I feel I have less and less freedom."[104]

There was an atypical element to *Mafalda*. While the comic strip was a product of the culture industry that had originally been conceived in the world of advertising and made use of globalized marketing strategies, in contrast to other major comics it had not gone the way of mass production, nor had it been distributed through syndicates. Quino never felt comfortable with the idea of working with an assistant, although he did try it. He continued to draw each and every one of his strips—often tracing them—and laboriously meeting every deadline. His methods were thus outdated and that made production increasingly more difficult. Also, as the years went by and Mafalda and friends grew, Quino incorporated the changes brought on by the passage of time, but he was keenly aware that he could not continue doing that indefinitely without distorting the essence of the characters and the storyline. In that sense, the conceit that the characters existed in real life implicitly carried the possibility of their death, so that when the comic strip ended, there seemed to be an obvious logic to the metaphor.

Even though Quino announced it as a momentary break—"a vacation" was what he called it—the decision gave substance to the fantasy and prompted a string of funereal speculations, ranging from the comical to the morbid, the light-hearted to the tragic. Imagining Mafalda's death seemed the logical conclusion to having given her "life." Upon hearing the news, in 1974 a Spanish journalist wrote, "Our Mafalda is dying," and noted that her death made Quino's creation more honest, as it went against the logic of mass production.[105] In Latin America, the death metaphor was tinged with a sort of magical realism. A headline in a Caracas newspaper proclaimed in 1977 that Quino had "murdered" Mafalda because he was jealous. When the word spread that there would be no new installments, incredulous readers demanded an explanation from the newspaper it was featured in, which in turn sought the opinion of leading Venezuelan cartoonists. In Pedro León Zapata's opinion, for example, Quino had been right to kill her—"she was obnoxious; it wasn't out of envy"— as he would now be able to concentrate on other projects. "Mafalda is dead, long live Quino!" he concluded. Nonetheless, even those who celebrated her "death" had been enthusiastic readers of the comic.[106]

The joke became part of the folklore surrounding the cartoon. In Mexico, it fit right in with that country's unique culture of celebrating death, where the living feast with the dead, sharing joys and sorrows. Mexico's natural and festive relationship with the dead is grounded on humor and it is incorporated firmly in its popular culture through caricatures, in particular through José Guadalupe Posada's famous *Calavera Catrina*, which has become the referential image of Death in Mexico. It is not surprising, then, that the fantasies of Mafalda's death were particularly popular there. Quino was still being asked about it in Mexico as late as 1997. At that year's Guadalajara Book Fair, where he was a guest speaker, he faced numerous readers, both young and old, who wanted to know how Mafalda had died. "Every time I visit [Mexico] people want to know if it's true that Mafalda was run over by a soup truck or a police car. I don't know where that idea came from; not from any strip of mine. It's entirely made up, a purely Mexican fantasy. . . . Mafalda didn't die, she's a cartoon and cartoons don't die."[107] But his words fell on deaf ears. In Mexico, the myth of Mafalda necessarily required imagining her death. More than a decade later, the idea was still strong. According to Alberto Fernández, in the literary magazine *Letras Libres*, everyone in Mexico knew that "Quino killed Mafalda." This was indeed a phrase that came up often in the interviews with Mexican readers I conducted for my research. However, there was no consensus as to how she died, and the contrasting of possibilities made the game of imagining her death more interesting. Some believed Quino had in fact drawn a strip in which Mafalda died under the wheels of an army truck, while others were convinced it had been a soup tank truck, and still others thought that regardless of what her creator may have wanted, a logical death for her would have been by strangulation at the hands of Manolito.[108]

In Mexico these fantasies can be seen as a tribute, as a way of incorporating the myth of Mafalda into Mexico's popular culture. In Salta, however, one of the most conservative and religious provinces of Argentina, Mafalda's death was used with an entirely different intention, namely as a cautionary tale for Catholics. A Jubilee poster in the year 2000 featured a comic strip that showed Mafalda in a succession of situations typical of the character, each captioned with variations of a similar phrase—"Too busy/distracted/preoccupied to think about God"—and ending in a scene with Mafalda in a coffin and the caption "Too late to think about God." The message was crystal clear.[109]

These macabre fictions nurtured the Mafalda myth, but its vitality lay in the multiple references to the cartoon, the constant reappropriations, and the new meanings ascribed to it by the legions of readers who had been forever captivated by her universal appeal. In 2009, the "intellectualized little girl" accompanied 100,000 women in Italy in a march against Silvio Berlusconi's sexism. In 2011, a giant Mafalda doll was placed in the middle of Plaza de Mayo for Cristina Kirchner's inauguration. Her image could be seen in student protests in Valencia during the Spanish economic crisis, and in 2017 in anti-Trump demonstrations in New York. In sum, Mafalda has become a global myth that can be appropriated by different groups around the world who draw on her symbolic power to highlight their demands and to make sense of the dilemmas faced in the twenty-first century.

CONCLUSION

In 2014 *Mafalda* turned fifty and the celebrations exceeded every expectation. The birthday was announced in countless magazines, newspapers, blogs, and web pages worldwide. Tributes followed one another in rapid succession to the beat of prizes, exhibits, events, and new editions. In France Quino was awarded the Legion of Honor, that country's highest order of merit, and in Spain he received the prestigious Prince of Asturias Prize for Communications and Humanities, while in Argentina he opened that year's edition of the Buenos Aires Book Fair, and multiple events were held across Latin America to celebrate his work. These tributes had a huge impact. The latest editions saw a new boost in sales, the number of followers of the official Mafalda Facebook page climbed to seven million (having doubled in only four years), street vendors everywhere in Argentina sold bootleg merchandise featuring Mafalda and friends, and the main character's image was held up as a symbol by demonstrators protesting femicide in Uruguay and homophobia in New York, among other causes. *Mafalda* is still, without a doubt, the most popular Latin American comic strip in the world.

What are the reasons behind its enormous popularity and staying power? What social significations has the comic strip had and how have these changed over the years? These questions were at the heart of what prompted me to write this book. As I set out to answer them I focused on three dimensions. First, I examined the comic strip itself, because Quino's creativity, his clever humor, and the quality of his artwork are essential elements of *Mafalda*'s great appeal. Second, I looked at the conditions of production of the comic strip and the various individuals (publishers, agents, translators, journalists, curators) and institutions involved that made its publication, circulation, and dissemination possible. And third, I considered the appropriations, uses, and significations of the comic strip by a range of subjects (individuals, institutions, and organizations) throughout its history and around the world. With those dimensions in mind, I embarked on a purely historical reconstruction of *Mafalda*, in the belief that it would help explain the social phenomenon produced by the comic strip. Understanding that phenomenon would, in turn, provide insight into major historical processes of the recent past. For that reason I organized each chapter around a different issue that has been important in the field of historiography in the last few decades. The first issue involves the discussion on how to conceptualize the middle class in the 1960s in connection with the processes of social modernization, conflicts concerning the family, and generational and gender clashes. This discussion is particularly relevant because the political and social importance this class unquestionably had in the 1960s enables us to separate the question of its origins and examine the polarized views that placed this social group's sympathies either to the left or to the right of the political spectrum. The second issue focuses on political polarization and radicalization to explore how they affected culture and society in Argentina, providing insight in this sense for all of Latin America. The third issue poses the question of the place of Latin American cultural productions in the world, exploring the conditions and interventions that made the emergence and circulation of a "progressive," "antiestablishment," and "rebellious" culture possible. The fourth returns to the role of cultural productions and their social meanings in Argentina under the country's dictatorship and subsequent democratic transition. The last issue considers the disputes around the legacy of the antiestablishment generation and the symbolic and material effects of the global rise of neoliberalism. Following this brief outline of what I set out to explore in this book, I would now like to summarize my leading findings.

I have posited that humor is an extremely rich avenue for exploring the middle class's social and cultural modernization and identity in the 1960s. Using implicit references, omitted lines, and open endings, Quino's humor played with the blurring of the line between the public and the private as established by bourgeois modernity. He did this by illuminating the political through the familiar, and vice versa. The character of Mafalda allowed him to use the contrast between irony and naïveté to maximum effect. With great intuition, the illustrator abandoned the boy character he had initially included in his strip—a Charlie Brown–type character—and left only the little girl as the protagonist who catalyzed the gender and generational clashes emerging in Argentine society. The main character's concerns—and the situations she encountered—echoed and questioned the country's social and cultural modernization. What is interesting in this sense is that the comic strip went against the grain of the sugarcoated views that were on the rise at the time—such as those advanced by Latin America's political and cultural elites—and brought into play the limitations and frustrations, and even the impossibilities, of modernization. I highlighted this angle in particular to show that the comic strip was born at the intersection (produced as a result of Quino's unique working method) of the field of culture and humor, local and global political processes, and the social conditions of its readers. Quino drew on radically new social "materials"—to use Raymond Williams's expression—that were shaping Argentine society in the 1960s and, by doing so, he shone a light on the professional and intellectualized middle class that read his comic strip. The result he achieved was also new. This humor demanded a reflective self-perception from its audience, and it triggered a social experience that emerged from reading the comic strip, but at the same time exceeded it, and nurtured a sense of belonging to a community. It is in this sense that I have argued that *Mafalda* operated on reality to shape that identity, giving it an image and a voice.

I was interested in showing how the comic strip's structure was modified to accompany the changes in the material demands of its production—for example, as it went from appearing daily in a newspaper to being featured in a weekly magazine—and how it dialogued with the social and political contexts. Thus, for example, the structure, argument, and social meaning of the comic strip was redefined with the introduction of Susanita and Manolito, which allowed Quino to take up two widely circulated prototypes with enormous symbolic power. Mafalda, the character, gained substance as the counterpoint to these two new characters, who were, in turn, defined as mutually opposing. She thus distanced herself from the "anti-popular" middle class (Susanita) and the "social climbers" (Manolito), and that distance completed her ideological definition. In this way, the cast of characters created a choral view that offered an unprecedented representation of this social sector: a heterogeneous middle class pierced by ideological and cultural differences that nonetheless did not prevent it from being considered a "single" class, defined by its social ties and shared experiences. With this conceptualization, I am proposing a way of thinking about the middle class that takes into account its heterogeneity and its ideological differences and conflicts, and a perspective for studying it that connects the material with the symbolic, the private with the public, and experiences with identity. *Mafalda* portrayed an image of Argentine society centered on the middle class, but that view was, at the same time, strained by the problematization of social injustices and inequalities. This expanded the scope of the comic strip, so that it spoke to the working classes as well. It also favored a manifold and varied identification, in which the most salient identity was, of course, associated with the younger generations and social protest. This association was furthered by the main character's ideological stance, which combined Third Worldism in international affairs, antiauthoritarianism at the national level (which made it possible to avoid the Peronism/anti-Peronism dichotomy), and universal concerns (such as social injustice, inequality, and war), while continuing to blur the line between domestic life and politics.

Moreover, I analyzed how the comic strip gained further complexity as of 1968 when it moved to the magazine *Siete Días*, both in terms of humor (with the addition of marginalia), the new characters that represented the greater rebelliousness of the youngest generation (Guille) and the more politicized sectors (Libertad), and the echoing of political and social struggles. I argued that with these new developments the comic strip worked with the dilemmas faced by Argentine society, and it influenced controversies and helped define positions. And in the discussions it prompted, the cartoon was caught in a crossfire. On the one hand, the character of Mafalda was criticized because she was seen as a dangerous subversive and as representing the rebelliousness of the new generations. On the other, she was reproached for her moderate political stance and her petit bourgeois attitude.

I have stressed how the massive scale of these discussions reveals the extent to which political radicalization had taken hold in the country, with the growing importance of the revolutionary intellectual and the renewed criticism leveled against the middle class by exponents of the long-standing sociopolitical tradition in sociology. In this sense, this analysis shows the central importance of understanding the middle class in its historicity. This entails conceiving the middle class dynamically, within a rapidly moving historical process, and examining the way that process affected individual lives, the positions adopted by different actors, and social identities, in the contingent intersection of long-term structures and turbulent social and political junctures.

I described in detail this context, in which rising authoritarianism and repressive violence pierced *Mafalda*, because the rapid changes in the "speakable" in public opinion and the fierce ideological battles between the left and the right are key elements for understanding the heightened confrontations and the way in which cultural productions were read and used in those struggles, and how they operated in them. The differences that divided the organizations that opposed the status quo in Argentina (as in the rest of Latin America) were so significant that they could not be viewed as a unified and coherent movement. However, their common denominators could be expressed through humor, through a cultural production such as the "ideology-denting stick," which became a "watchword" for the antiauthoritarian and antiestablishment sensitivity that linked various political actors and social subjects. The importance of that image as representative of a common identity is evident in the intelligence services' use of an adulterated version of the poster in 1975 in an effort to win over certain sectors of the middle class and as a way of co-opting a symbol of the "enemy"—that is, of individuals who opposed the repressive power of the state. Following the 1976 coup d'état, this strategy of appropriation was taken to extremes when, after brutally murdering a group of Pallottine priests and seminarians in an act of revenge, members of the repressive forces used the original poster to send a threatening message to opponents, in an attempt to turn that symbol into a macabre instrument of terror.

The comic strip's antiauthoritarian political meaning, underscored by these appropriations, was again evidenced by the censoring of part of the dialogue of the *Mafalda* movie that came out in 1981, near the end of the dictatorship, although the comic strip in print form continued to be published uncensored throughout this period. In this book, however, I have proposed an approach for understanding cultural productions during the dictatorship based on a nonbinary logic that goes beyond thinking in terms either of repression or resistance. This approach had three elements. First, I sought to illustrate the paradoxes that existed, such as the absurd situation in which a soldier momentarily suspends his repressive role to express his admiration for the comic strip and request a Mafalda drawing from a political prisoner he is guarding, in the mistaken belief that he is the cartoon's creator. I also took into consideration the contradictions in the policies of the dictatorship and the cracks left by its repressive action. The second element of this approach involved identifying the subjective, intimate, and private resignifications of the comic strip during the period of state terrorism. I have argued that *Mafalda* was an object and an experience that enabled the survival and transmission of a certain aesthetics and sensitivity, of an ideology, social relations, and affective environments that opposed the dictatorial state of affairs. The third element of the approach entailed taking into account that while the coup d'état caused a fracture in Argentine society, that fracture did not mean an absence of continuity. In particular, it involved recognizing the significance of the proximity the subjects felt with respect to their experiences prior to the coup. For them, what they experienced (and how they interpreted it) was marked by the closeness (the proximity in time) of the previous intellectual climate and debates. This was evident in the discussions prompted by the screening of the *Mafalda* movie in 1981. From this angle, the return to democratic rule in 1983 brought to the fore again major issues from the 1960s, including the relationship between political commitment and the field of humor. If, in the past, Quino had been reluctant to put his artwork explicitly at the service of a political goal, in the context of a recovered but frail democracy, he decided to use his creation to further the cause of strengthening democracy. The comic strip's identification with the democratic creed, to which broad sectors of society adhered, renewed *Mafalda*'s social success. The twenty-fifth anniversary was commemorated with a massively attended exhibit and the publication of previously unpublished material. Moreover, the celebrations fueled a new resignification of the strip among the public, as Quino imagined that Mafalda could have been among the country's disappeared. The public was receptive to this interpretation because it helped process the tragic fate that had befallen the protest generation symbolized by the "intellectualized little girl."

The local dimension then gave way to an examination of how a Latin American comic strip that was not marketed through syndication schemes was able to achieve major international success. My conclusion is that such success was possible due to a combination of favorable contexts, contingencies, and unique appropriations. In the first place, Quino's working method allowed him to interact fluidly and dynamically with the field of humor and sociocultural processes on a transnational scale. His open and conceptual humor, which combined references to everyday life with atemporal reflections (on issues such as injustice, inequality, and human relations), facilitated its circulation in different contexts despite having a strong local component. This dynamic operated in the framework of a certain change of direction in cultural exchanges, which repositioned the "South" with respect to the "North" in the 1960s and '70s, as Latin America came to be seen as spearheading Third World efforts to build a new world order. Second, I took into account the importance of readers (the new antiestablishment generations, the displaced working and middle classes) who could laugh at themselves with that conceptual humor that played with the ruptures caused by modernization, political repression, and later the rise of neoliberalism. Third, I examined the sales strategies involved. In this sense, I highlighted the important role played by small ventures and the forging of informal networks through personal interactions, which provided a vehicle for cultural and political identities and subjectivities. This link between market, ideology, and subjectivity on a global scale turned out to be key. In those processes, Southern Cone immigrants and exiles were instrumental, as they drove the production and consumption of *Mafalda*. But the comic strip transcended them and built a readership in each country it entered. So, while that diaspora facilitated the comic strip's entry into those markets, *Mafalda* was quickly resignified by their national and local dynamics and processes. That is, it took on new meanings that were not dependent on connections with its original public.

Finally, I posited that in the last twenty-five years the social signification of *Mafalda* (both the character and the comic strip) was redefined as it was linked to social memory concerns at a global scale. The book editions, compilations and new formats, short films, exhibits, and various objects contributed to keep *Mafalda* alive for the public and created new social, geographical, and virtual spaces for it. Its enormous media appeal was enhanced with every new production. In the 1990s, against the backdrop of the triumph of neoliberalism and the collapse of the Soviet bloc, *Mafalda* emerged as a myth, that is, a story—embodied in an image—that, in the words of Mircea Eliade, was a "most precious possession," offering exemplary models. The commemorative milestones (the birthday celebrations) and ritual spaces (exhibits, squares, statues) were decisive in the construction of that myth and in the intergenerational transmission (both inside and outside Argentina) of a sensitivity that seemed defeated. The comic strip was thus a vehicle for nostalgia and a legacy of resistance. *Mafalda* became a symbol that reasserted the value of political commitment, collective action, and social utopias as a way of countering the cult of individualism, capitalism, and the "end of history."

With the 2001 crisis in Argentina, the social phenomenon that *Mafalda* had become reached new heights. By then its cast of characters had long since taken on a life of their own, with readers treating them as flesh-and-blood individuals. Not for the first time, the public and the media engaged in a collective game of imagining the fate of Mafalda and her gang of friends. Played out in a global scenario and with the participation of numerous people and institutions, this game traced the supernatural condition of the myth, which involved characters that were not subject to the laws governing human life and challenged the categories used to organize reality. Mafalda straddled major Western dichotomies: male/female, child/adult, fiction/reality, eternity/historicity. Her liminal nature even prompted a macabre imagery—which had its epicenter in Mexico—that fed a myth whose strength lay in the multiple invocations, constant reappropriations, and new meanings that were made possible by the universal projection of the comic strip.

In sum, the comic strip was born inextricably linked to the historical processes of Argentina in the 1960s, which were, to a greater or lesser extent, connected with a global dimension. It had been crafted by an artist who could give form to universal characters and forge an open, polysemic, and versatile humor that prompted an ironic and sarcastic reflection on reality, by contrasting the acerbic nature of the strip's commentary on that reality with the innocence of the child characters who delivered it. That formula, which still stirs readers and demands that they engage actively in the production of the laughable, became an experience and an identity for subjects across time and space. There have been as many meanings, appropriations, and resignifications of *Mafalda* as there have been readers—readers who have been transformed by the act of reading the comic strip, as only art can do. That paper-and-ink universe contains relationships, problems, and reflections that have allowed these readers to grow, learn about themselves and others, and often make sense of their own existence, and which have catalyzed social and political issues that left a brutal mark on the second half of the twentieth century.

NOTES

INTRODUCTION

1   Bakhtin, *Rabelais and His World*. For an analysis of later developments in this respect, see Burucúa, *La imagen y la risa*.

2   Berger, *Redeeming Laughter*, 109–222.

3   Freud, *Jokes and Their Relation to the Unconscious*.

4   For a discussion on the social history of humor, see Swart, "'The Terrible Laughter of the Afrikaner.'"

5   Williams, *The Sociology of Culture*, 13.

6   Ginzburg, *The Cheese and the Worms*; and Chartier, *Cultural History*. For a Latin American approach, see also Rubenstein, *Bad Language, Naked Ladies, and Other Threats to the Nation*.

7   I found the following works particularly suggestive in this sense: Rapp, "Household and Family"; and Davidoff and Hall, *Family Fortunes*.

8   There are numerous contributions in this direction. A pioneering work is Kuznesof and Oppenheimer, "The Family and Society in Nineteenth-Century Latin America." For more recent overviews, see Gonzalbo Aizpuru, *Familias iberoamericanas*; and Pablo Rodríguez, ed., *La familia en Iberoamérica 1550–1980*. Also particularly useful for my research has been Owensby, *Intimate Ironies*; and Milanich, *Children of Fate*. There is extensive literature on the subject for Argentina in particular. See Míguez, "Familias de clase media"; Nari, *Políticas de maternidad y maternalismo político*; Cosse, *Estigmas de nacimiento*; Cosse, *Pareja, sexualidad y familia en los años sesenta*; and Losada, *La alta sociedad en la Buenos Aires de la* Belle Époque.

9   See Cosse, *Pareja, sexualidad y familia*, 14–15. With respect to everyday life and politics in Argentina, see Cosse, Manzano, and Felitti, *Los sesenta de otra manera*; Manzano, *The Age of Youth in Argentina*; and Felitti, *La revolución de la píldora*. For other Latin American countries, see Tinsman, *La tierra para el que la trabaja*; and Langland, "Birth Control Pills and Molotov Cocktails."

10 Appadurai, *Modernity at Large*; and Giddens, *Runaway World*. More recently, see López and Weinstein, *The Making of the Middle Class*.

11 For an example of this perspective, see Zolov, *Refried Elvis*. On the Left and the use of transnational networks, see Markarian, *Left in Transformation*; and on mass culture, see Cosse, "Cultura y sexualidad en la Argentina de los sesenta." For an overview, see Shukla and Tinsman, *Imagining Our Americas*.

12   Fraser, *1968: A Student Generation in Revolt*; Gould, "Solidarity under Siege"; and Lumley, *States of Emergency*, 39–40.

13   Masotta, *La historieta en el mundo moderno*, 145; Steimberg, *Leyendo historietas: Estilos y sentidos en un "arte menor*,*"* 174–76; Latxague, "Lire Quino."

14   There are numerous studies from this point of view, including, on the political and social context, Sasturain, "Mafalda en tres cuestiones" and "Mafalda sin libertad," in *El domicilio de la aventura*, 167–77; Foster, "Mafalda: An Argentina Comic Strip," on national identity; Foster, "Mafalda: Ironic Bemusement," in *From Mafalda to Los Supermachos*, 53–64, for a somewhat different focus; Wainerman, *La vida cotidiana en las nuevas familias*, 69–71, on everyday life; and with respect to urban aspects, Fernández L'Hoeste, "From Mafalda to Boogie."

15   Vázquez, *El oficio de las viñetas*; Levín, *Humor político en tiempos de represión*; Burkart, *De Satiricón a Hum®*; and Manzano, "'Contra toda forma de opresión.'" Pioneering studies include Rivera, "Historia del humor gráfico argentino"; and Matallana, *Humor y política*.

1. MARKS OF ORIGIN

1   Quino, *Mafalda inédita*, n.p.

2   Williams, *The Sociology of Culture*, 24.

3   See Parker, *The Idea of the Middle Class*; Owensby, *Intimate Ironies*; and Adamovsky, *Historia de la clase media argentina*. For an overview of this historiography, see Garguin, "El tardío descubrimiento de la clase media en Argentina"; and Visacovsky and Garguin, eds., *Moralidades, economías e identidades de clase media*.

4   See Parker and Walker, eds., *Latin America's Middle Class*; and Adamovsky, Visacovsky, and Vargas, eds., *Clases medias*.

5   For a pioneering study, see Altamirano, "La pequeña burguesía, una clase en el purgatorio."

6   See, for example, Walker, *Waking from the Dream*, and López, "Conscripts of Democracy"; Cosse, "*Mafalda*"; and articles in Cosse, ed., "Dossier: Clases medias, sociedad y política en la América Latina."

7   See Garguin, "'*Los Argentinos Descendemos de los Barcos*'"; and Guano, "The Denial of Citizenship."

8   Germani, *Política y sociedad en una época de transición*; and Germani, *Estructura social de la Argentina*.

9   Adamovsky, *Historia de la clase media argentina*. For a similar view, see Garguin, "El tardío descubrimiento de la clase media en Argentina."

10   See, for example, Zanca, "Reseña: Ezequiel Adamovsky, *Historia de la clase media argentina*; and López, "Reseña: Ezequiel Adamovsky: *Historia de la clase media argentina*."

11   For a more in-depth discussion, see Cosse, "Clases medias e historia reciente," 13–20.

12   See the classic works by Sigal, *Intelectuales y poder en Argentina*; and Terán, *Nuestros años sesentas*. See also Plotkin, *Freud en las pampas*. For more recent

research, see Cosse, *Pareja, sexualidad y familia*; and Manzano, *The Age of Youth in Argentina*. For a comprehensive view on everyday life, see Cosse, "Everyday Life in Argentina in the 1960s."

13 Thompson's signal work of class history is *The Making of the English Working Class*.

14 For this same approach, see Davidoff and Hall, *Family Fortunes*.

15 "Encuestas. Adiós a los *self-made men*. Una nueva clase empresaria en escena," *Primera Plana* (Buenos Aires), November 5, 1963, no. 52, 5.

16 For more details on *Primera Plana*, see Terán, *Nuestros años sesentas*, 151–59; Mazzei, *Medios de comunicación y golpismo*; Plotkin, *Freud en las pampas*, 149–87; and Cosse, "Cultura y sexualidad en la Argentina de los sesenta."

17 "La batalla de los semanarios parece planteada en todos los frentes," *Primera Plana* (Buenos Aires), October 27, 1964, 32–33.

18 The data on circulation is from the Instituto Verificador de Circulaciones. I thank Pascual Orellana for giving me access to its records.

19 For a full account of Quino's career, see Quino, *Toda Mafalda*, 655–59.

20 As shown by Germani with data from the 1947 census (*Estructura social de la Argentina*, 149, 198).

21 Torrado, *Estructura social de la Argentina (1945–1983)*, 187–202.

22 Based on data from Ministerio de Educación y Justicia, Departamento de Estadística Educativa (Argentina), *Enseñanza Media: Años 1914–1963*, vol. 1, 62–204; and vol. 2, 282–413; and Instituto Nacional de Estadística y Censos de la República Argentina, *Censo Nacional de Población, Familias y Vivienda, 1970*, vol. 2, tables 5, 21. For a comprehensive overview, see Cosse, "Everyday Life in Argentina in the 1960s."

23 Plotkin and Neiburg, "Elites intelectuales y ciencias sociales en la Argentina de los años 60."

24 In this regard, see Altamirano, "La pequeña burguesía." The quote by Viñas is from Altamirano, "Las dos Argentinas," 101–2.

25 Enrique Arrosagaray, "Ese hombre, de joven fue Felipe," *Página/12* (Buenos Aires), May 5, 1999, 29. I was unable to pinpoint the exact dates of these gatherings, but they began as early as the late 1950s and probably continued into the early 1960s.

26 On the exclusionary and homogeneous nature of this model, see Cosse, *Estigmas de nacimiento*.

27 I elaborate further on this in Cosse, *Pareja, sexualidad y familia*.

28 I examine these issues at length in Cosse, *Pareja, sexualidad y familia*; and Cosse, "Argentine Mothers and Fathers and the New Psychological Paradigm of Child-Rearing (1958–1973)."

29 See Cosse, *Pareja, sexualidad y familia*.

30 In addition to the works already cited, see Manzano, *The Age of Youth in Argentina*; Sergio Pujol, "Rebeldes y modernos"; and Ehrlich, "Rebeldes, intransigentes y duros en el activismo peronista, 1955–1962."

31 See Fernandez and Taylor Huber, "Introduction: The Anthropology of Irony."

32   See Nari, *Políticas de la maternidad y maternalismo político*.

33   See Recchini de Lattes, *La participación económica femenina en la Argentina desde la segunda posguerra hasta 1970*; Dirección Nacional de Estadística y Censos (Argentina), *Censo Nacional de Población. 1960*, vol. 2, xxxvii–xxxix; and Instituto Nacional de Estadística y Censos (Argentina), *Censo Nacional de Población, Familias y Vivienda. 1970*, vol. 2, 19 (table 6).

34   "La mujer pop. El posible y espantoso futuro," *Confirmado* (Buenos Aires), no. 51 (June 9, 1966), 38–43. I elaborate on this in Cosse, *Pareja, sexualidad y familia*.

35   Quino, "Mafalda," *Primera Plana* (Buenos Aires), no. 102 (October 20, 1964), 64. Capital letters in the original. Reproduced in Quino, *Mafalda inédita*, n.p.

36   Quino, "Mafalda," *El Mundo* (Buenos Aires), June 27, 1965; and March 19, 1965, 8.

37   In Buenos Aires, the proportion of men employed by the service sector rose from 16 percent in 1960 to 23 percent in 1970. See Torrado, *Estructura social de la Argentina*, 127; Dirección Nacional de Estadística y Censos (Argentina), *Censo Nacional de Población 1960*, vol. 2, 202–3 (table 21); and Instituto Nacional de Estadística y Censos de la República Argentina, *Censo Nacional de Población, Familias y Vivienda, 1970*, vol. 2, 221 (table 26).

38   Quino, "Mafalda," *El Mundo* (Buenos Aires), June 6, 1964, 8.

39   Cosse, "La emergencia de un nuevo modelo de paternidad en Argentina (1950–1975)"; and Cosse, *Pareja, sexualidad y familia*, 177–92.

40   Andrew Graham-Yooll, "Mafalda: The Star with No Illusions," *Buenos Aires Herald*, October 2, 1967, 8.

41   Quino, "Mafalda," *Primera Plana* (Buenos Aires), no. 104 (November 3, 1964), 45.

42   On Cold War ideology, see May, *Homeward Bound*. For Argentina, see Franco, *Un enemigo para la nación*.

43   See Ginzburg, *The Cheese and the Worms*.

44   See Mazzei, *Medios de comunicación y golpismo*.

45   "El País: La clase media juzga al gobierno," *Primera Plana* (Buenos Aires), no. 101 (October 13, 1964), 5–8.

46   Quino, "Mafalda," *Primera Plana* (Buenos Aires), no. 108 (December 1, 1964), 26.

47   See Pateman, *The Sexual Contract*.

48   Quino, "Mafalda," *El Mundo* (Buenos Aires), March 24, 1965, editorial page.

49   Quino, "Mafalda," *Primera Plana* (Buenos Aires), no. 109 (December 8, 1964), 20.

50   See Sebreli, *Buenos Aires, vida cotidiana y alienación*; and Jauretche, *El medio pelo en la sociedad argentina*. For an analysis of these anxieties at the turn of the twentieth century, see Losada, *La alta sociedad en la Buenos Aires*.

51   Quino, "Mafalda," *Primera Plana* (Buenos Aires), no. 120 (December 8, 1964), 36.

52   Quino, "Mafalda," *Primera Plana* (Buenos Aires), January 19, 1965, 46.

53   See Lang, "The Limits of Irony."

54   See Ulanovsky, *Paren las rotativas*, 40–47; and Saítta, *El escritor en el bosque de ladrillos*. For a historical account, see "37 años de diálogo con Ud.," *El Mundo* (Buenos Aires), May 14, 1965, 31–33.

55 This data is drawn from "Sexta Encuesta de Opinión Pública," January 1962, from the Max von Buch Library, Universidad de San Andrés, Buenos Aires, José Enrique Miguens Collection, table 37. The figures are based on my calculation.

56 Quino, *Mafalda inédita*, n.p. Quino joked about this involuntary similarity between the two characters, blaming it on his subconscious and even referencing it in one of his strips on *El Mundo*, on December 16, 1966.

57 For example, the first strip showed Mafalda on her first day of school lecturing her mother on the importance of education to avoid becoming a frustrated and mediocre woman like her. Quino, "Mafalda," *El Mundo* (Buenos Aires), March 15, 1965, editorial page.

58 Quino, *Mafalda inédita*, 43–44.

59 On this shift, see Sasturain, *El domicilio de la aventura*, 170–71. On the early importance of Jiggs and Maggie's family-centered strip in Argentina, see Gené, "Varones domados."

60 Quino, "Mafalda," *El Mundo* (Buenos Aires), March 29, 1965, 8; and Quino, "Mafalda," *El Mundo* (Buenos Aires), July 6, 1965, 8.

61 See Garguin, "*Los Argentinos Descendemos de los Barcos.*"

62 "Mafalda," *Dinamis* (Buenos Aires), no. 14 (November 1969), 55.

63 Landrú, "Landrú y los ejecutivos: Sir Jonás, el executive," *Primera Plana* (Buenos Aires), no. 290 (July 16, 1968), 83; and Landrú, "Landrú y los ejecutivos: Sir Jonás, el executive," *Primera Plana* (Buenos Aires), no. 301 (October 1, 1968), 48.

64 See Gombrich, "The Mask and the Face" and "The Visual Image."

65 See Quino, "Mafalda," *El Mundo* (Buenos Aires), May 3, 1965; and Quino, "Mafalda," *El Mundo* (Buenos Aires), July 18, 1965, editorial page.

66 Quino, *Mafalda 1*, strip 110.

67 "Mafalda," *Dinamis* (Buenos Aires), no. 14 (November 1969), 55.

68 Landrú, "Señora gorda," *El Mundo* (Buenos Aires), March 10, 1965, 1. On the upper class, see Losada, *La alta sociedad*.

69 Sebreli, *Buenos Aires, vida cotidiana y alienación*; and "Bestseller" and "Libros: La ciudad de arriba abajo," *Primera Plana* (Buenos Aires), no. 90 (July 28, 1964), 44.

70 See, for example, Germani, *Política y sociedad*.

71 See Sasturain, *El domicilio de la aventura*, 170–71.

72 See, for example, Quino, "Mafalda," *El Mundo* (Buenos Aires), November 29, 1967, 11; and Quino, "Mafalda," *El Mundo* (Buenos Aires), June 30, 1966, 13.

73 Quino, "Mafalda," *El Mundo* (Buenos Aires), July 23, 1965, editorial page.

74 "Bienvenida, Mafalda," *El Independiente* (La Rioja), April 4, 1968, n.p.; and "Mafalda, una nena entre la rebeldía y el establishment," *Grandes Chicos* (Buenos Aires), May 1972, n.p. These articles were consulted in Quino's personal archive (hereafter cited as APQ), Buenos Aires, press clippings file. In some cases I was unable to access the original publication that featured the articles found in the files consulted. In such cases, if the copy had no page number it is indicated with "n.p."

75 Oscar Steimberg, "Historietas: El lugar de Mafalda," *Los Libros* (Buenos Aires), no. 16 (March 1971), 6–7.

76 Quino, *Toda Mafalda*, strip 287, p. 119.

77 See, for example, Quino's installments of "Mafalda" in *El Mundo* (Buenos Aires) on March 2, 1967, 13; December 6, 1967, 5; December 10, 1967, 5; and December 20, 1967, 5.

78 Mónica Maristain, "Quinomanía," *Página/12* (Buenos Aires), "Radar" supplement, no. 392 (February 22, 2004), 1–7.

79 Quino, "Mafalda," *El Mundo* (Buenos Aires), March 31, 1965, 4.

80 Quino, *Toda Mafalda*, strip 109.

81 Graham-Yooll, "Mafalda: The Star with No Illusions."

82 Quino, "Mafalda," *El Mundo* (Buenos Aires), June 15, 1966, 16.

83 Quino, *Toda Mafalda*, strips 29, p. 55; 79, p. 67; 109, p. 74; 163, p. 87; 478, p. 165; and 781, p. 243.

84 On the Peronist movement and women's involvement in politics, see Barry, *Evita capitana*. Regarding the debates on women's political rights after 1955, see Valobra, "Derechos políticos femeninos en la Junta Consultiva Nacional." For information on the number of women in Congress, see Marx, Borner, and Caminotti, *Las legisladoras*, 51–52.

85 See Quino's installments of "Mafalda" in *El Mundo* (Buenos Aires) on May 10, 1965; May 11, 1965; May 12, 1965; May 16, 1965; May 17, 1965; May 18, 1965, editorial page.

86 Alasdair Lean, "Quino's Dreadful Niece Punctures a Failed Planet," *Buenos Aires Herald*, March 7, 1970, 12; and Adriana Civita, "Mafaldito," *Claudia* (Buenos Aires), no. 185 (May 1969), 34–37.

87 Quino, "Mafalda," *El Mundo* (Buenos Aircs), June 29, 1966, 14; and testimony by Carlos Martínez (audio and video recording), Buenos Aires, 2007, in Memoria Abierta, archive of the Acción Coordinada de Organizaciones de Derechos Humanos, Argentina.

88 See "Señaló Illia dos realizaciones de su gobierno: Energía y reforma agraria," *El Mundo* (Buenos Aires), June 27, 1966, 11; "Queremos precisamente que todos puedan expresar sus discrepancias, dijo el doctor Illia," *El Mundo* (Buenos Aires), June 6, 1966, 10; "Exhortó Illia a desterrar polémicas estériles, odios y enfrentamientos," *El Mundo* (Buenos Aires), June 26, 1966, 12; and Ulanovsky, *Paren las rotativas*, 169.

89 Alicia Colombo, interview by the author, May 30, 2013, Buenos Aires.

90 Gillespie, *Soldados de Perón*, 91–92.

91 "Mafalda, infancia y realidad," *Acción* (Buenos Aires), May 16, 1973, n.p.

92 See Avellaneda, *Censura, autoritarismo y cultura*; Terán, *Nuestros años sesentas*, 151–59; and Manzano, "Sexualizing Youth."

93 Pablo Llonto, "Mafalda 10 años sin arrugas," *Gatopardo* (Mexico City), October 2004, 136–42.

94 Quino, "Mafalda," *El Mundo* (Buenos Aires), December 24, 1966, n.p. Article consulted in the archive of the newspaper *Clarín* (hereafter ADC).

95 Miguel Brascó, "Esperable éxito inesperado," *Adán* (Buenos Aires), February 1967, 25.

96 Miguel Brascó, "Mafalda se incorpora a 'Córdoba,'" *Córdoba*, December 31, 1965, 5; and "Quino," *El Mundo* (Buenos Aires), December 24, 1966, n.p.

97 For a historical overview, see Brennan and Gordillo, *Córdoba*, 15–79.

98 "Y aquí está," *Córdoba*, January 3, 1966, 5.

99 Alicia Colombo, interview by the author, May 30, 2013, Buenos Aires; and "Chiche" Linari (whose press agency provided services to various newspapers outside the capital), interview by the author, January 20, 2013, Buenos Aires.

100 Ana María Fouga, "Mafalda, embajadora de la niñez contemporánea," *El Colono* (Santa Fe, Argentina), July 28, 1970, n.p. (APQ).

101 "Mafalda," *Dinamis* (Buenos Aires), no. 14 (November 1969), 55.

102 On this neighborhood rhetoric, see Armus, "El viaje al centro."

103 Quino, *Toda Mafalda*, strip 1659, p. 466.

104 Quino, *Mafalda 7*, strip 1289, p. 367.

105 Cortázar, "Casa tomada"; and Rozenmacher, "Cabecita negra." See an analysis by Altamirano, "La pequeña burguesía," 100–102.

106 Deleuze, "Humor, Irony, and the Law," 81–90.

2. CONTROVERSIAL *MAFALDA*

1   Cristina Irala, "Este es mi papá," *Gente* (Buenos Aires), February 1, 1968, 18.

2   See Levín, *Humor político en tiempos de represión*; and Burkart, *De Satiricón a Hum®*.

3   Bergson, *Laughter*, 7–8.

4   Irala, "Este es mi papá," 18.

5   Graham-Yooll, "Mafalda: The Star with No Illusions," 8.

6   "Mafalda, niña terrible se ofrece," *Confirmado* (Buenos Aires), February 29, 1968, 28.

7   "Quino, humorista y algo más," *Siete Días* (Buenos Aires), no. 43 (March 5, 1968), 46–47. On the negotiations with *Crónica* and *Clarín*, see "Mafalda, niña terrible se ofrece," and Sergio Kiernan, "Mafalda cumplió 25 años," *La Semana* (Buenos Aires), August 24, 1988, 34–35.

8   On photojournalism in Argentina, see Gamarnik, "El fotoperiodismo en Argentina: De *Siete Días Ilustrados* (1965) a la Agencia SIGLA (1975)."

9   Norberto Firpo (editor in chief of *Siete Días*), interview by the author, January 13, 2011, Buenos Aires. The data on the number of copies sold weekly is drawn from the Instituto Verificador de Publicaciones.

10 Scarzanella, *Abril*, 129–30.

11 "Quino, humorista y algo más," 46–47.

12 Cosse, "*Claudia*."

13 Scarzanella, *Abril*, 119–20.

14 Scarzanella, *Abril*, 135.

15 Quino, *Mafalda inédita*, n.p.

16 Adriana, "Mafaldito," *Claudia* (Buenos Aires), no. 145 (May 1969), 56.

17 "Quino, humorista y algo más," 46–47.

18 Quino, *Todo Mafalda*, 336.

19 Quino, "Mafalda," *Siete Días* (Buenos Aires), no. 162 (June 15–21, 1970), 38; and Quino, "Mafalda," *Siete Días* (Buenos Aires), no. 157 (May 11–17, 1970), 38.

20 Quino, "Mafalda," *Siete Días* (Buenos Aires), no. 61 (July 9, 1968), 38; Quino, "Mafalda," *Siete Días* (Buenos Aires), no. 65 (August 5, 1968), 31; Quino, "Mafalda," *Siete Días* (Buenos Aires), no. 66 (August 2, 1968), 42; Quino, "Mafalda," *Siete Días* (Buenos Aires), no. 213 (June 14, 1971), n.p.

21 "Correo de los lectores," *Siete Días* (Buenos Aires), no. 163 (June 22, 1970), 20; Quino, "Mafalda," *Siete Días* (Buenos Aires), no. 268 (July 3–9, 1972), 10–18; Quino, *Al fin solos*; Quino, *Y digo yo*; and Quino, *¿A dónde vamos a parar?* Many of these vignettes were also featured in *Todo Mafalda*.

22 "Mafalda, niña terrible se ofrece," 28.

23 "La maratón de los estudiantes," *Siete Días* (Buenos Aires), no. 75 (October 14, 1968), 10–11; "Todo el 68," *Siete Días* (Buenos Aires), December 30, 1968, 89–94.

24 Quino, "Mafalda," *Siete Días* (Buenos Aires), no. 63 (July 23, 1968), 31.

25 I examine these issues at length in Cosse, "Argentine Mothers and Fathers and the New Psychological Paradigm of Child-Rearing (1958–1973)."

26 Quino, *Toda Mafalda*, strips 938 and 939, 285.

27 Latxague, "Lire Quino," 378; and Quino, "Mafalda," *Siete Días* (Buenos Aires), no. 90 (January 27, 1969), 27.

28 Quino, "Mafalda," *Siete Días* (Buenos Aires), no. 104 (May 5, 1969), 47.

29 Quino, "Mafalda," *Siete Días* (Buenos Aires), no. 112 (June 30, 1969), 34.

30 Quino, "Mafalda," *Siete Días* (Buenos Aires), no. 116 (July 28, 1969), 56.

31 Quino, "Mafalda," *Siete Días* (Buenos Aires), no. 67 (August 19, 1968), 31.

32 Avellaneda, *Censura, autoritarismo y cultura*, 42–43.

33 On the enemy within, see Franco, *Un enemigo para la Nación*. On the linking of political and sexual issues, see Manzano, "Sex, Gender, and the Making of the 'Enemy Within' in Cold War Argentina." On the family-centered perspective, see Cosse, *Pareja, sexualidad y familia*, 151–53. Regarding the effect these views had on armed groups, see Cosse, "Infidelities."

34 "El derrocamiento de Illia," *Siete Días* (Buenos Aires), no. 63 (July 23, 1968), 50–55.

35 "La censura ya tiene candidatos," *Revista Extra* (Buenos Aires), February 1969, n.p. Article consulted at the archive of Ediciones de la Flor (hereafter AEDF), press clippings file.

36 "Dulce y venenosa," *Visión* (New York), September 6, 1968, 76; and "Extravagario," *Primera Plana* (Buenos Aires), no. 304 (October 22, 1968), 72.

37 Horacio, "¡Quino tuvo una nena!," *El Popular* (Montevideo), October 24, 1970, n.p. Article consulted at APQ.

38 Guillermo Saccomano, "A mí no me grite," *Página/12* (Buenos Aires), November 14, 1993, 30.

39 As told by Quino in an interview by Carlos Ulanovsky on the radio program *Reunión Cumbre*, Radio Nacional (Buenos Aires), August 4, 2012.

40 "Mafalda: Ideal de alumna entre las noveles maestras," *El Mundo* (Buenos Aires), November 17, 1967, 32.

41 *Siete Días* (Buenos Aires), no. 138 (December 29, 1970).

42 "Hechos y protagonistas," *Siete Días* (Buenos Aires), no. 87 (January 6, 1969),14. The launch was probably held on December 30, 1968. No precise sales figures are available from the publishing house Jorge Álvarez.

43 Archive of the Instituto Torcuato Di Tella (hereafter AITDT), Visual Arts Center series, folio 767.

44 Masotta, *La historieta en el mundo moderno*, 10–11.

45 Vázquez, *El oficio de las viñetas,* 77–98.

46 Entel, Lenarduzzi, and Gerzovich, "La Escuela de Frankfurt en América Latina."

47 Longoni and Mestman, *Del Di Tella a "Tucumán Arde,"* 97, 163–73.

48 Longoni and Mestman, *Del Di Tella a "Tucumán Arde,"* 173.

49 *Revista de Letras y Artes de Rosario*, editorial, reproduced in *Crónica* (Buenos Aires), January 21, 1968, n.p. Article consulted at AITDT, Visual Arts Center series.

50 Quino, "Mafalda," *Siete Días* (Buenos Aires), no. 62 (July 16, 1968), 25.

51 "El Che en Historietas" and "Hechos & Protagonistas," *Siete Días* (Buenos Aires), no. 79 (November 11, 1968), 14.

52 Here I draw on the analysis by Vázquez, *El oficio de las viñetas*, 114.

53 Quino, "Mafalda," *Siete Días* (Buenos Aires), no. 72 (September 23, 1968), 43.

54 Quino, "Mafalda," *Siete Días* (Buenos Aires), no. 76 (October 21, 1968), 30; Diego Marinelli, "He convivido con la censura desde que empecé a trabajar," *Clarín* (Buenos Aires), July 28, 2004, available online at http://www.edant .clarin.com/diario/2004/07/28/sociedad/s-03101.htm (accessed January 10, 2011); "Italia también festeja los 25 años de Mafalda," *Nuevo Sur* (Buenos Aires), December 12, 1989, 19.

55 I draw here on Avellaneda, *Censura, autoritarismo y cultura*; Cosse, "Germán Leopoldo García y *Nanina*"; and Manzano, "Sexualizing Youth."

56 See this explanation in Quino, *Todo Mafalda*, 603. He also cut the strip in which Mafalda's father is at work and his boss threatens to fire him, accusing him of being a communist for saying that if the Pope had had children he would have never said television was good for the family.

57 "Periodismo y gobierno: El ojo de la cerradura," *Siete Días* (Buenos Aires), no. 72 (September 23, 1968), 54–56.

58 Quino, "Mafalda," *Siete Días* (Buenos Aires), no. 76 (October 21, 1968), 30.

59 On media coverage of current events during this period, see Varela, *La televisión criolla*, 227–37.

60 Quino, "Mafalda," *Siete Días* (Buenos Aires), no. 80 (November 18, 1968), 28.

61 "Todo el 68: El veredicto de los intelectuales," *Siete Días* (Buenos Aires), no. 86 (December 30, 1968), 84–85.

62 Quino, "Mafalda," *Siete Días* (Buenos Aires), no. 76 (October 21, 1968), 30; Quino, "Mafalda," *El Mundo* (Buenos Aires), August 8, 1965, editorial page.

63 Caimari, *Mientas la ciudad duerme*.

64 "Gobierno: Tiempo de minigolpes," *Siete Días* (Buenos Aires), no. 100 (April 7, 1969), 18–19.

65 Quino, "Mafalda," *Siete Días* (Buenos Aires), no. 101 (April 14, 1969), 33.

66   Quino, "Mafalda," *Siete Días* (Buenos Aires), no. 109 (June 8, 1969), 36.

67   Quino, "Mafalda," *Siete Días* (Buenos Aires), no. 111 (June 23, 1969), 34.

68   Quino, "Mafalda," *Siete Días* (Buenos Aires), no. 116 (July 28, 1969), 56.

69   "Mayo: De corceles y de aceros," *Siete Días* (Buenos Aires), no. 108 (June 2, 1969), 14–20.

70   Adriana Civita, "Mafaldito," *Claudia* (Buenos Aires), no. 145 (May 1969), 34–36.

71   Cano, "El movimiento feminista argentino en la década del '70"; and Vassallo, "'Las mujeres dicen basta.'"

72   Quino, "Mafalda," *El Mundo* (Buenos Aires), May 11, 1965, editorial page.

73   Quino, "Mafalda," *Siete Días* (Buenos Aires), no. 77 (October 28, 1968), 58; Teresa Villalba Rodríguez, "Cartas al Director: Un Trapo," *El País* (Madrid), February 25, 1997, available online at http://elpais.com/diario/1997/02/25 /opinion/856825209_850215.html (accessed February 10, 2012).

74   Quino, "Mafalda," *Siete Días* (Buenos Aires), February 16, 1970, 40.

75   "En este número," *Siete Días* (Buenos Aires), no. 113 (July 7, 1969), 30.

76   Gillespie, *Soldados de Perón: Los montoneros*, 119–25.

77   "Joan Manuel Serrat: 'La guitarra no es un fusil,'" *Siete Días* (Buenos Aires), no. 147 (March 2, 1970), 38.

78   Quino, "Mafalda," *Siete Días* (Buenos Aires), no. 212 (June 7, 1971), 79.

79   I draw here on Gilman, *Entre la pluma y el fusil*, esp. 233–63.

80   Mónica Maristain, "Quino," *Radar* (Buenos Aires), year 7, no. 392 (February 22, 2004), 4–7. (*Radar* is a supplement in *Página/12*.)

81   Montanaro, *Francisco Urondo*, 83.

82   Quino, "Ajedrez," *Panorama* (Buenos Aires), December 8, 1970, 82.

83   "Un grupo de extremistas asaltó el banco ubicado en 17 y 70," *El Día* (La Plata), December 16, 1970, 1, 8.

84   Tomás Eloy Martínez, "Esta semana," *Panorama* (Buenos Aires), no. 185 (November 10, 1970), 1.

85   "Personajes: 'Discepolada,'" *Panorama* (Buenos Aires), December 22, 1970, 80.

86   Oscar Giardinelli, interview, *Semana Gráfica* (Buenos Aires), March 13, 1971, 25–26.

87   Dorfman and Mattelart, *How to Read Donald Duck*. The book was originally published in Chile in 1971 as *Para leer al Pato Donald: Comunicación de masa y colonialismo*, and first appeared in print in Argentina in 1972. On the discussions it prompted, see Sarowsky, *Del laboratorio chileno a la comunicación-mundo*, 99–115. See also Grimson and Varela, "Recepción, culturas populares y medios."

88   Sarowsky, *Del laboratorio chileno a la comunicación-mundo*, 75–79, 115.

89   Oscar Steimberg, "Historietas: El lugar de Mafalda," *Los Libros* (Buenos Aires), no. 16 (March 1971), 6–7. I draw on the original version, with slight variations, in Steimberg, *Leyendo historietas: Textos sobre relatos visuales y humor gráfico*, 93–99.

90   J. C. M., "Mafalda," *La revista de los Jueves* (Buenos Aires), July 8, 1971, 18. (*La revista de los Jueves* was a supplement to *Clarín*.)

91 Juan Sasturain sensed the importance of this contradiction between storyline and social context in his article "Mafalda en tres cuestiones," *Superhumor* (Buenos Aires), no. 9 (September 1981), 50–51, reproduced in Sasturain, *El domicilio de la aventura*, 169–71.

92 Quino, "Mafalda," *Siete Días* (Buenos Aires), no. 203 (April 5, 1971), 75.

93 Quino, "Mafalda," *Siete Días* (Buenos Aires), no. 206 (April 26, 1971), n.p. Drawn from APQ.

94 Quino, "Mafalda," *Siete Días* (Buenos Aires), no. 207 (May 3, 1971), n.p. Drawn from APQ.

95 O'Donnell, *El Estado burocrático autoritario*, 408–9, 416.

96 "Investigación especial: Cuánto cuesta vivir dignamente," *Siete Días* (Buenos Aires), no. 224 (August 30, 1971), 54–56; "Costo de vida: ¿Adónde vamos a parar?," *Siete Días* (Buenos Aires), no. 247 (February 7, 1972), 74–75.

97 Quino, "Mafalda," *Siete Días* (Buenos Aires), no. 151 (March 30, 1970), 32.

98 Quino, "Mafalda," *Siete Días* (Buenos Aires), no. 152 (April 6, 1970), 32.

99 Quino, "Mafalda," *Siete Días* (Buenos Aires), no. 218 (July 19, 1971), 29.

100 Quino, "Mafalda," *Siete Días* (Buenos Aires), no. 230 (October 11, 1971), 71.

101 "Quino," *Panorama* (Buenos Aires), no. 244 (December 28, 1971), cover.

102 Valeria Manzano, "'Contra toda forma de opresión,'" 9–42.

103 Quino, "El día, un dibujito un pedido," *El Día* (Buenos Aires), April 12, 1970, n.p. Article consulted at APQ.

104 See Cosse, *Pareja, sexualidad y familia*, 191–92.

105 Rodrigo Fresán, "La extraña del pelo largo," *Verano 12* (Buenos Aires), February 19, 2010, 1–10, 12. (*Verano 12* is a supplement to *Página/12*.)

106 Quino, *El mundo de Mafalda*, 27.

107 I thank Antonio Torres of the Comics Club for generously showing me his collection of *Mafalda* toys.

108 "Mafalda en el diván," *La Nación* (Buenos Aires), September 11, 1971, 12. The two experts were Ema Kestelboim (National University of La Plata) and María Lelia Ivancovich (University of Buenos Aires).

109 "Mafalda, una nena entre la rebeldía y el establishment," *Grandes Chicos* (Buenos Aires), May 1972, n.p. Drawn from APQ.

110 "La juventud y la política," *Siete Días* (Buenos Aires), no. 213 (June 14, 1971), 8–12.

111 Tomás Eloy Martínez, "La ideología de la clase media: Los del medio, mayoría domesticada y consumidora, enemiga de todo cambio," *La Opinión* (Buenos Aires), November 1–4, 1972, 8–9.

112 "Historia tendenciosa de la clase media," *Siete Días* (Buenos Aires), no. 234 (November 1971), 73. On the optimism in left-wing criticism of the middle class and for a detailed analysis of this play, see Adamovsky, *Historia de la clase media argentina*, 393–403.

113 Quino, "Mafalda," *Siete Días* (Buenos Aires), no. 272 (July 31, 1972), 68.

114 Tomás Eloy Martínez, "Viaje al planeta Quino," in Quino, *El mundo de Mafalda*, 112–21.

115   Quino, "Mafalda," *Siete Días* (Buenos Aires), no. 207 (May 3, 1971). The reference is drawn from APQ.

116   Quino, "Mafalda," *Siete Días* (Buenos Aires), no. 276 (August 28, 1972), 98; Quino, "Mafalda," *Siete Días* (Buenos Aires), no. 277 (September 4, 1972), 98.

117   Quino, *Todo Mafalda*, strips 815 (250), 1079 (316). I could not access the *El Mundo* and *Siete Días* numbers that featured these strips.

118   Trillo and Bróccoli, *El humor gráfico*, 106–7.

119   "Correo de los lectores," *Siete Días* (Buenos Aires), no. 226 (September 13–19, 1971), 26.

120   Freud, "Humour."

121   "Los humoristas y la idea fija," *Siete Días* (Buenos Aires), no. 234 (November 8–14, 1971), 58–62; "Correo de los lectores," *Siete Días* (Buenos Aires), no. 226 (September 13, 1971), n.p.

122   Osvaldo Soriano, "Quino, Pensar no es divertido," *La Opinión Cultural* (Buenos Aires), December 3, 1972, 1–5. (*La Opinión Cultural* is a supplement to the newspaper *La Opinión*.)

123   Quino, "Mafalda," *Siete Días* (Buenos Aires), no. 253 (March 20, 1972), 94.

124   Quino, "Mafalda," *Siete Días* (Buenos Aires), no. 291 (November 28, 1972), 98.

125   Quino, "Mafalda," *Siete Días* (Buenos Aires), no. 291 (November 28, 1972), 90; Quino, "Mafalda," *Siete Días* (Buenos Aires), no. 303 (March 5, 1973), 90.

126   Burkart, *De Satiricón a Hum®*, 69–76.

127   Juan Sasturain noted that Quino found it hard to "cope with the noises that came from the street." See his article "Mafalda en tres cuestiones," reproduced in Sasturain, *El domicilio de la aventura*, 172. Regarding the growth of the far right, see "El escuadrón de la muerte en acción," *Siete Días* (Buenos Aires), no. 147 (March 2–8, 1970), n.p.

128   Quino, "Mafalda," *Siete Días* (Buenos Aires), no. 295 (January 8–14, 1973), n.p.; Quino, "Mafalda," *Siete Días* (Buenos Aires), no. 296 (January 15–21, 1973), 4–7.

129   Quino, "Mafalda," *Siete Días* (Buenos Aires), no. 301 (February 19, 1973), n.p.

130   Quino, "Mafalda," *Siete Días* (Buenos Aires), no. 319 (June 25, 1973), 82.

131   The last strip in the newspaper *Río Negro* was published on December 1, 1973: "El adiós de Mafalda," *Río Negro*, December 1, 1973, 11; in the daily *Córdoba*, the last strip was featured on February 3, 1974.

132   Pablo Hernández, interview by the author, June 14, 2012, Buenos Aires.

133   Hernández, *Para leer a Mafalda*.

134   Hernández, *Para leer a Mafalda*, 28, 73.

135   Hernández, *Para leer a Mafalda*, 110.

136   Jorge Giertz, "Mafalda es una pequeño burguesa," *Cuestionario* (Buenos Aires), no. 33 (January 1976), 46–47.

137   Transcribed version of the radio program broadcast by the National Library on January 6, 1976, at 7 P.M. I thank Pablo Hernández for giving me access to the transcription.

138   Jorge B. Rivera, "¡Sonaste Maneco! Historia del humor gráfico argentino (1)," *Crisis* (Buenos Aires), no. 34 (February 1976), 16–24.

139 "¡Los cabecitas negras!," *El Caudillo* (Buenos Aires), no. 7 (December 28, 1973), 22.

140 "El chiste de la semana," *El Caudillo* (Buenos Aires), March 1, 1974, 23. This was the only time that the magazine used cartoons published in other media. In the first scene the two cavemen were about to fight to see who was a more authentic representative of the people. The second showed a group of tourists looking at ruins and one of them asking a guard what the ruins had been, to which he responded, "A people." When I asked Quino about this use of his work he told me he was unaware of it at the time. Quino, interview by the author, May 30, 2013, Buenos Aires.

141 For new approaches in studies on the Peronist right, see Besoky, "La derecha peronista en perspectiva."

142 This article was reproduced two months later by a newspaper in Vedia, a small town in the province of Buenos Aires, and from there it was cut out by a member of Montoneros who saved it in the guerrilla group's files. "¿Mafalda en la escuela . . . ?," *Alberdi*, no. 2716 (August 16, 1975), n.p. I could not locate the original version published by *Educación Popular*, only a cutout from the Montoneros files, which is kept by the organization Memoria Abierta.

143 *Alberdi* featured work by poets such as José Cedrón, Leónidas Barletta, and Raúl González Tuñón. The director's son, Rodolfo Joaquín Álvarez, was shot to death some time later while he was handing out political flyers in La Plata. See Dalter, "El periódico de Alberdi (1923–1976) y sus poetas."

144 Mónica Maristain, "Quino," *Radar* (Buenos Aires), year 7, no. 392 (February 22, 2004), 4–7; Pablo Llonto, "Mafalda 10 años sin arrugas," *Gatopardo* (Mexico City), October 2004, 142–48. The information on the minister's request was provided by Quino in an interview by the author, May 30, 2013, Buenos Aires.

3. GLOBAL *MAFALDA*

1 See Hofmeyr's contribution to "*AHR* Conversation: On Transnational History"; and Saunier, "Learning by Doing."

2 Daniel Divinsky (director of Ediciones de la Flor), interview by the author, March 22, 2010, Buenos Aires.

3 Graham-Yooll, "Mafalda: The Star with No Illusions," 8; "Los números de Mafalda," *Superhumor* (Buenos Aires), no. 9 (September 1981), 49; interview with Daniel Divinsky. Data based on information from Quino's official website, http://www.quino.com.ar/publicaciones-historicas/libros-mafalda (accessed March 28, 2014), in addition to other sources consulted during my research.

4 See, among others, Giddens, *Runaway World*, 6–19, 51–66.

5 The full complexity of these redirections can be seen in literature and art. See Gilman, *Entre la pluma y el fusil*; and Plante, *Argentinos de París*.

6 Lumley, *States of Emergency*, 39–40.

7 Ginsborg, *A History of Contemporary Italy*, 220–40; and Pasqualini, "Psychoanalysis to the People!"

8 Ravoni and Riva, *Il libro dei bambini terribili per adulti masochisti*, 407–10.

9 Ginsborg, *A History of Contemporary Italy*, 298–306.

10 *Corriere della Sera* (Milan) article reproduced in Enza Mandelli, "Mafalda," *Wheeling Paths*, http://www.wheelingpaths.com/index.php/collezionismo/collfumetti/65-mafalda (accessed September 10, 2013).

11 Eco, "Elogio di Franti," in Ravoni and Riva, *Il libro dei bambini*, 292–93.

12 Isidoro Gilbert, "Crónica de una decepción," *Revista Ñ* (Buenos Aires), January 19, 2014, 12. (*Revista Ñ* is a supplement to *Clarín*.)

13 Lumley, *States of Emergency*, 40.

14 Gilbert, "Crónica de una decepción."

15 Sergio Kiernan, "Mafalda cumplió 25 años," *La semana* (Buenos Aires), August 24, 1988, 34–35.

16 Forgacs, *L'industrializzazione della cultura italiana (1880–2000)*, 24–25.

17 Eco, *Apocalípticos e integrados*, 42, 166–67, 224, 257. Originally published in Italian in 1964.

18 Novelli, "Trent'anni di Letteratura," 8. Marcelo Ravoni, who passed away in 2004, was Quino's agent in Europe until 2001. Quipos is still operating and is run by Rossana and Coleta Ravoni, whom I thank for giving me access to this pamphlet.

19 Umberto Eco, "Mafalda, o del Rifiuto," in Quino, *Mafalda, la contestataria*, 1–2. My analysis is based on the Spanish translation of Eco's prologue published in Quino, *El mundo de Mafalda*, 63.

20 Eco, "Mafalda, o del Rifiuto."

21 The strip in question is number 168, featured, for example, in the *Toda Mafalda* edition.

22 Montironi, "In viaggio con Mafalda dall'a Argentina all'Italia."

23 Drawn from the analysis by Montironi in "In viaggio con Mafalda," 57, 85.

24 Quino, *Mafalda, la contestataria*, n.p. The original is strip no. 295 in *Toda Mafalda*.

25 E. Don, "Mafalda contesta," *La Stampa* (Turin), no. 61 (March 14, 1969), 3.

26 Dario Natoli, "Il rifiuto di Mafalda," *L'Unità* (Rome), March 26, 1969, 10.

27 Ginsborg, *A History of Contemporary Italy*, 316–17.

28 Lumley, *States of Emergency*, 313–34.

29 This information is drawn from http://www.paeseserastory.it (accessed October 10, 2013).

30 "Da Oggi un nuovo fumetto, Mafalda contestataria," *Paese Sera* (Roma), February 9, 1970, 3.

31 Barbieri, "Il fumetto in Italia."

32 This information is drawn from http://www.slumberland.it/contenuto.php?tipo=rivista&id=9 (accessed April 30, 2012).

33 Stefano Reggiani, "Il Salone dei Comics a Lucca: Fumetti e i cimeli di capitan Salgari," *La Stampa* (Turin), November 4, 1973, 9; and by the same author, "Dall'ambizioso Asterix a Mafalda: Fumetti chewing-gum," *La Stampa* (Turin), April 27, 1973, 15.

34 "'Mafalda,' la creación de Quino, ha conquistado Italia," *La Opinión* (Buenos Aires), November 23, 1973, 21.

35 "Andanzas de una estrella de la historieta, el cine y la TV," *La Nación* (Buenos Aires), March 28, 1973. Article consulted at APQ.

36 Tusquets, *Confesiones de una editora poco mentirosa*, 139.

37 This draws on the analysis by Catelli, "La élite itinerante del boom."

38 Carr, *España*, 212–17.

39 Carr, *España*, 226–30.

40 Merino, *El cómic hispánico*, 97–144.

41 See Gubern, *El lenguaje de los cómics*; and http://www.tebeosfera.com /documentos/prensa/bang_boletin_informativo_martin_editor_1968.html (accessed January 10, 2014).

42 Tusquets, *Confesiones de una editora*, 140. Miguel García, telephone interview by the author, October 7, 2013, Buenos Aires/Madrid.

43 Conde Martín, *Historia del humor gráfico en España*, 135–39.

44 Miguel García, interview by the author.

45 Tusquets, *Confesiones de una editora*, 142.

46 "Libros más vendidos," *ABC* (Madrid), October 28, 1972, 66; "Libros que se recomiendan," *La Vanguardia* (Barcelona), December 2, 1971, 52; "Perich y Mafalda, nueva frontera para el humor," *ABC* (Madrid), February 2, 1971, 11.

47 Santerbas, "El mundo de Mafalda," *Triunfo* (Madrid), no. 454 (February 13, 1971), 46.

48 "Mafalda niña contestataria," *Cambio 16*, April 3, 1972, 11–13.

49 Ana María Moix, "Los Complejos del padre de Mafalda," *Triunfo* (Madrid), no. 503 (May 20, 1972), 43.

50 Coll Garcés, "'Mafalda.'"

51 Joan Fuster, "La risa va por los barrios," *La Vanguardia* (Barcelona), March 12, 1972, 13; "Desconcertante Emma Cohen," *La Vanguardia* (Barcelona), April 2, 1972, 27; and "También es noticia," *La Vanguardia* (Barcelona), May 1, 1973, 23.

52 It was published by the San Sebastián publishing house Buru Lan Ediciones and its directors were José Aramburu and Luis de Apraiz.

53 *El Globo* (San Sebastián), no. 1, March 1973, front page. I was able to review all the issues of this magazine thanks to Antonio Torres, who generously gave me access to his collection. I contacted Torres upon José María Gutierrez's suggestion. I thank them both.

54 "Hola amigos," *El Globo* (San Sebastián), no. 1, March 1973, 1.

55 "Mafalda," *El Globo* (San Sebastián), no. 1, March 1973, 2–3.

56 "Mafalda," *El Globo* (San Sebastián), no. 1, March 1973, 4–11.

57 "Libros recibidos," *ABC* (Madrid), May 2, 1974, 63, online version. http://heme roteca.abc.es/nav/Navigate.exe/hemeroteca/madrid/abc/1974/05/02/063.html.

58 Ferran Monegal, "Esther Tusquets y el libro infantil," *La Vanguardia* (Barcelona), January 31, 1974, 49.

59 José Alejandro Vara, "La repelente niña Mafalda," *ABC* (Madrid), March 9, 1984, 89.

60 Jensen, "Suspendidos de la historia/exiliados de la memoria. El caso de los argentinos desterrados en Cataluña (1976– . . .)," 258–310.

61 Jensen, "Suspendidos de la historia," 258–72.

62 Eduardo Blaustein, "Nena qué va a ser de ti," *Página/12* (Buenos Aires), October 19, 1988, 10.

63 Miguel García, interview by the author.

64 "Quino," *El País* (Madrid), August 2, 1977, http://elpais.com/diario/1977/08/02/sociedad/239320818_850215.html (accessed February 8, 2012).

65 This is also an accurate description of the 1970s. It is based on a letter in the archive of Ediciones de la Flor (AEDF), dated Mexico, November 2, 1976. The signature is illegible.

66 Rubenstein, *Bad Language, Naked Ladies, and Other Threats to the Nation*, 14–24; Soto Díaz, *Un paseo por la historieta Mexicana*, 32–53. On political cartoons, see Acevedo, *La caricatura política en México en el siglo XIX*.

67 Merino, *El cómic hispánico*, 209–17.

68 Monsiváis, "De los cuentos de hadas a los cómics." On *Los agachados*, see Foster, "Los Supermachos: Golpe de estado en San Garabato," in Foster, *From Mafalda to Los Supermachos*, 89–99.

69 Zolov, *Refried Elvis*.

70 Guevara González, *La educación en México*, 32–63.

71 Zermeño, *México*; Rodríguez Kuri, "Los primeros días."

72 Guevara González, *La educación en México*, 52–59.

73 Frazier and Cohen, "Defining the Space of Mexico '68."

74 Maria Idalia, "Sobre Alterio y Brandoni pesa amenaza de muerte en Argentina" and "Mercedes Sosa no saldrá del país," *Excélsior* (Mexico City), June 15, 1975, 2; "Diorema cultural," *Excélsior* (Mexico City), October 8, 1975, 4.

75 Yankelevich, "México," 188.

76 Sara Moira, "En Chile la represión ha sido más dura para la mujer," *Excélsior* (Mexico City), June 22, 1975; Grammático, "La I Conferencia Mundial de la Mujer."

77 "Novedades," *La Onda* (Mexico City), no. 17 (October 7, 1973), 3; Elena Poniatowska, "Cambiar su estructura mental: Principal batalla de la mujer," *Novedades* (Mexico City), July 9, 1974, 4. On the children's market, see Sosenski, "Producciones culturales para la infancia mexicana"; and Sosenski, "El niño consumidor."

78 "Nuevo álbum de 'Quino' al caricaturista argentino, 'padre de Mafalda,'" *Excélsior* (Mexico City), January 4, 1975, n.p. Article consulted at the Documentation Center of the newspaper *Excélsior* (hereafter CDDE), Quino folder.

79 "Mafalda," *Excélsior* (Mexico City), June 1, 1975, n.p. (CDDE).

80 "El legado del caricaturista Armando Guerrero Edwards," *El Proceso* (Mexico City), February 14, 2005, http://www.proceso.com.mx/?p=225310 (accessed February 10, 2012).

81 Quino, "Mafalda," *Revista* (Mexico City), September 6, 1976, n.p. (*Revista* was the comics supplement to the newspaper *Excélsior*.)

82 I thank Marcela Gené for her input on this.

83 Antonio Soria, "Casi medio siglo de Mafalda," *La Jornada Semanal* (Mexico City), March 11, 2012, http://www.jornada.unam.mx/2012/03/11/sem-antonio

.html (accessed August 8, 2012). (*La Jornada Semanal* is a supplement to *La Jornada*).

84 Sealtiel Alatriste, telephone interview by the author, December 12, 2012, Buenos Aires/Mexico City.

85 Guillermo Schavelzon, telephone interview by the author, February 8, 2013, Buenos Aires/Madrid.

86 Guillermo Schavelzon, interview by the author.

87 "Derechos del *Excélsior*, solo sobre la tira cómica Mafalda," *Excélsior* (Mexico City), September 4, 1977, n.p. Article consulted at CDDE.

88 "Experimentales: Mafalda," *La Onda* (Mexico City), September 9, 1979, 9.

89 Eduardo Camaño, "El dibujante argentino Quino desautoriza la escenificación de su personaje Mafalda," *Excélsior* (Mexico City), September 6, 1979. Article consulted at CDDE.

90 "México: Estreno teatral de Mafalda," *Conjunto: Revista de teatro latinoamericano* 43 (January–March 1980), 139. According to this account, the play opened in June.

91 Eduardo Camacho, "Representan nuevamente a Mafalda a pesar de la oposición de su autor," *Excélsior* (Mexico City), September 29, 1979, n.p. Article consulted at CDDE. Interview with Andrés Accorsi, http://www.tebeosfera.com/1/Documento/Recorte/Comiqueando/Quino.htm (accessed March 10, 2014).

92 Camacho, "Representan nuevamente a Mafalda a pesar de la oposición de su autor."

93 Fernando Meraz, "Humorismo, refugio contra la amargura," *Excélsior* (Mexico City), November 6, 1981, n.p. Article consulted at CDDE.

94 "Medalla de oro," *Excélsior* (Mexico City), November 6, 1981, n.p. Article consulted at CDDE.

95 Meraz, "Humorismo, refugio contra la amargura."

96 Jorge Tovar, telephone interview by the author, March 3, 2013, Buenos Aires/Mexico. The artist could not recall the exact date of this exhibit but thought it probably took place in 1981, which is the date on the photograph on file in CDDE.

97 See Yankelevich, "México."

98 Martín Zamor (born in Mexico City in 1967), interview by the author, October 10, 2011, Mexico; and Mabel Domínguez (born in Mexico City in 1968), interview by the author, October 8, 2011, Mexico. The names have been changed to protect the subjects' privacy.

99 Mario García (born in La Plata, Argentina in 1957), interview by the author, January 10, 2014, Buenos Aires; and Rosana Muñoz (born in Buenos Aires in 1972), interview by the author, June 22, 2013, Buenos Aires.

100 Antonio Soria, "Casi medio siglo de Mafalda," *La Jornada Semanal* (Mexico City), March 11, 2012, 1–4.

101 The comic strips were published in book format in the following languages: Italian, French, Portuguese (both Brazilian and Iberian varieties), German, Finnish, Norwegian, Swedish, Dutch, Danish, Catalan, Galician, Basque, Greek,

Turkish, Hebrew, Korean, Chinese, English, Japanese, and Indonesian. See, for example, Andrew Graham-Yooll, "Friend," *Radar* (Buenos Aires), April 25, 2004, 3 (*Radar* is a supplement to *Página 12*).

4. ANTIESTABLISHMENT VOICE IN TURBULENT TIMES

1   There is abundant literature on this subject. See, for example, Filc, *Entre el parentesco y la política*; and Azpiazu, Basualdo, and Khavisse, *El nuevo poder económico en la Argentina de los años 80*. For more recent studies, see Novaro and Palermo, *La dictadura militar 1976–1983*; Crenzel, *Memory of the Argentina Disappearances*; Franco, *Un enemigo para la nación*; Cosse, *Pareja, sexualidad y familia*, 150–69; and Manzano, "Sex, Gender, and the Making of the 'Enemy Within' in Cold War Argentina."

2   See Levín, *Humor político en tiempos de represión*; and Burkart, *De Satiricón a Hum®*.

3   This is based on data from Kimel, *La masacre de San Patricio*, and accounts in the film *4 de julio: La masacre de San Patricio*, dir. Juan Pablo Young and Pablo Zubizarreta (Buenos Aires: Aguafuertes Film, 2007).

4   This account is also based on Kimel, *La massacre de San Patricio*, and *4 de julio*.

5   Available online at http://www.palotinos4dejulio.com.ar/ (accessed December 10, 2014). The diary excerpts are heard in *4 de julio*.

6   Kimel, *La masacre de San Patricio*, 17–19, 23–24.

7   Kimel, *La masacre de San Patricio*, 78.

8   Kimel, *La masacre de San Patricio*, 33.

9   Kimel, *La masacre de San Patricio*, 51.

10 Court file labeled "Expediente 7970, 1er cuerpo, año 1977, Juzgado Nacional de 1ª instancia en lo criminal y comercial, Barbeito, Salvador; Kelly, Alfredo; Leaden, Alfredo, Dufau, Pedro; Barletti, José Emilio; víctimas de homicidio (art. 79 CP)." The case is still open in Federal Court No. 12, under Sergio Torres.

11 Rodolfo Capalozza, interview by the author, September 22, 2013, Buenos Aires.

12 Statements by Quino on the television program hosted by Santo Virgilio Biasatti, http://www.tn.com.ar/programas/otro-tema/quino-con-santo_273691 (accessed January 10, 2014).

13 For the official press release, see "Asesinan a tres sacerdotes y a dos seminaristas en la parroquia de San Patricio, en Belgrano," *Clarín* (Buenos Aires), July 5, 1976, 5.

14 Andrew Graham-Yooll, interview by the author, July 17, 2013, Buenos Aires.

15 Roberto Cox, "Nuevo hombre ¿pero la misma política?," *Buenos Aires Herald*, July 6, 1976, editorial page.

16 "Ultiman en Tucumán a dos guerrilleros," *Clarín* (Buenos Aires), July 9, 1976, 5; "Ultiman a siete subversivos," *Clarín* (Buenos Aires), July 6, 1976, 4; "Ultimaron a 19 extremistas en 3 enfrentamientos," *Clarín* (Buenos Aires), July 3, 1976, 1.

17 Mignone, *Iglesia y dictadura*.

18 Press clippings are attached to the petition; Letter from José Divinsky and Elisa S. de Miler addressed to the president, "Al presidente de la Nación Argentina," dated March 14, 1977, in Buenos Aires. Consulted at AEDF.

19 Avellaneda, *Censura, autoritarismo y cultura.*

20 Daniel Divinsky, interview by Judith Gociol in Gociol, "Soy un escritor solapado."

21 "No deje que los animales sean más," October 24, 1969. Advertisement consulted at AEDF, press clippings file.

22 Daniel Divinsky, "Breve historia de la Editorial de la Flor," manuscript. Consulted at AEDF. He made the same statement in several interviews in the press.

23 "Esta noche acuéstese con . . . un libro de la Flor," unpublished, July 1971. Advertisement consulted at AEDF, press clippings file.

24 Avellaneda, *Censura, autoritarismo y cultura*, 38.

25 On these Catholic leagues, see Vázquez Lorda, "Intervenciones e iniciativas católicas en el ámbito familiar," 76–110.

26 Gociol and Invernizzi, *Un golpe a los libros*, 63, 214.

27 "Prohibiciones: La novela de un italiano," *Análisis*, no. 585 (June 2–8, 1972). Consulted at AEDF, press clippings file.

28 Untitled, *La Opinión* (Buenos Aires), February 5, 1977. Consulted at AEDF, press clippings file.

29 Complaint filed by Divinsky, addressed to Jorge Rafael Videla, Buenos Aires, February 11, 1977. Consulted at AEDF, miscellaneous file.

30 Gociol and Invernizzi, *Un golpe a los libros*, 33–34.

31 Letter to the president of the Sociedad Argentina de Escritores, dated Buenos Aires, February 24, 1977. Signed by Silvina Ocampo, Eduardo Gudiño Kieffer, José Bianco, Ulyses Petit de Murat, Juan José Hernández, Héctor Yánover, Ramón Plaza, and Luisa Mercedes Levinson, plus an illegible signature. Consulted at AEDF, miscellaneous file. Other letters of support arrived from different places in Latin America and Europe.

32 Divinsky in Gociol, "Soy un escritor solapado," http://www.me.gov.ar/monitor/nro11/conversaciones.htm, accessed January 27, 2014.

33 Eduardo Blaustein, "Nena qué va a ser de ti," *Página/12* (Buenos Aires), October 19, 1988, 10–11.

34 Martín Pérez, "A Quino podemos hacerlo," *Radar* (Buenos Aires), July 29, 2012 (*Radar* is a supplement to *Página/12*), http://www.pagina12.com.ar/diario/suplementos/radar/9-8112-2012-07-29.html (accessed December 10, 2013).

35 The newspaper *Río Negro* published its last *Mafalda* strip on December 1, 1973. "El adiós de Mafalda," *Río Negro*, December 1, 1973, 11. *Córdoba* published its last strip on February 3, 1974.

36 Ministerio de Justicia y Derechos Humanos (Argentina), *Informe de Ediciones*, file 179376.

37 Leila Guerriero, "Mafalda, vida de esta chica," *El País* (Madrid), March 13, 2012, www.cultura.elpais.com/cultura/2012/03/13/actualidad/1331659623_507858.html (accessed January 10, 2014).

38 Manuel Díaz, interview by the author, September 27, 2012, Buenos Aires.

39 Investigative report by Fons De Poel broadcast on the program *Brandpunt*, KRO-NCRV, The Netherlands, posted on YouTube as *Un horrible secreto: La*

historia de Rey Piuma, www.youtube.com/watch?v=zGVbxZiy_1s (accessed January 15, 2014).

40 María Rinifort, interview by the author, February 8, 2014, Buenos Aires.

41 Mario Amado, interview by the author, August 19, 2013, Buenos Aires.

42 Miguel Rep, in Quino, *Toda Mafalda*, 28.

43 Novaro and Palermo, *La dictadura militar 1976–1983*, 89–90.

44 "Humorista: Quino obtuvo una distinción," *La Nación* (Buenos Aires), August 1, 1977. Consulted at ADC.

45 See Crenzel, *Memory of the Argentina Disappearances*.

46 Novaro and Palermo, *La dictadura militar 1976–1983*, 166. For a discussion of how that moment was perceived, see Juan Corradi, "The Mode of Destruction." On media support, for example, in the women's magazine *Para Ti*, see Bontempo, "La construcción del consenso en torno al golpe de Estado de 1976"; and Margulis, "La piel busca sus formas."

47 Novaro and Palermo, *La dictadura militar 1976–1983*, 334–56.

48 Freud, "Humour."

49 Burkart, *De Satiricón a Hum®*, 55.

50 Abel González, "El buen humor de Quino," *Revista Clarín* (Buenos Aires), March 30, 1980, 4. (*Revista Clarín* is a supplement to *Clarín*.)

51 "Quino, sobre la mesa," *Clarín* (Buenos Aires), September 1980 (exact date illegible). Consulted at ADC, press clippings file.

52 "Mafalda, ahora dibujada para cine argentino," *Clarín* (Buenos Aires), May 1981 (exact date illegible). Consulted at ADC, press clippings file.

53 "Pase y vea," *Superhumor* (Buenos Aires), no. 9 (September 1981), 1.

54 Juan Sasturain, "Mafalda en tres cuestiones," *Superhumor* (Buenos Aires), no. 9, September 1981, 51.

55 Foster, *From Mafalda to Los Supermachos*, 61.

56 Sasturain, "Mafalda en tres cuestiones," 50.

57 Sasturain, "Mafalda en tres cuestiones," 50–51.

58 Oscar Steimberg, "Acerca de Mafalda según Quino, Sasturain y otros," *Superhumor* (Buenos Aires), no. 11 (November 1981), 8–9.

59 "Los números de Mafalda," *Superhumor* (Buenos Aires), no. 9 (September 1981), 49.

60 Carlos Exequiel Bellio, "Letter to the National Film Director," Museo del Cine, Buenos Aires, December 12, 1978, signed by María A. V. de Villa; and script of *Mafalda, la película*, 21, 24, 35. See also *El mundo de Mafalda* (film, Daniel Mallo), 1981.

61 "Mafalda, marxista," *Última Hora* (Buenos Aires), July 31, 1975, n.p. Consulted at ADC.

62 Juan Sasturain, "Esta Mafalda llega cuando la fiesta ha terminado," *Clarín* (Buenos Aires), December 10, 1981, 4–5.

63 Néstor Tirri, "El cine nacional," *Clarín* (Buenos Aires), December 4, 1981, 5.

64 "Gente recomienda: Mafalda," *Gente* (Buenos Aires), December 1981, 90.

65 "Estadística: Las películas que se exhiben," *La Razón* (Buenos Aires), December 23, 1981, 11.

66 "Otro importante premio internacional para Quino," *Convicción* (Buenos Aires), June 20, 1982, n.p. Article consulted at ADC.

67 On this, see Novaro and Palermo, *La dictadura militar 1976–1983*, 382–410.

68 "Mafalda," *Río Negro*, February 21, 1982, 19. The newspaper also started featuring a weekly humor page penned by Quino.

69 Pisani et al., *100 años, Río Negro*, 28–29, 226–27.

70 Carlos Torrengo, interview by the author, December 13, 2013, Buenos Aires.

71 Steinberg, "Acerca de Mafalda según Quino, Sasturain y otros," 8–9.

72 For an overview of the conflict, see Novaro and Palermo, *La dictadura militar 1976–1983*, 411–56.

73 On this climate of euphoria, see Romero, *Breve historia contemporánea de la Argentina*, 333–35.

74 Salomón et al., *Quinta Bienal Argentina del humor y la historieta*.

75 Quino, *Mafalda inédita*, n.p.

76 "Mafalda: Un alegato a la paz y la libertad," *Tiempo Argentino*, February 25, 1984, 9.

77 Quino, "La Argentina en dibujitos," *Tiempo Argentino*, July 21, 1985, n.p. Consulted at ADC.

78 Daniel Datola, "El hombre que ignora el verano," *La Razón* (Buenos Aires), July 30, 1985, 28.

79 Ricardo Parrota, "Mafalda, en gallego," *Clarín* (Buenos Aires), August 20, 1984, 27.

80 "El dibujante Quino, creador de Mafalda, indignado por la utilización de sus viñetas como emblemas franquistas," *El País* (Madrid), April 10, 1985, 21.

81 "El dibujante Quino."

82 Carlos G. Santa Cecilia, "La propaganda franquista usa los dibujos de Quino," *La Razón* (Buenos Aires), April 12, 1985, n.p; "Mafalda con emblemas franquistas," *La Razón* (Buenos Aires), April 11, 1985, n.p. Article consulted at ADC.

83 Eduardo Longoni, interview by the author, December 3, 2013, Buenos Aires.

84 "Quino, premiado," *La Razón* (Buenos Aires), April 11, 1987, n.p.; "Galardonaron a Quino," *Clarín* (Buenos Aires), June 7, 1988, 41; "Quino fue galardonado," *ABC* (Madrid), June 10, 1988, 52.

85 "Mafalda festeja sus 25 años, contando episodios de su vida," *Semanario* (Buenos Aires), October 18, 1988, n.p. The research for the book was conducted by Sylvina Walger and the compilation was edited by Alicia and Julieta Colombo.

86 Norma Morandini, "Los 25 años de Mafalda," *Cambio 16* (Madrid), no. 862 (June 6, 1988), 203–4.

87 Blaustein, "Nena qué va a ser de ti."

88 Leonardo Tarifeño, "Se supo: Mafalda cumple veinticinco años," *El Cronista Comercial*, September 28, 1989, n.p. Consulted at ADC.

89 José Manuel Vaquero Oviedo, "El creador de 'Mafalda' defiende el cine infantil y juvenil," *El País* (Madrid), June 26, 1979, 33.

90   "Quino," *Revista Confederal* (Buenos Aires), September 1988, 4–5.

91   Adair, *In Search of the Lost Decade.*

92   "El indulto abolla la democracia, dijo Quino," *Nuevo Sur* (Buenos Aires), November 8, 1989, n.p. Article consulted at ADC.

5. *MAFALDA*, THE MYTH

1   Eliade, *Myth and Reality*, 1, 14, 184–85; Eco, "Il Mito di Superman."

2   Halbwachs, *On Collective Memory.*

3   Nora, "Generation."

4   Norma Morandini, "Los 25 años de Mafalda," *Cambio 16* (Madrid), no. 862 (June 6, 1988), 203–4.

5   Mar Correa, "El regreso de Mafalda," *ABC* (Madrid), March 31, 1989, 91.

6   Carlos Ares, "Mafalda cumple 25 años," *El País* (Madrid), November 2, 1988, 42–43; Javier Coma, "Menores de edad, mayores de mente," *El País* (Madrid), November 2, 1988, 43; Horacio Eichelbaum, "Mafalda nos hace cosquillas," *El País* (Madrid), November 2, 1988, 43.

7   "Mafalda por Quino," *La Vanguardia* (Barcelona), October 3, 1989, 15.

8   Hobsbawm, *The Age of Extremes*, 406, 416.

9   Giusi Quarenghi, "Così ho ucciso a Mafalda," *L'Unità* (Rome), December 8, 1984, 15.

10   "Italia también festeja los 25 años de Mafalda," *Nuevo Sur* (Buenos Aires), December 12, 1989, 19.

11   Sealtiel Alatriste, telephone interview by the author, December 12, 2012, Buenos Aires/Mexico City; Guillermo Schavelzon, telephone interview by the author, February 8, 2013, Buenos Aires/Madrid.

12   Mauricio Ciechanower, "Entrevista a Joaquín Lavado (Quino): Mafalda, esa famosa y tremenda criatura," *Plural* (Mexico City), no. 209 (February 1, 1989), 62–73.

13   Alex Grijelmo, "Mafaldalandia se instala en Madrid," *El País* (Madrid), November 11, 1991, 31.

14   I draw here partly from Stern, "Paradigmas de la conquista." Stern also identifies a third paradigm, conquest as a power relationship that was challenged, which did not receive as much attention in public debates.

15   Alex Grijelmo, "Mafalda se ha hecho española," *El País* (Madrid), January 17, 1990, 28.

16   "Joya," *Flash* (Madrid), May 29, 1992, 9.

17   Information obtained from the current website of the exhibit, available at http://www.expo92.es (accessed January 10, 2014).

18   The short film by Juan Padrón is mentioned in Quino, *El mundo de Mafalda*, 123, but I was unable to access a copy of it.

19   Alex Grijelmo, "Quino: Bienvenido a casa," *El País* (Madrid), October 15, 1995, 26–28.

20   Grijelmo, "Mafaldalandia se instala en Madrid," 31.

21   Grijelmo, "Mafaldalandia se instala en Madrid," 31.

22 Daniel Samper, "Quino en el país de Mafalda," *Cambio 16* (Madrid), April 13, 1992.

23 Soledad Alameda, "Padre de la criatura," *El País* (Madrid), ca. March 1992, 19–26. Article consulted at the archive of the newspaper *La Vanguardia*.

24 Maite Rico, "La niña del pelo tieso" and "Cuerpos represivos," *El País* (Madrid), April 22, 1992, 2.

25 Enrique Arrosagaray, "Este hombre, de joven fue Felipe," *Página/12*, May 5, 1999, 28–29.

26 Quino, *Toda Mafalda*, strip 781, 243.

27 This anecdote is recounted in several articles with few variations. This is drawn from Mónica Maristain, "Quinomanía," *Radar* (Buenos Aires), no. 392 (February 22, 2004), 1–7. (*Radar* is a supplement to *Página/12*.) See also Mauricio Vincent, "Mafalda descubre el 'amol' en Cuba," *El País* (Madrid), February 20, 2007, 43.

28 "Premian a Quino en Cuba," *La Nación* (Buenos Aires), November 28, 1985, n.p. Article consulted at ADC.

29 "Quino critica la acumulación de poder de Castro," *Excélsior* (Mexico City), June 4, 1999, n.p. Article consulted at CDDE.

30 *Quinoscopio 2* and *Quinoscopio 3* were awarded Second Coral Prize at the International Latin American New Cinema Festival held in Havana in 1986, and Best Short Film at the International Imagination and Fiction Film Festival held in Madrid in 1987. *Quinoscopio 6* received an honorable mention from the judges at the Leipzig International Documentary and Short Film Festival in 1988, and the Pitirre Prize at the San Juan International Film Festival in Puerto Rico in 1990. The information is drawn from http://www.juanpadron.cu/premios.html (accessed January 20, 2014).

31 Gabriela Saidón, "Quinoscopios," *Clarín* (Buenos Aires), October 7, 1993, n.p.; "Mi temática es siempre la lucha entre débiles y poderosos," *La Maga* (Buenos Aires), October 20, 1993, 16.

32 Roque Casciero, "Somos nostálgicos de los ideales de los '60," *Página/12* (Buenos Aires), September 22, 2000, 25.

33 "Treinta años después," *Página/12* (Buenos Aires), March 8, 1995, n.p.; "Las autonómicas recuperan a Mafalda," Paz Álvarez, *El País* (Madrid), February 25, 1995, available at http://www.elpais.com/diario/1995/02/25/radiotv/793666802_850215.html (accessed October 8, 2013).

34 "Quino expone dibujos inéditos," *Río Negro*, February 15, 1995, n.p.

35 "Quino, inteligencia y política desde el humor," *Río Negro*, January 19, 1998, 31.

36 "Tengo cosas de Mafalda, Susanita y Felipe," *La Nación* (Buenos Aires), August 29, 2000, 6.

37 Juan Cruz, "Mafalda vacila al vampiro," *El País* (Madrid), October 12, 2008, 37. The vampire's words in Spanish were "¡Hola, Mafaldita! ¿Qué tú haces, *mijita*, tan solita *pol* Madrid?"

38 Judith Gociol, "Historia de Felipe," *Clarín* (Buenos Aires), April 23, 1995, 9.

39 "Mafalda no murió," *Noticias* (Buenos Aires), April 12, 1997, 10.

40 "Ahora Mafalda aparece en un diario de los EEUU," *Clarín* (Buenos Aires), May 8, 1995, 33; "Mafalda divierte en Estados Unidos," *Crónica* (Buenos Aires), May 9, 1995, 31.

41 "Quino dio un portazo en apoyo a Castro," *La Nación* (Buenos Aires), August 28, 1995, 4.

42 Vincent, "Mafalda descubre el 'amol' en Cuba"; "Pasión por Mafalda en La Habana," *Clarín* (Buenos Aires), February 13, 2007, n.p. Consulted at ADC.

43 Hobsbawm, *The Age of Extremes*, 585.

44 Hobsbawm, *The Age of Extremes*, 10–11.

45 Quino, *I Pensieri di Mafalda* (Turin: Lo Scarabeo, 1993), with four thematic volumes on everyday life, economy and politics, pessimism and optimism, and Mafalda and company; Quino, *Il mondo di Mafalda* (Milan: Bompiani, 1994); "Quino, a la Feria de Bolonia," *Excélsior* (Mexico City), April 6, 1994, n.p. Article consulted at ADE.

46 Karmentxu Marín, "Mafalda," *Clarín* (Buenos Aires), April 1, 1994, n.p. Article consulted at ADC.

47 Quino, *Tutto Mafalda*, 587.

48 "Tanti auguri," *Página/12* (Buenos Aires), August 21, 1994, n.p. Consulted at ADC.

49 Manuel Vicent, "Imágenes," *El País* (Madrid), July 31, 1994, n.p.; Ángel de la Peña Tejerina, "Hipocresías," *El País* (Madrid), August 10, 1994, available at http://www.elpais.com/diario/1994/08/10/opinion/776469604_850215.html (accessed October 10, 2012).

50 "Quinosofía: Personajes/Joaquín Lavado," *Clarín* (Buenos Aires), October 24, 1993, 20.

51 Patricia Kolesnicov, "Su filosofía," *Clarín* (Buenos Aires), October 18, 2000, 39.

52 Casciero, "Somos nostálgicos."

53 On these processes of impoverishment, see Minujin and Kessler, *La nueva pobreza en la Argentina*; and Svampa, *Los que ganaron*.

54 In addition to the works cited above, see Guano, "Spectacles of Modernity"; and Adamovsky, *Historia de la clase media argentina*, 421–38.

55 "Mi temática es siempre la lucha entre débiles y poderosos," *La Maga* (Buenos Aires), October 20, 1993, 16; Diego Fischerman, "De qué se ríe Quino," *Página/12* (Buenos Aires), October 15, 1993, 27.

56 Miguel Rep, "Menem y Quino," *Página/12* (Buenos Aires), October 12, 1993, 26.

57 Carolina Muzi, "Con ojos de Quino," *Clarín* (Buenos Aires), October 15, 1993, 15.

58 "Quinosofía."

59 "Mafalda cumple 30 años," *El Cronista* (Buenos Aires), September 29, 1994, n.p. News item drawn from ADC.

60 "Quino que se vengan los chicos," *Clarín* (Buenos Aires), July 22, 1994, 15.

61 "Mafalda," *Clarín* (Buenos Aires), ca. November 1994, n.p. Consulted at ADC, date illegible.

62 Jorge Schvarzer, "La clase media partida al medio," *Página/12* (Buenos Aires), September 28, 1994, 18.

63   Luis Alberto Quevedo, "Ahora veranean en el patio," *Clarín* (Buenos Aires), September 28, 1994, 19.

64   Daniel Samper Pizano, "Aguante, Mafalda," *Clarín* (Buenos Aires), May 16, 1993, 32–35.

65   "Mafalda: La genia del genio," *Revista Viva* (Buenos Aires), October 2, 1994, 17–24. (*Revista Viva* is a supplement to the newspaper *Clarín*.)

66   "Hola Córdoba!" (advertisement), *La voz del Interior* (Córdoba), September 20, 1995, 13. With this ad, the paper announced the regular publication of the comic strip. Alba Lampón, interview by the author, August 23, 2012, Buenos Aires.

67   For more data, see Podestá, "La crisis de desocupación en la Argentina (1993–1998)," 7.

68   On the effects of this state of affairs on the middle class, see Visacovsky, "Imágenes de la 'clase media' en la prensa escrita argentina durante la llamada 'crisis del 2001–2002.'" See also Adamovsky, *Historia de la clase media*, 449–74.

69   "Quisimos mostrar solidaridad de una manera equivocada europea," *Página/12* (Buenos Aires), January 22, 2002, available at http://www.pagina12.com.ar /diario/cultura/7-1058-2002-01-22.html (accessed April 7, 2002); "Quino: Mafalda no es 'saqueadora,'" *La Nación* (Buenos Aires), January 20, 2002, available at https://www.lanacion.com.ar/368028-quino-mafalda-no-es-saqueadora (accessed May 7, 2014). Consulted at ADC.

70   "España otorgó gran distinción al humorista Quino," *Clarín* (Buenos Aires), October 18, 2000, 38; "Distinguió la Universidad de Alcalá a Quino," *Excélsior* (Mexico City), October 18, 2000, n.p.; "El creador de Mafalda cumple hoy 70 años," *La Voz del Interior* (Córdoba), July 17, 2002, 4.

71   "Mafalda abre la colección Biblioteca Clarín," *Clarín* (Buenos Aires), December 14, 2003, 40.

72   Oscar Steimberg, "Una nena con mundo propio," *Clarín* (Buenos Aires), December 14, 2003, 40.

73   Quino, *In viaggio con Mafalda*; Quino, *De viaje con Quino*.

74   Carlos Alegri and Virginia Messi, "Mafalda da la cara," *Somos* (Buenos Aires), October 19, 1988, n.p. Article consulted at ADC.

75   Andrew Graham-Yooll, interview by the author, July 17, 2013, Buenos Aires.

76   "Friend," *Radar* (Buenos Aires), April 25, 2004, 3. (*Radar* is a supplement to *Página/12*.)

77   Ezequiel Martínez, "Quino, sin medias tintas," *Clarín* (Buenos Aires), September 25, 2004, 6–8.

78   The Buenos Aires distinction was stipulated under Law 1567 of December 9, 2004, and sanctioned on January 12, 2005; "Quino fue declarado Ciudadano Ilustre," *Los Andes* (Mendoza), August 2, 2005; "La legislatura declaró a Quino ciudadano ilustre," *Clarín* (Buenos Aires), December 10, 2004, 55; María Luján Picabea, "Quino: 'Esos homenajes me comprometen a portarme bien,'" *Clarín* (Buenos Aires), August 17, 2005, 10.

79   See "Historia de Plaza Mafalda," *La voz de Colegiales* (Buenos Aires), August 22, 2013, available online at http://www.barriocolegiales.blogspot.com.ar/2013/08 /la-historia-de-plaza-mafalda.html (accessed January 10, 2014).

80 The strips were reproduced by a team of artists formed by Marta Inés Tapia Vera, Paula Franzi, Eduardo Iglesias Bickles, and Fabián Herrera. See Daniela Bordón, "Para ver a Mafalda en la plaza," *Pagina/12* (Buenos Aires), August 20, 2005, 3.

81 "La sabiduría de Mafalda revive en una plaza de Colegiales," *Clarín* (Buenos Aires), August 20, 2005, 40.

82 "Mafalda y los personajes de Quino llegan al subte," *La Nación* (Buenos Aires), August 31, 2008, 2; Juan Manuel Bordón, "Quino visitó el taller donde se hace el mural de Mafalda," *Clarín* (Buenos Aires), August 21, 2008, 21.

83 "Mafalda ya es la niña terrible del subte," *Clarín* (Buenos Aires), November 20, 2008, 31.

84 Quino, *Toda Mafalda*. A special two-volume edition was published for this collection. See "Distribuirán un millón de libros en escuelas medias," *La Prensa* (Buenos Aires), August 11, 2007, n.p. Article consulted at APQ.

85 Alba Lampón, interview by the author, August 23, 2012, Buenos Aires.

86 Marta Platía, "Cumple 75 años Quino, un pensador que hace historias," *Clarín* (Buenos Aires), July 17, 2007; "'El mundo según Mafalda' sale de gira hasta 2010," *La Voz del Interior* (Córdoba), October 2, 2008, article consulted at the archive of the newspaper *La Voz del Interior* (hereafter ADLVI). There is also a description of the exhibit online at http://www.planetacultural.com.ar/index .php/coberturas-menu/580-se-inauguro-la-muestra-el-mundo-segun-mafalda -en-el-centro-cultural (accessed January 10, 2014).

87 Mariana Pérez, interview by the author, November 10, 2012, Buenos Aires.

88 Resolution no. 19, UPEPB/09, dated April 17, 2009, *Boletín Oficial de la Ciudad de Buenos Aires*, 25–27.

89 Pablo Irrgang, interview by the author, March 12, 2014, Buenos Aires.

90 Irrgang, interview by the author.

91 Irrgang, interview by the author.

92 Turner, *From Ritual to Theatre*, 24–27.

93 "Correo de lectores," *El Globo* (Madrid), no. 11 (January 1974), 37–38.

94 "Mafalda: La genia del genio," *Revista Viva*, October 2, 1994, 17–24. (*Revista Viva* is a supplement to the newspaper *Clarín*.) I was unable to find any record of the proposal in the legislature's documentation center, but neither did I find anything to contradict the report.

95 "Mafalda da la cara," *Somos* (Buenos Aires), October 19, 1988, n.p. Article consulted at ADC. (Italics in the original.)

96 Quino, *Tutto Mafalda*, 558–61.

97 Quino, *Tutto Mafalda*, 564–65.

98 Pilar Rahola, "El catecismo de Mafalda," *La Nación* (Buenos Aires), May 8, 2007, 10.

99 Javier Barroso, "Mafalda toma vida," *El País* (Madrid), September 26, 2000, 24.

100 Pedro Triguero-Lizana y Gómez, "Mafaldas y Manolitos," *El País* (Madrid), October 7, 2000, available online at http://www.elpais.com/diario/2000/10 /07/madrid/970917884_850215.html (accessed January 10, 2012).

101 Eduardo Pogoriles, "Ahora Mafalda habla en coreano," *Clarín* (Buenos Aires), July 14, 2002, 43; Susana Parejas, "Quino, el papá de Mafalda festeja hoy, en

París, sus 75 años," *Clarín* (Buenos Aires), July 17, 2007; Leonardo Tarifeño, "Se supo: Mafalda cumple veinticinco años," *El Cronista Comercial* (Buenos Aires), September 28, 1989.

102 Andrés Padilla, "Quino atribuye el éxito de Mafalda a que la sociedad no ha cambiado," *El País* (Madrid), November 19, 1999, 56.

103 Alberto Mazzei, "Correo de los lectores," *Siete Días* (Buenos Aires), no. 226 (September 13, 1971), 25.

104 "Veinticuatro horas de la vida de . . . Quino," *La Vanguardia* (Barcelona), ca. April 1972, n.p. Consulted at ADLV.

105 F. Monegal, "Esther Tusquets y el libro infantil," *La Vanguardia* (Barcelona), January 31, 1974, 49; "Mafalda se acaba," *La Vanguardia* (Barcelona), April 21, 1974, n.p. News item drawn from ADLV.

106 "Quino 'asesinó' a Mafalda por celos," *Crónica* (Buenos Aires), January 26, 1977.

107 "Tiempos difíciles por esta maldita globalización: Quino," *Excélsior* (Mexico City), December 3, 1997.

108 Alberto Fernández, "La muerte de Mafalda: Narrativas postelectorales desde la izquierda," *Letras Libres* (Mexico City), July 25, 2012, available at http://www.letraslibres.com/blogs/polifonia/la-muerte-de-mafalda-narrativas-postelectorales-desde-la-izquierda (accessed March 10, 2014). Information drawn from http://www.mx.answers.yahoo.com/question/index?qid=20080522183710AAhjjs1 (accessed January 10, 2014), and https://mx.answers.yahoo.com/question/index?qid=20090125172705AAwfKlf (accessed March 10, 2013).

109 Casciero, "Somos nostálgicos."

BIBLIOGRAPHY

MAFALDA BOOKS, FILMS, AND TELEVISION SHOWS
Books

Quino (Joaquín Salvador Lavado). *¿A dónde vamos a parar?* Buenos Aires: Ediciones de la Flor, 1973.

Quino (Joaquín Salvador Lavado). *Al fin solos*. Buenos Aires: Ediciones de la Flor, 1971.

Quino (Joaquín Salvador Lavado). *De viaje con Quino*. Mexico: Tusquets, 2004.

Quino (Joaquín Salvador Lavado). *In viaggio con Mafalda*. Rome: Touring, 2004.

Quino (Joaquín Salvador Lavado). *Mafalda: Oltre le estrisce . . .* 2008. Milan: Salani, 2012.

Quino (Joaquín Salvador Lavado). *Mafalda 1*. 1966. Buenos Aires: Jorge Álvarez, 1966. Repr. Buenos Aires: Ediciones de la Flor, 1988.

Quino (Joaquín Salvador Lavado). *Mafalda 2*. 1967. Buenos Aires: Ediciones de la Flor, 1992. Originally published under the title *Así es la cosa Mafalda*.

Quino (Joaquín Salvador Lavado). *Mafalda 3*. 1968. Buenos Aires: Ediciones de la Flor, 1989.

Quino (Joaquín Salvador Lavado). *Mafalda 4*. 1968. Buenos Aires: Ediciones de la Flor, 1988.

Quino (Joaquín Salvador Lavado). *Mafalda 5*. 1969. Buenos Aires: Ediciones de la Flor, 1989.

Quino (Joaquín Salvador Lavado). *Mafalda 6*. 1970. Buenos Aires: Ediciones de la Flor, 1988.

Quino (Joaquín Salvador Lavado). *Mafalda 7*. 1971. Buenos Aires: Ediciones de la Flor, 1989.

Quino (Joaquín Salvador Lavado). *Mafalda 8*. 1972. Buenos Aires: Ediciones de la Flor, 1988.

Quino (Joaquín Salvador Lavado). *Mafalda 9*. 1973. Buenos Aires: Ediciones de la Flor, 1989.

Quino (Joaquín Salvador Lavado). *Mafalda 10*. 1973. Buenos Aires: Ediciones de la Flor, 1989.

Quino (Joaquín Salvador Lavado). *Mafalda inédita*. Buenos Aires: Ediciones de la Flor, 1988.

Quino (Joaquín Salvador Lavado). *Mafalda, la contestataria*. Milan: Bompiani, 1969.

Quino (Joaquín Salvador Lavado). *El mundo de Mafalda*. Barcelona: Lumen, 1992.

Quino (Joaquín Salvador Lavado). *Toda Mafalda*. Buenos Aires: Ediciones de la Flor, 1993.

Quino (Joaquín Salvador Lavado). *Todo Mafalda*. Barcelona: Lumen, 1992.

Quino (Joaquín Salvador Lavado). *Tutto Mafalda*. 2009. Milan: Salani, 2010.

Quino (Joaquín Salvador Lavado). *Y digo yo*. Buenos Aires: Ediciones de la Flor, 1971.

Ravoni, Marcelo, and Valerio Riva. *Il libro dei bambini terribili per adulti masochisti*. Milan: Feltrinelli, 1968.

Films and Television Shows

De Poel, Fons. Investigative report broadcast on the television program *Brandpunt*, KRO-NCRV, The Netherlands, 2012. Posted on YouTube as "Un horrible secreto—Daniel Rey Piuma," 2013. https://www.youtube.com/watch?v=zGVbxZiy_1s.

Mallo, Daniel, dir. *Mafalda, la película*. Argentina, 1981.

Padrón, Juan, dir., and Quino (Joaquín Salvador Lavado). *Mafalda y sus amigos*. Cuba–Spain, 1993.

Young, Juan Pablo, and Pablo Zubizarreta. *4 de julio: La masacre de San Patricio*. Buenos Aires: Aguafuertes Film, 2007.

ARCHIVES

Argentina

Note: Unless otherwise specified, the following archives are in Buenos Aires.

ADC. Archive of *Clarín* (newspaper).

ADLVI. Archive of *La Voz del Interior* (newspaper), Córdoba.

ADRN. Archive of *Río Negro* (newspaper).

AITDT. Archive of Instituto Torcuato Di Tella, Library of Universidad Torcuato Di Tella.

APQ. Personal archive of Quino (Joaquín Salvador Lavado).

Archive of Secretaría 23, Juzgado Criminal y Correccional Federal 12.

Círculo Sindical de la Prensa y la Comunicación de Córdoba, Documentation Center, Córdoba.

Editorial Perfil, Documentation Center.

José Enrique Miguens Collection, Special Collections and Archives, Max von Buch Library, Universidad de San Andrés, Victoria, Argentina.

Torres, Antonio, Club del Comic. Private collection.

Spain

El País (newspaper), Documentation Center, Madrid

La Vanguardia (newspaper) archive, Barcelona

Mexico

CDDE. *Excélsior* (newspaper), Documentation Center, Mexico City
Editorial Tusquets archive, Mexico City

NEWSPAPERS AND MAGAZINES
Argentina

Boletín del Consejo Deliberante   *Hum*®
   de la Ciudad de Buenos Aires   *Los Libros*
Boletín Oficial de la Ciudad de   *El Mundo*
   Buenos Aires   *La Nación*
Buenos Aires Herald   *La Opinión*
El Caudillo   *Panorama*
Clarín   *Primera Plana*
Crisis   *La Razón*
Cuestionario   *Siete Días*
El Día   *Superhumor*
Gente   *La Voz del Interior*

Spain

ABC   *El Globo*
Bang   *El País*
Cambio 16   *La Vanguardia*

Italy

Il Mago   *La Stampa*
Il Messaggero   *L'Unità*

Mexico

El Día   *Novedades*
Excélsior   *La Onda*
El Imparcial   *Plural*
El Nacional

INTERVIEWS

Alatriste, Sealtiel, telephone interview by the author, December 12, 2012, Buenos
    Aires/Mexico City.
Amado, Mario, interview by the author, August 19, 2013, Buenos Aires.
Capalozza, Rodolfo, interview by the author, September 22, 2013, Buenos Aires.
Chirichella, Francisco, interview by the author, August 8, 2013, Buenos Aires.
Colombo, Alicia, interview by the author, May 30, 2013, Buenos Aires.

Díaz, Manuel, interview by the author, September 27, 2012, Buenos Aires.

Divinsky, Daniel, interviews by the author, January 10, 2010, Buenos Aires, March 22, 2010, Buenos Aires, and February 10, 2014, Buenos Aires.

Domínguez, Mabel, interview by the author, October 8, 2011, Mexico City.

Firpo, Norberto, interview by the author, January 13, 2011, Buenos Aires.

Flores, Verónica, telephone interview by the author, January 10, 2013, Buenos Aires/Mexico City.

Fuentes, Vanessa, telephone interview by the author, September 3, 2012, Buenos Aires/Mexico City.

García, Mario, interview by the author, January 10, 2014, Buenos Aires.

García, Miguel, telephone interview by the author, October 7, 2013, Buenos Aires/Madrid.

Giovannucci, Iván, telephone interviews by the author, January 14, 2013, Buenos Aires/Milan, and January 16, 2013, Buenos Aires/Milan.

Graham-Yooll, Andrew, interview by the author, July 17, 2013, Buenos Aires.

Hernández, Pablo, interview by the author, June 14, 2012, Buenos Aires.

Irrgang, Pablo, interview by the author, March 12, 2014, Buenos Aires.

Lampón, Alba, interviews by the author, August 23, 2012, Buenos Aires, and December 10, 2013, Buenos Aires.

Linari, "Chiche," interview by the author, January 20, 2013, Buenos Aires.

Longoni, Eduardo, interview by the author, December 3, 2013, Buenos Aires.

López de la Madrid, Claudio, telephone interview by the author, September 19, 2013, Buenos Aires/Barcelona.

Morero, Sergio, interview by the author, September 20, 2012, Buenos Aires.

Muñoz, Rosana, interview by the author, June 22, 2013, Buenos Aires.

Pérez, Mariana, interview by the author, November 10, 2012, Buenos Aires.

Quino (Joaquín Salvador Lavado), interview by the author, May 30, 2013, Buenos Aires.

Rinifort, María, interview by the author, February 8, 2014, Buenos Aires.

Sabino, Rolando, interview by the author, August 8, 2013, Buenos Aires.

Sasturain, Juan, interview by the author, March 13, 2014, Buenos Aires.

Schavelzon, Guillermo, telephone interview by the author, February 8, 2013, Buenos Aires/Madrid.

Suppo, Sergio, interview by the author, May 14, 2013, Córdoba.

Torrengo, Carlos, interview by the author, December 13, 2013, Buenos Aires.

Tovar, Jorge, telephone interview by the author, March 3, 2013, Buenos Aires/Mexico City.

Tovar, Luis, interview by the author, October 9, 2010, Mexico City.

Zamor, Martín, interview by the author, October 10, 2011, Mexico City.

GOVERNMENT AND OTHER OFFICIAL DOCUMENTS

Dirección Nacional de Estadística y Censos (Argentina). *Censo Nacional de Población 1960*. Buenos Aires, 1963.

Instituto Nacional de Estadística y Censos de la República Argentina (INDEC). *Censo Nacional de Población, Familias y Vivienda, 1970*. Buenos Aires, ca. 1970.

Ministerio de Educación y Justicia, Argentina. *Enseñanza Media: Años 1914–1963.* Vol. 1: *Ciclo Básico, Bachillerato y Bachilleratos Especializados.* Prepared by Departamento de Estadística Educativa. Buenos Aires, n.d.

Ministerio de Educación y Justicia, Argentina. *Enseñanza Media: Años 1914–1963.* Vol. 2: *Enseñanza Normal, Comercial y Especial.* Prepared by Departamento de Estadística Educativa. Buenos Aires, 1965.

Ministerio de Justicia y Derechos Humanos, Argentina. *Informe de Ediciones.* Prepared by Dirección Nacional de Derechos de Autor. File no. 179376, 1982.

PUBLISHED SOURCES

Acevedo, Esther. *La caricatura política en México en el siglo XIX.* Mexico City: Círculo de Arte, 2000.

Adair, Jennifer. *In Search of the Lost Decade: Everyday Rights in Post-Dictatorship Argentina.* Berkeley: University of California Press, forthcoming.

Adamovsky, Ezequiel. *Historia de la clase media argentina: Apogeo y decadencia de una ilusión, 1919–2003.* Buenos Aires: Planeta, 2009.

Adamovsky, Ezequiel, Sergio Visacovsky, and Patricia Beatriz Vargas, eds. *Clases medias: Nuevos enfoques desde la sociología, la historia y la antropología.* Buenos Aires: Ariel, 2014.

Altamirano, Carlos. "Las dos Argentinas." In *Peronismo y cultura de izquierda,* 27–48. 1997; reprint, Buenos Aires: Temas Grupo Editorial, 2001.

Altamirano, Carlos. "La pequeña burguesía, una clase en el purgatorio." In *Peronismo y cultura de izquierda,* 81–105. 1997; reprint, Buenos Aires: Temas Grupo Editorial, 2001.

Appadurai, Arjun. *Modernity at Large: Cultural Dimensions of Globalization.* Minneapolis: University of Minnesota Press, 1996.

Armus, Diego. "El viaje al centro: Tísicas, costureritas y milonguitas en Buenos Aires, 1910–1940." In *Entre médicos y curanderos: Cultura, historia y enfermedad en América Latina moderna,* edited by Diego Armus, 221–58. Buenos Aires: Norma, 2002.

Avellaneda, Andrés. *Censura, autoritarismo y cultura: Argentina 1960–1983.* Vol. 1. Buenos Aires: Centro Editor de América Latina, 1986.

Azpiazu, Daniel, Eduardo Basualdo, and Miguel Khavisse. *El nuevo poder económico en la Argentina de los años 80.* Buenos Aires: Editorial Legasa, 1986.

Bakhtin, Mikhail. *Rabelais and His World.* Translated by Helene Iswolsky. Bloomington: Indiana University Press, 1984.

Barbieri, Daniele. "Il fumetto in Italia." Paper presented at the conference "Contemporary Italy: The Construction of Identities," University of Warwick, October 29, 1995.

Barry, Carolina. *Evita capitana: El partido peronista femenino, 1949–1955.* Buenos Aires: EDUNTREF, 2009.

Berger, Peter L. *Redeeming Laughter: The Comic Dimension of Human Experience.* New York: Walter de Gruyter, 1997.

Bergson, Henri. *Laughter: An Essay on the Meaning of the Comic*. New York: Macmillan, 1914.

Besoky, Juan Luis. "La derecha peronista en perspectiva." *Nuevo Mundo Mundos Nuevos,* 2013. Accessed March 20, 2014. https://journals.openedition.org/nuevomundo/65374.

Bontempo, Paula. "La construcción del consenso en torno al golpe de Estado de 1976: La revista *Para Ti,* 1974–1976." Buenos Aires: unpublished manuscript, 2008.

Brennan, James, and Mónica Gordillo. *Córdoba: El Cordobazo, el clasismo y la movilización política*. La Plata: De la Campana, 2008.

Burkart, Mara E. *De Satiricón a Hum®: Risa, cultura y política en los años setenta*. Buenos Aires: Miño y Dávila, 2017.

Burucúa, José Emilio. *La imagen y la risa*. Mérida: Editorial Periférica, 2007.

Caimari, Lila. *Mientras la ciudad duerme*. Buenos Aires: Siglo XXI, 2012.

Cano, Inés. "El movimiento feminista argentino en la década del '70." *Todo es Historia*, no. 183 (August 1982): 84–93.

Carr, Raymond. *España: De la Restauración a la democracia, 1875–1980*. Barcelona: Ariel, 1983.

Catelli, Nora. "La élite itinerante del boom: Seducciones transnacionales en los escritores latinoamericanos (1960–1973)." In *Historia de los intelectuales en América Latina: Los avatares de la "ciudad letrada" en el siglo XX*, vol. 2, edited by Carlos Altamirano, 712–32. Buenos Aires: Katz, 2010.

Chartier, Roger. *Cultural History: Between Practices and Representations*. Ithaca, NY: Cornell University Press, 1988.

Coll Garcés, Oriol. "'Mafalda': Análisis estético, sociológico y lingüístico de un fenómeno de masas." Undergraduate thesis, Universitat de Barcelona, 1973.

Conde Martín, Luis. *Historia del humor gráfico en España*. Lleida, Spain: Editorial Milenio, 2002.

Corradi, Juan. "The Mode of Destruction: Terror in Argentina." *Telos* 54, no. 3 (1982): 61–76.

Cortázar, Julio. "Casa tomada." In *Bestiario*, 9–18, 1951; reprint, Buenos Aires: Minotauro, 1969.

Cosse, Isabella. "Argentine Mothers and Fathers and the New Psychological Paradigm of Child-Rearing (1958–1973)." *Journal of Family History* 35, no. 2 (2010): 180–202.

Cosse, Isabella, "Clases medias e historia reciente: Problemas y enfoques de estudio." In "Clases medias, sociedad y política en la América Latina," edited by Isabella Cosse. *Contemporánea* (Universidad de la República, Uruguay), no. 5 (2014): 13–20.

Cosse, Isabella. "*Claudia*: La revista de la mujer moderna en la Argentina de los años sesenta (1957–1973)." *Revista Mora* (IIEGE and Universidad de Buenos Aires) 17, no. 1 (2011). Accessed March 10, 2014. http://www.scielo.org.ar/scielo.php?script=sci_arttext&pid=S1853-001X2011000100007.

Cosse, Isabella. "Cultura y sexualidad en la Argentina de los sesenta: Usos y resignificaciones de la experiencia transnacional." *Estudios interdisciplinarios de América Latina y el Caribe* 17, no. 1 (January–June 2006): 39–60.

Cosse, Isabella, ed. "Dossier: Clases medias, sociedad y política en la América Latina." *Contemporánea* (Universidad de la República, Uruguay), no. 5 (2014): 13–91.

Cosse, Isabella. "La emergencia de un nuevo modelo de paternidad en Argentina (1950–1975)." *Estudios Demográficos y Urbanos* 24, no. 2 (May–August 2009): 429–62.

Cosse, Isabella. *Estigmas de nacimiento: Peronismo y orden familiar.* Buenos Aires: Fondo de Cultura Económica, 2006.

Cosse, Isabella. "Everyday Life in Argentina in the 1960s." *Oxford Research Encyclopedia of Latin American History* (July 2017). Accessed April 20, 2018. doi:10.1093/acrefore/9780199366439.013.316.

Cosse, Isabella. "Germán Leopoldo García y *Nanina*: Claves de lectura para una novela de los 60." *Revista de Literatura Hispamerica* 96 (2004): 103–14.

Cosse, Isabella. "Infidelities: Morality, Revolution, and Sexuality in Left-Wing Guerrilla Organizations in 1970s Argentina." *Journal of the History of Sexuality* 23, no. 3 (September 2014): 415–50.

Cosse, Isabella. "*Mafalda*: Middle Class, Everyday Life, and Politics in Argentina (1964–1973)." *Hispanic American Historical Review* 94, no. 1 (2014): 35–75.

Cosse, Isabella. *Pareja, sexualidad y familia en los años sesenta.* Buenos Aires: Siglo XXI, 2010.

Cosse, Isabella, Valeria Manzano, and Karina Felitti. *Los sesenta de otra manera: Vida cotidiana, género y sexualidades en la Argentina.* Buenos Aires: Prometeo, 2010.

Crenzel, Emilio. *Memory of the Argentina Disappearances: The Political History of Nunca Más.* New York: Routledge, 2012.

Dalter, Eduardo. "El período de Alberdi (1923–1976) y sus poetas." *Razón y Revolución*, no. 10 (Spring 2002). Accessed March 10, 2014. http://www .razonyrevolucion.org/textos/revryr/arteyliteratura/ryr10-05-Dalter.pdf.

Davidoff, Leonore, and Catherine Hall. *Family Fortunes: Men and Women of the English Middle Class, 1780–1850.* London: Routledge, 2002.

Deleuze, Gilles. "Humor, Irony, and the Law." In *Masochism: Coldness and Cruelty and Venus in Furs*, 81–90. New York: Zone Books, 1991.

Dorfman, Ariel, and Armand Mattelart. *How to Read Donald Duck: Imperialist Ideology in the Disney Comic.* New York: I. G. Editions, 1984. Published in Spanish as *Para leer al Pato Donald: Comunicación de masa y colonialismo.* 2nd ed. Buenos Aires: Siglo XXI, 1972.

Eco, Umberto. *Apocalípticos e integrados.* Buenos Aires: Tusquets Editores, 2008. First published in Italian in 1964 (*Apocalittici e integrati,* Milan: Bompiani), and in Spanish in 1965.

Eco, Umberto. "Il Mito di Superman." In *Demitizzazione e immagine*, edited by Enrico Castelli, 131–48. Padua: Cedam-Casa Editrici Dott. Antonio Milani, 1962.

Ehrlich, Laura. "Rebeldes, Intransigentes y duros en el activismo peronista, 1955–1962." Master's thesis, Universidad Nacional de General Sarmiento e Instituto de Desarrollo Económico y Social, Buenos Aires, 2010.

Eliade, Mircea. *Myth and Reality.* New York: Harper and Row, 1963.

Entel, Alicia, Víctor Lenarduzzi, and Diego Gerzovich. "La Escuela de Frankfurt en América Latina." In *Escuela de Frankfurt: Razón, arte y libertad*, 201–34. Buenos Aires: EUDEBA, 1999.

Felitti, Karina. *La revolución de la píldora: Sexualidad y política en los sesenta*. Buenos Aires: Edhasa, 2012.

Fernandez, James W., and Mary Taylor Huber. "Introduction: The Anthropology of Irony." In *Irony in Action: Anthropology, Practice, and Moral Imagination*, edited by Fernandez and Taylor Huber, 1–2. Chicago: University of Chicago Press, 2001.

Fernández L'Hoeste, Héctor D. "From Mafalda to Boogie: The City and Argentine Humor." In *Imagination beyond Nation*, edited by Eva P. Bueno and Terry Caesar, 81–106. Pittsburgh: University of Pittsburgh Press, 1998.

Filc, Judith. *Entre el parentesco y la política: Familia y dictadura, 1976–1983*. Buenos Aires: Editorial Biblos, 1997.

Forgacs, David. *L'industrializzazione della cultura italiana (1880–2000)*. Bologna: Il Mulino, 1994.

Foster, David William. *From Mafalda to Los Supermachos: Latin American Graphic Humor as Popular Culture*. Boulder, CO: Lynne Rienner, 1989.

Foster, David William. "Mafalda: An Argentina Comic Strip." *Journal of Popular Culture* 14, no. 3 (1980): 497–508.

Franco, Marina. *Un enemigo para la nación: Orden interno, violencia y "subversión," 1973–1976*. Buenos Aires: Fondo de Cultura Económica, 2012.

Fraser, Ronald. *1968: A Student Generation in Revolt*. London: Pantheon, 1988.

Frazier, Lessie Jo, and Deborah Cohen. "Defining the Space of Mexico '68: Heroic Masculinity in the Prison and 'Women' in the Streets." *Hispanic American Historical Review* 83, no. 4 (2003): 617–60.

Freud, Sigmund. "Humour." 1927. In *The Future of an Illusion: Civilization and Its Discontents and Other Works (1927–1931)*, vol. 21 of *The Standard Edition of the Complete Psychological Works of Sigmund Freud*, edited by James Strachey, 159–66. London: Hogarth Press, 1961.

Freud, Sigmund. *Jokes and Their Relation to the Unconscious*. 1905. In vol. 8 of *The Standard Edition of the Complete Psychological Works of Sigmund Freud*, edited by James Strachey. London: Hogarth Press, 1961.

Gamarnik, Cora. "El fotoperiodismo en Argentina: De *Siete Días Ilustrados* (1965) a la Agencia SIGLA (1975)." PhD diss., Facultad de Ciencias Sociales, Universidad de Buenos Aires, 2015.

Garguin, Enrique. "El tardío descubrimiento de la clase media en Argentina." *Nuevo Topo / Revista de historia y pensamiento crítico*, no. 4 (September–October 2007): 85–108.

Garguin, Enrique. "*Los Argentinos Descendemos de los Barcos*': The Racial Articulation of Middle Class Identity in Argentina (1920–1960)." *Latin American and Caribbean Ethnic Studies* 2 (September 2007): 161–84.

Gené, Marcela. "Varones domados: *Family strips* en los años veinte." In *Travesías de la imagen: Historias de las artes visuales en la Argentina*, vol. 1, edited by María

Isabel Baldasarre and Silvia Dolinko, 95–118. Buenos Aires: Centro Argentino de Investigadores de Artes and EDUNTREF, 2011.

Gené, Marcela, and Laura Malosetti Costa. *Impresiones porteñas: Imagen y palabra en la historia cultural de Buenos Aires*. Buenos Aires: Editorial Edhasa, 2009.

Germani, Gino. *Estructura social de la Argentina: Análisis estadístico*. 1955. Buenos Aires: Solar, 1987.

Germani, Gino. *Política y sociedad en una época de transición*. Buenos Aires: Editorial Paidós, 1962.

Giddens, Anthony. *Runaway World*. New York: Routledge, 2003.

Gillespie, Richard. *Soldados de Perón: Los montoneros*. Buenos Aires: Grijalbo, 1987.

Gilman, Claudia. *Entre la pluma y el fusil: Debates y dilemas del escritor revolucionario en América Latina*. Buenos Aires: Siglo XXI, 2003.

Ginsborg, Paul. *A History of Contemporary Italy: Society and Politics, 1943–1988*. New York: Palgrave Macmillan, 1990.

Ginzburg, Carlo. *The Cheese and the Worms: The Cosmos of a Sixteenth-Century Miller*. Baltimore: John Hopkins University Press, 1980.

Gociol, Judith. "Soy un escritor solapado." Interview with Daniel Davinsky. *El monitor*, no. 11 (2007), 58–62. Accessed January 27, 2014. http://www.bnm.me.gov.ar /giga1/monitor/monitor/monitor_2007_n11.pdf.

Gociol, Judith, and Hernán Invernizzi. *Un golpe a los libros: Represión a la cultura durante la última dictadura militar*. Buenos Aires: EUDEBA, 2003.

Gombrich, Ernst H. "The Mask and the Face: The Perception of Physiognomic Likeness in Life and Art." In *Art, Perception and Reality*, edited by Ernst H. Gombrich, Julian Hochberg, and Max Black, 1–46. Baltimore: John Hopkins University Press, 1972.

Gombrich, Ernst H. "The Visual Image: Its Place in Communication." *Scientific American* 272 (1972): 82–96.

Gonzalbo Aizpuru, Pilar, ed. *Familias iberoamericanas: Historia, identidad y conflictos*. Mexico City: El Colegio de México, 2001.

Gould, Jeffrey L. "Solidarity under Siege: The Latin American Left, 1968." *American Historical Review* 114, no. 2 (April 2009): 349–72.

Grammático, Karin. "La I Conferencia Mundial de la Mujer: México, 1975. Una aproximación histórica a las relaciones entre los organismos internacionales, los Estados latinoamericanos y los movimientos de mujeres y feminista." In *Hilvanando historias: Mujeres y política en el pasado reciente latinoamericano*, edited by Andrea Andújar, Débora D'Antonio, Karin Grammático, and María Laura Rosa, 101–13. Buenos Aires: Luxemburg, 2010.

Grimson, Alejandro, and Mirta Varela. "Recepción, culturas populares y medios: Desplazamientos del campo de comunicación y cultura en Argentina." In *Audiencias, cultura y poder*, edited by Alejandro Grimson and Mirta Varela, 43–98. Buenos Aires: EUDEBA, 1999.

Guano, Emanuela. "The Denial of Citizenship: 'Barbaric' Buenos Aires and the Middle-Class Imaginary." *City and Society* 16, no. 1 (2004): 69–97.

Guano, Emanuela. "Spectacles of Modernity: Transnational Imagination and Local Hegemonies in Neoliberal Buenos Aires." *Cultural Anthropology* 17, no. 2 (2002): 181–209.

Gubern, Román. *El lenguaje de los cómics*. Barcelona: Península, 1972.

Guevara González, Iris. *La educación en México: Siglo XX*. Mexico City: Universidad Nacional Autónoma de México, 2002.

Halbwachs, Maurice. *On Collective Memory*. 1925. Chicago: University of Chicago Press, 1992.

Hernández, Pablo. *Para leer a Mafalda*. Buenos Aires: Meridiano, 1975.

Hobsbawm, Eric. *The Age of Extremes: The Short Twentieth Century, 1914–1991*. London: Michael Joseph, 1994.

Hofmeyr, Isabel. "*AHR* Conversation: On Transnational History." *American Historical Review* 111, no. 5 (December 2006): 1441–64.

Jauretche, Arturo. *El medio pelo en la sociedad argentina (Apuntes para una sociología nacional)*. Buenos Aires: Peña Lillo, 1966.

Jensen, Silvina Inés. "Suspendidos de la historia/exiliados de la memoria: El caso de los argentinos desterrados en Cataluña (1976– ...)." PhD diss., Facultat de Filosofia i Lletres, Universitat Autonoma de Barcelona, 2004.

Kimel, Gabriel. *La masacre de San Patricio*. Buenos Aires: Ediciones Dialéctica, 1989.

Kuznesof, Elizabeth, and Robert Oppenheimer. "The Family and Society in Nineteenth-Century Latin America: An Historiographical Introduction." *Journal of Family History* 10, no. 3 (1985): 215–34.

Lang, Berel. "The Limits of Irony." *New Literary History* 27, no. 3 (1996): 571–88.

Langland, Victoria. "Birth Control Pills and Molotov Cocktails: Reading Sex and Revolution in 1968 Brazil." In *In from the Cold: Latin America's New Encounter with the Cold War*, edited by Gilbert M. Joseph and Daniela Spenser, 308–49. Durham, NC: Duke University Press, 2008.

Latxague, Claire. "Lire Quino: Poétique des formes brèves de la littérature dessinée dans la presse argentine (1954–1976)." PhD diss., L'Université de Grenoble, 2011.

Levín, Florencia. *Humor político en tiempos de represión: "Clarín," 1973–1983*. Buenos Aires: Siglo XXI, 2013.

Lomnitz, Claudio. *Idea de la muerte en México*. Mexico City: Fondo de Cultura Económica, 2006.

Longoni, Ana, and Mariano Mesman. *Del Di Tella a "Tucumán Arde": Vanguardia artística y política en el 68 argentino*. Buenos Aires: EUDEBA, 2010.

López, Ricardo. "Conscripts of Democracy: The Formation of a Professional Middle Class in Bogotá during the 1950s and Early 1960s." In *The Making of the Middle Class: Toward a Transnational History*, edited by Ricardo López and Barbara Weinstein, 161–95. Durham, NC: Duke University Press, 2012.

López, Ricardo. "Reseña: Ezequiel Adamovsky, *Historia de la clase media Argentina: Apogeo y decadencia de una ilusión, 1919–2003*." *Anuario Colombiano de Historia Social y de la Cultura* 36, no. 2 (2009): 209–14.

López, Ricardo, and Barbara Weinstein. *The Making of the Middle Class: Toward a Transnational History*. Durham, NC: Duke University Press, 2012.

Losada, Leandro. *La alta sociedad en la Buenos Aires de la* Belle Époque: *Sociabilidad, estilos de vida e identidades.* Buenos Aires: Siglo XXI, 2008.

Lumley, Robert. *States of Emergency: Cultures of Revolt in Italy from 1968 to 1978.* London: Verso, 1990.

Manzano, Valeria. *The Age of Youth in Argentina: Culture, Politics, and Sexuality from Perón to Videla.* Chapel Hill: University of North Carolina Press, 2014.

Manzano, Valeria. "'Contra toda forma de opresión': Sexo, política y clases medias juveniles en las revistas de humor de los primeros '70." *Cuadernos del CISH. Sociohistórica* 29 (2012): 9–42.

Manzano, Valeria. "Sex, Gender, and the Making of the 'Enemy Within' in Cold War Argentina." *Journal of Latin American Studies* 47, no. 1 (February 2015): 1–29.

Manzano, Valeria. "Sexualizing Youth: Morality Campaigns and Representations of Youth in Early 1960s Buenos Aires." *Journal of the History of Sexuality* 14, no. 4 (2005): 433–61.

Margulis, Paola. "La piel busca sus formas: Un estudio cultural sobre la representación del cuerpo en *Para Ti* durante la década del 70." Undergraduate thesis, Facultad de Ciencias Sociales, Universidad de Buenos Aires, 2004.

Markarian, Vania. *Left in Transformation: Uruguayan Exiles and the Latin American Human Rights Networks, 1967–1984.* New York: Routledge: 2005.

Marx, Jutta, Jutta Borner, and Mariana Caminotti. *Las legisladoras: Cupos de género y política en Argentina y Brasil.* Buenos Aires: Siglo XXI and Iberoamericana, 2007.

Masotta, Oscar. *La historieta en el mundo moderno.* Barcelona: Ediciones Paidós, 1970.

Matallana, Andrea. *Humor y política: Un estudio comparativo de tres publicaciones de humor político.* Buenos Aires: EUDEBA, 1999.

May, Elaine Tyler. *Homeward Bound: American Families in the Cold War Era.* New York: Basic Books, 1988.

Maynes, Mary Jo. "Cultura de clase e imágenes de la vida familiar." In *Historia de la Familia Europea: La vida familiar desde la Revolución Francesa hasta la Primera Guerra Mundial (1789–1913)*, vol. 2, edited by David Kertzer and Marzio Barbagli, 297–337. Barcelona: Paidós, 2003.

Mazzei, Daniel H. *Medios de comunicación y golpismo: El derrocamiento de Illia (1966).* Buenos Aires: Grupo Editor Universitario, 1997.

Merino, Ana María. *El cómic hispánico.* Madrid: Cátedra, 2003.

Mignone, Emilio. *Iglesia y dictadura: El papel de la iglesia a la luz de sus relaciones con el régimen militar.* Buenos Aires: Universidad Nacional de Quilmes and Página/12, 1999.

Míguez, Eduardo. "Familias de clase media: La formación de un modelo." In *Historia de la vida privada en Argentina*, vol. 2, edited by Fernando Devoto and Marta Madero, 21–45. Buenos Aires: Taurus, 1999.

Milanich, Nara. *Children of Fate: Childhood, Class, and the State in Chile (1850–1930).* Durham, NC: Duke University Press, 2009.

Minujin, Alberto, and Kessler, Gabriel. *La nueva pobreza en la Argentina.* Buenos Aires: Planeta, 1995.

Monsiváis, Carlos. "De los cuentos de hadas a los cómics." *Revista de la Universidad de México* (July 1963): 8–15.

Montanaro, Pablo. *Francisco Urondo: La palabra en acción. Biografía de un poeta y militante*. Rosario, Argentina: Homo Sapiens, 2003.

Montironi, Silvia. "In viaggio con Mafalda dall'a Argentina all'Italia." Undergraduate thesis, Facoltà di Lettere e Filosofia, Università di Macerata, 2007–8.

Nari, Marcela. *Políticas de maternidad y maternalismo político: Buenos Aires, 1890–1940*, 51–71. Buenos Aires: Biblos, 2004.

Nora, Pierre. "Generation." In *Realms of Memory: Rethinking the French Past*, vol. 1, edited by Pierre Nora, 498–531. New York: Columbia University Press, 1996.

Novaro, Marcos, and Vicente Palermo. *La dictadura militar 1976–1983: Del Golpe de Estado a la Restauración Democrática*. Buenos Aires: Paidós, 2003.

Novelli, Luca. "Trent'anni di Letteratura." ca. 2002.

O'Donnell, Guillermo. *El Estado burocrático autoritario*. Buenos Aires: Editorial Belgrano, 1982.

Owensby, Brian P. *Intimate Ironies: Modernity and the Making of Middle-Class Lives in Brazil*. Stanford, CA: Stanford University Press, 1999.

Parker, David S. *The Idea of the Middle Class: White-Collar Workers and Peruvian Society, 1900–1950*. University Park: Pennsylvania State University Press, 1998.

Parker, David S., and Louise E. Walker, eds. *Latin America's Middle Class: Unsettled Debates and New Histories*. Lanham, MD: Lexington Books, 2013.

Pasqualini, Mauro. "Psychoanalysis to the People! Alienation, Anguish, and the Unconscious in a Review of the Italian Left, 1961–9." *Psychoanalysis and History* 15, no. 1 (2013): 45–67.

Pateman, Carole. *The Sexual Contract*. Stanford, CA: Stanford University Press, 1988.

Pisani, Ítalo, ed. *100 años, Río Negro*. Bahía Blanca, Argentina: Editorial Río Negro, 2012.

Plante, Isabel. *Argentinos de París: Arte y viajes culturales durante los años sesenta*. Buenos Aires: Edhasa, 2013.

Plotkin, Mariano. *Freud en las Pampas*. Buenos Aires: Sudamericana, 2003.

Plotkin, Mariano, and Federico Neiburg. "Elites intelectuales y ciencias sociales en la Argentina de los años 60: El Instituto Torcuato Di Tella y la Nueva Economía." *Estudios interdisciplinarios de América Latina y el Caribe* 14, no. 1 (January–June 2003). Accessed November 10, 2013. http://eial.tau.ac.il/index.php/eial/article/view/932.

Podestá, Jorge. "La crisis de desocupación en la Argentina (1993–1998)." Documento de trabajo, no. 17, 7. Buenos Aires: Programa de Investigación sobre el Movimiento de la Sociedad Argentina, 1999.

Pujol, Sergio. "Rebeldes y modernos: Una cultura de los jóvenes." In *Nueva Historia Argentina: Violencia, proscripción y autoritarismo (1955–1976)*, edited by Daniel James, 283–328. Buenos Aires: Editorial Sudamericana, 2003.

Rapp, Rayna. "Household and Family." *Feminist Studies* 5, no. 1 (Spring 1979): 178–81.

Recchini de Lattes, Zulma. *La participación económica femenina en la Argentina desde la segunda posguerra hasta 1970*. Cuadernos del CENEP, no. 11, 26–63. Buenos Aires: Centros de Estudios de Población, 1980.

Rivera, Jorge B. "Historia del humor gráfico argentino." In *Medios de comunicación y cultura popular*, edited by Aníbal Ford, Jorge B. Rivera, and Eduardo Romano, 106–40. Buenos Aires: Legasa, 1985.

Rodríguez, Pablo, ed. *La familia en Iberoamérica 1550–1980*. Bogotá: Convenio Andrés Bello and Universidad Externado de Colombia, 2004.

Rodríguez Kuri, Ariel. "Los primeros días: Una explicación de los orígenes inmediatos del movimiento estudiantil de 1968." *Historia Mexicana* 53, no. 209 (July–September 2003): 179–228.

Romero, Luis Alberto. *Breve historia contemporánea de la Argentina*. Buenos Aires: Fondo de Cultura Económica, 1994.

Rozenmacher, Germán. *Cabecita negra*. 1961. Buenos Aries: Jorge Álvarez, 1963.

Rubenstein, Anne. *Bad Language, Naked Ladies, and Other Threats to the Nation: A Political History of Comic Books in Mexico*. Durham, NC: Duke University Press, 2003.

Saítta, Sylvia. *El escritor en el bosque de ladrillos: Una biografía de Roberto Arlt*. Buenos Aires: Debolsillo, 2008.

Salomón, Antonio José, ed. *Quinta Bienal Argentina del humor y la historieta: El humor hacia la democracia, 1976–1984*. Cordoba: Municipalidad de Córdoba, ca. 1984.

Sarowsky, Mariano. *Del laboratorio chileno a la comunicación-mundo: Un itinerario intelectual de Armand Mattelart*. Buenos Aires: Biblos, 2013.

Sasturain, Juan. *El domicilio de la aventura*. Buenos Aires: Colihue, 1995.

Saunier, Pierre-Yves. "Learning by Doing: Notes about the Making of *The Palgrave Dictionary of Transnational History*." *Journal of Modern European History* 6, no. 2 (2008): 159–80.

Scarzanella, Eugenia. *Abril: Da Perón a Videla. Un editore italiano a Buenos Aires*. Rome: Nova Delphi, 2013.

Sebreli, Juan José. *Buenos Aires, vida cotidiana y alienación*. 1964. Buenos Aires: Siglo Veinte, 1966.

Shukla, Sandya, and Heidi Tinsman, eds. *Imagining Our Americas*. Durham, NC: Duke University Press, 2007.

Sigal, Silvia. *Intelectuales y poder en Argentina: La década del sesenta*. Buenos Aires: Siglo XXI, 2002.

Sosenski, Susana. "El niño consumidor: Una construcción publicitaria de mediados de siglo XX." In *Ciudadanos inesperados: Procesos de formación de la ciudadanía ayer y hoy*, edited by Ariadna Acevedo and Paula López Caballero, 191–222. Mexico City: Cinvestav and El Colegio de México, 2012.

Sosenski, Susana. "Producciones culturales para la infancia mexicana: Los juguetes (1950–1960)." *Relaciones: Estudios de Historia y Sociedad*, no. 32 (Autumn 2012): 95–126.

Soto Díaz, Rubén Eduardo. *Un paseo por la historieta mexicana*. Buenos Aires: Ediciones El Escriba, 2008.

Steimberg, Oscar. "Acerca de Mafalda según Quino, Sasturain y otros." *Superhumor* (Buenos Aires), no. 11 (November 1981): 8–9.

Steimberg, Oscar. "Historietas: El lugar de Mafalda." *Los Libros* (Buenos Aires), no. 16 (March 1971): 6–7.

Steimberg, Oscar. *Leyendo historietas: Estilos y sentidos en un "arte menor."* Buenos Aires: Nueva Visión, 1977.

Steimberg, Oscar. *Leyendo historietas: Textos sobre relatos visuales y humor gráfico.* Buenos Aires: Eterna Cadencia, 2013.

Stern, Steve J. "Paradigmas de la conquista: Historia, historiografía y política." *Boletín del Instituto de Historia Argentina y Americana "Dr. E. Ravignani,"* no. 6 (1992): 7–39.

Svampa, Maristella. *Los que ganaron: La vida en los countries y en los barrios privados.* Buenos Aires: Biblos, 2001.

Swart, Sandra. "'The Terrible Laughter of the Afrikaner': Towards a Social History of Humor." *Journal of Social History* 42, no. 4 (Summer 2009): 889–917.

Terán, Oscar. *Nuestros años sesentas: La formación de la nueva izquierda intelectual argentina (1956–1966).* Buenos Aires: El Cielo por Asalto, 1993.

Thompson, E. P. *The Making of the English Working Class.* New York: Vintage Books, 1966.

Tinsman, Heidi. *La tierra para el que la trabaja: Género, sexualidad y movimientos campesinos en la Reforma Agraria Chilena.* Santiago: Lom Ediciones, 2009.

Torrado, Susana. *Estructura social de la Argentina (1945–1983).* Buenos Aires: Ediciones de la Flor, ca. 1983.

Trillo, Carlos, and Alberto Bróccoli. *El humor gráfico.* Buenos Aires: Centro Editor de América Latina, ca. 1972.

Turner, Victor. *From Ritual to Theatre: The Human Seriousness of Play.* New York: PAJ Publications, 1982.

Tusquets, Esther. *Confesiones de una editora poco mentirosa.* Barcelona: B de Bolsillo, 2012.

Ulanovsky, Carlos. *Paren las rotativas: Historia de los grandes diarios, revistas y periodistas argentinos.* Buenos Aires: Espasa, 1996.

Valobra, Adriana. "Derechos políticos femeninos en la Junta Consultiva Nacional." *Estudios Sociales*, no. 45 (2013): 169–201.

Varela, Mirta. *La televisión criolla: Desde sus inicios hasta la llegada del hombre a la Luna (1951–1969).* Buenos Aires: Edhasa, 2005.

Vassallo, Alejandra. "'Las mujeres dicen basta': Movilización, política y orígenes del feminismo argentino en los setenta." In *Historia, género y política en los '70*, edited by Andrea Andújar, Débora D'Antonio, Nora Domínguez, Karin Grammático, Fernanda Gil Lozano, Valeria Pita, María Inés Rodríguez, and Alejandra Vassallo, 62–88. Buenos Aires: Seminaria Editora, 2005.

Vázquez, Laura. *El oficio de las viñetas: La industria de la historieta en Argentina.* Buenos Aires: Paidós, 2010.

Vázquez Lorda, Lilia. "Intervenciones e iniciativas católicas en el ámbito familiar: La Liga de Madres y Padres de Familia (1950–1970)." Master's thesis, Universidad de San Andrés, 2011.

Viñas, David. *Dar la Cara*. 1962. Buenos Aires: Centro Editor de América Latina, 1967.

Visacovsky, Sergio. "Imágenes de la 'clase media' en la prensa escrita argentina durante la llamada 'crisis del 2001–2002.'" In *Moralidades, economías e identidades de clase media: Estudios históricos y etnográficos*, edited by Sergio Visacovsky and Enrique Garguin, 247–78. Buenos Aires: Ediciones Antropofagia, 2009.

Visacovsky, Sergio, and Enrique Garguin, eds. *Moralidades, economías e identidades de clase media*. Buenos Aires: Ediciones Antropofagia, 2009.

Wainerman, Catalina. *La vida cotidiana en las nuevas familias: ¿Una revolución estancada?* Buenos Aires: Lumiére, 2005.

Walker, Louise E. *Waking from the Dream: Mexico's Middle Classes after 1968*. Stanford, CA: Stanford University Press, 2013.

Williams, Raymond. *The Sociology of Culture*. Chicago: University of Chicago Press, 1981.

Yankelevich, Pablo. "México: Un exilio fracturado." In *Represión y destierro: Itinerarios del exilio argentino*, edited by Pablo Yankelevich, 187–222. Buenos Aires: Ediciones al Margen, 2004.

Zanca, José. "Reseña: Ezequiel Adamovsky, *Historia de la clase media argentina: Apogeo y decadencia de una ilusión, 1919–2003* (Buenos Aires: Planeta, 2009)." *Iberoamericana*, no. 41 (March 2011): 286–87.

Zermeño, Sergio. *México: Una democracia utópica. El movimiento estudiantil de 1968*. Mexico City: Siglo XXI, 1981.

Zolov, Eric. *Refried Elvis: The Rise of the Mexican Counterculture*. Berkeley: University of California Press, 1999.

INDEX

Civita, Adriana, 75
Civita, César, 57, 162
Colombo, Alicia, 6, 13, 48, 107, 128, 246
Copi, Raúl (Daniel Botana), 17
Cortázar, Julio, 52, 81, 128, 134, 194, 249
counterculture, 15, 61, 63, 65, 87, 102–3, 105, 106, 144
Crepax, Guido, 112, 113
Cuban Revolution, 3, 24, 45, 46, 63, 79, 104, 163; cultural strategies and *Mafalda*, 135, 177, 180–84

Delgado, Julián, 17, 39
democracy, 15, 45, 84, 160; *Mafalda* as a symbol of, 168, 211–12; return to, 137, 161–69; weakened, 30, 53, 66, 161, 169
dictatorship, 3, 8–9, 14, 47–48, 65, 117, 208, 211; *Mafalda* during the, 137–61. *See also* authoritarianism
disappeared, 9, 67, 79, 98–99, 133, 137–38, 139, 142, 143, 145, 150; denunciation of disappearances, 120, 133, 151, 160; disappeared activists, 9, 148; Mafalda as one of the disappeared, 159, 161, 163, 166–68, 172, 201, 212. *See also* human rights
Divinsky, Daniel, 13, 143, 144, 145, 146, 147, 168, 189, 192
Dorfman, Ariel, 82, 97, 128, 250

Eco, Umberto, 2, 5, 107, 111, 128, 153, 170, 185, 192
everyday life, 58, 59, 72, 115, 126, 135, 178, 212; middle class and, 7, 14, 28, 42, 53, 85–86, 112; and politics in the comic strip, 4, 7, 28, 32, 33, 36, 43, 48, 55, 110; working class and, 85, 175, 195
El Excélsior (México), 6, 122, 125, 126, 127, 131, 132
exile, 8, 9; Argentine exiles in Mexico, 127, 133–35; Argentine exiles in Spain, 115, 120–21; Latin American, 120–21, 124–25, 192, 212. *See also* immigration

family: changes in family relations, 10, 14, 36, 105, 111, 124, 125–26, 135, 208; family life, 14–15, 31, 33, 36, 43, 63, 71–72, 112, 115, 126; middle class families, 1, 20–29, 73, 85, 197; national security discourse and, 30, 66, 138, 144, 150; parent-children relations, 6, 10, 23, 32; politics and, 4, 14, 40, 110, 208; representation of the family in the strip, 38, 40, 41, 66, 123, 195; working class families, 5
fatherhood, 21, 22, 25, 32, 38–39, 43, 49; father-child relations, 62–64, 148; fathers depicted in the strip, 77, 195–97; modernization of, 28–29, 104–6; traditional style of, 27–28, 85–86. *See also* masculinity
Felipe (*Mafalda* character), 50, 60–61, 87, 88, 132, 185, 188, 202, 66, 71, 73, 93, 106, 176, 179; creation, 36, 163, 180–81, 183; identification, 148; relationship with another characters, 42, 43, 45, 51, 85. *See also* Timossi, Jorge
feminism, 77, 106, 111; feminist demands, 8–9, 76–77, 124; Mafalda as a symbol for feminists, 1, 76, 172, 174; struggles, 10, 77, 193. *See also* gender; women
Firpo, Norberto, 58, 221
Fontanarrosa, Roberto, 128, 147
Fromm, Erich, 23
Frondizi, Arturo, 19, 24, 31

Galeano, Eduardo, 99, 103, 121, 125, 140
García, Miguel, 116, 117, 121
García Lupo, Rogelio, 146
Gardel, Carlos, 1, 134, 166, 178
gender, 15, 20, 22, 24–25, 27, 29, 36, 66, 112, 124, 135; androgyny or ambiguity of, 24; conflicts, 2, 7, 208; inequality, 4, 125, 192–93. *See also* fatherhood; femininism; motherhood; masculinity; women

generation: generational gaps, 20, 23–24; intergenerational conflicts, 2, 4, 5–6, 7, 10, 22, 24–25, 27, 38, 41, 105–6, 108, 110, 182; intragenerational differences, 63–64; *Mafalda* readers across generations, 1, 10, 36, 87–88, 113, 121, 135, 147–49, 155, 162, 178, 195–97, 199–200, 208, 209, 213; 1960s generation, 9, 15, 18–19, 42, 135, 158–59, 166–68, 171–72, 184, 186; rebellious generations, 193, 210, 212, 147, 178, 187; subversion of generational order, 25, 30, 32, 42, 112; younger generations, 22, 24, 25–26, 29, 32, 42, 46, 53, 61–63, 71, 74–75, 86–87, 94, 122. *See also* youth
Germani, Gino, 14, 19, 34, 41, 57
Giardinelli, Oscar, 81
globalization, 8, 11, 24, 49, 102–36; global economy, 103–4, 184, 189, 208; global order, 32, 43, 44, 112; global scale of the strip, 8, 9, 10, 50, 170–71, 176–77, 192–93, 201, 206, 212–13; markets, 5, 104, 115, 121–22, 183
El Globo (Spain), 6, 116, 119, 201
Guevara, Ernesto "Che," 1, 69, 70, 78, 109, 124, 140, 167, 174, 175, 200
Guille (Mafalda's little brother), 66, 71, 90–91, 156, 158, 163, 176, 178, 179; creation, 61–62; intergenerational gaps, 62–64; rebellious attitude, 62, 63, 64–65, 70, 71–72, 73, 86–87, 210; relationship with readers, 201. *See also* generation

human rights, 72, 122, 137–38, 147, 148, 151, 161, 164, 165, 168, 169, 191; organizations, 159, 164
humor, 3–4, 7, 15–17, 20, 22, 25, 26, 32, 36–37, 38–39, 42–43, 51–53, 63, 76, 91, 94, 110, 123–24, 152, 156, 158, 182, 192–93, 207–13; cartoonists, 17, 31, 87, 92; conceptual humor, 5, 8–9, 33, 135–36, 138; humorous devices, 35, 43,

45, 61, 84, 181; politics and, 9, 31, 48, 54–55, 70–74, 92–93, 99, 101, 108, 117, 141, 143, 151, 161–63, 168, 197; shared codes, 46–47. *See also* laughter

Illia, Arturo, 31, 47, 66, 164
immigrants, 17, 57, 100, 138–39, 212; immigration, 13–14, 42, 120–25, 192; stereotypes of, 38–40, 82. *See also* exile
intellectuals, 16, 25–26, 29, 44, 46, 48, 57, 69, 72, 76, 77, 82, 104, 107–10, 111, 112–16; community of, 19, 58, 180; and mass culture, 68, 126–27; social and political commitment of, 54–55, 78, 80–81, 124, 133, 164–65, 181–82, 210; social networks, 8, 49, 57, 118, 192, 212
Irrgang, Pablo, 197

Jauretche, Arturo, 34, 41, 97

Landrú (Juan Carlos Colombres), 17, 31, 37, 38, 39, 41, 43, 92
Lanusse, Alejandro A., 83, 84
laughter, 3–4, 8, 28, 29, 48, 55, 61, 63, 67, 91–92, 101, 107, 118, 131, 135. *See also* humor
Levingston, Roberto M., 79, 83
Libertad (*Mafalda* character), 163, 176; creation, 76; exclusion from the film, 156, 158, 159; Libertad's family, 77, 149, 167; as a prototype of radicalized youth, 77–79, 93, 210; relationship with Mafalda, 100
Lugones, Susana "Pirí," 67, 144, 180

Mafalda (the character): antiauthoritarianism and, 47–48, 70–73, 84, 91–92, 96, 132–33, 167–69; childhood and, 23, 51–52, 148, 201–3, 213; denunciation of state repression, 139–42, 166–67, 211; gender constructions and, 15, 23–25, 63–64, 213;

Moix, Ana María, 116, 117

Moix, Terenci, 116

Monsiváis, Carlos, 123

Morandini, Norma, 166, 172, 173

Mordillo Menéndez, Guillermo, 113

motherhood: new style of, 41, 77; traditional role of women, 25–29, 40–41.
See also Susanita (*Mafalda* character);
women

Mugica, Carlos, 140, 143

El Mundo (Argentina), 6, 15, 37, 38, 41,
44, 46, 47, 48, 49, 52, 56, 61

neoliberalism, 3, 9, 109, 171, 184; in
Argentina, 137–38, 189; ideology,
171–75, 185, 191, 202, 208, 212–13;
policies, 138

Oesterheld, Héctor Germán, 70, 79, 113

Onganía, Juan Carlos, 8, 15, 31, 47, 48,
54, 65, 66, 69, 73, 78, 79, 90, 143, 162,
168, 181

Oski (Oscar Conti), 17

Padrón, Juan, 135, 163, 177, 180, 181, 182,
183, 236n18, 237n30

Perich, Jaume, 117

Perón, Juan Domingo, 18, 52, 53, 90, 94,
98, 147, 148

Perón, María Eva Duarte de, 203

Peronism, 94, 95; activists and organizations, 31, 139, 159, 169, 189, 210;
anti-Peronism, 19, 53, 83; Peronist
identity, 19, 34, 90, 96, 97; Peronist
governments, 14, 18, 57; Peronist resistance, 24, 77, 210

petite bourgeoisie, 8, 16, 83, 96, 210. *See
also* middle class

Pratt, Hugo, 68

Primera Plana (Argentina), 6, 12, 15, 16,
17, 20–25, 27–30, 35, 37, 48, 56

progressiveness: progressive public and
networks, 29, 46, 107, 117, 120, 126,
144; progressive sensitivity, 9, 46,

52–53, 136, 171, 177, 180, 192. *See also*
middle class

psychology: experts, 24, 88, 105; psychoanalysis, 30, 148, 166; psychological
trends in child-rearing, 14, 20, 23, 26,
28, 32, 105

publishing houses: Abril, 57–58, 144;
Bompiani, 108, 174; De la Flor,
103, 128, 143–49, 155, 168, 175, 192;
Feltrinelli, 104, 107; Haynes, 37,
Jorge Álvarez, 49, 66–67, 116, 127,
144, 223n42; Lumen, 115, 116–18, 127,
144, 179, 180; Mondadori, 108, 113,
114; Nueva Imagen, 127–28, 144, 175;
Rizzoli, 112; Tusquets, 115–17, 120,
128, 175

Quino (Joaquín Salvador Lavado), 6,
16, 37, 96, 113, 125, 142, 147, 171, 194,
197; drawing, 34–35, 37, 56, 65, 74,
82, 95, 126–27, 183, 192–93; education, 17, 57; exhibits, 68, 162, 176–80,
186–87, 193; family history, 6, 44,
107, 163, 174, 194; friends, 20, 37, 48,
58, 67, 88, 107, 163, 174, 180–81, 202;
humor style, 5, 37, 40–43, 49–50,
54–55, 66, 74, 83, 87, 91–92, 108–9,
136, 138, 160–62; Mafalda character
and, 9, 19, 24–26, 54, 56, 82, 119, 152,
161, 165–67, 172–73, 185, 196–97, 200,
204–5, 212; *Mafalda* strip and, 1, 4,
7, 12, 15, 18, 20–22, 43, 51–53, 90, 103,
121, 130, 135, 153, 167, 184–85, 192, 195,
201; other *Mafalda* characters and,
27, 36, 38–39, 42, 49, 61–63, 76, 119;
political commitments, 8, 31, 44, 46,
48, 62, 70–73, 76, 78–79, 80–84, 93,
97, 100–101, 117, 164, 168–69, 181, 211;
prizes, 102, 122, 150, 159, 165, 191, 203,
207; reflections on humor, 167, 168,
174; relationship with readers, 49, 56,
59, 67, 94, 128, 131–32, 155, 204; work
method, 10, 13, 29, 33, 50, 60, 77, 56,
207–9

radicalization: in Argentina, 14, 54–55, 68–88, 144, 156, 158, 165, 208–10; in Europe, 104–5, 166; in Latin America, 123–25, 135; in/and the middle class, 10, 15, 32, 46–48, 52–53, 76, 78, 87, 93, 98; radicalized youth, 8, 63, 104–5, 156, 172–73

Ravoni, Coleta, 107, 228n18

Ravoni, Marcelo, 10, 106, 107, 110, 111, 116, 155, 180, 228n18

Rey Piuma, Daniel, 148

Rico, Aldo, 164, 187

Rius (Eduardo del Río García), 123, 124

Rozenmacher, Germán, 52, 194

Sábat, Alfredo, 203

Sábat, Hermenegildo, 195, 197

Sasturain, Juan, xiv, 147, 152, 153, 155, 158, 201, 225n91, 226n127

Serrat, Joan Manuel, 78, 174, 178, 224n77

Schulz, Charles M., 60, 68, 192

Siete Días (Argentina), 6, 8, 55–56, 58–59, 60, 61, 62, 63, 64, 66, 67, 71, 75–76, 78, 84–85, 90, 91, 92, 95, 162, 201, 204, 210

Snoopy, 60–61

social protest, 69, 79, 83, 209

sociology: ideas, 41, 83, 105, 110, 112; sociologists, 14, 19, 41, 96, 98, 148

La Stampa (Italy), 6, 111

state terrorism, 7, 137, 142, 152, 161, 211; disappeared and repression by, 9, 138–43, denunciation of, 71, 120. *See also* violence

Soriano, Osvaldo, 92, 153

Susanita (*Mafalda* character), 61, 197; creation, 40–43, 61, 197; and the conservative middle class, 93, 95, 157, 185, 188, 109; racism, 52, 53, 86; relationship with Mafalda, 41, 52, 71, 77, 94–95, 111; relationship with Manolito, 42, 44, 185; traditional female role, 41–43, 157, 166, 194

Third World, 3, 8, 9, 32, 44, 46, 79, 104, 113, 118, 122, 136, 184, 209, 212; Movement of Priests for the Third World, 69, 139–40

Timossi, Jorge, 163, 180, 181, 183. *See also* Felipe (*Mafalda* character)

Tovar, Jorge, 132, 133, 231n96

Trillo, Carlos, 91

Tusquets, Esther, 115, 116, 120, 128

United Nations, 59, 122, 123

United States, 3, 49, 68, 82, 103, 118, 123, 160, 183, 192, 199

Urondo, Francisco "Paco," 19, 20, 78, 79, 81, 180

utopia, 3, 9, 78, 95, 104, 136, 166, 171, 173, 184, 185, 191, 213

La Vanguardia (Spain), 6, 117, 118, 120, 174

Vietnam, 44, 106, 109, 110, 111, 186, 193

Viñas, David, 19, 20, 41, 144

violence: Ezeiza massacre, 95; Pallottine massacre, 138–43; political violence, 2, 8, 54, 55, 69, 78, 81–83, 94–95; Tlatelolco massacre, 124; Trelew massacre, 91

Walsh, María Elena, 62, 203

Walsh, Rodolfo, 20, 78, 144, 180, 203

women: associations and movements of, 76–77, 125, 193, 206; demands and changes, 20, 25, 26, 29, 41, 46, 57, 58, 76–78, 125, 203; education and workforce, 25; family relations and, 23, 125; female ideals and styles, 26–27, 41; inequality, 125; magazines and press, 46, 49, 57, 58, 75, 77; representation of women in *Mafalda*, 20, 29, 46, 77, 149, 174, 185, 193, 203. *See also* feminism; gender; motherhood

working class: children and family of, 5, 40, 51, 85; images of, 69, 80, 97, 195;